琉球のことばと人
——エヴィデンシャリティーへの道——

伊豆山敦子 著

真珠書院

はしがき

　初めて琉球の言葉を耳にしたのは、今から半世紀以上前の事です。奄美大島・大和浜の語彙を学ぶ会に同席させて頂いたのが、その始まりでした。

　言語学を学ぶようになったのは、日本語を考えたかったからです。昭和30年前後、東京大学言語学科・服部四郎教授が、Bernard Bloch : Studies in Colloquial Japanese を用いて演習を行って居られました。フランス文学科在学中の幼稚な私は、言語学科在学の仲良し友人と一緒の時間を持ちたかったので、何気なくその授業に出席し、非常な衝撃を受けました。文化の高い（？）欧米（当時は欧米に学ばねば……の努力が常にありました。）を学ぶのに苦労していた私には、「日本語も欧米の言語も、同じレベルで検討する」というのが、とても新鮮でした。教養学部時代からフランス語を教えて頂いた、前田陽一教授の「東洋・日本を考える為に、フランス語を勉強する」というような、お考えにも影響を受けていました。卒業論文に選んだベルグソン（H. Bergson）には、その美しいフランス語で、「自分自身の言葉を考えるように」と教わりました。

　そのうち、上記の奄美研究会にもお誘い頂き、言語学科修士課程に入り、琉球語を専攻することに決めました。その時は、『落ち穂拾い』をするつもりだったのです。やがて、服部教授の知己で、沖縄・首里に孫娘と二人で住む真壁ツルさんが、私を居候させて下さり、沖縄で、1ヶ月程の楽しい夏を過ごしました。この経験は、論文にはならなくても、琉球語に対するカンを養うのに、とても役にたちました。後に、エヴィデンシャリティーに出会えたのも、これが基になっていたからでしょう。当時、既に首里語研究書はありましたが、それを理解していても、共通語翻訳による会話は、全く、巧くいかなかったのです。

（1）その成果は「長田須磨、須山奈保子：奄美方言分類辞典」に見られる。

その後、子育てその他に追われ、研究は、もう遠い遠い所に去りました。一段落した所で、再開。私のブランクの間に、本島は研究し尽くされたのではないかと思い、楽しみも兼ねて、宮古・八重山を巡りました。手に入る研究書で勉強してあるのに、解らないだらけの琉球諸方言。驚きの連続でした。

　そのうち縁あって、石垣島の宮良という集落に仲良しの友達ができたので、その離れ部屋を借りて、頻繁に逗留しました。「お帰りなさい。」という挨拶を頂くほどでした。そこで、姿を表してくれたのがEvidentialityでした。2003年3月出版の「琉球語文法研究」（「環太平洋の言語」成果報告書Ａ4‐024）の英文論文にはEvidentialityという語は無いけれど、事実は掴み、speakerの重要性を強調しています。その直後、Aikhenvald教授の著書に驚くという事になりました。後、英国の大学からの求めに応じて、与那国の文法を書き始めましたが、Evidentialityの範疇は、既に当然の前提でした（2011年発行予定）。

　服部先生、仲宗根政善先生が亡くなられた後、琉球語研究のあり方は変わりました。隆盛もしましたので、当然、グループに分かれる傾向もありました。学問は、本来、独りでやるものと思い込んでいた私は、無関係でしたが、これは大きな誤りでした。研究費のあり方も、研究事情を変えていたのです。世間に認められる地位はなくても、研究をすることには、差し支えないと思っていましたが、それは半ば正しく半ば間違いでした。

　調査に多額な費用が必要な訳ではありませんでした。話者への謝礼金は、どこでも皆無でした。ご縁あって、調査させて頂いた方々は、私と一緒に勉強するのが好きで、いつも逆にお礼の言葉を貰っていました。中でも、私を感激させたのは、宮古出身話者の次の言葉です。「御陰で、自分の言葉も、<u>規則のある立派な言葉だと解って、とても嬉しい。</u>」その方は、社会的に立派な仕事をされたのですが、若い時から、故郷以外の地（沖縄本島、本土）では、自分の言葉との大きな差異に、とても苦労されたのです。

　旅費は必ず必要でしたが、寄宿（無料）又は民宿の費用も多額ではありませんでした。しかし、論文を公表することは、とても難しいことだと身にしみました。研究費を貰った場合は公表義務があるでしょうが、特に地位を持

はしがき

たない私には、投稿するしかありません。ところが、新しい発見があると、この査読が通らないのです。理由としては、いつも、内容には全く触れず、「書き方が悪い」だけでした。残念なことに、どこが、どう悪いかの指摘もありませんでした。査読では、欠点を具体的に指摘して頂きたいものだと痛感しました。新しい地位の無い人の研究発表に関するサポートを、是非、望みたいものです。

そんな私に協力してくださる有難い方々も居られました。東京外国語大学 AA 研の湯川恭敏先生・梶茂樹先生には論文出版のお世話になりました。

国立国語研究所大西拓一郎氏の知己を得たのは、表現できないほど有難い事でした。「琉球の視点」から、最後の「Evidentiality」まで、この科研費グループの優秀な方々とご縁があったのは、不思議です。丁度、私のエヴィデンシャリティーへの歩みと重なっているのです。

今では、琉球語の気持ちまでが解るようになりました。Evidentiality への理解が、大きかったのです。この範疇は、文字のない言語では、殆ど必ずあると思い、早い時期に、台湾サオ語（オーストロネシア語）の研究者・新居田純野さんに伺ったところ、やはり、あると解り、納得したことがあります。

長い間、一緒に研究してきた新垣友子さんは、私が獨協大学で授業をしていた頃、大学院生でした。彼女は首里出身で、自分の父祖の言葉を研究したいとの事でした。その後、文部科学省特定領域研究、環太平洋の「消滅に瀕した言語」に関する緊急調査研究のプロジェクトで、琉球班には入れなかった私たち二人を、宮岡伯人、真田信治両先生が拾って下さり、感謝しながら、二人とも研究や発表に勤しみました。この時 Evidentiality へ、あと一歩のところまで、進むことができたのです。その後も新垣さんと二人で首里に関する研究(2)を出す事もでき、2010年、彼女は、「首里方言文法（Evidentiality を中心に）」研究で、英国エデインバラ大学から博士号を得ました。

多くの話者達の愛情と時間の賜物を、無にするのも申し訳ないので、ご縁のあった真珠書院にお願いして、島々の言葉に関する研究を出版することに

（2）「放送録音テープによる琉球首里方言」（2006）東京外語大学 AA 研

しました。英語のものを主にしたのは、理由があります。日本の中では受け入れられ難くても、言語の研究は文法研究を含め世界に繋がるものですから。

　沖縄各地で、美しい海を眺めながら、私は、そこの御先祖様がたに、何度も呼びかけたものです。「あなた方は自分達の言葉が解らないまま、消えてしまっていいのですか？」「ご自分の言葉を、私に、教えてください。」御先祖様がたは、願いを聞き入れ、（少なくとも重要な一部を）教えて下さったようです。

　沖縄各地には、沢山の方言があり、どこに行っても、殆ど必ず、皆、「ここの方言が一番良い方言だ」と、言います。人が言葉を持つ尊さ、人の感覚を、思考を、形にする尊さ。半世紀前、ベルグソンから得た種は、思いがけず、遥か彼方、琉球列島の Evidentiality に繋がっていたようです。

　琉球各地でお世話になった多くの方々、本当に有り難う御座いました。応援して下さった方々、どんなに感謝しても、しきれません。美しい島々で語られている魅力的な言葉。そしてそれを共有しながら生きて行く愛おしい人々。この著で、少しでも「人の持つ言葉」の尊さが伝えられることを願っています。

2011年1月

目　　次

はしがき ……………………………………………………… i

琉球の視点 ………………………………………………… 1
  A　解説
    1．伝統的琉球諸方言……………………………… 1
    2．琉球方言の文法 ……………………………… 3
    3．調査の着眼点 ………………………………… 4
    4．研究の現状を示す基本的文献（刊行順）……… 4
    5．調査を始める前に……………………………… 5
    6．調査を始める時………………………………… 7
  B　項目
    1．表記……………………………………………… 8
    2．代名詞 ………………………………………… 9
    3．名詞（固有名詞）附助詞 ……………………… 12
    4．動詞 …………………………………………… 14
    5．形容詞 ………………………………………… 25

The Grammar of Ishigaki Miyara Dialect in Luchuan ………… 27
    1．Introduction …………………………………… 28
    2．Transcription ………………………………… 35
    3．Pronouns ……………………………………… 38
    4．Nouns ………………………………………… 51
    5．Particles ……………………………………… 54
    6．Adjectives …………………………………… 59
    7．Verbs…………………………………………… 75

- 8. Copula 182
- 9. Compound sentences 192
- 10. Conditional expressions 201
- 11. Sample of Miyara dialect 209

琉球・宮古（平良）方言の文法基礎研究 225
- １．平良市の概要 225
- ２．表記 228
- ３．名詞（附助詞） 231
- ４．代名詞 236
- ５．話し手の優位性（モダリティー的側面） 245
- ６．形容詞 263

A Study on the Formation of Luchuan (Ryukyuan) Adjective Endings 287
- 1. The established theory on the formation of Luchuan adjectives 287
- 2. Differences in the adjective forms between Shuri and Yaeyama Miyara 288
- 3. Evidentiality and personal restriction in the Miyara adjective 291
- 4. Adjective forms of two dialects in Yaeyama 292
- 5. Discussion about a phonological change *s→h in adjective endings 295
- 6. Miyara verb *hu-N* "to do" 297
- 7. Interpretation of the phonological correspondence *s : k* in Yaeyama 299
- 8. *kiru-N* "to do" and *iru-N* "to do" in Yonaguni dialect 300
- 9. Change of the verb meaning "to do" into an affix

　　　　………………………………………………………… 305
　　10. Evidentiality and personal restriction in the Yonaguni
　　　　adjective ………………………………………… 306
　　11. Yonaguni *kiru-* "to do" and Miyara *hu-* "to do" … 307
　　12. Conclusion ……………………………………… 308

「ている」形への一考察（A Study on the Form "-te-iru" in
Japanese）……………………………………………………… 311
　　１．初めに ………………………………………… 311
　　２．普通態の「た」形と「ている」態の「た」形 …… 312
　　３．第一種動詞の「ている」形 …………………… 319
　　４．第四種動詞の「ている」形 …………………… 321
　　５．「ている」形と話し手 ………………………… 322
　　６．終わりに ……………………………………… 326

琉球・八重山（与那国）方言の文法基礎研究 …………… 329
　　１．与那国島の概要 ……………………………… 329
　　２．危機的な状況 ………………………………… 329
　　３．表記 …………………………………………… 332
　　４．人称代名詞と指示代名詞 …………………… 334
　　５．名詞と助詞 …………………………………… 342
　　６．話し手の認識と優位性 ……………………… 346
　　７．形容詞 ………………………………………… 357

琉球方言の母音調和的傾向（A Kind of Vowel Harmony in
Luchuan Dialects）…………………………………………… 371
　　１．初めに ………………………………………… 371
　　２．八重山方言の地域 …………………………… 371
　　３．助詞の母音交替 ……………………………… 371
　　４．石垣宮良方言の形容詞語尾 ………………… 379

5．その他の母音調和的現象……………………… 381
　　6．終わりに……………………………………… 383

Evidentiality―琉球語の場合― …………………………………… 385
　　1．Evidentiality（証拠様態）について ……… 385
　　2．宮良方言……………………………………… 386
　　3．宮古平良方言………………………………… 394
　　4．終わりに……………………………………… 399

琉 球 の 視 点

A　解　説

1．伝統的琉球諸方言

　奄美諸島から沖縄本島を経て先島諸島にいたる、南西諸島と呼ばれる地域の伝統的諸方言は、今日では消滅の危機に瀕している。

　1940年の統計類によると、その人口は以下のようであった[1]。
奄美大島11万、喜界島2万、徳之島4万6千、沖永良部2万5千、与論8千600、沖縄本島と離島50万、宮古6万5千、八重山3万5千
沖縄本島の詳細：国頭郡10万6千、中頭郡14万6千、島尻郡15万4千、那覇市6万5千、首里市1万9千

　1950年の各地区の人口は次のようであった[2]。
沖縄58万2,611人、宮古7万4,612人、八重山4万3,973人、大島21万9,024人、計92万余

　この当時の成人人口は大体方言話者を意味していたと考えてよい。中高年の婦人達は殆ど方言で生活するのが普通であった。

　2000年度の沖縄県統計年鑑によると、平成12年の県総人口は、132万1,024人。1950年から増加し続けている[3]。

　しかし、現在では、人口は方言の話し手を意味してはいない。1950年の10歳以上の人口は、1995年の55歳以上にあたる。上述の統計年鑑によると、1995年、沖縄県の総人口127万3,440人中、55歳以上の人口は、27万9,394人であ

---

(1) 世界言語概説、p.317
(2) 注1と同じ。
(3) これは、沖縄県の統計だから、奄美諸島の人口は含まれていない。

る。転出入を考え合わせると、方言話者は、この数より相当少ないと考えられる。仮に25万としよう。

この統計の市町村別は、10の市、本島の2郡37村、宮古郡5村、八重山郡2町、計54市町村に分かれているから、単純に25万人を54で割っても1町村あたり、4千600人程度である。

しかも、現在の行政区画と方言の違いとは一致しない。例えば石垣市の中には、市街地の方言の他に、川平、宮良、白保、その他異なる方言があり、竹富町という一つの区域の中に、黒島、竹富、小浜、波照間、鳩間、新城、古見、祖納、等々異なる方言がある。

同様に平良市の中には、狩俣のように異なる方言があり、下地町といっても、来間島のように異なる方言もある。

本島でも、今帰仁村のように大きな村は、与那嶺と天底で異なる。国頭村の中には、阿波、奥、辺土名、安田など各々異なる方言が多い。本島中部・南部の詳しい方言事情も、ほとんど報告されていない。こう考えると方言的には54行政区で割るわけにはいかない。

更にまた、方言の使用度は、その人の生活環境（その1世代前の両親との同居期間の有無、共通語地域での生活の長さなど）によって、異なっている。1世代前と違って、現在、共通語を用いないで公共生活をおくるわけにはいかないのである。無意識のうちに共通語に影響されるから、その選び分けが難しくなる。

このように考えれば、ある1方言の文法を調査するために、話者を探すのも難しくなってきている事情がわかるであろう。大都市の人口と小さな島の1集落の人口との差を思えば、話者の数が数人ということも珍しくないことが理解されるだろう。それ程、急速に話されなくなってきたのである。

このような理由で、今、琉球諸方言のどの方言にせよ、どの面にせよ、共時的研究は重要なのである。書かれることはなかったが、毅然とした1言語体系を持っている方言の研究は、日本語の研究にとっても、一般的な言語研究にとっても実り多いものにちがいない。そして、<u>どこの方言も調査者としての「あなた」を待っている</u>のである。

2．琉球方言の文法

　琉球方言の共時的文法研究は、残念ながら無いに等しい。教育のための研究書も作られたが、それらは方言話者が共通語を学ぶためのものであり、琉球諸方言を学ぶ為のものではなかった。つまり共通語の方からのみ、眺められていたのである。実用的な目的の為なのであるから、しかたがないことであった。

　更に、方言研究は歴史的関心が先行して、限られた形だけが採り上げられ、論じられていた。特に音韻・語彙的な関心は強く、そのお陰で辞書は刊行されたが、文法を１言語システムとして研究されることは無いに等しかった。共通語（ないし上代語）に翻訳されることが主要であった。

　動詞・形容詞など、活用する語に関する研究は本土の枠組みでのみ記述され、それ以外は殆ど顧慮されず、テンス・アスペクト・ムードなどは、本土方言と異なるにも拘わらず殆ど研究されていない。

　更に、琉球諸方言は変化に富んでいた。島嶼に広がっていたせいもあり、同じ琉球方言の中でも互いに解らないといわれるほどの違いさえある[4]。それらが、どのように異なり、どのように似ているか、文法的な枠組みで明示されたこともなかった。

　近年まで、島々への交通に時間がかかり、十分な調査ができなかったのだから、これもしかたがないことかもしれないが、そのため、本土の国語・日本語研究者に十分な情報がなく、「日本語」の中で、琉球の諸方言がどのような位置をしめるのか、常に曖昧であった。

　主要方言でさえ、文法書といえるものはないのである。つまりその方言を話したいと思っても、参考になるような研究書が殆ど無い（または、手に入らない）のが実情である。従って、方言自体に焦点を当てた共時的調査が緊急に期待されている。

（4）同じ八重山でも、宮良の話者は、与那国方言はわからないし宮古方言も解らないと言う。

3．調査の着眼点

　方言は話し言葉である。その方言を「話せるように」と思えば多くのことを調べたくなる。「話せる」ということには、音韻・語彙・文法以外の社会的心理的文化的要素等も含まれるが、その中から、文法的要素を抽出するという試みも、楽しい良い訓練である。

4．研究の現状を示す基本的文献（刊行順）

Chamberlain, Basil Hall (1895) "Essay in Aid of a Grammar and Dictionary of the Luchuan Language". Tokyo, Z. P. Maruya & Co., Ltd
宮良当荘（1930）『八重山語彙　附八重山語総説』東洋文庫
岩倉市郎（1941）『喜界島方言集』中央公論
金城朝永（1944）『那覇方言概説』三省堂
服部四郎・金城朝永（1955）「琉球語」『世界言語概説　下巻』pp. 318-353 研究社
服部四郎（1959）『日本語の系統』岩波書店
服部四郎（1960）「奄美大島諸鈍方言の動詞・形容詞終止形の意義素」『言語学の方法』所収 pp. 401-412 岩波書店
鈴木重幸（1960）「首里方言の動詞のいいきりの形」『国語学』41
国立国語研究所（1963）『沖縄語辞典』大蔵省印刷局
平山輝男・中本正智（1964）『琉球与那国方言の研究』東京堂
平山輝男・大島一郎・中本正智（1967）『琉球先島方言の総合的研究』明治書院
柴田武（1972）『全国方言資料第10巻琉球編Ⅰ』pp. 17-55・『第11巻琉球編Ⅱ』pp. 24-60 日本放送協会
法政大学沖縄文化研究所（1975年～現在）『琉球の方言』（1 ～25号）
長田須磨・須山名保子（1977）『奄美方言分類辞典上巻・下巻』笠間書院
仲宗根政善（1983）『今帰仁方言辞典』角川書店
中松竹雄（1987）『琉球方言辞典』那覇出版社

亀井孝 et al.（1992）『言語学大事典』 4巻『琉球列島の言語』pp.771-814
　三省堂
池間苗（1998）『与那国言葉辞典』私家版
生塩睦子（1999）『伊江島方言辞典』 伊江村教育委員会

　以上の文献でも解るように語彙集・辞書が多く、文法は、あっても形の記述が主体で、解説は極めて少ない。

5．調査を始める前に
(1) その方言関連の事を、何でもいいから好きになろう。例えば、そこの景色、海や空の色、食べ物、芸能、話者の方等々何でもいいから何か一つ。（たくさんならもっといい。）
(2) 話者に出会う方法もいくつかある。一般的には教育委員会に頼むことが多いが、筆者にはその経験がない。もし、筆者同様の普通の人なら、いろいろな方法がある。
　　① 土地出身者でなければ、必ず宿を取らなければならないから、土地の人が経営する宿を選び、そこで紹介してもらう。
　　② 小さな「しま（村）」なら、しまなかのお店（新しいスーパーではない）、郵便局、JA等の方々、老人会の世話役の方、土地のタクシーやバスの運転手さん、島通いの船主さん等、その土地を知っている方との出会いから、協力して下さる話者が現れるだろう。
　　③ インターネットにも土地の情報がある。要するに、どこに行っても「方言方言」と喚けばいい。「案ずるより産むが易し」だから、ご縁のあった話者との出会いを大切にしよう。
(3) 「調査させて下さい」より「教えて下さい」にしよう。理由はあるが、単純に、もし自分が誰かに「あなたの言葉を調査させて下さい」と言われるのと「教えて下さい」と言われるのと、どちらが好ましいか考えてみよう。

　　　　後の資料の取り扱いや発表に関しても、話者は「先生」なのだ。全て<u>許可をお願いしよう</u>。
(4)　少なくとも話者の名前・年齢・男女別は記そう。それを<u>発表するかどうかは別問題</u>。前述のように許可を得よう。消滅の危機に瀕した言語の場合<u>年齢</u>は大切だから、発表できるように理解を得よう。男女別もできれば発表させて貰おう。
(5)　方言調査以外の雑談も、調査に関係ないと思わないで楽しく聞こう。すぐ、例文作りなどに役立つし、話者の背景を知ることも大切。また、親しみも増える。
(6)　<u>「あなたの話者を信じなさい。」</u>基本的に、話者が間違うことはない。間違うのは調査者の方だ。質問の仕方が悪かったり、解釈が悪かったり、話者の状態を観察せず無理したり、それから人間だから一寸したミスがあるのは当然だと思わなかったり等々。
(7)　必ず録音をしよう。できれば、初めから終わりまで全部（勿論<u>許可が必要</u>）。
(8)　解ったことがあった時は、話者の方にも伝わるように喜びを表そう。何を喜んでいるのか良く解らなくても、相手も同様に嬉しくなるものだし、感謝も伝わる。
(9)　調査時は、気楽になるような雰囲気にしよう。方言は普段着なのだから、調査者も普段着でやろう。話者が思わず同輩知人に話す積りになれるように。
(10)　言葉だけではなく、話者の表情その他も大切である。自信ありげか、興味なさそうか、昔懐かしそうか等々。解釈や、今後の調査の参考になる。
(11)　調査が、思うほどは、うまくいかなくても、こう思うことにしよう。「何かが好きになり、誰かと交流できたのは得がたい事だった。自分で方言に接することができただけでも収穫だった。この次は、この土台の上で、何かが得られるに違いない」と。そして例外なくその通りになる。

6．調査を始める時

(1) 具体的な人と場を設定する。「書く」「書かない」……というのは、既に抽象化である。<u>抽象化は話者の仕事ではない</u>。それは、<u>調査者の仕事</u>なのだ。（話者の内省を大切にすることとは違う。話者の内省は勿論尊重する。）

(2) 会話する人物を少なくとも<u>3人設定</u>しよう。話し手、聞き手、それ以外。

(3) 話し言葉では、ただ「書く」ということはない。何か書きたいものを見て「書く。」と言ったのか、「書く？」と尋ねたのか、<u>誰が誰に、どんな時、言ったのか明瞭</u>にする。

(4) 肯定・否定・質問などは、本土共通語と同じだと思わず、丁寧に調べる。

(5) 無い形、無い表現などは、<u>「無い」ということを確かめておく</u>。これこそ文献資料と異なる、フィールドワークの有利な点なのだ。

(6) 敬語を調べたいのでなければ、基礎的なものから調べた方がいい。現在では、既に、日常あまり方言を使わない場合が多いので、子供の時を思い出すように設定した方が好都合だろう。親兄弟姉妹・親しい親戚とその子供達の中から選ぶのが無難。夫婦間は敬語を使うことがあるから、注意。（親から子へ、夫から妻へ、が無難）

B 項目

調査項目

　注記のない実例は、八重山（石垣宮良）方言である。それ以外からも適宜異なる方言を採用し、未発表の事実も採用した。諸方言の共時的研究は未だ不十分だから、これらの項目以外も必要になるだろう。調査者に期待するところは大きい。

1．表記

　琉球方言は変化に富んでいる上、調査もまだ不十分だから、音韻が決定されていない方言もある。先行研究の記述が納得いかない時もある。その時は、音韻の決定が先決だと拘ることはない。それは疑問のままにして、先へ進もう。文法的な事実から観察が精密になったり、解釈ができたりすることもある。とにかく一応の<u>簡略音声表記</u>を心がけよう。

　ここでは印刷の都合で次のように書き換える。
Φ→hw/hu, ʃ→sj, dz/z→z, ʒ/dʒ→zj, tʃ→c, g→g, ŋ→G, 成節鼻音→N, 成節無声子音→Q, 無気喉頭化音→大文字, その他変種には大文字を随時使う。

全く知識のない方言を調査する際の注意事項
(1)　各方言間で音声面も異なりはするが、先行研究で大まかな見当をつけておく。但しそれにとらわれると、かえって難しくなることがある。自分の耳を信頼しよう。
(2)　基礎語彙（名詞）を集め、音韻的な問題点がどこにあるか大体の見当をつける。
(3)　本土方言の形の上での対応語を常に意識しておく。
(4)　話者の内省（音の異同）を尊重する。調査者は意識的に発音して、話者が「いい」と言ってくれるまで、練習する。すぐ出来なくても<u>努力だけはする</u>。

(5)　その音（韻）の見本となる単語を見つけておき、疑問の時には、それを照合する。
(6)　音韻論的解釈が十分出来なくても先に進もう。常に完璧は目指すけれど、到達できるかどうかは神仏の分野だと……。進むうちに解ることもある。言語は体系なのだから。

2．代名詞

通常のとおり、1人称、2人称それぞれの単数・複数形を採取する。
(1)　代名詞の形は語形変化する。私、私は、私の、私が、私を、私も等々の各変化形を取る。無助詞独立形は、「もしもし」と呼ばれ「私？」という場合。戸の外で（最近は電話で）、声で自分だと知らせる「誰？」への答えなど。2人称も同様にする（多くの場合平行的な形ではない）。

宮良の例を図示する。助詞つきは与那国からの例示である。

宮良	1人称	2人称	自己称	3人称	再帰
単数	ba:～banu	wa:～wanu	×	uri	na:ra
複数	banda:	wada:	baga:	uɴta:	naɴta:
うち	baɴca	waꝗca	baga:	×	naꝗca

（与那国）　uja ɴda iri kuja aGa iruɴ.　　　ɴda munu, aGa munu
　　　　　それはあんたがしてこれは私がする　あなたの物　私の物

ano: aTa ja buranuɴ.　　ɴda aTa ja bu:na: ?
私は　明日は　居ない　　お前は　明日は　いるか

anu ja numanuɴ.　　×aGa ja　（普通に勧められた時）
私　は　飲まない

ɴda Ga buru na ?　aGa ja buranuɴ.　　　u Ga buruɴ do.
あんた が 折るの か　私 は 折らない　　　彼 が 折る よ

kari Ga ja buttaɴtiɴ　　aGa ja buranuɴ.
彼 が は 折っても　　　　私 は 折らない

(2) 3人称は一寸難しい。指示代名詞との兼ね合いがある。3系列（コソア）のうちの一つが人称代名詞である可能性もある。単数複数が形態的に区別されることも頭に入れておく。現場指示と文脈指示。物も人も共通に指せるかどうか。文脈指示に多出するものに注意する。3系列のうちの1系列は、人を指し難いということもよくある。

(3) 1人称単数形「私」に当たる語が2個（以上）ある方言もある。それも文体的に異なるのではない。その場合は、複数形も各々単数形に対応して2形ある。歴史的に重要だから形だけでも採集する。また、「<u>私は</u>しない」と「<u>私が</u>する」の「私」が異なる方言もある。

（来間）

<u>a</u>ga kakadi　　　≒　　　<u>b</u>aga kakadi
私が　書く　　　　　　　　私が　書く

<u>b</u>aga kakadi / <u>a</u>ga kakadi　　aba kakadjan　（×<u>b</u>aga kakadjan）
私が　書く　私が　書く　私は　書かない

(4) 1人称複数形は特に注意する。あなた(達)に対する「私達」（baNda:）と、彼（等）に対する「私達（自己称）」（baga:）とが異なる（しかもさまざまなレベルで）方言が多い

① 「<u>彼等は</u>……するけど<u>私達は</u>……しよう。」（敵味方に分かれる場合など）

② 新しいお嫁さんに「ここが<u>私達の</u>畑（お墓）だよ」と教える。他人に言う時と比較。

（来間）

du:ta:　paka　(pari).　baNta:　paka　(pari)
自分達の　墓　畑　　私達の（まだ家族と認められていない感じ）

③ <u>孫に</u>「お家に行こう」。<u>友達に</u>「家にいらっしゃい」。「うち」にどう言うか。

baga: ge: hara.　　　　baNca ge: hara.
家　に　行こう（孫に言う）　うち　に　行こう（他人に言う）

④ 他村に嫁ぐ娘に「<u>私達の（村）</u>の風習はこうだけど、あちらは……」

(5) 3人称の<u>再起代名詞</u>的なものの存在を単数複数形（na:ra, natta:）ともに確かめる。（1・2人称にも同じ形があるのか、違う形を使うのかも確かめる。）

単・複を確かめるのには、個人使用の物と家族使用の物（家は普通複数）を考える。

「黙って持っていっちゃった」と思い違いする。「Aさんは<u>自分</u>のを持って行ったんだよ。」

（与那国）

  uja <u>sa:</u> munu.
  それは 彼自身の物 （彼が自分の物を持っていった）

借りた鍋 nabi を持っていった人がいる。勝手に持っていったかと思って、

  A：kari ɢa mutti hjuN. B：je: <u>ure:sji:</u> munu
  彼 が 持って行った えー あれは 彼ら自身(彼のうち)のもの

(6) 文体的に異なる形 ― 例えば2人称の敬語形 ― があるときは序にそれに伴う「はい」に当たる返事の形も採っておくと便利

（沖縄語辞典）ʔjaa, naa, ʔuNzu 他

返事（はい）の例（辺土名） u:, o:, i:, 3種類がある。

(7) 指示詞
  単数 kuri （uri） kari 人を指せるかどうか
  複数 kuɴta:(uɴta:) kaɴta:
  場所 kuma （uma） kama ①<u>こっち</u>へお出で。②一寸<u>そこ</u>まで。

(8) 副詞的代名詞（こう、そう、ああ）

指示詞と必ずしも並行的でない。

  <u>aNzji</u>, <u>kaNzji</u>, （×kuNzji, ×uNzji）
  そう こう

3．名詞（固有名詞）附助詞

基礎語彙表を使って調べる。勿論、動詞などと同時に調査してもいいが、調査を単純化するために、何十個くらいは知っていた方が便利である。基礎語彙表になくても次のような語彙は心がけておく。

十二支　：年齢が正確にわかるという利点もある。（お年寄りは数え年の場合もある）

数え方　（一つ、二つ……一人、二人……一束、一回……）

次の音の対応語：ワ行音（井草、亥、苧、襟など）、
　　　　　　　　エ段の音を含む語　イ段の音を含む語
　　　　　　　　語頭のハ行音対応語～カ行音対応語
　　　　　　　　ガ行音対応語
　　　　　　　　ラ行音（特に音節リ）

(1) 助詞「は」相当の語が接する時、名詞の語末音節は形を変えることが多い。それを先ず調べる。そのためには例文の作り易さから人名を用いるといい。その場合、嘗ては（昭和10年位まで）、戸籍名の他に方言名を持つのが常だったから、それを採取しながら「誰々はいる」「誰々はいない」のようにすると楽しい。人名は最終音節が限られているかもしれないが、全体の見当がつくから、その後で名詞の語末音節（含む成節的子音）全部を調べる。これにより、逆に名詞の語末音が判明することもある。

（平良西仲）

長母音　V:→＋ja　例 sjinsji:　先生→sjinsji: ja

短母音　a→a:　例 pana 花→pana:, u→o:　例 fumu 雲→fumo:,
　　　　i→ja: ami 雨→amja:

子音　　m→mma 例 num 蚤→numma, n→nna 例 in 犬→inna,
　　　　v→vva 例 pav 蛇→pavva

子音 z（２重母音の後部要素として記されることが多い）
　　　z→zza 例 maz 米→mazza, piz 針→pizza, tuz 鳥→tuzza

長子音　m:→mma 例 m:芋→mma (:)

短母音 I -bI ＋ -za kabI 紙→kabIza -gI ＋ -za mugI 麦→mugIza

```
          -kɪ  +  -za  kakɪ 垣→kakɪza    kɪ  +  -sa  iskakɪ 石垣→iskakɪsa
          -sɪ→   ssa junusɪ 人名→junussa-   tsɪ→   -ttsa matsɪ 人名→mattsa
          -zɪ→   -ttsa tuzɪ 妻→tuttsa
```

(2) 「これは……だ」という時も同様なことがある方言もある。
　　（黒島）ure: nu:ja.（これは何か）に対する返事
　　sabaɴ nawaja:.　kiɴ na waja:.　sa: jawaja:.　pe: jawaja:.
　　茶碗　だ　　　　着物　だ　　　茶　だ　　　　緋　だ
　　ki: jawaja.
　　木　だ
　　hata waja:.　para waja:.　usje waja:.　izo waja:.
　　肩（hata）だ　針（parɪ）だ　牛（usji）だ　魚（izu）だ

(3) 「へ」相当の語が接する時も同様なことが起こる方言もある。
　　（黒島）hama—ha, iso—ho, hanu piso ho,　usje he,　iɴ ha
　　　　　 あそこへ　磯　へ　あの人（pisu）へ，牛（usji）へ，犬（iɴ）へ

(4) 「が」相当の語の接し方も注意する。多くの方言で、物と人で異なる。
　　代名詞を含め留意しておく。
　　（沖縄語辞典）wa: ga,　ari ga,　siɴsii ga,　tui nu,　tiida nu,
　　　　　　　　 私　が　　彼　が　　先生　が　　鳥　が　　太陽　が

(5) 琉球の諸方言には「……だ」に相当するコプラがある。(2)であげたのが
　　その一例だから、名詞と一緒に採集してもいい。動詞のように語形変化を
　　するから注意。また、「ある」と同じ語がその役を担う方言もある。言い
　　切る時は普通現れない方言もある。

（言語学大辞典他）

首里	今帰仁	平良	石垣	与那国	名瀬
jaɴ	eɴ～jar-	jaɪ	jaɴ	aɴ	zja～ʔa-

4．動詞

常時必要な予備知識
①日本語動詞の5段・上下1段活用。「する」「来る」「ある」「いる」など変格活用動詞。
②日本語5段活用動詞終止形末尾母音の直前の子音（または母音）
③先に調べた代名詞の知識（行為者が誰かにより動詞形が異なる）

注意事項
①　語形変化を調べながらテンス・アスペクト・ムード等にも気を配る。各分野集中というのもいいが、それでは話者も楽しくない。ある程度は総合的にやって、見当がついてから各分野を集中的にしたほうが調査者も話者も慣れる。
②　本土方言の形と1対1で対応するとは限らない。重要動詞（含変格活用動詞）は特に注意。勿論文法的範疇も1対1で対応するとは限らない。対応しないと思って始めた方が安全である。
③　本土5段活用対応動詞、上下1段活用対応動詞、「する」「来る」「ある」「いる」など変格活用動詞は、常時注意している。5段動詞は、語幹末子音が軟口蓋音である方が区別（口蓋化・非口蓋化）を持っている可能性が高い。
④　「書く・書かない・書きたい・書く時・書けば・書け・書いた・書いて」などから始めても場合によってはいいが、それでは話者が楽しくない。調査者も共時的に大切な形を取りこぼす。なるべく臨場感があるような場面を設定した方がいい。既述したように、話者の内省は大切にするが、抽象化を話者に求めてはならない。
⑤　琉球諸方言では、多くの場合、話し手が重要である。話し手のmodus的な面（認識、判断のあり方）を常に注意する。自分（1人称）の行為か、相手（2人称）の行為か、話し合っている二人に無関係な他者（3人称）の行為か常に確かめる。質問文の時に明瞭になることが多い。
⑥　話し手が、その行為を見て（経験して）いるかどうかということは常に重要である。更に話し手が確認したかどうかも重要である。

項目

(1) 3人（以上）を設定する。その行為と話し手は、どういう関係であるかをはっきりさせておく。①話し手の行為か、②話し手とそれに属す人の行為か、③話し相手の行為か、④第3者の行為か。⑤物（現象）の行為—「咲く」「降る」「(風が) 吹く」「枯れる」—か、など。

① ba: kakuN. / ?　（wa: kakuN？　×wa: kakuN. atsuko kakuN. / ?
　　私　書く。／？　（あんた書く？　　あんた書く。敦子　書く。／？

② baNda: kakuN. baga: kakuN？　×baga: kakuN. cf. baga: kaka. ba:kaka.
　　私達　　書く　私達　書く？　　　　　　　　　　　　私達　書こう　私　書こう

③ wa: kakuN？　答えて　① ba: kakanu.　　×ba: kakanu do:.
　　あんた書く？　　　　　　私　書かない。

② baga: kakuN？　答えて　baga: kakanu do:. ×baga: kakanu.
　　私達　書く？　　　　　　私達　書かない。

⑤ hana sakuN. / ?　答えて　sakuN.
　　花　咲く。／？　　　　　咲く

①話し手とそれ以外では異なることが多い。

（平良西仲）肯定と否定

(a) ta: ga kakadi？　誰が書くのという質問に答えて
　　baga kakadi.　atsuko ga du kakɪ（gamata）.　×atsuko ga kakadi
　　私が　書く　　敦子　が　書く

(b) kaki　返事して　kakamba. ／ kakadjan.（話し手本人）
　　書け　　　　　　書かない　　書かない
　　しかし　　　　　karja: kakan　×kakadjan
　　　　　　　　　　彼は　書かない

(2) 質問がどんな風にできるか。2人称主体では、質問だけが可ということもある。①質問にならない形もある。②話し相手の行為と3人称の行為、③行為の確認、見ながらか、見えていないか、④3人称の行為を見ながら確認質問ができるかどうか。内省の参考例も付した。

①　ba: atugani kakjaN. ×wa: atugani kakjaN. / ?　×atsuko: atugani kakjaN？
　　私は　後で　書く

② （久場）
- (a) ?ja: kacumi？　しかし　×／？　　atsuko kacumi？
  あんた書く　　　　　　　　　　　敦子　書く
  　　　　　　　　　　　　　　　　　　この時は以下の方が好ましい

  atsuko ja kacuga ja:　答えて　kacu isani
  敦子　は　書くかな　　　　書くんじゃない
- (b) 敦子と一緒に隣室で手紙を書いているが、途中で出て来た人に
  ?ja:　tigami kaco:mi？　（動作見えない）
  あんた手紙　書いている
  atsuko kaco:ti：？　　　　　　　×atsuko kaco:mi？
  敦子　書いていた　　　　　　　　敦子　書いてる
- (c) ?ja: tigami kaci：？　　　　　　×atsuko kaci：？
  あんた手紙書いた（書き終わったと思っている）
  atsuko kacuti：？
  敦子　書いてた　（敦子が書いてるのを見たか）

③
- (a) taraNdaru muno:　wa:　kakiN？　　kakiN.
  頼んだ　物は　あんた書いてる？　書いてる（動作は見えない）
- (b) wa:　kakiN？（動作は見えない）×wa:　kakiN？（動作が見えている）
  あんた書いてる？（書いているのを見ながらでは不可。）
- (c) wa: tigami du kakiru? wa: tigami kaki duru？（共に動作が見えている）
  あんた手紙を書いているの？あんた手紙書いているの（書かなくてもいいのに）

④
- (a) A：atsuko: nakiN？　　　B：nakiN.
  敦子　泣いてる？　　　泣いてる。（泣いているらしい後姿を見ながら）

  そこで、敦子の所に行って　×atsuko: wa: nakiN？（動作は見えている）
  　　　　　　　　　　　　　敦子　あんた泣いてる

  内省「wa:　nakiN？というと泣くことを楽しんでいる気がする。」
- (b) （久場）泣いている人のところに行って　見ながら確認の質問は

できない。
　　　nu:ga naco:ru　　　　×　?ja: naco:mi?
　　　どうして泣いてるの　　　あんた泣いてるの？
　内省「泣くことを要求しているような気がする。泣くべきなのに泣いていないのか」
　(c)　(久場) 第3者どうしでも、動作を見ながらでは (b)同様
　　　×　atsuko naco:mi?
　　　A：are: naciru uNna:　　　B：naco:N do:
　　　　彼は　泣いているのね　　　　泣いているよ（理由が良くわかっている）

(3) 疑問詞のある質問文。いわゆる係り結びの形だが、注意して調べる。行為が具体的に決まっているかにどうかにより、異なることがある。係りを必ずしも必要としない。既に決定していても話し手が知らない場合に注意。質問文の動詞形と答えの動詞形にも注意する。

① ta: du kaku?　atsuko Ndu kaku. no:du kaku?　ba: unu zI: du kaku.
　　誰が　書くの　敦子が　書く。　何を　書く　私　この　字を　書く。

② ta: du kakja?　atsuko Ndu kakjaN.
　　誰が　書くの。　敦子が　書くの。(敦子が書くことが既に決まっている)

① zI: ja no: sa:ri (du) kaku?　hudi sa:ri (du) kaku.
　　字は　何　で　　　書くの。　筆　で　　　書く。

② kunu zI: ja no: sa:ri (du) kakja?　hudi sa:ri (du) kaku. ×kakja
　　この　字　は　何　で　　　書くの　筆　で　　　書く

② (平良西仲)
　　ta: ga kakja:?　答えて　kai / baga du kakI (ga mata). ×kakadi
　　誰　が　書くの(書く人が決まっている)　彼 / 私　が　書く

③ (平良西仲)
　　no: ju ga kakacca.　答えて　tigami ju. (du kakI)
　　何を　書くの　　　　　手紙　を　　　　　×kakadi　×kakacca

(4) 話し手がその行為（行動）を「見て（直接経験）」いるかどうかは重要である。基本的に見ていないというのは無いという方言が多い。多くの琉

球方言では、現在時制とは話し手の認識の上にあるのだが、過去というのも無限ではない。過去とは、話し手の経験中の過去であって、それ以外は伝聞にしなければならないという方言も多い。

① ami nu huiriki　　　　mukaina: kuN co:
　雨　が　降ってるから　迎えに　来るってよ（電話で言付けがあった）

② ba:maridakeNja kazji Ndu hukida co:.　Cf.　kIno: kazji Ndu hukida.
　私の生まれた時は風が吹いていたんだと　　昨日は　風　が　吹いた

(5) 相手を見ながら確かめる場合は、いわゆる係り結びがあるから、構文的に注意が必要である。他動詞と自動詞を意識的に調べる。

wa: tigami du kakiru？　wa: du tigami kakiru？　wa: tigami kaki duru？
あんた手紙を書いているの　あんたが　手紙書いてるの　あんた手紙書いてなんかいる

×wa: du nakiru？　　？wa: naki duru？
あんたが泣いてるの　　あんた泣いてなんかいるの（泣くこと無いのに）

(6) 「死ぬ」も必要だが「縁起が悪い」からなるべく鼠やゴキブリに例をとる。無意思動詞として「咲く」「降る」などとの共通性があることもある。

ba: tigami kakiruNkeN　　wa:　ikite ku:.
私　手紙　書いている間　あんた　行って来い

ba ikite kuNkeN wa: tigami kakiruN？
私　行って来る間あんた手紙書いている

×ba: sjiniruN.　×ujaNco: siniruN.　×ami huiruN.　×hana sakiruN.
私　死んでいる　鼠は　死んでいる　　雨　降っている　花　咲いている

(7) 動作を見ているか、見ていないか。また、相手から自分の行動が見えているかどうかが必要な条件であることは多い。「電話で話す（見えない）」というのも使い甲斐がある。確認しながら話すことになる。

①A：taraNdaru muno: kakiN？　B：kakiN. (道端、戸を隔てて等の会話)
　　　頼んだ　物は　書いてる　書いてる

A（電話で）：no: du hi: uru.　(hi:ru 可) cf.対面では普通 no: du hi:ru.
　　　　　　　何を　している　　　　　　　　　　　何をしている

　　　　　　taraNdaru muno: kakiN？
　　　　　　頼んだ　もの　書いてる
　　　Ｂ：kaki uruN.（kakiN 可、対面では kikiN）
　　　　　　書いている
　　　Ａ：atsuko: kakiN？（Aからは見えない）　B（見て）：kaki duru.（kakiN 可）
　　　　　　敦子は　書いている　　　　　　　　　　　　　　書いている
　②見ながらの叙述（質問文になるかどうかも確かめる）
　　　wa: kaki so:.　　　　　　　ba: kakaNtiN misjaN.
　　　あんたが書いている　　　　私は　書かなくて　いい（相手が書いているのを見ながら）
　　　ba: kaki so:.　　　　　　　wa: kakana:rja.（自分が書きながら）
　　　私　書いているの　　　あんた　書かないで
(8)　その行為が話し手にとって、望ましいか望ましくないか。意に反するか。同じ動作でも、異なることがある。
　①（辺土名）
　　(a)　敦子のお母さんが亡くなったので、友人がその親類の人に尋ねる。
　　　　　友人：atsuko maco:ti: na.　×nakiti: na　　親類：naco:taN.
　　　　　　　　敦子　　泣いてたか　　　　　　　　　　　泣いてた
　　(b)　敦子が非行少女で親に反抗して家出していた。ところが、親が亡くなったので帰ってきた。そこで同居の親類の人に尋ねる。
　　　　　Ａ：atsuko nakiti: na　　×naco:ti na　　　親類：nakitaN
　　　　　　　　敦子　　泣いてたか　　　　　　　　　　　　泣いてた
　　　　　Ａ：arigaN nakite:ssa ja:　　×nace:ssa ja:.
　　　　　　　あれまでも　泣いたんだね　　泣いたんだね
　　　　(b)は泣く行為が望ましい（ちゃんと泣いた）。
　②×wa: hwa:ja nakiN？（体が弱くて泣く力もない子が泣いてるかという時は可）
　　　あんたの　子　は　泣いてる（ちゃんと泣いてるか）
　③unu bi:ca:　　mata ki:caN.　　Cf. atsuko ki:Ta.
　　　この　酔っ払いまた　来ちゃった　　敦子　来た（敦子を待っていた）

④ kakaba muci harja.　　　　　　×sɪnaba（代わりに　sɪnuKa:）
　　　書いたら　持って行け　　　　　死んだら（死にたがっているよう）
(9)　話し手の判断と叙述。及びその質問のあり方。
　　① jagati ami hwo:ɴ. / ?　　　しかし　×ami hwo:ɴ ?
　　　間もなく　雨　降る（黒雲を見ながら）　　雨　降る
　　② atsuko kakɪ so:.　wa: higu kakja.　×　atsuko kakɪ so: ?
　　　敦子　書くよ　　あんた早く書け
　　③（平良西仲）kai ga kakɪm do:.　Cf. kai ga du kakɪ（ga mata）.（彼が書く）
　　　　　　　　彼が　書くよ（ほら今書こうとしてるよ。あんた早く行って書け）
(10)　初めての判断であるか（発見）、期待していたことであるか。思いがけないことか。
　　　遠くから来る人を見て、それが敦子だとわかった時、
　　　atsuko juɴ.　atsuko jaruɴ.　atsuko jarjaɴ.　atsuko jare:rjaɴ.
　　　敦子　だ　　敦子なんだ　　敦子なんだった　敦子　なんだったんだ
(11)　日常的な、習慣的なことかどうか。
　　① ba: mainitsɪ sjiɴbuɴ jumuɴ.
　　　私　毎日　新聞　読む
　　② ba: gaQko: ge: haru.
　　　私　学校　へ　行く（今学校へ行く子供が母に言う）
　　③（平良西仲）ba: ja mainitsɪ tigami ju kakɪ.　cf. baga kakadi. kari ga du kakɪ.
　　　　　　　　私　は　毎日　手紙　を　書く　私が　書く　彼が　書く
(12)　過去的な時制では、先ず過去の語（昔、昨日、去年、……の時）との共存を見る。
　　　mukasa:　ju:　tigami kakɪda.　　kɪnu du kakɪda.
　　　昔は　よく　手紙　書いた　　　　昨日　書いた
　　（上記は1・3人称ともに可、しかし書いたのを見知っていなければならない。同様な時は、見知っていない場合についても調べる。）
(13)　順番にする行動。（もう書いたか、まだか）
　　　全員が順番に黒板に出て書くことになっている。先生が生徒に確かめて、

先生：wa: kakiTa?　　　　　　生徒：me:da kakanu.
　　　あんた書いた(書き終わったか)　まだ　書かない(てない)
　　　(生徒は書きに出る)
Cf. 隣室で書いている人々のうち一人が途中で出て来た。もう済んだのか
　と思い、

A：wa: kakiTa?　　　B：me:da kakanu.
　　あんた書いた　　　　まだ　書かない（てない）(書いている途中)

⒁　瞬間的な認識。赤ちゃんが縁側から「落ちる」「落ちた」などが便利。
瞬間動詞でも、その落ちた（上から離れる時）／起きた（目を開けた時）
を確かめることも心がける。「落ちる」なら例えば上だけ見える窓から見
ている場合を考える。
（黒島）

utijaN!　　　　　　　uteheN
落ちた（飛行機が）　　落ちた(落ちそうだったものが遂に台風で)

ukijaN!　　　　　　　ukeheN
起きた（寝顔を見ている時）　起きていた（見たら目を開けていた）

⒂　動作・状態が起こった（ている）のが過去なのか、それを認識したのが
過去なのかを確かめる。話し手自身の行為と第三者の行為とでは異なる可
能性が高い。
敦子とBが同室で書いている。Bが出て来た。
A：atsuko: kakida?　　　　　　B：kakida（多分今でも書いてる）
　敦子 書いてた(敦子が書いてるのを見たか)書いてた（書いてるのを見た）

A：wa: kakida?　　　B：kaida.
　あんた書いてた　　　書いてた（終わっている）

⒃　現在の状態が、過去の行為存在を示すかどうか。
①話し相手が直接経験している。それを現在の状態から話し手が確認す
る。（話し手がそれを認識し、確認する。質問から始まる事が多い。ま
たは、独り言的）
　(a)　部屋から出て来た子供の目が赤くなって泣いた痕がある。

　　　　A：naki du:?　　　子供：naki du.
　　　　　　泣いたの　　　　　　泣いたの
　　　(b)　畑から濡れて帰ってきた人に（自家の周囲では雨は降らなかった）
　　　　A：ami hui du:?　　　B：hui du:.
　　　　　　雨　降ったの　　　　降った
②話し手は、行為の生起に関して全ての情報（記憶を含む）を用いてその
　行為が起こったと認識する。
　　　(a)　朝濡れた地面を見て、ami huie:N.　～　ami Ndu huie:ru.
　　　　　　　　　　　　　　　雨　降った　　　雨　が　降ったんだ
　　　(b)　自分が手紙を書いたかどうか忘れた。（当然、手紙はここに無い）
　　　　　A：ba: tigami kakIda kaja:.　B：wa: kake:so:.
　　　　　　　私　手紙　書いた　かね　　あんた　書いた
　　　　　　　　　　　　　　　　　（書くのは見なかったが手紙を見た）
　　　(c)　ba: taraNdaru muno: wa: kake:N?　kake:N.
　　　　　　私　頼んだ　ものは　あんた書いた　書いた（今その書類は見えない）
　　　(d)　tigami nu assoNga wa:du kake:ru?
　　　　　　手紙　が　あるけど　あんたが書いたの（手紙を見ながら言う）
　　　　　答えて　N: ba: du kake:ru.
　　　　　　　　　　うん私が書いたの　×　wa: kake:N?
　　　(e)　tigami nu attasoNga wa: du kake:da?
　　　　　　手紙　が　あったけど　あんたが書いたの（今その手紙は見えない）
　　　(f)　昔の忘れていたノートが出て来た。　ba: du kake:ru.
　　　　　　　　　　　　　　　　　　　　　　　　私　が　書いたんだ
　　　(g)　忘れていた場所に来て思い出し、　ba: manta Nga ke:N.
　　　　　　　　　　　　　　　　　　　　　　　私　前　に　来た（ことがある）
　　　(h)　犬の足跡があって床が汚れている。　iN nuN du arage:ru.
　　　　　　　　　　　　　　　　　　　　　　　犬　が　歩いたんだ
(17)　使役には、直接の使役と、人に言ってやらせる間接の使役の接辞があ
　　る。一段対応動詞に注意
　　　①　kak-u- 書く　kaka-hu- 書かせる　kaka-sjimiru- 人に言って書かせ

② uk-iru-　起きる　uka-hu-　起こす　uka-sjimiru-　人に言って起こす
　　③ ak-iru-　開ける　　×　　aki-sjimiru-　人に言って開けさせる

書く（実例は石垣宮良方言）
　例文は、話者との兼ね合いで場面を設定する。ある程度すると話者の方も面白がり、「こんな人もいるから」と条件をつけたり、後回しにしたり、遠慮したりといろいろな形、表現が出てくる。それらを整理して、次は形の規則性の方から確認していく。参考を記す。

● 何か書くことになった。（学校・会合・黒板に、書類を、記録等々わいわいがやがや）
　①「誰が書く？」「私が書く。」「私も書く。」「あんた書きなさい。」
　　「何を書くの」
　　"ta: du kaku ?"　"ba: du kaku."　"banuN kakuN."　"wa: kakja."
　　"no: du kaku."
　②「あんたも書く？」「私は書かない。」「書けばいいのに。」
　　「じゃ、書こう。」
　　"wanuN kakuN ?"　"ba: kakanu."　"kakja: misja:ru munu."
　　"anzuKa: kakuN."
　③「あんた書きたい？」「書きたくない。」「書く人がいないなら、私が書くよ」
　　"wa: kakIpusuN ?"　"kakIpusanu."　"kaku pItu urana:Ka: ba: kakuN."

●「敦子が書くよ」「敦子が書く？」「敦子は書かないよ」「敦子は書くだろう」
　　"atsuko: kakuN." "atsuko: kakuN ?" "atsuko: kakanu." "atsuko: kaku hazI."

● 書く人を敦子に決めたところで、光子が入ってきて問う。
　「誰が書くの？」「敦子が書くんだよ」
　　"ta: du kakja ?" "atsuko Ndu kakjaN."

●希望者が多い。「みんなで書こう」
"(baga:) ma:zoN kaka"
●グループ対抗「あの人達は早く書くけど、私達はゆっくり書こう」
"uQta: hajamari kakabaN baga: jurQtu kaka na:."
●順番に書くことになった。
「あんたもう書いた？」「まだ書いてない」「あんたは？」「書いた」
"wa: kakiTa?"　　　"me:da kakanu."　　"wa: kakiTa?"　"kakiTa."
「敦子は書いた？」　　「書いたよ。」
"atsuko: kakiTa?"　　"kakiTa."

●「敦子は書いた？」「今書いてるよ。」「陽子は書いてた？」「書いてる（のを見た）。」
"atsuko: kakiTa?"　"nama du kakiru."　"jo:ko: kakida?"　"kakida."

●書いたものを見ながら
「これは誰が書いたの」「敦子が書いたの（敦子が書くのを見た）」
"kure: ta: du kake:ru?"　"atsuko Ndu kakIda."
「これは誰が書いたの」「名前があるから、敦子が書いたんだ（書くのは見ていない）」
"kure: ta: du kake:ru?"　"na: nu ariki, atsuko Ndu kake:ru na:"

●道端で出会って、「頼んだもの書いてる？」「書いてる」
"taraNdaru muno: kakiN?"　"kakiN"
その書類を取りに行く。　「頼んだの書いた？」　　「書いてある。」
"taraNdaru muno: kake:N?"　"kake:N."
取りに来た時まだ書いている最中
戸を隔てて見えないとき "nama kakiN."　見えるとき "nama du kakiru"

●「頼んだもの書かなくてよくなった。書いちゃった？」「あら。書いちゃった。」
"taraNdaru muno: kakaNtiN misjaN. wa: kakiCaN?"　"agajo: kakiCaN."

●「何処で書く？」、　「何で書く？」、　「どう書く？」
"zImaNga du kaku?"　"no: sa:ri du kaku"　"no: ba hi du kaku/kakja: ?"

このくらいでひとまず整理して足りない形を調べる。
例えば　書く　　kakiN　：　kakuN,
　　　　　　　　　：　　　：　　　（kakiruN)
　　　　起きる　ukiN　：　ukiruN,
　　　　　　　　　　　　　　　　（×　ukuN)

4形の関係を上表のように見れば、kakiruN, ukuN, があるかどうか知りたくなる。すると、kakiruN は限られた用法でも実在するが、ukuN は無いということがわかる。

勿論状況に応じて他の動詞を用いることも心がける。

5．形容詞
注意事項
①語幹と語尾に注目する。
②語尾の形に注意する。方言により異なる。

項目
(1)　語尾が動詞と同様か異なるか。違った語尾があるか。どのような違いか。
　①　sane-he-N　嬉しい（と感じる）　kake:-N　書いてある（と認める）
　　　sane-he:-da-ru　嬉しい　　　　　kake:-da-ru　書いてある
　　　sane-he:-da　嬉しかった　　　　kake:-da　書いてあった
　②　2種の語尾（佐和田）
　　(a)　pukarasImunu:　嬉しい　pukarasImunu atam　今日は嬉しかった
　　(b)　pukarasIkam　嬉しい　pukarasIkatam　嬉しかった
　③（伊良部）
　　　Nmaham　美味しい（食べてから言う）　　Nmamunu
　　　fufumunu　黒い　　　　　　　　　　　×　fufuham

25

④（黒島）　haijaN　美しい　　sanijaN　うれしい
　　　　　　akahaN　赤い　　　ma:haN　うまい
⑤形容詞語尾の母音が、語幹末音と呼応することがある。

語幹	a	u/o	i/e	I	i:
語尾	-haN	-hoN	-heN	-saN	-sjaN

takahaN（広い），pIsohoN（広い），kaiheN（美しい），sI:saN（すっぱい），p:sjaN（寒い）

(2) 主観的形容詞（大体シク活用に対応）と客観的形容（大体ク活用に対応）が形として異なる（首里、黒島）場合もあるが、接辞で異なる時もある。

① ba: saneheN.　　atsuko: sanehe huN.　　×atsuko saneheN.
　　私　嬉しい　　敦子は嬉しくする（喜ぶ）

② ba: sanehe:du aQta.　　atsuko: sanehe:du sIta.
　　私　嬉しかった　　　敦子は　嬉しくした（喜んだ）
　×ba: sanehe:du sIta.　　×atsuko: sanehe:du aQta.

(3) この「する」を意味する動詞との結合は琉球方言に広くあるので注意する。

(4) 動詞と同様な語尾を持つ場合は動詞との整合性に注意する。
　　kju: ja pi:sjadaru.　　外に出て冷たい風にあたって　pi:sjaN.
　　今日は　寒い　　　　　　　　　　　　　　　　　　　寒い

The Grammar of Ishigaki Miyara Dialect in Luchuan

The area of Luchuan dialects

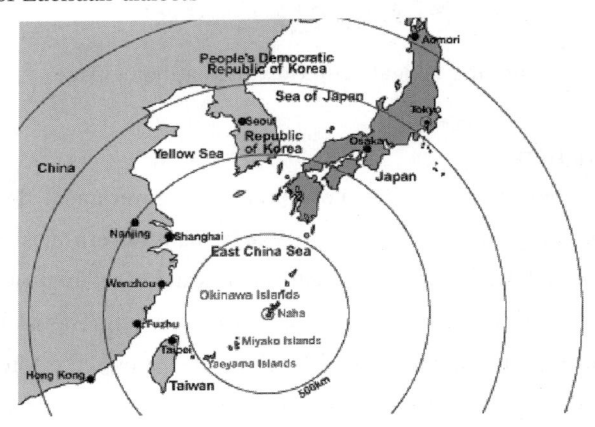

Okinawa prefecture

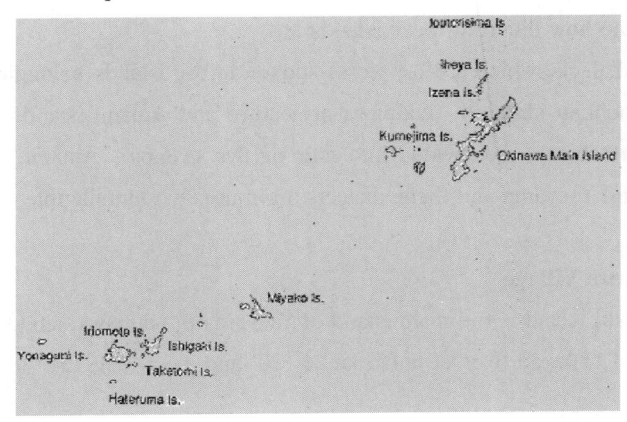

From the Okinawa prefectual Government home page

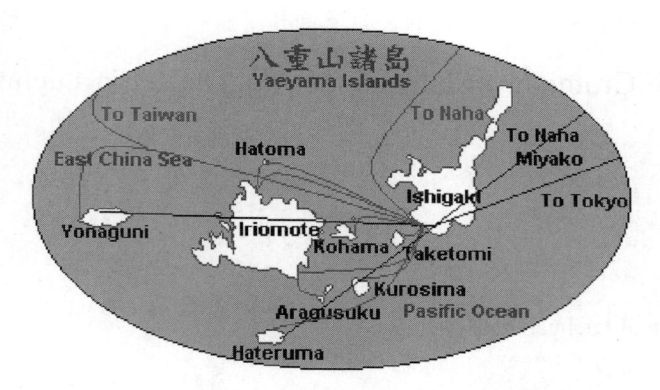

From the Ishigaki city Government home page

1. Introduction

On its home page, the Okinawa prefecture government described its area as follows: "Okinawa Prefecture, Japan's southwestern most prefecture, consists of 49 inhabited and 110 uninhabited islands scattered over an area 1,000 from east to west and 400 km from north to south. The islands are divided into three major groups: the Okinawa island group, the Miyako island group, and the Yaeyama island group. Okinawa island is by far the largest, followed in turn by Iriomote island, Ishigaki island and Miyako island." We can imagine how different these islands are.

The dialects, which are (or were) spoken in the islands belonging to the former Luchuan kingdom (Okinawa prefecture and Amami islands of Kagoshima prefecture), are divided into four or five [1] groups: Amami, Okinawa, Miyako and Yaeyama and these dialects are mutually unintelligible.

1. 1. Miyara Village

Ishigaki Island is the main island of Yaeyama in Okinawa, situated in the south west of Japan. It is at north lat.24° 20' and west long.124° 9'. Ishigaki

---

(1) Yonaguni dialect might be independent from Yaeyama group.

Island is 1952 km from Tokyo, 411 km from Naha-Shuri which was the capital of Luchuan Kingdom. The distance from Naha to Ishigaki is almost the same as from Tokyo to Kyoto. Considering this great distance, we can easily conceive of varieties in the Luchuan language.

Ishigaki city includes all of Ishigaki Island, and it comprises a number of villages, whose histories are not yet clarified. Before the Meiji Restoration (1867), there were many waves of immigration, so while some villages are old, others were founded recently.

One of the small villages, now a part of Ishigaki city, is Miyara, situated along the seaside in 8 km south-east from the central part of Ishigaki city.

"Miyara" is first documented in Japanese history, in the book "*Miyako-Yaeyama ryōtō ezu chō*"[2] published in 1611. In 1771,[3] Miyara Village was almost destroyed by a tsunami, and of the 1221 inhabitants at the time, only 171 survived the disaster. After that, 320 people from Kohama Island immigrated to Miyara to construct a new village. Linguistically, while we have no record of what Miyara dialect was like before the disaster, the Kohama immigration has led to today's Miyara dialect being similar to that of Kohama. Even now, the people of these two villages have some cultural exchange when conducting local festivals.

"*Miyako-Yaeyama ryōtō ezu chō*" also described about "Shiraho" which is another village of Miyara. "The district of Miyara includes two villages, that is, Miyara and Shiraho." Shiraho was also destroyed with the same tsunami. At that time, the population of Shiraho was 1574, and only 28 people survived. Later on, 418 people from Hateruma Island immigrated to Shiraho and they reconstructed this village. Therefore, Shiraho dialect is basically as same as Hateruma dialect. That is to say, two different dialects are (better to say were) spoken in the same district.

---

(2) "Miyara son shi (History of Miyara Village)" (1986, pp.11–13).
(3) The third year of the Meiwa period, making this disaster the "Meiwa Tsunami".

Ishigaki Island is known for sight seeing because of its beautiful ocean, but Miyara is not a sight seeing place. It is in the farm area. In recent times, Miyara is changing into a suburb of the central part of Ishigaki city. As the result, the number of Miyara dialect speakers is getting fewer and fewer.

The population of Miyara was about 1,000 in 1931, and about 1,500 in 2,000. The residential area of Ishigaki city is getting wider and wider. Even old traditional houses are sometimes sold out. New residents are enjoying the life in Miyara, but the increased population does not mean that there are more speakers of the dialect. The traditional dialect is spoken mainly by people who are 60 years old or more.

1. 2. Miyara dialect

Miyara village fortunately has a conservative tendency to keep old traditions. People maintain rigid discipline for festivals ; they would not like to change their festivals into simple events.

Their most important festival, in which *"akamata and kuromata"* play an active part, is common to 4 villages (Miyara, Kohama, Aragusuku, Iriomotekomi). Accordingly it is considered that these four villages might have some relation in their history.

Thanks to this tendency, their traditional dialect has been kept pretty well. In addition Miyara dialect has a beautiful phonetic and grammatical system that does not lose its important features.

Speakers are proud of "tenderness" of their dialect. It is said in this area that it is impossible to quarrel when speaking in Miyara dialect. They are also proud of their good pronunciation when singing traditional folk songs. These days, even young men and women are interested in Yaeyama folk songs. As a result, they are also interested in their pronunciations because most of young people have some difficulty to sing folk songs with good traditional pronunciation.

Miyara speakers feel that Shika (central part of Ishigaki city) dialect is similar to their own. Shika dialect has a role of common language in the Yaeyama district. People of both Miyara and Shika can communicate with each other using their mutually intelligible dialects.

1. 3. Endangered Luchuan

We can easily observe an endangered dialect in any places where traditional Luchuan dialects are spoken. The situation of Miyara is but one example, which we will discuss here.

As stated, immigrants from other islands rebuilt Miyara and Shiraho after the Meiwa tsunami. That, and their subsequent independence, is why these sister villages have very different dialects in spite of their close proximity.

After Meiji Restoration in 1868, the Japanese Government created a law making education compulsory, and a primary school was founded in this district. It happened that only one school was founded in Shiraho village for children of both Miyara and Shiraho. In the Taishō period (about 1920), children of both villages used to go to school in Shiraho and they learned there common Japanese for the first time. Children from both villages were able to make friends communicating in common Japanese, though they spoke only their dialect at home.

The people of Miyara, however, wanted to have a school in their village, and at last, Miyara School was founded in 1942.[4]

With the modernization since Meiji Era, a small local community became larger and its dialect came to be deprived of its power. People have to communicate each other in the larger community, e.g. army and commerce. They need a common language.

Family register and school education made useless traditional names such as *"ja:nu na:*(name of the house ≅ family name)" and *"kanasɪ na:*(lovely

---

(4) *Miyara-son-shi* (history of Miyara village) (pp.331-357)

name=given name ≅ nickname)". For example, those who were born in the 1910s have "*kanasɪ na:*" besides personal name of family register. Those who were born in the end of the 1920s were not given "*kanasɪ na:*" any more. Some people in Okinawa still have their traditional names but never use them.

In the 1930s, young men and women enjoyed singing folksongs in the open spaces. They improvised songs and they could often find their sweethearts or lovers in singing and dancing and addressing with "*kanasɪ na:*" They used to help each other in building houses, in cultivating fields, in any tasks singing *zjiraba* (songs for work). They conversed always in their dialect. The whole life was with their dialect.

The Pacific War unexpectedly contributed to the spread of common Japanese. A young men's association was activated and young people were educated to speak the common language. It was necessary for them to communicate in an emergency in common Japanese.

After the war, the educational system was changed in Japan. In the 1950s, a new junior high school was founded in Shiraho for children of both Miyara and Shiraho. Miyara dialect and Shiraho dialect are so different that the students communicated neither in Miyara dialect nor in Shiraho dialect, but in common Japanese. Senior high schools are only in the central part of Ishigaki city, and with pupils with different dialects coming to senior high school from all districts and islands in Yaeyama, the result is unification of dialects, or rather abandonment of their own dialects.

This is the situation in which people today form relationships and marry. They speak common Japanese more and more. For example, a couple consisting of a man from Miyara and his wife who comes from Naha of Okinawa will naturally expect that their children be educated in common Japanese, because difference between Naha and Miyara is bigger than that between Tokyo and Kyoto. The rich dialectal varieties themselves have ironically made them endangered.

Polite expressions in dialects also influenced this decline. It is difficult for young generation to choose among levels of polite expressions. An anecdote in Kume-island[5] will tell the situation. A young boy was scolded for using a vulgar word when he addressed his uncle in next village. This poor young boy did not know that the honorific word in his village is used to look down on the hearer in the next village.

People speak the common language when conducting commercial activities. They avoid using their dialects for fear of misunderstanding.

Children are surrounded by the common language in nursery school. Parents and grand parents follow suit and they speak the common language also at home.

It is admirable that old people have the ability to acquire the common language. These days, generation gap is getting bigger and bigger, and with lonely old people most interested in their health, those who are working for medical treatment such as doctors and nurses usually speak common language. It is impossible to adapt every local dialect for public use in hospitals ; therefore old people have to master common language. Everyone needs to communicate in order to live well. Old people are not exception.

If a language has too much variation, it might be get endangered very quickly when it meets another sister language with strong power. Luchuan dialects are endangered in such a way.

Luchuan rapidly lost its power for the external-internal and social-commercial reasons. People have to learn a different language. It is desirable for them to enter into the world of common Japanese language as soon as possible. The old traditional dialects are becoming useless for their social lives.

It seems that the radio did not have such a great influence on the language in Okinawa. In the 1950s, Luchuan classic music and folk songs were sent almost every day on the wired radio system in Shuri, the capital of Oki-

---

(5) It is situated near to Okinawa and its dialect is not Yaeyama branch.

nawa. Perhaps, however, the majority of households did not have the radios. At that time, housewives of a certain age would not address their conversation a girl who spoke only the common language. Now, 50 years later, however, even a 100-year old woman will not hesitate to speak the common language.

Moreover, television broadcasts spread over whole Okinawa with great power. In addition to NHK, commercial broadcasting began to go on the air in 1993 in the whole area of Yaeyama. Cheerful talk and funny action in the common language! They speak in such an amusing and entertaining way, even in the common language! The barrier disappeared completely.

It is difficult to teach Luchuan dialect in school. Luchuan is different from common Japanese language in both its phonological and grammatical system. In school, children have to learn the curriculum on the basis of the common language. "Why should children learn old useless things?" say supporters of common Japanese. Mothers' wish that "children could be rich in vocabulary" prevents them from teaching children their traditional dialect.

It does not necessarily follow that Luchuan native teachers are interested in the local dialect. Luchuan has a lot of varieties. The teacher's dialect may be too different to stimulate an interest in the new dialect. In addition, it is decided that the teacher always moves after a short period on an isolated island.

In the 1920s, teachers sometimes spoke to first year pupils in local dialect. Old people once said that children could master speaking common language in third year. Children were usually enjoying going to school. After school they used to work very hard at feeding horses and pigs, cooking, washing clothes and farming. They used to baby-sit even before school age.

Home life is now changed. It is occasionally found that grandparents have made progress in speaking their common language after grandchildren's staying during summer vacation. Social life has changed entirely. Now it is impossible for grandparents to teach their own dialect to their grandchildren.

Nowadays we can see dialect speech festivals in several villages and towns. These events help to protect dialects from disappearing. Children might learn at least to respect old people who speak their traditional dialect.

In 2001, a traditional song festival was held in Miyara Public Hall. They tried to speak only their dialect in public. This was successful although they needed efforts and they hope to continue revival activities like this.

Miyara dialect might go extinct without ever having been studied fully. It is very regrettable that this beautiful dialect, which includes numerous facts that are important for general linguistics and the history of Japanese language, is disappearing.

2. Transcription

Broad transcription is here employed to write Miyara dialect. For the convenience of printing, some phonetic symbols are changed as follows:

Φ → hw~hu, ʃ → sj, dz/z → z, ʒ/dʒ → zj, tʃ → c, g → g, ʔ → ʼ

syllabic nasal phone → N, syllabic voiceless consonant → Q,

non-aspirated glottalized consonant → capital letter

This dialect does not have one syllable word with short vowel. Short vowel [e] and [o] appear only in special environments: before [N] and word or morpheme final position where they are lengthened.

The following is a list of phonological correspondence between Common Japanese and Miyara dialect. It will be useful to understand quickly phonological system of this dialect. It seems that Miyara has neither [e] nor [o] respectively corresponding to Japanese [e] and [o], although it has usually long [e:] and [o:].[6]

---

(6) Short [e] and [o] can appear in the position preceding [N] and word final position

CJ	k*i*mo (lever)	k*u*ci (mouth)	k*e* (hair)	k*o* (powder)	k*i* (tree)
Miyara	k*ɨ*mu	huts*ɨ*	ki:	k*u*:	k*ɨ*
CJ	s*i*ima (island)	s*u* (nest)	se*N* (thousand)	s*o*N (loss)	
Miyra	s*ɨ*ma	s*ɨ*:	s*ji*N	s*u*N	
CJ	c*i* (blood)	ts*u*na (rope)	t*e* (hand)	t*o*: (ten)	
Miyara	ts*ɨ*:	ts*ɨ*na	ti:	tu:	
CJ	h*a*na (flower)	h*i* (fire)	h*u*ka- (deep)	h*e* (wind)	h*o* (sail)
Miyara	h*a*na	p*ɨ*:	h*u*ka-	p*i*:	p*u*:
CJ	(w) *i* (reed)⁽⁷⁾	(w)*e*- (drink)	(w)*o*- (break)	z*ji* (letter)⁽⁸⁾	z*ji* (earth)
Miyara	b*ɨ*:	b*i*-	b*u*-	z*ɨ*:	z*ɨ*:

It is shown that there are two kinds of vowels which correspond to /i/ of Common Japanese. The one corresponds to /i/ and /e/. The other corresponds to only /i/, never to Japanese /e/. The latter is usually described as [ɨ],⁽⁹⁾ that is, central vowel. As a matter of fact, this vowel is not "central", at least not in Yaeyama.

In Miyara, it is a tense unrounded front close vowel, but the preceding consonant is never palatalized. The preceding velar consonants ([k], [g]) are articulated in back position in comparison with those of Tokyo dialect. The preceding labial consonants ([p], [b]) are articulated with lip spread sideways and with very weak plosion. They seem to be easily changed into affricates ([Φ], [β]).

This vowel is articulated in the position so close to [s] that we hear the glide [s] after voiceless consonants [k] [p], and the glide [z] after voiced consonants [g] [b]. They sound very curious to those who do not have such consonants with glide in their dialect even in Yaeyama. In this paper, this

---

(7) In ancient Japanese, these word had [w] in initial position.
(8) In ancient Japanese, the initial sound of the word "letter" was fricative but that of "earth" was affricate.
(9) Karimata (1992, p.863)

vowel is designated by symbol [ɪ].

On the contrary, [i] is a little bit wide and lax front vowel articulated in rather back position in comparison with [ɪ] and is pronounced with rather neutral lips. Its preceding consonants are always palatalized.

[ɪ] can not stand in initial position although it can in Aragusuku dialect (a branch of Yaeyama Dialect). It never stands after [h, t, d, n].

It is considered that the syllables with this [ɪ] are phonologically opposed to those which have [i], as non-palatalized versus palatalized. That is to say, this kind of oppositions might be interpreted as the oppositions of consonants, not of vowels. They might be designated as /ki̱/:/kji/, /pi̱/:/pji/ etc. In this paper, however, [i] and [ɪ] is used to designate this phenomena according to the traditional interpretation. The syllable with [b, p, (m), s, z, ts, k, g] have this kind of opposition. As far as [mɪ] is concerned, only one of the oldest who is near 100 years old has it for special one word.(10)

Miyara dialect does not have glottal stop which is usually observed in Okinawa Main Island where vowels have a glottal stop in word initial position.

In Miyara dialect, close vowels are often devocalized after voiceless consonants. Sometimes even an open vowel, e.g. [a], is devocalized.(11) Devocalization accompanies strong aspiration. Some morphemes, however, are never devoiced but always pronounced in full voice and sometimes with laryngealization. Young people pronounce it as a syllabic consonant. This phenomenon is also going to disappear without researching in detail.

The articulation point of syllabic nasal [N] is a little forward and close to velar. It is articulated as the more steady sound than that of Tokyo. It is never changed into a nasalized vowel before vowels and semivowels. We can often hear the glide like [ʔ] before [j]. In general, the vowels before syllabic

---

(10) For the word meaning "serpent" in the twelve horary signs.
(11) The devocalization will be related to the accent. It is not yet studied.

nasal are pronounced a little longer.

There is no voiceless palatal fricative [c] even before [i]. Yaeyama dialects, not only Miyara but also many other dialects do not have it. Instead, they have [h].

Word final vowels are often lengthened[12] without phonological meaning.

3. Pronouns
3. 1. Personal pronouns

Common Japanese does not have personal pronouns in the precise meaning. It has several first person pronouns according to the speaker: *boku* for boys, *atashi* for girls, *watakushi* for polite use, *ore* for men's slang, *watashi* for neutral use etc. In Luchuan dialects, however, there is only one word for first person pronoun. It is important that both men and women use the same word for the first person though the honorific system always makes distinction of sex and the kin terms differ with the sex. Miyara dialect does not have any honorific word for second person though Shuri and other dialects have one.

Neither second person nor third person has distinction of sex.

3. 1. 1. Special categories of personal pronouns

We generally find two kinds of first person plural in Luchuan dialects of wide area from Amami to Yonaguni. It was reported since long[13] that a number of Luchuan dialects have two kinds of first person plural. So far as I know, they are Amami (Kikai Island), northern part of Main island of Okinawa (Nakijin, Hentona, etc.), its southern part (Itoman), Kume Island (Gima and

---

[12] It is observed especially at the end of sentences or phrases.
[13] The oldest is Iwakura (1941)

Torishima), Miyako Islands (Ikema, Irabu, Tarama, Kurima, etc.), Yaeyama Islands (Shika, Miyara, Shiraho, Kuroshima, Yonaguni, etc.).

Some of contemporary scholars classify 1st person plural pronouns as "exclusive we" and "inclusive we". However, this opposition is not "exclusive versus inclusive" but rather "we, the opposite of second person versus we, the opposite of third person". The so-called inclusive one means "we, speaker's group", that is, the speaker and anyone participating in the speaker's action, or otherwise associated with the speaker. This is not necessarily linked to family or other "in-groups" often distinguished in common Japanese. In this paper, we will use the term "speaker's group (SG)"[14].

Another notable category is reflexive pronoun (oneself, the said person, the person in question). A number of Yaeyama dialects have this category. In general, however, speakers of these dialects use it only for the third person contextually designated, and not for the first person or the second person. It indicates the persons who are not in the presence of the people having the conversation, or who do not participate in the conversation.

In Miyara dialect, there are special words to denote the family community, e.g. my (or our) family (members)[15].

3. 1. 2. Forms of pronouns
Pronouns

	1st	2nd	SG	3rd	3rd person reflexive
Sg	ba:/banu	wa:/wanu	---	uri	na:ra
Pl	banda:	wada:	baga(:)	uQ-ta:	naQ-ta:

banu and *wanu* are independent forms

---

(14) The details of this topic were described in Izuyama (1992).
(15) The members are not necessarily all living together.

Family community

1st	2nd	SG	3rd	3rd reflexive
baN-ca	*waQ-ca*	*baga(:)*	---	*naQ-ca*

Morpheme *-ca* is suffixed to personal name and derives a word meaning his/her family community ; e.g. *atsuko-ca*: 'atsuko's family'.

The third person pronoun has some relation with the demonstrative pronoun. It will be discussed later. The structure of pronoun is important to consider co-occurrence restriction of verbal form in accordance with actors.

3. 1. 3. Illustrative sentences[16]

(1) First person singular

  (a) A : *'ja: ja:*   B : *banu?*
                      1-IND

     A : Hello!   B : Me?

  (b) *ba: kak-u-N.* (c) *kure: ba: munu.* (d) *banu N kak-u-N*
[17]
    1-NOM-TOP writeAC-CON-N this-TOP 1GEN thing 1-IND also write-AC-CON-N

    'I write.'   'This is my thing.' 'I also write.'

    (○ *ba: ja* × *ba: nu* × *banu nu* / *ba: nu* × *banu ja*)

       TOP   NOM   GEN / GEN   TOP

  (e) *banu ju sa: ri har-i.* (f) *banu ju N sa: r-i har-i.*

    1-IND ACC bring-and go-IMP   1-IND ACC also bring and go-IMP

    'Accompany me.'   'Accompany me, too.'

  (g) *banu N sa: ri har-i.* = (f) (without particle *ju*)

  (h) *banu ge: hir-i.* (i) *ba: du kak-u.*

    1-IND DAT give-IMP   1-NOM FOC write

    'Give me.'   'I write.' (It is me who writes.)

---

(16) The English of the examples might sound unnatural but I have left them this way to reflect the original Miyara grammar.

(17) Form *"ba:"* can be translated into Japanese as +*ga* (nominative) and/or +*wa* (topic).

(2) Second person singular
- (a) A: *taru rja*.   B: *banu*   A: <u>wanu</u> *du aQ-ta?!*
  'Who is it?'   'It's me.'   'It is you?!'
- (b) <u>wa:</u> *kak-ja:*. (c) *kure:* <u>wa:</u> *munu*. (d) <u>wanu</u> *N kak-ja:*.
  2-NOM/TOP IMP-write this-TOP 2-GEN thing 2-IND also write-IMP
  '(You) Write!'   'This is your thing.'   'Write, you also.'
  ×<u>wanu</u> *ja*   ×<u>wanu</u> *nu*
  2-IND TOP   2-IND NOM/GEN
- (e) <u>wanu</u> *jo: (=ju+ja)   sa:r-i   har-a*.
  2-IND ACC-TOP   bring and   go-IREA
  'I/we will accompany you (even if I/we do not accompany any other person).'
- (f) <u>wanu</u> *ge: hir-u-N*.
  2-IND DAT giveCON-N
  'I give (it) to you.'
- (g) <u>wa:</u> *du kak-u?*   ×<u>wa:</u>   *du   kak-u*.
  you-NOM FOC write-CON   you-NOM FOC write-CON
  'Do you write?'   'You write.'

(3) Third person singular
- (a) <u>uri</u> *nu/N du kak-u*.   (b) *kure:* <u>uri</u> *nu munu*.
  3 NOM FOC write-CON   this-TOP 3 NOM thing
  'He writes.'   'This is his thing.'
- (c) <u>uri</u>   *du   sa:r-i har-u*.
  3   FOC bring-and go-CON
  'I (we/he/she/they) accompany him.'
- (d) <u>ure:</u> *kak-u hazI*.   (e) <u>uri</u> *N   kak-u hazI*.
  3-TOP write-ATT certainy   3 also write-ATT certainty
  'He ought to write.'   'He also ought to write.'
- (f) <u>uri</u> *N   sa:r-i har-ja*.   (g) <u>uri</u> *ju N   sa:r-i har-ja*.
  3 also   bring&go-IMP   3 ACC also bring&go-IMP

'Accompany him also.'   'Accompany him also.'

(f) & (g) are almost same. The accusative marker "ju" is often omitted.

(4) Plural forms

(a) An old couple is telling about an old work song to Izuyama (author).
unu zjiraba: <u>baNda:</u> du izji-da.
This song-TOP 1-pl FOC sing-PST
'Speaking of this zjiraba, we are used to sing it.'

(b) The old couple recalls an old work song in the above case, and looking at each other :
unu zjiraba: <u>baga:</u> du izji-da na:.
This song-TOP SG FOC sing-ST-PST FP
'We were used to sing this song. Isn't it?'

(c) Two groups were going to the same place. Group-A was overtaken by group-B. Then a member of group-A said to his group members :
<u>uQta:</u> hajamari ha-r-a-ba-N <u>baga:</u> juruQtu har-a na:.
3 pl-TOP hurry and go-though   SG-TOP slowly go-VL FP
'Let's walk slowly, though they are hurrying along.'

(d) And he shouts to group-B :
<u>wada:</u> har-ir-ja:. <u>baNda:</u> juruQtu ku(:)-N.
2-pl-Top go-EP-IMP 1-pl-Top slowly come-AC-CON-N
'You go on hurrying up. We follow slowly.'

(e) After a while, another member of group-A says on second thought to his group :
<u>baga:</u> N hajamari usjik-i har-a na:.
SG also hurry and catch up and go-VL FP
'Let's catch them up hurrying and go (together).

(f) Speech at the party celebrating "old people's day"
<u>baga:</u> me:ramura: mukasI gara takame:ra di
SG-GEN Miyara-village-TOP oldtimes from high-Miyara AP
na: taci du uriki, <u>baga:</u> me:ramura murazju: nu

42

name rose FOC left-because, SG-GEN Miyara-village whole village GEN
pItu, gaNzjoho:ar-ir-i, co:me:sjikir-i...
person, healthy be-IMP, long-life do-IMP

'Our Miyara village has made its name as "Great Miyara" from old times, so I say to the people of whole village : "be healthy and enjoy long life..." '

(g) Three people arranged to meet and go somewhere but Masako did not come at the promised time.

   A : *masako: kuN-ba* <u>*baga*</u> *har-ir-u-N* ?   B : *di: har-a.*
     masako-TOP come-NEG-CND SG go-EP-CON-*N*   come on go-VL

    ' Masako does not come , so will we start ?   'come on. Let's go.'

In this case, B cannot answer "*hariruN*". "*hariruN*" means "only speaker goes, not hearer".

(5) Words for family community (home or house)

  (a) To the friends.   (b) To the friends
   <u>*waQca:*</u> *ge: har-a.*   <u>*baNca:*</u> *ge har-u-N* ?
   Your-house to go-VL   my/our house to go-AC-CON-*N*
   'Let's go to your house.'   'Won't you come to our house?'

  (c) To the members of family (e.g. grand children who live in other place)
   <u>*baga:*</u> *ge har-a.*
   SG to go-VL
   'Let's go home.'

   "<u>*baga:*</u> *ja*: " is not chosen in this case. "*ja*: (house)" is always omitted.
   SG-GEN house (our house)

  (d) Miyara speakers do not use first person singular to indicate their house. To indicate the house as building, not home, they use only plural forms as follows.

  (d-1) <u>*wada:*</u> *ja: ja zINga du ar-u?*
     2-pl-GEN house TOP where-in FOC is-CON
     'Where is your house?'

(d-2) *uma du* <u>*wada:*</u> *ja : ?*   *kuma:* <u>*baNda:*</u> *ja:*.
　　This place FOC 2-pl-GEN house this place-TOP 1-pl-GEN house
　　'Is this your house?'　　　　'This is our house.'
(e) Pointing at the field or the tomb belonging to one's own family :
(e-1) The hearer is the daughter in law who has recently got married to the son.
　　<u>*baga:*</u> *nu hatagi / haka dara:*.
　　SG GEN field / tomb　FP
　　'(It's) our field / tomb.' 'It is the field/tomb belonging to our family.'
(e-2) The hearer is the friends or acquaintances.
　　<u>*baNca*</u> *nu hatagi / haka dara:*.
　　Our family GEN field / tomb FP
　　'(It's) our field/tomb.' 'It is the field/tomb belonging to our family.'
(f) Referring member of family
(f-1) <u>*baga:*</u> *nu ja:niNzju*
　　SG　GEN　house-member
　　Our family member　(speaking among the family)
(f-2) <u>*baNca*</u> *nu ja:niNzju*
　　Our family GEN house-member
　　Our family member　(speaking to another family member)

(6) Reflexive pronoun

　　The reflexive pronoun has co-occurrence relation with the third person pronoun. The *u-series (uri , uQta:)* can co-occur with it but *ka-series (kari, kaQta:* referring to someone at a distance from both the speaker and the hearer) can not. It seems that the latter does not have anaphoric usages. The following are the examples :

　(a) Looking at one's friend passing away,
　　(a-1) *banu jo: sa:rana:-te* <u>*na:ra / naN*</u> *taNga: du har-u*.
　　　　I ACC-TOP ask-NEG-and REF-sg alone FOC go-CON
　　　　'(He/she) is going (somewhere) him/herself alone without asking me

(to go together).'

(a-2) *banu jo: sa:rana:-te <u>naQta</u> taNga: haQ-so:.*
I ACC-TOP ask-NEG-and REF-pl alone go-AC-INF-so:
'(They) are going (somewhere) themselves alone without asking me (to go together).'

(b) Atsuko took and brought back a big pan with her from the kitchen. The man who was there and saw it told to others "A girl took back the thing of this house." The others know that it belongs to her. The answer is following :

atsuko: <u>na:ra</u> munu du muc-i haQ-ta.
Atsuko-TOP REF-sg thing FOC bring and go-AC-PST
'Atsuko bought back her own thing'.

(c) A : *ure: ta: munu?*
It-TOP Q-sg-GEN thing
'Whose (thing) is it?'

B : *atsuko nu munu.*
Atsuko GEN thing
'(It is) Atsuko's (thing).'

Pointing another thing

uri N <u>na:ra</u> munu jaQ-soNga muc-i har-a-na:-da.
It also REF-sg thing COP- but bring-and go-NEG-PAST
'It is Atsuko's, too. But she did not bring it back.

(d) Reflexive expression about family (home, house)

(d-1) Seeing a stranger(s) to enter into the house opposite, someone says "Thief!"

Answering to him : *<u>naQca:</u> ge: du pe:r-i har-u.*
REF to TOP enter-and go-AC-CON
'(He) is going into his own house.'

(d-2) *uma: <u>naQca:</u>.*
that-place-TOP REF

45

'That is his own (their own) house.'

(d-3) unu ja: ja   naQta: ja: . (= naQca:)

  that house TOP his own (their own) house.

  'That house is his own house.'

(d-4) uQta: naQca: ge: du pe:r-u.

  3-pl-TOP REF   to FOC enter-AC-CON

  'They are entering into their own house.'

We have to notice that there is no *uQca:* (these persons' house) but there is *uQta: ja:*.

(e) Comparison with the word *du:* 'oneself'

(e-1) For third person :

  atsuko: ja na:ra ha:na: -te du banu ju h-i: di anN-ta.

  Atsuko TOP herself do-NEG-and FOC 1sg ACC do-IMP AP say-PAST

  'Atsuko said to me "Do it." though she herself did not do it.

(e-2) For second person : (Speaking directly to Atsuko)

  du: ja h-a:-na-:te   banu ju h-i: di anz-u ?

  Oneself TOP do-NEG-and 1sg ACC do-IMP AP say-AC-CON

  'Do you say to me "Do it!" though you yourself do not do it?

(e-3) Exceptional case : *na:ra* for the second person

  na:ra h-i:-te   sIs-a-nu   ho:rI ba h-i:!

  REF do-PF-and know-NEG pretense AF do-ST-INF

  'You made a pretense of ignorance though you yourself did it.'

(f) Examples of the word *du:* (oneself)

(f-1) ba: du: ja   du: sa:ri   du a:r-o:.

  I-GEN body TOP oneself with FOC wash-CON

  '(I) wash my body by myself.'

(f-2) du: nu du: ja du: sa:ri du a:r-o:.

  Oneself GEN body TOP oneself with FOC wash-CON

  'Everybody washes his body by himself.'

(f-3) na: du: du: nu munu

Each own GEN thing

'Each person's own thing'

(f-4) *na: du: du: nu ja: ge du har-u.*

Each one GEN house to FOC go-CON

'Everybody goes to his own house.'

(g) In addition, it means "spontaneously" concerning phenomena of the nature.

unu ki: ja na:ra du: sa:ri mu-ir-u.

This tree TOP REF body with grow-EP-CON

'This tree has grown by itself.' (Nobody sowed its seeds.)

3. 2. Interrogative and indefinite pronouns

3. 2. 1. Human (who)

Sg.		Pl.	Family
Independent	NOM/GEN		
taru	ta:	taQta:	taQca

Examples :

(a) *taru r-ja:?*
Q-IND COP-REA
'Who is it?'

(b) *taQta: jar-ja?*
Q-pl COP-REA
'Who are they?'

(c-1) *ta: du kak-u?*
Q FOC write-CON
'Who writes it?'

(c-2) *ure: ta: du kak-i:?*
this-TOP Q FOC wrote-ST-INF
'Speaking of this, who wrote it?'

(d) A : *ure: ta: munu.*
This-TOP Q-GEN thing
'Whose is this?'

B : *ure: atsuko nu munu.*
This-TOP atsuko GEN thing
'This is Atsuko's.'

(e) *taru du sa: r-i har-u?*
Q-IND FOC bring-and go-CON
'Whom do you bring with you?'

(f) *kunu kwa:sa:* <u>taru</u> *ge: (du) h-ir-u ?*
   This cookie-TOP Q-IND to (FOC) giveEP-CON
   'Speaking of this cookie, to whom shall I give it?'

(g) <u>taQca</u> *nu jumi jar-ja?*
   Q-family GEN daughter in law COP-REA
   Which house are you belonging to as the daughter in law?

(h) Indefinite usage

(h-1) <u>*taro:*</u> *jar-a-ba-N akkoN hwo:-Ka pi: pIS-I du h-u: na:.*
   Q-TOP COP-though sweet potato eat-CND wind break-INF FOC do-CON FP
   'Anyone breaks wind when he eats sweet potato.'

(h-2) <u>*taro:*</u> *N du sI:bus-a-nu.*
   Q-TOP even FOC do-can-NEG
   'Nobody can do it.'

(h-3) <u>*taro:*</u> *N ur-a-nu.*   (i-4) <u>*taniNgasa:*</u>*N du ur-u.*
   Q-TOP even be-NEG   Somebody FOC be-CON
   'Nobody is there.'   'Somebody is there.'

3. 2. 2. Interrogative (what, which, where) and indefinite pronouns

what	which	where
no:	zIri	zIma

zIma has weak forms : *zINge (zIma + Nge)* and *zINga (zIma + Nga)*

Illustrated examples

(a) <u>*no:*</u> *nu N-du aQ-ta?*   (b) <u>*no:*</u> *du kak-u?*
   What NOM FOC be-PAST   What FOC write-AC-CON
   'What happened?'   'What do you write / what do I write?'

(c) <u>*no:*</u> *N nar-a-nu.*   (d) <u>*zIri*</u> *N du masI?*
   What even turn out-NEG   Which NOM FOC better
   'Nothing can be done about it.' 'which do you like better?'

(e) <u>*zIri*</u> *du tur-u?*

which FOC takeAC-CON
'Which do you take?

(f) zIma ge: du har-u?   (= zINge du har-u?)
where to FOC go-AC-CON   where-to FOC go-AC-CON
'Where do you go?'

(g) zINga du ar-u?   (= zIma Nga du ar-u?)
where-in FOC be-CON   where- in FOC be-CON
'Where is it/ are they?'

(h) no:niNgasa: (i) zImaNgasa:
'something'   'somewhere'

3. 3. Demonstrative

	CJ	This-here		that-over there
Singular	ko-re, so-, a-	kuri	(uri)	kari
Plural	ko-re-ra etc.	kuQta:	(uQta:)	kaQta:
Place	ko-ko, so-, aso-	kuma	(uma)	kama
Attributive	ko-no, so-, a-	kunu	unu	kanu
Adverbial	koo, soo, aa	kanzji	×	anzji

uma has weak forms : *Nge (uma+ge)* and *Nga (uma+ga)*

Ku-series is used for referring to something (/someone) near both the speaker and hearer. *Ka*-series is used for referring something (/someone) in the far distance from both the speaker and hearer. The series used in common Japanese (*ko-, so-, a-*) do not always correspond with the Miyara series (*ku-, u-, ka-*).

A number of contemporary researchers point out that it is hard to distinguish demonstrative *u-* from *ku-*. However, we find some difference between these two series.

People hardly refer to someone visible by *kuri*[18] but can do by *uri / kari*.

49

The series *ku-* can be used for referring to someone when they need the contrast like "*kuriN kariN* (both this man and that man)". The word meaning oneself (*na:ra* or *naQta:*) can be used with *u-* but not with *ku-*. It is considered that the series *u-* originally has the anaphoric usage. It is often observed that the plural form *uQta:* is used for the anaphoric usage. It seems that *ku-* and *ka-* might not have it.

Ku- and *u-* are hardly distinguished from each other referring to some place. We could find some examples of usage which indicate their anaphoric nature.

The origin of the word *aNzji* (in that way) would be the verb *anz-*. *aNzji* is a conjugated form as verb[19] meaning "to say/do so".

Examples:

(a) weak form of *uma*

(a-1) *Nge   k-u:.*

　　　Here-to come-IMP

　　　'Come here. (Come near to my side)'

　　　Miyara speakers say that the full form *kuma ge:* should be all right. However, it is hardly heard in daily conversation.

(b) Greetings (around the one's house)

(b-1) A :   *zINge (jar-ja)?*　　　(=*zINge du har-ja?*)

　　　　　where-to (COP-REA)　　where-to FOC go-REA

　　　　　'Where are you going?'　'Where are you going?'

　　B :   *na:i uma ge:*　× *kuma ge:*　× *kama ge:*

　　　　　just there to

　　　　　'just walking distance'

(b-2) A :   *zIma Nga du (har-i:)?*

　　　　　where in FOC (go-ST-INF)

　　　　　'Where were you?'

---

(18) *kuri* can be used only to refer to the child.

B : *uma Nga du har-i-da*   × *kuma Nga* × *kama Nga*
　　There in FOC go-ST-PST
　　'I was just nearby'

(c) Demonstrative adverb

(c-1) *aNzjiru   zjiraba,*　　　*aNzjiru munu,*
　　　that-sort work-song　　　that-sort thing
　　　'work song of that sort'　'thing of that sort'

(c-2) *kaNzj-ir-u zjiraba,*　　　*kaNzjiru munu,*
　　　'work song of this sort'　'thing of this sort (holding in one's hand)'

(c-3) *aNzji kaNzji h-i: jo:.*   (There is neither *uNzji* nor *uNzjiru*.)
　　　that-way this-way do-IMP FP
　　　'Do somehow or other.'

(c-4) *aNzji.* (response)
　　　in that way
　　　'Is that so?'
　　　cf. *aNsoNga*   (there is neither *uNsoNga* nor *kaNsoNga*.)
　　　　　However

4. Nouns

4.1. Declension

When the particle *ja* which marks the topic, is added to nouns or proper nouns,[20] it is united with their final sound, modifying it. This phenomenon is widely observed in Luchuan, e.g. Shuri, Hirara etc. and it is important from the historical point of view.

The declensional types are classified with the final sound of the noun and proper noun.

---

(19) It has the adjectival form '*anzji-ru* + noun' like the verb.
(20) It happens to be added to the particle.

(1) Long vowel   word + *ja* (topic particle)   (cf. CJ topic particle *wa*)
Examples :

ha: ja,   ki: ja,   su: ja,   tsI: ja,   naKe: ja,   gaQko: ja
teeth   tree   tide   blood   crybaby   school

(2) Short vowel

The Short vowel lengthens into long vowel. Except for the case of [a], this vowel changes itself.

(a) a → a: *han-a:*   (*hana*)   flower
(b) i → e: *am-e:*   (*ami*)   rain
(c) u → o: *kIm-o:*   (*kImu*)   liver
(d) I → a: *har-a:*   (*harI*)   needle

It is important to notice that the case of final sound [I] has a special feature of pronunciation. The older people want to keep the non-palatalization of consonant. For instance, *kI* → *ka:* is articulated as if its [I] is devocalized and disappeared like "*k'a:*" instead of simple *ka:* and *bI* → *ba:* is articulated as "*b'a:*". These old speakers are conscious of such distinctions.

As far as alveolar consonants [r, s, z, ts] are concerned, they do not have such distinctions.

Examples :   (d-1) *kab(I)a:*   (*kabI*)   paper
             (d-2) *huk(I)a:*   (*hukI*)   core of adan (name of a plant)
             (d-3) *tura:*   (*turI*)   bird
             (d-4) *usa:*   (*usI*)   cow
             (d-5) *tuza:*   (*tuzI*)   wife
             (d-6) *hutsa:*   (*hutsI*) mouth

(3) Syllabic [N] word + *ja*

The word-final [N] is not changed into a nasalized vowel before semi vowel [j]. [N] is a steady regular uvular nasal sound articulated closer to the front part of the tongue in comparison with Tokyo dialect. We often hear the glide [ɲ] before [j].

Examples :　(a) *iN ja*　　(*iN*)　dog

　　　　　　(b) *zjiN ja*　　(*zjiN*)　money

4. 2. Plural formation suffixes

　　Miyara dialect, like many other Luchuan dialects, has plural formation suffixes ; common Japanese doesn't. Which suffix is used depends on the word. The shapes of the suffixes differ depending on the dialect, but the contents of each group remain almost unchanged regardless of which dialect one is speaking.

Examples :

(1)　*-da:*

　(a) *aNni-da:*　　(b) *a:ja-da:*　　(c) *aQpa-da:*　　(d) *aQci-da:*

　　　mothers　　　　fathers　　　　grandmothers　　grandfathers

(2) *-nu-me:*

　(a) *hwa: -nu-me:*　(b) *uja-nu-me:*　(c) *jarabi-nu-me:*　(d) *dusɪ-nu-me:*

　　child-GEN-PL　　　parent-s　　　　infant-s　　　　　friend-s

　(e) *sji:zja-nu-me:*　　(f) *utudu-nu-me:*　　(g) *bunarɪ-nu-me:*

　　elder (brother-&-sister)-s　younger (brother-&-sister)-s　sister-s

　(h) *bigirɪ-nu-me:*　　(i) *sɪtu uja-nu-me:*

　　brother-s　　　　　　father-&-mother-s-in-law

　　　cf. *sɪtubara* (honorific word of *sɪtu uja*) has no plural form.

(3) *-ta:*

　(a) *birama-ta:*　　(b) *me:rabi-ta:*

　　　lad-s　　　　　maiden-s

　　The plural forms of Luchuan dialects can indicate not only real plural numbers but also "something and others of the same kind".

5. Particles

I will here explain only main particles in order to understand illustrative examples.

(1) *nu*

nu is roughly equivalent to common Japanese *ga* marking the nominative case. Shuri dialect has both *ga* and *nu* for nominative marker. Miyara dialect, however, has only this *nu* for the nominative marker. Miyara speakers intuitively think that common Japanese *ga* is equivalent to their focus particle *du* which is said corresponding to Japanese ancient *kakari-musubi* particle because *nu* is accompanied with *du* in most cases.

(2) *nu*

This particle marks genitive although its phonological form is the same as that of nominative particle. This phonological form corresponds with common Japanese *no* which means also genitive. This particle has co-occurrence restriction with the first and second person pronouns. They do not appear with *nu*. The one same word form is used as topic, nominative, and genitive in these pronouns. It seems that *nu* does not indicate the so-called subject, but rather the verb's agent.[21]

(3) *ju*

This particle marks accusative but it does not appear except in special cases. On the other hand, *ju-N* (ACC-also) often appears in daily conversations. *ju* is translated *(w)o* in common Japanese..

(4) Question

There is not any particle to indicate the yes-no question. It is usually indicated by rising intonation. However, there is an interrogative particle *kaja:*. It marks doubt and is not used for the direct question. We have to add "*i*" which indicates a request for agreement with the speaker, added only to the volitional. *kaka i?* 'Shall I write?'

---

[21] cf. the *no* in common Japanese *watashino iku toki* 'when I go,....'

(5) *ja*

This particle corresponds functionally to Japanese wa which marks the topic.

(6) *N*　　This particle adds the meaning "also" just like CJ *mo*.

(7) *ba*

This particle appears in the position of nominative case and accusative case, together with the particle du in most cases. It is considered that ba is not a case particle and it belongs to the same class as *ja* (adverbial particle).

ba has the co-occurrence restriction with the verbal conjugational categories[22]. Because of this restriction, it does not appear so often in a nominative position. That is why most contemporary researchers report that ba is equivalent to the accusative marker.[23]

It is important for the history of Japanese language that there is *ba* besides *ja* in Luchuan, because *ba* corresponds phonemically with *wa* in Japanese.

(8) *ge*

This particle marks the dative (including direction). Its usage roughly corresponds to that of Japanese particle *ni* & e (to, toward).

(9) *Nga*

This particle marks the place where something is. Both *Nga* and *ge* can occur with the verb *har-* (go) but with a different verbal conjugational category. In most of cases, it is translated as "in, on, under, up, above..." etc.

(10) *du*

This is very important particle to understand the Luchuan syntax. This particle is said to originate in ancient *kakari-musubi*, and it correlates in some ways with verbal conjugational forms. In this paper, it is called focus particle. Interrogative words such as who (*ta:*), what (*no:*), which (*zIru*),

---

[22] It does not appear in the active.
[23] Nohara (1986)

where (*zIma*) are almost always accompanied with this particle.
Examples :

(a) *ta:　du　kak-u?*　　(b) *ba:　du　kak-u.*
　　who FOC write-AC-CON　　I FOC write-AC-CON
　　'Who will write it?'　　'I will write it.'

(c) *wa:　du　kak-u?*
　　you FOC write-AC-CON
　　'Will you write it?'

(d) *ba:　kak-a-nu.　atsuko N-du (=nu du) kak-u.*
　　1sg-TOP write-NEG　atsuko NOM-FOC write-AC-CON
　　'I will not write it.'　'Atsuko will write it.'

(e) *wa: tigami kak-u-N?　ba:　kak-u-N.*
　　you letter write-AC-CON-N　I write-AC-CON-N
　　'Will you write a letter?'　'I will write it.'

(f) *wanu N tigami kak-ja.*
　　you-IND also letter write-IMP
　　'Write a letter, you too.

(g) *kure: wa: munu?　　N: ba: munu. /　araN. atsuko nu munu.*
　　this-TOP you-GEN thing　yes 1GEN thing　no atsuko GEN thing
　　'Is this yours?'　　'Yes, it's mine.'　'No, it's Atsuko's.'

(h) The particle *ba* is used in the environment that the predicate verb takes a certain conjugational category (it is called "stative" in this paper). In most cases, it marks accusative and accompanies the focus particle *du*. However, it can mark the nominative in the case that the marked noun(s) is/are undesirable for the speaker. Since *du* can appear just once in one sentence, *ba*, rather than *du*, accompanies the second noun.

(h-1) *banu　ba　maQts-a-hi:!*
　　　　I-IND　AP　wait-CAS-ST-INF
　　　　'You keep me waiting!
　　　　watashi o matasete! (CJ)

Cf. *aNta naze watashi o mataseta?* (CJ)
　　wa: no:di banu maQts-a-sɪ-ta?
　　you-TOP why 1-IND wait-CAS-AC-PAST
　　'Why did you keep me waiting?'

(h–2) *ba: bune Ndu banu ba sɪsabu ge: sɪko: -da.*
　　I-GEN father NOM-FOC 1-IND AP Shiraho to send-AC-PST
　　'My father sent me to Shiraho.' (*du* can not be used twice in one sentence.)

(h–3) *ami ba hwu-i zɪma ge: har-ar-a-nu.*
　　rain AP fall-ST-INF where to go-POT-NEG
　　'Rain is falling and I/we can not go anywhere.'
　　ame ga huri doko he mo ikarenu. (CJ)

(h–4) *ami ba hwu-i hatagi sjirar-a-nu.*
　　rain AP fall-and field do-POT-NEG
　　'It is raining and I/we can not cultivate fields.'

(h–4') The speaker is waiting for the rain because of the dry weather.
　　ami nu hwu-i haNtaha-ru.
　　rain NOM fall-ST-INF busy-CON
　　'Rain (welcome rain) is falling and I/we are busy (working in the field).
　　ame ga huri isogashii. (CJ)

(h–5) *ami Ndu hwu-ir-u.*　　cf. *ami ba du hwu-ir-u.*
　　rain NOM-FOC fall-EP-CON　　rain AP FOC fall-EP-CON
　　'Rain is falling.'　　　　'Rain is falling.'

(h–6) In the case that there are two similar clauses in one sentence, *ba* can appear in the second clause.
　　ami nu hwu-i, uri ba h-i:, haNtaha-ru
　　rain NOM fall-ST-INF welcome rain AP do-ST-INF busy-CON
　　'(A welcome) rain is falling (/ has fallen) and I/we are busy.

(h–7) *kɪno: ami ba hwu-i na:.*

yesterday rain AP fall-ST-INF FP

'Yesterday it was raining, wasn't it? (So I/we could not go to the field.)

(h-8) *jana huca <u>nu</u> hana <u>ba</u> sak-ir-u.*

bad grass GEN flower FOC bloom-EP-CON

'The flowers of weed are in bloom.' (So I have to take them out.)

cf. *hana <u>Ndu</u> sak-ir-u. mi: -na: har-a.*

Flower NOM-FOC bloom-EP-CON to see go-VL

'The flowers are blooming' 'Let's go to see'

(h-9) *jana huca <u>nu</u> hatagi Nga hana <u>ba</u> sak-i.*

bad grass NOM field in flower AP bloom-ST-INF

'The flowers of weed are in bloom in the field.'

(h-10) *ui-pɪtu <u>ba</u> nar-i no: N nar-a-nu.*

old person AP become-ST-INF what even become-NEG

'I have got old and nothing can be done.'

(i) Particles of place and direction

They depend on the verbal conjugational category.

(i-1) *wa: zɪNga <u>du</u> har-i: ?*

you-TOP what- place-in FOC go-ST-INF

'Where have you been?'

(i-2) With the verb *har-*'go' Nga is not acceptable in its active forms.

Atsuko is away from home, and her friend asked her family :

atsuko: zɪNge <u>du</u> har-i: ?

atsuko-TOP where-to FOC go-ST-INF

'Where has Atsuko gone?'

cf. *zɪN<u>ge</u> <u>du</u> har-<u>u</u>?*   × *zɪN<u>ga</u> du har-<u>u</u>?*

where to FOC har-AC-CON

'where will you go?'

6. Adjectives
6. 1. Historical study of Luchuan adjectives

According to Chamberlain (1895, p.117), the Luchuan adjective originates in ancient Japanese {...*sa* (noun formation suffix) + *ari* (be)}. Since then, it is an established theory which is accepted for almost all of dialects that {stem of adjective + *sa* (noun formation suffix) + *ari* ('be')}[24] is the origin of adjective, and the details of various dialects are left almost unknown.

This theory is based on the comparison between ancient Japanese and Luchuan, that is to say, the comparison between characteristics of Shuri adjective and those of Japanese. In short, following 4 items explain this theory:[25]
(1) According to adjectival conjugation, there are two groups. The one has -sa and -*ku*. The other has -*sja* and -*siku* as follows :

> *Shushikei* (conclusive)   *renyôkei* (adverbial)
> -*sa*/-*sja*   -*ku*/-*siku*

(2) It seems that -*sj*- /-*sik*- type corresponds to *shiku*-type in Japanese.
(3) The morphemes added to stem-s have the same forms as the verb *aN* ('be').
(4) -*sa* /-*sja* form can be used as a noun.

We have to examine first (1) & (2). The following table shows traditional Japanese categories and endings of two dialects.

In Miyara, there is no distinction between -s-type and -*sik*-type which corresponds respectively with *ku*-type and *shiku*-type in Japanese.

Renyôkei (adverbial) of Miyara is used in different way from that of common Japanese. It is used with the verb *h-u*- ('do') in many cases.

uQ-sja sju- and *sanehe hu-*" ('happily do') means "be glad". *takaha hu-* (make something high) can be used to make a fence.

---

(24) Karimata(1992, p.870) etc.
(25) Hattori (1955, pp.346-351)

	Shûshi (constative)	*renyô* (adverbial)	Negative
	high	highly	not high
Shuri	taka-*saN*	taka-*ku*	taka-*ko: neeN*
Miyara	taka-*haN*	taka-*ha* (*huN*)	taka-*ha ne:nu*
	happy	happy (*renyô* + *suru* (do))	not happy (*renyô* + *suru* (do-NEG))
Shuri	*uQ-sjaN*	*uQ-sja sjuN*	*uQ-siko: neeN*
Miyara	*sane-heN*	*sane-he huN*	*sane-he ne:nu*

Examples :

(a) *takaha-N!* (The speaker has just recognized that it is high.)

(b) *takaha ja:* (The speaker is looking up for the first time and is struck.)

(c) *takaha daru* (The speaker state his knowledge that it is high.)

(d) *sanehe-N*.　　*ba: sanehe-N*
　　(I am) happy.　I-TOP happy

(e) × *ure: sanehe-N*.　　(f) *ure: sanehe h-u-N*
　　he-TOP happy　　　　　he-TOP happy-ADV do-AC-CON-N
　　'He is happy'　　　　　'He feels happy'

Now we have to examine (3) and (4). The morphemes added to stem-s have the same as the verb *aN* ('be') in Shuri dialect. In Miyara, however, they are not always same as the verb *aruN* ('be').

60

The Grammar of Ishigaki Miyara Dialect in Luchuan

	Miyara		Shuri	
	Be	High	Be	High
Constative	a-ru-N	taka-h-a-N	'a-N	taka-s-a-N
question	a-ru-N?	taka-h-a-N?	'a-mi	taka-s-a-mi
past	aQta	taka-h-a:da	'a-taN	taka-s-a-taN
past question	aQta?	taka-h-a:da?	'a-tii	taka-s-a-tii
attributive	a-ru	taka-h-a-ru	'a-ru	taka-s-a-ru
+nu	——	taka-h-a-nu	——	taka-s-a-nu

(The name of category is tentative.)

There is a category "+ *nu*" both in Shuri and Miyara; and it is used very often in the final position of sentences. It indicates some personal feelings. Examples: (a) *ure: takaha-nu.* (in the case that someone gives up buying)

    this-TOP high

    '(since) this is high (price)…'

  (b) *ure: Nmaha-nu.* (in the case that someone recommends foods)

    this-TOP delicious

    'It is delicious.'

Now we have to examine *-sa -sja* form of Shuri dialect, which can be used as a noun even though its usages are restricted. Examples are following:[26]

(a) *waNnee 'ukaasja-du 'uhusa-ru (du…ru : kakari-musubi)*

  I-TOP danger many

  'I am in dangerous condition.' (Someone is sick.)

(b) *'anu muinu takasa*

  that mount high

  'That mount is high!'

We can not find such a usage in Miyara dialect.

---

[26] *"Okinawago jiten"* (p.84)

6. 2. Basic structure of Miyara adjectives

(1) The role of speaker

Miyara dialect does not have any particle to indicate questions as stated (such as Common Japanese *ka*). The N-form called *shushikei* (I named it 'constative' or 'conclusive +N' in this paper) appears as the predicate and the rising intonation gives it the meaning of question. When the speaker wants to say to oneself his feeling, N- form does not appear. The morpheme N seems to indicate the speaker's recognition or judgment.

	Statement	Interrogative
(to the hearer)	*takaha-N.* 'It's high'.	*takaha-N?*
(to oneself)	*takaha:* 'It's high(!)'	×
(to oneself)	*takaha ja:* high + FP 'It's high!'	×

(2) Two groups of adjective

We can not make distinction between -*ku*- and -*shiku*-conjugation in Miyara adjectives but we find two groups according to their syntactic features : the one is <u>descriptive adjective</u> and the other is <u>emotive adjective</u>. They show restrictions of co-occurrence with the personal pronoun.

Example of emotive adjective

<u>*sane-he-N*</u>   versus   <u>*sanehe h-u-N*</u>

happy-N   happy do-AC-CON

'(I am) happy.'   '(Someone) feels happy'

(a) <u>*ba: sanehe-N*</u>.

   'I am happy.'

(b) <u>*wa: sanehe-N?*</u>   × <u>*wa: sanehe-N*</u>. × <u>*ure: sanehe-N*</u>.

   'Are you happy'

Accompanied with the verb *h(u)*-meaning 'to do', the adjective can appear with any person.

    (c) <u>ure:</u> saneh-e du hi:r-u./? (<u>ba:</u> sanehe du hi: ru. <u>wa:</u> sanehe du hi:ru?)

    he-TOP happy FOC do-EP-CON

    'Does he feel happy?' ('I feel happy.' 'Do you feel happy?')

The speaker knows his own emotion but can not judge other's emotional state. The Japanese adjective *ureshii* 'happy' can not co-occur with third person, but the verb *yorokobu* (feel happy) can with any person.

We have to research various Luchuan dialects besides Shuri and to compare them for the historical studies.

6. 3. Forms of adjectives

Miyara adjectives have the ending -*haN* whereas Shuri has the ending -*saN*. Moreover, Miyara adjective ending has a kind of vowel harmony.[27]

The vowels of their conjugational endings correlate with those of final syllable of stem.

Stem	a	u/o	i/e	I	i:
Ending	-haN	-hoN	-heN	-saN	-sja

---

(27) Izuyama (1996)

English	Miyara	English	Miyara
red	akaha̱N	delicious	Nmaha̱N
bad	janaha̱N	black	hw(u)hwo̱ho̱N
weak	jo:ho̱N	wide	pɪso̱ho̱N
solid	ko:ho̱N	itchy	bjo:ho̱N
strong	co:ho̱N	far	to:ho̱N
blue	auho̱N	big	maihe̱N
cool	pirige̱he̱N	cute	ap(p)are̱he̱N
bitter	Ngaha̱N	dirty	jane̱he̱N
pretty	kaihe̱N	happy	sane̱he̱N
cold	pi:sja̱N	sour	sɪ:sa̱N
heavy	ihwhwa(ha)N	ticklish	ko:ho̱N
hot	ats(ɪ)sa̱N	light	karuho̱N
thin	pɪs(ɪ)sa̱N	thinned	pɪsa: pɪsa(h)iN
yellow	kɪNkɪi		

The reduplication of stem is widely spread in the Luchuan adjectives as well as in common Japanese. It is shown in the last example of the above table.

In the reduplication, the long vowel of the first part is characterized by a special voice tone with laryngealization.

6. 4. Conjugation

The conjugation of the adjective is parallel with that of the verb in Miyara dialect. The traditional categories which are generally chosen to describe its forms are difficult to explain the system of Miyara adjective.

The conjugational paradigm shows that the various morphemes are added to the infinitive forms with -ha (/-he/-ho). These forms are different from those of ar-u-N (to be) but are almost identical with the paradigm of the derived verb category (consecutive) later mentioned. This is also important for the historical study of the adjective. The list is following:

The endings are divided into three groups.

The Grammar of Ishigaki Miyara Dialect in Luchuan

(1) The infinitive form + N, so:, ru. These morphemes are mutually exclusive.
(2) The {infinitive + r-u} form seems to have its own conjugation.
(3) The {infinitive + da}[28] form seems to have its own conjugation.

Category[29]	high	write-[30]
negation	takaha (ne:nu)	×
constative	takaha-N	kak-e:-N
declarative	takaha-so:	kak-e:-so:
conclusive	takaha-ru	kak-e:-ru
realis	takaha-rja	kak-e:-rja:
durative	takaha-ri-ri	kak-e:-ri-ri
rational	takaha-ri-ki	kak-e:-ri-ki
conditional	takaha-ra-ba	kak-e:-ra-ba
confirmative	takaha-da	kak-e:-da
predicative	takaha-da-ru	kak-e:-da-ru
causal	takaha-da-ra:	kak-e:-da-ra:
past	takaha du aQta	×

6. 5. Usage

The adjectives are classified into two groups : the **descriptive** (*takaha-* etc.) and the **emotive** (*sanehe-* etc.). In some dialects — Kuroshima, for instance — they are formally distinguished by their endings. Miyara adjectives, however, are classified on the bases of their syntactical restriction and their usages, mainly in forming the collocation with *h-u-* (to do) and the past formation as follows.

(1) Infinitive. Declaration (no question sentence)
(1-1) Zero suffix. Monologue.

---

(28) *da-* is considered as follows. da<*du + *a. We can take *da-*etc. as an auxiliary which has its own conjugation.
(29) The category is tentatively named. We have to consider whole system of verbs and adjectives.
(30) The consecutive form of the verb *kak-* 'write'.

(a) *taka-ha:.* 'It is high!'
   Someone says to himself looking up a high building or a high stairway.
(b) *sane-he:.* 'I am happy!'
   Someone says to himself when he succeeds in something.
(c) *Nma-ha:.* 'This is delicious.'
   Someone mutters to himself eating delicious food.
(d) *kunu mitsɪ nu to:-ho:.* 'This is a long way.'
    this   way NOM far
   Someone mutters walking a long way.

(1-2) with final particles :
  (a) *Nma-ha jo:.*   'This is delicious.'
     (The hearer is not yet eating. He hears this word and then he will eat.)
  (b) *Nma-ha ja:.*   'This is delicious.'
     (The speaker does not necessarily expect the answer.)

(2) Negation : infinitive + *ne:nu*
  (a) *taka-ha   ne:nu.* 'It is not high'
              NEG
  (b) *sane-he ne:nu.* 'I am not happy.'
      happy   NEG
  (a') *taka-ha ne:na:-da* 'It was not high.'
       high   NEG-PAST
  (a") *taka-ha ne:na:-da ar-a-nu?* 'It was not high, was it?' (Speaker thinks it was high.)
       high NEG-PAST be-NEG

(3) Adverbial : Forming collocation with *h-u-*(do) or *nar-*(become)
  (a) *taka-ha h-u-N.*   (b) *sane-he(:) h-u-N.*
      high do-AC-CON-N   happy do- AC-CON-N
     'I/someone make(s) something high.' 'Someone is happy (feels happy).'
  (c) *pi:-sja nar-i.*   'It is getting cold.'
      cold become-ST-INF

(d) *ure: Nma-ha du h-u:.* 'His look tells his food is delicious.'
he-TOP delicious FOC do-CON According to his look, he feels his food is delicious.

(e) *ba: Nma-ha du h-u:.* 'I feel that this is delicious.'
I-TOP delicious FOC do-CON

(4) Infinitive + *so*: (This form can not appear in the question.) The statement (to the hearer)

(a) *taka-ha-so:.*   (b) *sane-he-so:.*
'It is high'   'I am happy.'

(c) *Nma-ha-so:.* 'It is delicious.' (The speaker declares it to the hearer.)

    cf. *aQ-so:.*   'Here it is.'

be-AC-INF-so:(The speaker tells it indicating something to the hearer.)

(d) *Nma-ha-so: na:* . 'It is delicious, isn't it?'
              FP   (The speaker expects hearer's agreement.)

(e) *Nma-ha-so: ja:.* 'It is certainly delicious, I bet you.'
              FP   (to the hearer who hesitates to eat, thinking it is not delicious.)

(5) infinitive + *N* (constative) This form indicates the speaker's recognition or judgment.

(a) *taka-ha-N./?*
high CNS
'It is high./?' 'I recognize it is high.' 'Do you think it is high?'

(b) *wa: sane-he-N?*   × *wa: sane-he-N*.   × *ure: sane-he-N./?*
you TOP happy-CNS   you   he
'Are you happy?'   'you are happy.'   'He is happy.'

(6) infinitive + *ru* (conclusive)

(6-1) conclusive (predication)

(a) *uri du taka-ha-ru.*   (b) *ma: nu ki: du sane-he:-ru.*
this FOC high-CON   grandchild NOM come- FOC happy-CON
'This is high.'   'Grandchild came and I am happy.'

(c) zɪri (N)du Nma-ha-ru ?   (d) kuri (N)du Nma-ha-ru.
    which NOM-FOC delicious   this NOM-FOC deliciousCON
    'Which is delicious?'   'This is delicious.'
(e) kju: ja ma:nu me: nu ki: sane-he:-ru. (×sane-he:ru?)
    today TOP grandchildren NOM come-and happy-CON
    'Today our grandchildren have come and I am happy.'

(6-2) attributive
    (a) taka-ha-ru hazɪ   (b) sane-he: -ru hazɪ
        high-ATT certainty   happy- ATT certainty
        'something ought to be hight'   'someone must be happy'
    (c) Nma-ha-ru munu
        delicious-ATT thing 'delicious food'
    (d) Nma-haru-ka: kam-u.
        delicious- ATT-CND eat-CON 'If it is delicious, I will eat.'

(7) infinitive + -rja: (realis)
    (a) taka-ha-rja: (b) sane-he:-rja:
        high-REA   happy-REA
        'As it is high '   'As I am happy'
    (c) taka-ha-rja: ka:-nu.   (d) ba: sane-he-rja: budurɪ h-u-N.
        High-REA buy-NEG   I-TOP happy-REA dance do-CNS
    'It (price) is high, and so I do not buy.' 'I am happy, and so I will dance.'
    (e-1) zɪri (N) du Nma-ha-rja: ? (e-2) kuri N du Nma-ha-ru.
          which NOM FOC delicious-REA   this NOM FOC delicious-CON
          'Which is delicious?'   'This is delicious.'

(8) infinitive + -ri-ri (durative)
    (a) taka-ha-ri-ri   (b) sane-he:-ri-ri
        be-high-and   be-happy-and
        'It is high so...'   'I am happy so...'
    (c) Nmaha-ri-ri taka: ni hwo:-da.
        delicious-DR much eat-PAST

'It was delicious and I ate a lot.'

(9) infinitive + -ri-ki (rational)

(a) *taka-ha-ri-ki ka:nu*.
expensive-RAT buy-NEG
'It is expensive, therefore I will not buy.'

(a') *takaha-ri-ki ka:na:da*.
expensive-RAT buy-NEG-PAST
'It was expensive, therefore I did not buy.'

(b) *Nma-ha-ri-ki hwai ja:*.
delicious-RAT eat-IMP FP
'It is delicious. So eat, please.'

(c) *sane-he:-ri-ki ...*
happy-RAT
'Because I am happy'

(10) infinitive + -ra-ba (conditional)
The condition is always desirable for speaker.[(31)]

(a) *taka-ha-ra-ba*
be-expensive-COND
'If it is expensive'

(b) *sane-he:-ra-ba*
be-happy-COND
'In the case of being happy'

(c) *Nma-ha-ra-ba du kamu*.
delicious-if FOC eat-CON
'If it is delicious, I will eat.'

(d) *kai-he:-ra-ba du iru*.
Pretty-CND FOC take-CON
'If it is pretty, I will take.'

(e) *jassa(:)-ra-ba kauN*.   (The cheaper is better, therefore it is acceptable.)
cheap-CND buy-CNS
'If it is cheap, I will buy.'

(e') ×*taka-ha-ra-ba ka:nu*.   Instead, attributive+Ka *taka-ha-ru-Ka: ka:nu*
expensive-CND buy-NEG
'I will not buy it if it is expensive.'

expensive-ATT-CND buy-NEG
'I will not buy in the case that it is expensive.'

(f) *taka-ha-raba na:*.
tall-CND FP
'(I wish that) I were tall.' (Everybody wants to be tall.)

---

(31) Izuyzma (2000)

(11) infinitive + -da (confirmative)
   (a) *taka-ha-da*   (b) *sane-he:-da*
       expensive-*da*   happy-feeling-*da*
       '(I have confirmed) being expensive.' 'I have confirmed being happy.'
(12) infinitive + -d-ar-u (predicative)
   (a) *taka-ha-d-ar-u*   (b) *sane-he:-d-ar-u*
       expensive-*d-ar-u*   happy-*daru*
       '(I think) It is in expensive state.' 'My situation is happy'
(13) infinitive + -d-ar-a (causal)
   (a) *taka-ha-d-ar-a: ka:-na:-da*.   × *taka-ha-d-ar-a: ka:-nu*
       expensive-*dara* buy-NEG-PAST   expensive- buy-NEG
       'As it was expensive, I did not buy it.'
   (b) *sane-he:-d-ar-a:*   (c) *Nma-ha-dara: hwo:-da.*
       happy-being-*dara*:   delicious- *dara*: eat-PST
       'As I am/was happy'   'As it was delicious, I ate it.'
(14) infinitive + *du aQ-ta* (Past)
   (a) *taka-ha du aQ-ta*   (b) *sane-he: du aQ-ta*
       expensive FOC be-PAST   happy FOC be-PAST
       'It was expensive'   'I was happy.'

Notes on the usage:
(1) We have to note the difference between constative and predicative. The constative -*N* indicates the speaker's recognition but the predicate -*dar-u* denotes the state generally recognized.
  (a) While shopping, Atsuko asks her friend, who knows what the market price is:
      Atsuko: *ure: taka-ha-dar-u?*
              this-TOP expensive-*dar-u*
              'Is this expensive?'

Friend (finding another poster and pointing) :

    kare: *jaQsa-N*.

    that-over-there cheap-*N*

    'That is cheap.'

(b) *kju: ja nIsI kazji ba nar-i*   *pi:-sja-dar-u*.

    today TOP north wind AP become-DUR   cold-*dar-u*

    'Today the wind has changed in the north and it is cold.'

(c) *kju: ja atsI-sa-dar-u / pi:-sja-dar-u*.

    today TOP hot-   / cold- *dar-u*

    'Today it is hot / cold.'

(c') Someone went out and the north wind blew, so he said : *pi:-sja-N!*

                                                            cold-CNS

    (He felt cold suddenly.) 'It's cold.'

(d) *wa: sane-he:-dar-u?*   (cf. *wa: sanehe-N?* 'Are you happy?')

    you-TOP happy-

    'Are you happy?' This expression is ironical. It will be continued :

(d') *sane-he haNtiN mi-sja:-ru munu*.

    happy do-NEG-and-even good-ATT Fm-N

    'It is better that you have not felt happy.' 'You should not have felt happy.'

(2) The forms of (11)-*da* & (14)-*du aQ-ta* are said to be "past". We have to examine the notion of past. The collocation *sanehe h(u)-* occurs with the third person. It may occur with the first person but usually not. We will take following examples :

sanehe:-da versus *sanehe: du aQ-ta* versus *sanehe du hi:-da /sI-ta / he:-ru*

happy-CNF   happy FOC bePST   happy FOC do-various "past"

(2-1) The form -*da* is not a simple past.

    (a) The speaker's friend is happy because a grandchild was born recently.

    (a-1) *waQca Nga ma: nu mar-i sanehe:-da ?*   × *sanehe du hi:da?*

71

your-house in grandchild NOM was born- and happy-*da* happy FOC do-PST

'You have a new born grandchild in your family and you are happy? 'You have felt happy?'

This sentence means "<u>Still now</u> you <u>are</u> happy". "*sanehe:da*" means the confirmation of "being in happy situation".

(a-2) *waQca Nga ma: nu mar-i <u>sanehe-N</u> ?* × <u>*sanehe du h-i:r-u*</u>?

your-house in grandchild NOM was born- and happy-CON happy FOC do-CON

'You have a new born grandchild in your family and you are happy? 'You are feeling happy?'.

Both (a-1) and (a-2) is all right in the same situation. However (a-3) is not acceptable.

×(a-3) *waQcaNga ma: nu mar-i <u>sanehe: du aQ-ta</u>?*

your-house in grandchild NOM was born- and happy FOC be-PST

'You have a new born grandchild in your family and you felt happy?'

(a-4) *haruo na:sI-ta-keN ja <u>sanehe: du aQ-ta</u>.*

haruo have-PAST-case TOP happy FOC be-PST

'When I had Haruo, I was happy.' (It is 30 years ago. Haruo is the speaker's first baby.)

(b) The speaker hears a baby crying and sees diapers in the neighbor's house.

(b-1) *uQta Nga ma: nu mar-i <u>sanehe: du h-e:-r-u</u> na:.*

they in grandchild NOM was-born-and happy FOC do-CSC-CON FP

'It seems they have a grandchild and they must have felt happy, I guess.'

(b-2) When the speaker meets the neighbor:

wa: <u>sanehe: du sI-ta</u> / <u>h-i:-da</u>? ×*wa: sanehe du h-e:-r-u?*

you-TOP happy FOOC do-AC-PAST/ do-ST-PST

'You felt / were feeling happy?'

(2-2) Restriction of the collocation with the person

(a) *ba: sanehe:-da*.   ×*ba: sanehe h-i:-da*.
   'I was happy.'
(b) *ba: sanehe: du aQ-ta*.   ×*ba: sanehe: sI-ta*.
   'I was happy.'
(c) *atsuko: sanehe: du hi:da/sIta* .   ×*atsuko: sanehe: du aQta*.
   Atsuko-TOP happy TOP do-PAST
   'Atsuko was feeling / felt happy.'

The morpheme *-da* indicates confirmation of the state which might not be changed still now. It does not indicate the past.

The collocation *du aQ-ta* implies that the speaker confirmed the state in past. Neither *sanehe-N* nor *sanehe du aQ-ta* occurs with the third person. Nobody knows the inside of the others. The speaker can not judge the other's heart or feeling but only his look or appearance.

We have some adjectives which are not clearly distinguished according to the meaning of their stems.

(d) *kIno: haNtaha-da?*   /   *haNtaha du aQ-ta?*
   yesterday busy-CNF   busy FOC be-PST
   Were you busy yesterday?'   'Were you in busy situation?'
(e) *kIno: aQtsa:-da ?*   /   *aQtsa: du aQ-ta?*
   Yesterday-TOP hot-CNF   hot FOC be-PST
   'Was it hot yesterday?'   'Was it hot weather?'

(3) Additional explications of *da / du aQ-ta etc*.

This collocation has its own conjugation as *du + a- (to be)*.

1. *Nmaha-d-aru*   'It is delicious.'

2. *Nmaha-d-arjaN*
   Nmaha ne:nu Ndi umui-da-soNga Nmaha-d-arjaN.
   delicious-NEG AP think-CNF-but delicious-FOC-REA-N
   'At first it seemed to me not delicious but unexpectedly I found it delicious.'

3. *Nmaha du aQ-ta*   'It was delicious.'

    Nmaha ne:nu Ndi umui-da-soNga Nmaha: *du aQ-ta*.
    delicious-NEG AP think-CNF-but delicious FOC be-PST
    'It didn't look delicious, but I found it delicious.'
    4. *no:di kai ku:na:-da* ?   *takaha du aQ-taro:*
    Why buy-and come-NEG-CNF   high FOC be-*taro:*
    'Why didn't you buy and come?'   'It was expensive, I know.'
    5. *ja:ha du ar-e:-r-u*
    hungry FOC be-CSC-CON 'I was hungry and still now you can guess it.'
(4) Personal restriction
    1. *(wa:) no:di harana:-da?*   *(ba:) haNtaha du aQ-taro:*.
    you-TOP why go-NEG-CNF   I-TOP busy FOC be-PST
    'Why didn't you go?'   'I was busy, I know.'
    1'*atsuko: no : di har-ana:-da?* atsuko: *hanta ba du h-i:-da*. × *haNtaha du aQ-taro*:
    Atsuko-TOP why go-NEG-CNF   Atsuko-TOP busy AP FOC do-ST-PST
    'Why did not Atsuko go?'   'Atsuko was working a lot'
    2 *wa: ja:ha du aQ-ta* ?   × *atsuko: ja:hadu aQ-ta?*
    you hungry be-PST   Atsuko-TOP hungry be-PST
    'Were you hungry'
    3 *atsuko: ja:ha du aQ-ta*.   *kaja:*.
    Atsuko-TOP hungry FOC be-PST FP
    'I wonder whether Atsuko was hungry.'
    4 *atsuko: ja:ha du are:ru na:*.   *a:ri NboN ba hwai-so:* .
    Atsuko-TOP hungry TOP be-CSC-CON FP   in haste meal AP eat-ST-INF-*so:*
    'Atsuko must be hungry. She is eating meal in haste.'

6. 6. Attributive usage of the stem

The adjective stem modifies the noun. This is very productive.

　　(1) *hukaha-*　　*huka-ka:*　　　(2) *asaha-*　　*asa-ka:*
　　　　deep　　　　deep well　　　　　shallow　　shallow well

(3) janaha-   jana-huca   (4) auho-   au-huca
     bad   bad grass   green   green   grass
(5) araha-   ara-munu   ara-kIN
     new   new goods   new dress
(6) hwhwuho-   hwuhwu-ja: hwhwu-kIn
     old   old house   old dress
(7) kanaha-   kanasI -na:
     cute   cute name (given name)

6. 7. Derivative words with adjectival endings

Some important words derived from the verb have adjectival ending. Some of them are listed below.

	ending	stem (write)	
+	-Taha-	kakI-Taha-	to be anxious of writing
+	-Qtsanehe-	kakI-Qtsanehe-	to be easy to write
+	-pIsa-	kakI-pIsa-	to want to write
+	-kisja-	kakuN-kisja-	to be likely to write

7. Verbs

The morphological study on Luchuan verb has been based on the grammatical category in common Japanese. The grammarians are most concerned with the conjugation of the verb and are interested in historical researches. Shuri dialect is compared with ancient Japanese and it results in the assertion that the Luchuan conclusive form *kacuN* (write) originates in ancient Japanese *kaki (w)ori* {*kaki* = adverbial form of *kaku* (write) + *(w)ori* (be ; CJ *iru*)}.[32]

---

(32) Hattori (1955, p.333), Uemura (1992, pp.804–805), Shimabukuro (1992, pp.825–826), Takahashi (1992, pp.876–881)

Even though it can explain Shuri dialect, it cannot explain the verb system in Miyara. If we want to reconstruct the parent language of Japanese and Luchuan, we must first reconstruct proto-Luchuan.

A synchronic study on the dialects is necessary also for the historical research, and with systematic study on the grammar of an endangered language like Miyara dialect becoming more and more difficult, it is now quite urgent.

7. 1. Comparison between Japanese and Miyara dialect

The verbs are classified into two groups on the basis of the verbal conjugational form which the negative morpheme -nu is suffixed to, even though there are some exceptions of irregular verb.

1		2	
ba: kak-uN	ba: kak-a-nu	kure: ut-ir-uN	kure: ut-u-nu
I write.	I do not writ.	This falls.	This does not fall.
ba: jum-uN	ba: jum-a-nu	ba: ak-ir-uN	ba: ak-u-nu
I read.	I do not read	I open.	I do not open.

These two groups correspond to the Japanese conjugational group. The verbs belonging to the Group 1 correspond to the verbs of *4dan-katsuyô* with a few important exceptions and the members of Group 2 mostly belong to the *1dan-katsuyô*. Each verb stem has only one negative form.

Let us compare the Miyara verbs to the ancient Japanese verbs.[33] The forms listed are not so called *syûshikei but renyôkei* because Miyara verb infinitive corresponds with it in ancient Japanese.

The form with * is the form that would be expected by phonological rules. The syllable *mɪ* is kept only by the oldest speaker in the word *mɪ:* (serpent), but it is not kept in verbs like *jumɪ*. The alternant (*jum-a:* ,*sɪn-a:-*,

---

(33) Jidaibetsu kokugo daijiten jodaihen (1967)

The Grammar of Ishigaki Miyara Dialect in Luchuan

ar-a:-) tells us that Miyara once had the expected form.

Miyara does not have *nI* for phonological restriction. Yet we can not deny the probability that it originates in non-palatalized syllabic [n].

meaning	Ancient Japanese		Miyara	
write / read	4-dan	—*kaki₁ / yomi₁*	—*kakI / juN (*jumI)*	—1-group
die	*na-hen*	—*shini*	—*sIN (*sInI)*	—1-group
wear/tide is out	*kami-1dan*	— *ki₁ / pi₁,₂*	—*kIsI /pIsI*	—1-group
see	*kami-1dan*	—*mi₁*	—*mi:*	—2-group
receive / open	*shimo-2dan*	—*uke₂ / ake₂*	—*uki /aki*	—2-group
fall / get up	*kami-2dan*	—*oci₂ / oki₂*	—*uti / uki*	—2-group
come	*ka-hen*	—*ki1*	—*kI*	—irregular
do	*sa-hen*	—*si*	—*sI*	—irregular
be	*ra-hen*	—*ari*	—*arI (aQ)*	—irregular
be / sit	*kami-2/kami-1*—*wi₁,₂*		—*birI (biQ)*	—1-group
?	—*urI (uQ)*	—1-group		
?	—**jarI (jaQ)*	—irregular		

Notes

(1) *Kami-1dan* verbs correspond to two groups of Miyara verbs. We have few examples of these verbs ; however, a phonological environment might have participated in it. The verbs belonging to Group 1 have a voiceless consonant in initial position and the syllable is devoiced. On the other hand, the verbs of Group 2 begin with voiced consonants and the syllable is not devoiced.

(2) Japanese word *wi* meaning "to be / sit" appears in both *kami-1* and *kami-2*. This is meaningful for the correspondence between Japanese and Luchuan dialects. The corresponding word *biru-* (to sit) is expected as *m-iru*-(to see) to belong to Group 2 ; however the fact is that it belongs to Group 1.

77

(3) The initial phoneme of the word *wi* (to be) in ancient Japanese do not corresponds with Miyara *ur-* (to be). It must be **b-*. Since this is a very important word, this exceptional correspondence must be investigated.

(4) Miyara Group 2 corresponds to both *kami-2dan* and *shimo-2dan* ; however it is subdivided in two separate groups which respectively correspond to *kami-2dan* and *shimo-2dan*.

(5) A number of Luchuan dialects have a copula which does not have a direct corresponding word in ancient Japanese.

(6) It is important to note the correspondence of vowels in the verbs of *ka-hen, 4-dan, 1-dan* and *2-dan* .

7. 2. Conjugation
7. 2. 1. Categories of traditional grammar

Luchuan dialect morphological studies are usually based on the traditional Japanese categories, with two categories added to the six traditional ones. They are *ishi-kan'yû* (intention or suggestion) and *chûshi* (suspensive) or *keizoku* (durative). The former is the independent form of irrealis and the latter corresponds to *renyô (adverbial) form or te-form* in Japanese.

According to this framework, each one verb stem has three types of conjugation as follows. Only the first type is usually considered conjugation like in common Japanese ; and the others have been neglected.

Type 1	irrealis	adverbial	conclusive	attributive	realis	imperative	durative
kak-(write)	kak-a	kak-I	kak-u-N	kak-u	kak-ja	kak-i	kak-i
uki-(rise)	uk-u	uk-i	uk-ir-u-N	uk-ir-u	uk-ir-ja	uk-ir-i	uk-i
aki-(open)	ak-u	ak-i	ak-ir-u-N	ak-ir-u	ak-ir-ja	ak-ir-i	ak-i

Notes

(1) Irrealis form in the common Japanese appears always with the negative particle. Miyara irrealis form has its independent use, while it expresses negation with the negative particle added ; it expresses suggestion when used alone. That is the reason why the category volitional is usually

added besides the negative in Luchuan studies.

(2) As described, Yaeyama dialects have tow kinds of the first person plural pronoun. If the agent is the speaker's group as a unit (*baga:*), it always accompanies the verb form of independent irrealis which means "Let us...". This independent form can occur with first person singular expressing his intention. Note, however, that Luchuan speakers can not use this form in monologues, whereas in common Japanese we can use irrealis (volitional) – *ô* form without a listener : *"tegami kakô* (I will write a letter)".

(3) The negative particle *nu* is suffixed to irrealis : *kaka-nu* (not write), *utu-nu* (not fall). However, its usage is not necessarily the same as in the common Japanese.

(4) The particle *ba* marking condition is suffixed to irrealis. Note that it shows some elements of modality in expressing conditions.

(5) Conclusive, attributive and realis form

These three forms function in different way in comparison to common Japanese. The conclusive form of this dialect is said "attributive form + *N*" as in other dialects. In Miyara, however, the reaslis form also can take "*N*" and appears in the predicate to express the action or state which has already been decided, but has not yet actualized. On the other hand, the attributive form also has a function of predicate.

(6) Durative (or suspensive) becomes a subject of discussion. Contrary its name, it appears in the predicate.

If we choose the traditional category to describe the morphological system of Miyara dialect, we have to add two more conjugational types. I only show them in the following tables.[34]

    Type 2 *kakiN* (←*kakuN* 'write') & *utiN* (←*utiruN* 'fall')
    Type 3 *kake:N* (←*kakuN* 'write') & *ute:N* (←*utiruN* 'fall')

---

(34) Their details are described in Izuyama (2002).

Type 2

irrealis	adverbial	conclusive	attributive	realis	imperative	durative
kak-ir-a-	kak-i	kak-i-N	kak-ir-u	kak-ir-ja	kak-ir-i	kak-ir-i-/kak-ir-ir-i
ut-ir-a-	ut-i	ut-i-N	ut-ir-u	ut-ir-ja	(---)	ut-ir-i-/ut-i-te

Type 3

irrealis	adverbial	conclusive	attributive	realis	imperative	durative
kak-e:-ra-	kak-e:-	kak-e:-N	kak-e:-ru	kak-e:-rja	--	kak-e:-ri-
ut-e:-ra-	ut-e:-	ut-e:-N	ut-e:-ru	ut-e:-rja	--	ut-e:-ri-

This framework is difficult to explain the whole system. It is hard to find the reason why the conclusive of type 1 is only assigned to the conclusive form in predicate among *kak-u-N, kak-i-N, kak-ja-N, kak-u* and *kak-ja*.

7. 2. 2. Paradigm of Miyara verbs

A tentative framework of conjugation is shown below.

I Regular verb

The verbs are divided into two groups based on their conjugational patterns, as stated above :

Group 1 (-a-nu)		Group 2 (-u-nu)	
ba: kak-uN	ba: kak-a-nu	kure: ut-ir-uN	kure: ut-u-nu
I write.	I do not write.	This falls.	This does not fall.
ba: jum-uN	ba: jum-a-nu	ba: ak-ir-uN	ba: ak-u-nu
I read.	I do not read	I open.	I do not open.

Group 1 kak-(write)	Infinitive (renyô)(35) (adverbial)	Conclusive (rentai) (attributive)	Imperative (meirei)	Realis (izen)	Irrealis (mizen)
active	kak-I	kak-u	--	--	kak-a
stative epistemic	kak-i kak-ir-i-	-- kak-ir-u	kak-i kak-ir-i	kak-ja kak-ir-ja	-- kak-ir-a

The Grammar of Ishigaki Miyara Dialect in Luchuan

Group 2 uk-(get up)	Infinitive (renyô) (adverbial)	Conclusive (rentai) (attributive)	Imperative (meirei)	Realis (izen)	Irrealis (mizen)
stative	uk-i	--	--	--	uk-u(uka-)[36]
epistemic	uk-ir-i-	uk-ir-u	uk-ir-i	uk-ir-ja	uk-ir-a

Consecutive : derived group (including Group 1 and 2)

	Infinitive	Conclusive	Realis	Irrealis	Stem
Group 1	kak-e:-r-i-	kake:-r-u	kak-e:-r-ja	kak-e:-r-a	kake:-
Group 2	uk-e:-r-i-	uke:-r-u	uk-e:-r-ja	uk-e:-r-a	uke:-

In Groups 1 and 2, morpheme -N can be added to the conclusive, the realis and the stative-infinitive to express the speaker's judgment or recognition. In the derived group, it can be added to the realis and the stem.

Notes

(1) Most of stems end in the consonants. There are a few single-consonant stem words : k(u)- (come) and h(u)- (do). m(i)- (see) may be also added in it.

(2) The verbs of Group 1 have conjugational patterns for active and for stative. The stem final consonant of Group 1 verbs has palatalized-nonpalatalized opposition. Group 2 does not have it ; it has only stative. The active infinitive determines other forms generally. There is a big difference between the active and the stative in the syntactic construction. That is a reason why Miyara dialect is rich in the aspectual phase.

(3) The epistemic is considered to be derived from the stative ; it obtains a function of the recognition by suffixation of -ir-.

(4) The negative morpheme -nu is suffixed to irrealis. Since each stem has only one negative form, we can generally predict other forms based on it.

---

(35) The word in brackets is name of traditional category.
(36) This is the stem of derived word. e.g. uka-h-u- 'wake up' It can not be independent word.

However, we have to pay attention to the vowel stems of Group 1 as follows.

	Irrealis	Active-Conclusive	Stative-Infinitive
(a) Eat	*hwa:*	*hwo:*	*hwai*
Not eat	*hwa:-nu*	Another example:	*a: ra:-nu* 'not wash'
(b) (It) rains.	*hwo:*	*hwo:*	*hwui*
(It does not) rain	*hwo:-nu*	Another example:	*to:-nu* 'not ask'
(c) buy	*ka:*	*kau*	*kai*
not buy	*ka:-nu*	Another example:	*a:-nu* 'qurrel'

The vowel stem verb belonging to Group 1 has the same form in both infinitive and conclusive for the active but for the stative-infinitive it has -*i* as if it corresponds to palatalized final consonant of the consonant stem. In the vowel stem verbs, the stative-infinitive only functions to form compound words, not active-infinitive.

(5) The stem final consonants -*r*, -*m*, -*n* are changed in the infinitive of active. The same phenomenon is called *onbin* in Japanese. The form in the parentheses is expected one. The form with -*r* has its alternant *tura:(turI +ja)* so underlying form should have -*rI*. The form with * is phonologically impossible but it is assumed on the base of *numa:(=nuN ja)*.

Stem	Infinitive
tur- (take ; CJ *tor-*)	*tuQ-* *(turI)*
har- (go)	*haQ-* *(harI)*
num- (drink ; CJ *nom-*)	*nuN-* (**numI*)
kam- (eat)	*kaN-* (**kamI*)
sIn- (die ; CJ *shin-*)	*sIN-* (**sInI*)

(6) The stem final consonants of Group 1 are palatalized in stative. If the vowel [I] is in the syllable next to the last, it is also palatalized and changed in [i].

Active infinitive	*asabI* (play)	Stative infinitive	*asabi*
	tatsI (stand)		*taci*

iz<u>I</u> (say)	*iz̲ji*
us<u>I</u> (push)	*us̲ji*
k<u>I</u>s<u>I</u> (wear)	*kis̲ji*
p<u>I</u>s<u>I</u> (tide is out)	*pis̲jj*
s<u>I</u>k<u>I</u> (hear)	*s̲jiki*
s<u>I</u>N (die)	*s̲jini*
s<u>I</u>s<u>I</u> (grind)	*s̲jis̲ji*

(7) The morpheme *N* belonging to the speaker is suffixed to the sative infinitive and also to the conclusive in all except consecutive, and finally to the realis in all. The consecutive stem is accompanied with morpheme *N* and *so*: just like the adjective.

(8) The infinitive has limited usages in the epistemic and consecutive. It is suffixed with the rational suffix *-ki* like *kak-ir-i-k*i. Although it is not shown in the table, Group 1 epistemic- infinitive can take *-ri* again for the same usage as the infinitive like *kakiri-ri*.

(9) Group 1 and 2 are not distinguished in the consecutive.

   The verbs with consonant stem : consecutive stem = stative infinitive stem + e:

   The verbs with vowel stem : consecutive stem = stative infinitive + e:

(10) Although it is not shown in the table, the consecutive infinitive can be added with *-ri* like *kake:ri-ri* and be used as durative. It is interesting for the historical studies.

(11) The consecutive irrealis can not be independent. It is always suffixed with *-ba* (conditional). The consecutive realis appears with wh-question.

(12) The forms of past

   The forms of past = Active / stative infinitive + *da* (/ta)

   The active past of Group 1 vowel-stem verbs = conclusive + *da*

   The epistemic does not have past form.

(13) The Perfect = stative infinitive +T-a /C-a

II Irregular verb
(1) *k-* (to come)

	Infinitive	Conclusive	Imperative	Realis	Irrealis
Active	kɪ	ku:	ku:	---	ku:
Stative	ki:	———	———	kja:	———
Epistemic	ki:ri	ki:ru	ki:ri	ki:rja	ki: ra-

All verbs except *k-* (come) have a final vowel *-i* as the imperative form. Only *k-* is exceptional. This imperative form of *k-* can be accompanied the particle *ba* instead of *ja* in regular verbs, like *k-u-ba(:)*.

It is difficult to decide whether the vowel of active conclusive is long or short. The speakers' introspection is varied depending on the speaker. The following are examples of these forms suffixed.

+*-so:*	*kɪ-so:*	*ki: -so:*	declarative
+*-soNga*	*kɪ-soNga*	*ki:-soNga,*	but
+*du (h-)*	*kɪ-tu hu:*	*ki: du*	focus
+*-кa:*	*ku:-кa:*	×	condition
+*-nu*	*ku:-nu*	×	negation
+*-ki*	*ki:-ki*		reason

It seems that the vowel [i] is long in the stative and [ɪ] is short in the active. As far as [u] is concerned, it is long in the other cases.

(2) *h-* (to do)

	Infinitive	Conclusive	Imperative	Realis	Irrealis
Active	sɪ	hu:	———	———	ha:
Stative	hi:	———	hi:	hja:	———
Epistemic	hi:ri	hi: ru	hi:ri	hi:rja	hi:ra-

This is only one exceptional verb which has a stem alternant *s-*. It has a stem which consists of one consonant like *k-* (to come). The following shows length of vowels in the forms suffixed.

The Grammar of Ishigaki Miyara Dialect in Luchuan

+-so:	sIso:	hi:so:	declarative
+-soNga	sIsoNga	hi:soNga	but
+du (h-)	sItu hu:	hi: du	focus
+-Ka:	hu:Ka:	×	condition
+-nu	ha:nu	×	negation
+-ki	×	hi:ki	reason

It seems that the vowel [i] is long in stative-infinitive and [I] short in active-infinitive.

(3) *ar-* (to exist, to be)

	Infinitive	Conclusive	Imperative	Realis	Irrealis
Active	arI(aQ)	aru	——	——	ara
Stative	ari	——	ari	arja	——
Epistemic	ariri	——	ariri	——	——

This is exceptional in regard to the suffixation of speaker's morpheme -N. It is not suffixed to the stative-infinitive of *ari-*. There is neither *ari-N* nor *ari-da*.

An example of epistemic infinitive :

gaNzjuho: ariri co:me: sjikiri.

healthy be-DUR long-life do-IMP

'I wish (you) healthy life and long life.'

In luchuan dialects, negative form *ara-nu* does not mean 'something/ someone does not exist' ; rather, it means 'A is not B' or 'it is not so'. The word *ne:nu* means 'not exist'.

This verb also functions as an important auxiliary verb.

(4) *ur-* (to exist for living things ; CJ *or-* / *ir-*)

	Infinitive	Conclusive	Imperative	Realis	Irrealis
Active	urI(uQ)	uru	——	——	ura
Stative	uri	——	uri	urja	——
Epistemic	uriri	——	uriri	——	urira-

The speaker's morpheme *N* is not suffixed satative-infinitive. There is neither *uri-N* nor *uri-da*. There is a durative imperative: *uriri* (Continue to be there.). Since the common Japanese does not have this kind of imperative, this fact deserves a consideration. This verb also functions as an auxiliary verb.

(5) *aN-/aNz-* (to do /say so)

	Infinitive	Conclusive	Imperative	Realis	Irrealis
Active	*aN-, aNzI*	*aNzu*		———	*aNza*
Stative	*aNzji*	———	*aNzji/aNri*	*aNzja*	———
Epistemic	*aNzjiri*	*aNzjiru*		*aNzjirja*	*anzjira*

This verb has a special form of past *aN-ta* in addition to the regular past form *aNzI-da* and *aNzji-da*. There is also *aN-so:*. These are special forms.

The stative infinitive is used as an agreeable response: *aNzji?* (Is that so?)

(6) Copula

	Infinitive	Conclusive	Imperative	Realis	Irrealis
Active	*jaQ-*	*ju(:)/jaru*	———	———	*jara-*
Stative	*jari*	———	———	*jarja*	———
Consecutive	*jare:ri*	*jare:ru*	———	*jare:rja*	*jare:ra-*

It will be explained later, in the chapter on the copula.

7.3. Predicate and verbal forms
7.3.1. Emotive predicate

This category includes negative (not do), imperative (Do!), prohibitive (must not do), intentional (will do) and suggestion (Let's do). The last two might be put together as the volitional.

The Grammar of Ishigaki Miyara Dialect in Luchuan

	Negative	Volitional	prohibitive	imperative
Write	kak-a-nu	kak-a	kak-ɪ-na	kak-i/kak-ja (kak-ir-i/kak-ir-ja)
Rise	uk-u-nu	uk-u/uk-ir-a	uk-i-na	uk-ir-i/uk-ir-ja
Open	ak-u-nu	ak-u/ak-ir-a	ak-i-na	ak-ir-i/ak-ir-ja

Note on the forms

(1) The negative form has its own conjugation where the stem alternates with -na.

Examples :

Imperative : kak-a-na:-r-ja.   uk-u-na:-r-ja.   ak-u-na:-r-ja.
'Don't write.'   'Don't get up."   "Don't open."

Past : kak-a-na:-da.   uk-u-na:-da.   ak-u-na:-da.
'did not write'   'did not get up'   'did not open'

Irrealis : wa: kake:ru-ka   ba: kak-a-na:-ra i ?
You write-CSC-CON-CND   I write not Irrealis Q
'Since you have written, I will not write, shall I?'

With rational suffix : kak-a-na:-ki   uk-u-na:-ki   ak-u-na:-ki
The independent irrealis form is used as the suggestive.

(2) The irrealis form accompanies *mba* to express the speaker's intention. This *mba* has a special rising intonation : *kaka-mba*. 'I will write.'

(3) In the verbs belonging to Group 2, the epistemic-irrealis form can be used to express intension and request but negative morpheme nu can not be suffixed to it.

uk-ir-a. 'Let's get up.'   ak-ir-a 'Let's open.'   ×uk-ir-a-nu ×ak-ir-a-nu

(4) The prohibitive form is infinitive + *na*. The stative infinitive of Group 1 can not form the prohibitive.

(5) The imperative has the same phonological form as the stative-infinitive in the Group 1. Its epistemic infinitive form also functions as the imperative. In the Group 2, only the epistemic infinitive functions as the imperative. The stative-infinitive does not function as the imperative. There are two

endings for imperative forms : *-i* and *-ja*. The latter has a slightly tender feeling.

Notes on usage

(1) The negative form is inaccurately translated into Japanese as negative "*kaka-nai* (not write)". In CJ, we have another form of negation ,"*kaite-(i) nai*" In this dialect, there is only one form of negation for each verb stem. Examples :

    Mr. A has left the room where he was writing something.

    B :   *wa:*   <u>*kak-i-Ta*</u>?   A : *me:da* <u>*kak-a-nu*</u>.   × <u>*kak-i ur-a-nu*</u>
          You   write-PF   still   write-NEG   write-be-NEG
          'Have you written?'   'I do not write yet'   'I have not yet written'.

(2) The volitional (independent irrealis form) is not used as the monologue. As far as the intention is concerned, "*ba: kak-a.* (I will write.)" is stronger than "*ba: ka-ku-N.*(I write.)". The following are the examples.

(a) <u>*kak-a*</u>   *i* ?   The speaker wants to have the listener's agreement.
    write-REA Q
    'I will write. O.K.?'

(b) The irrealis co-occurs with the 1st person plural speaker's group to express the suggestion.

    baga   <u>*kak-a*</u>.   .
    SG   write-IREA
    'Let's write.'

(c) *ar-*(be) has the desiderative usage of irrealis which we do not find in CJ.

    gaNzjuho: <u>*ar-a*</u>   *na:*
    healthy   be-IREA FP
    'I wish you good health'

(3) The verbs belonging to Group 2 have two forms of the volitional : stative and epistemic. These two forms are not identical in their meaning. The

stative-irrealis is in high degree of requirement. The speakers recently feel that the former sounds more old-fashioned.

Examples:

(a) Two men are trying to open the door which is hard to open. The stronger man says:

madagir-i.   ba: ak-u.   (Epistemic irrealis *ak-ir-a* is acceptable.)
move-IMP   I   open-IREA

'Move aside. I open.'

(b) Someone is knocking the door at midnight. The husband says to his wife:

wa: nim-ir-ja.   ba: uk-u.(Epistemic irrealis *uk-ir-a* is acceptable.)
you   sleep-EP-IMP I   get up

'(You) keep sleeping. I get up.'

(4) In the case that the imperative formation is semantically difficult, the desiderative (imperative form + *jo:*) functions as well.

(a) *ami   hu-i   jo:*.
     rain   fall-IMP FP

'I wish it would rain.'

(b) *pI: muir-i   jo:*.
    fire   burn-IMP FP

'I wish it could catch fire.'

(c) *gaNzju-ho: ar-i   jo:*
    healthy   be-IMP FP

'I wish you good health.'

7. 3. 2. Factive predicate

We will take up here the main verb forms which participate to compose sentences.

(1) The verb forms with N are paired with those without N as follows.

	Conclusive	Stative-Infinitive	Realis
Group1 Active 'write'	*kak-u-N* *kak-u*	*kak-i-N* *kak-i*	*kak-ja-N* *kak-ja*
Group2 Epistemic 'rise'	*uk-i-r-u-N* *uk-i-r-u*	*uk-i-N* *uk-i*	*uk-i-r-ja-N* *uk-i-r-ja*
Group1 Epistemic 'write'	*kak-i-r-u-N* *kak-i-r-u*	—— ——	*kak-i-r-ja-N* *kak-i-r-ja*
Consecutive Group1 'write'	*(kak-e:-N)* *kak-e:-r-u*	—— *kak-e:-r-i*	*kak-e:-r-ja-N* *kak-e:-r-ja*
Group 2 'fall'	*(ut-e:-N)* *ut-e:-r-u*	—— *ut-e:-r-i*	*ut-e:-r-ja-N* *ut-e:-r-ja*

The consecutive stem can not be independent. It is always accompanied with *-N /-so: /- ru*. That is to say, *kake: / ute:* can not appear independently as a word.

In consecutive, three morphemes *-N /-so: /-ru* are mutually exclusive. The consecutive conclusive *kake:ru* is an independent word but it does not have *N*-added-form like *kake:ruN*.

(2) The final consonants of verb stem can be palatalized or non-palatalized ; these two cases correspond to the stative and active forms, respectively.

On the other hand, the verbs of Group 2 have only the stative-infinitive whose final syllable is always palatalized. In the consecutive, they do not have this opposition.

Examples : The verbs : *kak-* (to write) & *uk-* (to get up)

Suffixed with morphemes *so:* (decralative) and *da* (past).

Group 1 Active Stative	*kak-I-so:* *kak-i-so:*	*kak-I-da* *kak-i-da*	*kak-I-da-so:* *kak-i-da-so:*
Group 2 (Stative) Stative	*(uk-i-so* *uk-i-so:*	*uk-i-da* *uk-i-da*	*uk-i-da-so:)* *uk-i-da-so:*
Group 1 Consecutive Group 2 Consecutive	*kak-e:-so:* *uk-e:-so:*	*kak-e:-da* *uk-e:-da*	*kak-e:-da-so:* *uk-e:-da-so:*

(3) There is a group of forms with *N* which do not have their counterpart, forms without *N*. This category is a kind of perfect.
Example :

| Group 1 (write) | *kak-i-Ta* | *kak-i-Ca-N* |
| Group 2 (get up) | *uk-i-Ta* | *uk-i-CaN* |

Notes on the tables
   (a) It shows that the verb forms with *N* appear in the predicate.
   (b) In the framework of traditional grammar, the so-called conclusive forms are formed in a different way between Group 1 and Group 2 (*kak-u-N* & *uk-ir-u-N*). In the above table, the simplest predicate form (stative-infinitive + *N*) is composed in the same way for the both groups (*kak-i-N* & *uk-i-N*).
   (c) Not all verbs of Group 1 appear in the epistemic. They have restriction in the aspect and modality.
   (d) The morpheme *so:* is suffixed also to the adjective and the copula. It is considered a basic morpheme like *N*. Both of them can be added to the stative-infinitive and consecutive. They are mutually exclusive there. *N* is incompatible with *da*.
   kakida-so:/ kakIda-so:/ kake:da-so:
   ×*kakida-N / kakIda-N / kake:da-N*

7. 3. 3. Active Infinitive

The active infinitive form has a nominal function in addition to the verbal function. Moreover, it can modify nouns. This is the basic form of verb.

Unlike the stative infinitive, the active-infinitive (*kakI*) cannot accept the morpheme *N* as a suffix. This means that the form *kak-I-N* does not occur.

(1) The verbs of Group 1 have opposing final syllables when deriving words. That is to say, there is an opposition {active-infinitive versus stative-infinitive}.

Active-infinitive (non-palatalized)		Stative-infinitive (palatalized)	
kakI-	to write	*kaki-*	
kakI-pIsuN	wish to	*kaki-hiri*	Please write for me.
kakI-TahaN	want to	*kaki-miri*	Try to write.
kakI-busuN	able to	*kaki-sjisjiN*	can write.
kakI-QtsaneheN	easy to	*kaki-meN*	have written (experience)
kakI-kIsuN	finish to	*kaki-sjike:N*	have written
kakI-TaNna:	while	*kaki-te:-gara*	after having writen

The morphemes added to the active-infinitive (*-pIsuN, -TahaN, -busuN, -QtsaneheN, -kIsuN and -TaNna:*) are not independent words by themselves; the suffixes need to be added for these morphemes to have meaning. Only the forms with suffixes added can function as derived verbs or adjectives. (Consider CJ *kakitai* "want to write"; the *-tai* suffix indicates "want", but cannot be used to mean "want" without a verb affixed to it.)

On the other hand, the forms which are composed of stative-infinitive collocated with other forms function as compound words. In this case, however, the rear morphemes have their own meaning as independent words (analogous to words like CJ *kudasai* "please"; it can be used independently, or it can be suffixed to a word like *kaite-kudasai* meaning "please write"). The morphemes in the above table mean:

-hiri 'Give me.' *-miri* 'Look.' *-sjisjiN* 'be done' *-meN* ' have seen' *-sjikeN* 'have set'

(2) The active-infinitive, as an independent word, can be used as a noun. The noun declension, in which the particle *ja* (approximately equivalent to CJ *wa*) can be added to the stem to form a topic and change its final consonant, was already described in Chapter 4.

Examples:

(a) **kak^Ia:**   *sI-soNga*   *zI: ja pita.* (←*kakI*)

CJ *kakiwa   suru-ga   ji wa heta*
write-INF-TOP do-AC-INF-but letter TOP bad
'I write letters but my letters are bad.' 'I certainly write letters but my writing is poor.'

  (a') **huk¹a:**   *aQ-soNga* ...   (←*kukɪ* 'core of plant *adan*')
    core of adan-TOP exist-but
    'There are cores of adan but...

  (b) **tura:**   *sɪ-soNga*   (←*tur-* 'take')
    take-Top do-AC-INF-but
    'Taking is o.k. but...'

  (b') **tura:** *uQ-soNga*... (←*turɪ* 'bird')
    bird-TOP exist-AC-INF-but
    'The bird exists but...

  (c) **kakɪ** *du h-u:*.   (c') *sjigutu du h-u:*.   (*sjigutu* 'work')
    write-INF FOC do-AC-CON   work FOC do-AC-CON
    'Certainly to write.'   'I do work.'

(3) Other nominal usages of the active-infinitive

  (a) *nakɪ*   *nu   sɪk-ari-da-soNga wa: du   nak-i:?*   (*nak-* 'cry')
    cry-AC-INF NOM be-heard-past-but you FOC cry-ST-INF
    'I heard you crying ; were you crying?'

  (b) *ba: sjiguto: zɪ: kakɪ*.
    my work-TOP letter write-INF
    'My work is writing characters.

(4) Verbal usages

  (a) A : *kju: ja no: du h-u:*.   B : *asab-ɪ*. (blunt response) (*asab-* 'play')
    today TOP what FOC do-AC-CON   play-INF
    'What do you do today?'   'Playing.'

  (b) A : *kju: ja   no: du h-ja:*.   B : *hatagi ka: sɪ*. (*ka: h-* 'cultivate')
    today TOP what FOC do-REA   field cultivate-AC-INF
    'What do you do today?   'Cultivating field'

(c) Explication of "*juima: rɪ* (mutual help)"

kju: ja baNca: nu to:sa turɪ.
today TOP our house NOM grass take-AC-INF
"Today we pick the grass at our house (in our fields),'

aǫtsa: sjizuko:ca: nu to:sa turɪ. uri du juima:rɪ.
tommorrow Shizuko's house GEN grass take-AC-INF this FOC cooperation
'Tomorrow, we'll pick the grass at Shizuko's house. This is called *juima: rɪ*.'

(5) The active-infinitive with N does not appear in general as independent form but it appears in a compound and some idioms.

(a) *aNmanu ami ba hui asabIN sjigutu nu tsɪrɪ tamar-ir-u.*
too much rain AP fall-INF play-even work NOM much pile-EP-CON
'Since it has been raining and (we've been) playing, work has piled up.'

(b) *dugu hatagi ba ka:sIN bugar-i dur-u.*
too much field AP cultivate-even get-tired-INF AX-CON
'I have got tired from cultivating the fields too much.'

(6) In the compounds

kakIN-guriheN 'difficult to write'

(Such morphemes as *guriheN* or *NguriheN* do not exist independently.)

cf. *kakuN-kisjaN* '(Someone) seems to write'

(Such morphemes as *kisjaN* or *NkisjaN* don't exist independently.)

(7) Attributive usage

We can not say it is productive but not petrified at all.

Infinitive modifier		conclusive (attributive) modifier
(a) *pɪk-* *pɪkɪ-usɪ*	(a')	*pɪku usɪ*
to grind hand mill		mill to grind
(b) *tsɪk-* *tsɪkɪ-usɪ*	(b')	*tsɪku usɪ*
to pound mortar		mortar to pound
(c) *ka:h-* *ka:sɪ-pɪtu*	(c')	*ka:hu pɪtu*
to sell seller (peddler)		person selling (salesperson)

(d) *kau-* *kai-pɪtu*   (d') *kai-na: ku:* *pɪtu*
    to buy   person to buy on order   person coming to buy

(e) *ka:h-* *hatagi ka:sɪ pɪtu*   (e') *hatagi ka:hu pɪtu*
    to cultivate   field cultivate person   field cultivate-ATT person
    'farmer'   'person cultivating field'

(f) *ka:h-* *ta:* *ka: sɪ* *pɪtu*   (f') *ta: ka:hu pɪtu*
    rice field cultivating person   rice field cultivating person
    'farmer engaged in cultivating rice field'   'person cultivating rice field'

(g) *huk-* *ja: hukɪ pɪtu*   (g') *ja: huku pɪtu*
    to thatch   house thatching person   person thatching house
    house thatcher   person who is thatching a house

(h) *ptso-* *tamunu putsui pɪtu*   (h') *tamunu putso: pɪtu*
    to pick up   fire wood picking person   person picking up fire wood

7. 4. The role of the speaker

All sentences are based on the speaker, with construction differing depending on whether or not the speaker has experienced the action being described. Sentences are always accompanied more or less with the speaker's modal elements. Because Miyara dialect does not have any writing system, and it is thus impossible to convey information without a speaker, the speaker is indispensable in any speech acts.

N-suffixed form is called conclusive form in the traditional category. We have to examine it. The followings should be taken in consideration:

(1) The verbs with N are paired with those which do not have *N* morpheme.

(2) *N*-forms occur with the second person pronoun only in question.

(3) *N*-forms can not appear in wh-question.

(4) *N*-forms appear only in non-past tense. An exceptional form *-caN* does not have its counterpart *-ca*.

7. 4. 1. Speaker and N suffixed form

N-forms have a co-occurrence restriction with the personal pronouns. *N*-forms depend on the speaker. They occur with the second person pronoun *wa*: only in question. The examination of following sentences indicates the feature of these forms.

(A) The agent is a human being.

   (a) *ba: kak-u-N*.   *Atsuko: kak-u-N*.   × *wa: kak-u-N*.

     I write-AC-CON-N   Atsuko-TOP write-AC-CON-N   you write-AC-CON-N

     'I will write.'   'Atsuko will write.'   'you will write'

   (b) A :   *ba: kak-u-N*?   B :   *wa: kak-ja:*.

            I write-AC-CON-N   you write-IMP

            'Shall I write?'   'You write!'

   (c) A :   *Atsuko: kak-u-N*?   B :   *kak-u-N*.

            Atsuko-TOP write-AC-CON-N   write-AC-CON-N

            'Will Atsuko write?'   '(She will) write.'

   (d) A :   *wa: ka-ku-N*?   B :   *ba: kak-u-N*.

            you write-AC-CON-N   I write-AC-CON-N

            'Will you write?'   'I will write.'

(e) The epistemic conclusive of Group 2 are same in this point.

   Ex. *uk-ir-* (get up)

ba: uk-ir-u-N. *atsuko: uk-ir-u-N*. *wa: uk-ir-u-N*?

Answer: *ba: uk-ir-u-N*.   ×*wa: uk-ir-u-N*.

'I get up.' 'Atsuko gets up.' 'Do you get up?' 'I get up.' You get up.

    These facts tell us that *N*-form can hardly occur with the second person ; the second person does not occur with realis added *N*-form even in question.

   (f) *ba: atugani kak-ja-N*.   ×*wa: atugani kak-ja-N*./?

      I later write-REA-N   you later write-REA-N

      'I write later.'   ' Do you write later?'

(f) *ure: kak-ir-ja-N!*　　　　×*wa: kak-ir-ja-N.*
　　he-TOP write-EP-REA-N　　　you write-EP-REA-N
　　'He is writing!'　　　　　　'You are writing.'
(g) *ba: kak-i-Ca-N.*　　*wa: kak-i-Ta?*　　×*wa: kak-i-Ca-N?*
　　I write-ST-INF-PF-N　you write-ST-INF-PF　you write-ST-INF-PF-N
　　'I accomplished to write.' 'Did you finish writing?' 'Did you finish writing?'

(B) The agent is not human.
  (a) A: *kunu ki: ja hana sak-u-N?*　B: *hana sak-u-N.* / *sak-a-nu.*
　　 this tree TOP flower bloom-AC-CON-N flower bloom-AC-CON-N / bloom-NEG
　　 'Flower blossoms on this tree?' 'Flowers blossom' 'They do not blossom.'
  (b) The case of rain is different from that of flower.
　　× *ami hwo:-N?*
　　　rain fall-AC-CON-N
　　　'Does rain fall?' 'Does it rain?'

This kind of question is not asked to any person, because no one can answer it using their own experience. It is possible, however, to say the same thing in using the final particle *kaja:* which expresses doubt.

  (b') *ami hwo:-N kaja:*
　　　rain fall-AC-CON-N FP
　　　'I wonder whether it rains or not.'

It is considered that these questions with *N*-form expect the speaker's judgment, that is, the personal judgment or recognition of the person answering. Negation indicates also speaker's judgment.

The speaker can not judge the hearer (*wa:*) better than the hearer himself. Nobody can judge that it rains.[37] Nobody asks such a silly question.

"*ami hwo:-N.*" means "I judge that it rains." Some speaker says that a weather forecaster may answer it. We can judge by experience whether this tree blossoms or not, whether Atsuko writes or not.

---

(37) "*jagati ami hwo:N?* (Is it rain in a little while?)" is acceptable.

97

In this sense, speech is entirely dependent on the position / presence of the speaker. Since *N*-form marks the speaker's recognition or judgment, we have to reconsider the conventional idea in which this form is assigned to the predicate conclusive corresponding to the common Japanese conclusive (e.g. *kaku* 'write' / *huru* 'rain') where the speaker can be unnamed and neutralized.

7. 4. 2. Speaker and speaker's group (*baga:*)

If *N*-forms depend on the speaker, the verb forms with *baga:* ought to show it also.

(1) The verb forms co-occurring with *baga:* are as follows.

  (a) *baga: ka-ku-N?*   × *baga: kak-u-N.*   × *baga: ka-ka-nu.*
    we-SG write-AC-CON-*N*   we-SG write-AC-CON-*N*   we-SG write-not
    'Will we write?'   'We will write.'   'We will not write.'

  (b) *baga: kak-a. (/ kak-a-Nba)*
    we-SG write-irrealis (write-irrealis-*Nba*)
    'Let's write.'

  (c) *baga: kak-I-so:.*
    we-SG writeAC-INF-*so*:
    'It is an established fact that we write.

(2) The verb forms which occurs with *baga:* are restricted. The following examples are focused on the *N*-forms in order to know the relation to the speaker.

  (a) A: *uQta: har-i-ki baga N ma:zoN har-u-N ?*
       they go-INF-*ki* SG also together go-AC-CON-*N*
      'Since they went, will we also go together?'
    B: *baga: har-a-nu do:. uQta: taNga: har-a-hi:.*   × *baga: har-a-nu.*
      SG go-NEG FP   they alone go-CAS-IMP
      'Let's not go.   Let them only go.'   × *ba: har-a-nu do:.*

(b) Three girls arranged to meet by appointment.

(b-1) A :   atsuko: ku-N-ba   baga har-ir-u-N ?
            atsuko-TOP come-NEG-CND SG go-EPS-CON-N
            'Since Atsuko did not come, are we going?'

     B :   di: har-a   ×har-ir-u-N.
            INT   go-IREA   go-EPS-CON-N
            'Now let' go'

If B' answer is "*hariruN*", it means that only B will go and A will keep waiting.

(b-2) atsuko ku-N-keN   wa: maC-ir-u-N?   ba: maNnari har-a i?
      atsuko come-while you wait-EP-CON-N   I before go-IREA Q
      'Until Atsuko comes, will you wait?   I will go ahead. O.K.?'

(b-3) atsuko: kuN-keN haruo nu mac-i-ri-ki baga hutara: har-a.
      Atsuko come-while Haruo NOM wait-EP-INF-RAT we-SG two-TOP go-IREA
      'Until Atsuko comes, Haruo is waiting. So, we two, let's go.
      cf. ba: mac-i-ra-ba   wada: hutara: maNnari har-ir-ja.
           I wait-EP-IREA-CND you-pl two-TOP before go-EP-IMP
           'Since I am waiting, you two go ahead.'

(3) A number of girls arranged to meet by appointment. Atsuko has not come yet.

   (a) atsuko: me:da ku:-na:-ki baga: maNnari har-ir-u-N ?
       atsuko-TOP yet come-NEG-RAT we-SG before go-EPS-CON-N (proposal)
       'Since Atsuko did not come yet, will we go before her?'

   (b) baga: har-ir-a   (na:).   × har-iru-N.
       SG-TOP go-EP-IREA (FP)
       'We will go.' / 'Let's go.'

   (c) me:sItu   mac-i m-ir-u-N?   (proposal)
       a short while waite-and see-EP-CON-N
       'Will we try to wait a while?'

99

(d) _ba: me:sɪtu mac-i m-ir-u-N_.   _wada: har-ir-ja_.
I short while wait-and see-EP-CON-N   2-pl-TOP go-EP-IMP
'I will try to wait a while. You go. (_ba_: is necessary to prevent misunderstanding.)

(e) _jagati k-u: hazɪ jar-i-ki   me:sɪtu   mac-i m-ira_.
soon come-ATT certainty COP-RAT   a short while wait-and see-EP-IREA
'She will come soon, so we will try to wait a while.'

(f) _wada: har-ir-ja:_.   _baNda: hutara: atugani k-u:-N_.
you-pl go-EP-IMP   we-pl two-TOP after   come-AC-CON
'You go. The two of us will go later.'

(4) One of neighbors has a celebration and is having a party. A woman says to her friend:

(a) _joi ja: ge wa: har-u-Ka: banda: joi nu munu   muc-i har-i h-ir-u-N_?
party house to you go-CON-CND our   gift bring-and go-and give-EP-CON-N
'If you go to the house having the party, would you bring for me our gift to them?'

(b) Listening to her, her husband says to her:

baga haQso:.   _baga muc-i ha-ra Nba_.   _no:di pɪtu taram-ja:_.
we-SG go-AC-INF-so: we-SG bring go-AC-IREAFP why other person ask-REA
'We are going. We will go and bring it ourselves. Why have you asked another person (to do it)?'

(5) In the conversation between wife and husband.

(a) _joi ja: nu ari-ki baga har-u-N_?   _har-a-nu_?   ×_haranu_.
party house NOM be-cause SG go-AC-INF-CON-N go-NEG
'There is a house having a party. Will we go, or won't we?'

(b) Answering:

har-a-ba du jar-u sa. / _baga: har-a-N-tiN   misja-N_. ×_baga ha-r-anu_.
go-IREA-CND FOC COP FP we-SG go-NEG-even good-N
'We have to go.'   It's OK if we don't go. (We need not go.)'

(6) In the conversation between wife and husband.

   (a) *tigame: pıtu taram-i kak-a-h-u-N?*   (b) *baga kak-a Nba.*
       letter-TOP other ask-and write-CAS-CON-N   SG write-IREA FP
       'Shall we ask someone to write a letter?'   'We will write it.'

It is clear that the morpheme *N* belongs to the speaker in the above sentences.

7. 4. 3. Speaker and *so:* suffixed form

The sentences where the forms with *so:* are in predicate can not take the rising intonation as the question sentences. That is to say, the forms with *so:* do not occur in questions.

The *N*-form can be accompanied with final particles (dara : , kaja : ...). However, the *so:*-form is accompanied only with a final particle *na:* (asking agreement). Generally speaking, a sort of objectivity is assigned to it. The morpheme *so:* is mutually exclusive with *N* and *ru*. It seems that it does not have relation with the speaker's judgment or recognition. The speaker describes (declares) with *so:* the state as it is.

(1) Active infinitive + *so:*

   (a) *unu pıtu nu kak-I-so: .*   *wanu N higu kak-ja.*
       that man NOM writeAC-INF-*so*:   you also quickly write-IMP
       'That man is going to write.   Write in a hurry, you, too.'
   (b) *wa: kak-a-na:r-ja. ba: kak-I-so:.*
       You write-NEG-IMP I write-AC-INF-
       'Do not write. I am going to write.'

For younger generation, this *so:*-form does not occur with the first person.

   ? (c) *wa: zjo:zI jaQ-so:. wa: kak-I-so:. ba: kak-i-sjisj-a-nu*
       you skilful COP   you write-*so:*   I write-can-NEG
       'You are good.   You are going to write. I can not write.'

The older generation does not have such a usage. Instead, *wa:kak-ja:*.
                                                              you write-IMP
                                                              'Do write.'

(d) It has a usage as noun.

(d-1) *unu pɪtu nu* <u>*aN-so:*</u>   *ja   atar-i dur-u*.
   that man NOM say-AC-INF-*so:* TOP hit-and AX-CON
   'What he said comes true.'

(d-2)   <u>*kak-I-so:*</u>   *masɪ*.
   write-AC-INF-*so:* better
   'It is better to write.'

This active-infinitive-*so:* form is difficult to occur with second person / (first person). It shows that this morpheme does not indicate the judgment but the declaration.

(2) Stative infinitive + *so:*

Someone or something is described very often by this form when it is in view of the speaker. The *so:*-form appears without restriction of person. In many cases, the agent is always translated into the common Japanese with *ga* (nominative), even though that sentence does not include its equivalent word or it does include *wa* (topic)-equivalent-word.

The verb of Group 2 has only one infinitive (palatalized stem) but it can functionally work as it is active infinitive in meaning. Note the usages of the verbs corresponding *Shimo2-dan* group.

Examples:

(a) Looking at someone writing : *m-i: m-ir-i*.   *ure:* <u>*kak-i-so:*</u>.
                              see-and look-IMP   he write-ST-INF-*so*:
                              'Look! He is writing'

(b) Writing something : *wa: kak-aN-tiN misja-N*.   *ba:* <u>*kak-i-so:*</u>.
                     you write-NEG-even-if good   I write-ST-INF-*so:*
                     'You do not need to write (it). I am writing (it).'

(c) To someone writing   *wa: <u>kak-i-so:</u>.*   *ba: kak-aN-tiN misja-dar-u.*
                           you write-ST-INF-*so:*   I write-NEG-even-if good-AX
                           'You are writing.'   Then I need not write.'

(d) In the morning, their son did not come to the dining room.
     A : *nim-i dur-u kaja*
        sleep-INF AX FP
        'I doubt whether he is sleeping.'
    B (after going to his bedroom) :   *nim-i ur-a-nu. <u>uki-so:</u>.*
                                   sleep-INF AX-NEG rise-INF-*so:*
                                   'He is not sleeping but is awake.'

(e) Toshio (small child) is on the top of the tree. Watching it, someone cries to his mother :
    Tosjio: jagati ki:gara <u>uti-so:</u>.   *kacim-ir-ja:.*
    Toshio soon tree-from fall-INF-*so:*   catch-IMP
    'Toshio looks like fall from the tree. Catch hold of him at once.'

(f) Looking at a child who fell down to the ground.   *du: sa:ri <u>uki-so:</u>* .
                                             by himself rise-INF-*so:*
                                             'He will get up by himself.'

(g) The verb corresponding to *shimo 2-dan* verb.
    jadu <u>ba</u> <u>aki-so:</u>.   (Looking at a person opening sliding doors.)
    sliding-door open-INF-*so:*
    '(Someone) is opening the sliding doors.

(g') *jadu <u>aki-so:</u>.*   (Looking at the house whose door was opened)
    sliding door open- INF-*so:*
    'The sliding door is open.'

(h) Looking at the bird flying out :   *<u>piNgi-so:</u>.*
                                    escape-ST-INF-*so:*
                                    'It is flying away!'

(i) Someone's bird repeats to fly out.

mata piNgi-so:. (Looking at the empty cage)
again escape-ST-INF-*so:*
'It has flied out again.'

7.5. Stative-infinitive

The following is to be noted.
(1) The verbs of Group 1 have two stems for the infinitive (active *kak<u>i</u>* stative *ka<u>ki</u>*).
(2) The verbs of Group 2 show in stative-infinitive their simplest forms e.g. ut-i which does not appear as the traditional conclusive, that is, *ut-ir-u-N*.
(3) Unlike the active-infinitive, the stative-infinitive is accompanied by the morpheme *N* which expresses speaker's recognition.
(4) Using the traditional grammatical category, this form is labeled as suspension, conjunctive or continuative, and its independent predicative usages have not been reported. It is considered the form corresponding to Common Japanese suspensive-form (*kaki / kaite, oci / ocite*). However, this infinitive form is very important in the syntax of this dialect. The modal-aspectual characteristics of Luchuan dialects might originate from the opposition of active versus stative.

7. 5. 1. Arising of action

The stative-infinitive indicates the state where the action has taken place. The action itself has arisen without any relation to the speaker, but the speaker perceives it and knows that it has arisen. The following are examples:

(1) Pointing the characters:

A: *kure: ta: du ka<u>k-i:</u>* .
this-TOP who FOC write-ST-INF
'Speaking of these characters, who wrote them?'

B : ba: du kak-i:.   /   tosjio Ndu kak-i:.
    I FOC write-ST-INF   Toshio NOM-FOC write-ST-INF
    'I did.'   'Toshio did.'

C : wa: du kak-i:?   zjo:zI jaQ-so: na: .
    you FOC write-ST-INF   good COP-AC-INF-so: FP
    'Did you write (them)?   They are good, aren't they?'

(2) Guessing that the action must have arisen :

  (a) nak-I nu sIk-ar-i-da-soNga wa: du nak-i:? ×wa: nak-i:?
     cry-AC-INF NOM hear-PSS-PST-but you FOC cry-ST-INF
     'I heard you crying.   Did you cry?' (Now he is not crying. He stopped it.)

  (b) mi: nu akam-i-soNga wa: du nak-i:?
     eye NOM redden-ST-INF-but you FOC cry-ST-INF
     'Your eyes have turned red. Have you cried?'

  (c) terebi nu utu nu sIk-ar-i-da-soNga wa: du m-i:?
     television GEN sound NOM hear-PSS-PST-but you FOC see-ST-INF
     'I heard sounds of television. Were you watching it?'

  (d) mizI nu tamar-i-soNga ami (N)du hu-i?
     water NOM stay-ST-INF-but rain-(NOM)FOC fall-ST-INF
     'There's water here (water has collected). Was it raining?' (Someone found that the road was pitted with puddles.)

  (e) Ms. A came to pick up her child, and at the gate she heard a child crying. Wondering whether it was her child or not, she asked
    A : ba: hwa: Ndu nak-i:?
      my child NOM-FOC cry-ST-INF
      'Was my child crying?'
    B : wa: hwa: Ndu nak-i:.
      your child NOM-FOC cry-ST-INF
      'Your child was crying.'

(3) A friend of my daughter sent her a letter of consolation. When I met him, I said with thanks :

    wa: *tigami du* <u>*kak-i:*</u> ?
    you   letter FOC write-ST-INF
    'You wrote her a letter, didn't you?'

(4) When B's friend (Ms. A) came to B's place, B was writing letters. So Ms. A came back without saying anything. The next day :

    A : *wa: uNja*   *tigami du*   <u>*kak-i:?*</u>
         you that time letter FOC write-ST-INF
         'Were you writing letters then?'

    B : *N:. Ndahu kata nu aQ-ta-ra: du tigami kak-i-da(/* <u>*kak-i:*</u>*)*
         yes send-ATT side NOM be-PST-CAU FOC letter write-ST-PST(/-INF)
         'Yes, I had some people to write to, so I was writing letters.'

(5) I said to my friend "I am going write a letter". The next day :

    Friend :   *kIno:*   *wa:*   *tigami* <u>*kak-i:?*</u>
               yesterday-TOP you letter write-ST-INF
               'Yesterday did you write a letter?'

    I :   *N:*   *kIno:*   *tigami kak-i-da* (/ <u>*kak-i:*</u>)
          yes yesterday-TOP letter write-ST-PST (/ write-ST-INF)
          'Yes, I wrote a letter yesterday.'

(6) Mr. A came from another island or is calling on the telephone from another island.

    A : *kIno:*   *kazji Ndu* <u>*huk-i:?*</u>
    Yesterday-TOP wind NOM-FOC blow-ST-INF
           'Yesterday was the wind blowing?' (It means a typhoon.)

    B : *kazji Ndu* <u>*huk-i:.*</u>
        wind NOM-FOC blow-ST-INF
        'The wind was blowing.'

(7) Atsuko's friend visited her but she was away from home. He asked to her mother :

The Grammar of Ishigaki Miyara Dialect in Luchuan

(7-1) atsuko: zINge   du   har-i:?
Atsuko-TOP where-to FOC go-ST-INF
'Where did Atsuko go?'   (CJ *itta no / itte iru no?*)

(7-2) Later, he visited again and she was there. He asked to her :
zINga   du   har-i:?
where-in FOC go go-ST-INF
'Where were you?'   (Cj *itta no / itte ita no?*)

(8) She wrote a letter of congratulation and sent it, without knowing that her husband had already written and sent one. He heard about it.

Husband :   wanu N   tigami   (du)   kak-i:?
you also letter (FOC) write-ST-INF
'You also wrote a letter?'

Wife :   banu N   kak-i:
I also write-ST-INF
'I wrote one, too.'

(9) There are a lot of people on the road.

A :   no: nu Ndu ar-i:?   (/ no: nu du ar-i:? / no: Ndu ar-i:?)
what NOM FOC be-ST-INF
'What's happening?'

B :   kazji nu Ndu   ar-i:.
fire NOM FOC be-ST-INF
'There was a fire.'

(10) Mr. B found what Mr. A was searching for.

A :   Nga du ar-i:?   B :   aQ-ta.   /   Nga du ar-i:.
there FOC be-ST-INF   be-AC-PST / there FOC be-ST-INF
'Is it there?'   'It is.'   /   'It is there.'

(11) Looking at a mess after the party :

A :   waQca   Nga   ju:zji   Ndu   ar-i:?
your house in party NOM-FOC be-ST-INF
'Was there a party in your house?'

107

B : *ju:zji* Ndu <u>*ar-i.*</u>   /   <u>*aQ-ta.*</u>
   party NOM-FOC be-ST-INF / be-AC-PST
   'There was a party.'   /   'There was.'

(12) The telephone rang. The housewife went to answer it, and coming back she said :

   cakusI   nu jumi gara   du   deNwa   nu   <u>ar-i:.</u>
   elder-son GEN wife from FOC telephone NOM be-ST-INF
   'The wife of my elder son gave me a phone call.'

(13) *kama Nga zjiN nu <u>ut-i-da.</u>   ba: tur-i   <u>k-i:.</u>*
   over there in money NOM drop-ST-PST I take-ST-INF come-ST-INF
   Over there, I found the money on the ground. I picked it up and have brought it.'

(14) Some money dropped down from the pocket of a drunk. Looking at it :

   A : *unu   pItu   gara   zjiN   nu   <u>ut-i:.</u>*
      that person from   money NOM drop-ST-INF
      'That person dropped some money.' (The money dropped from the pocket.)

(14-a) In the case that the speaker found the money lying on the road

   kanga   zjiN nu <u>ut-i-da.</u>
   over-there-in money NOM drop-ST-PST
   'There was the money (which must have dropped down from someone's pocket).

(14-b) *kaNga   zjiN   nu   <u>ut-i:</u>   ba: tum-i   kI-ta.*
   over-there-in money NOM drop-ST-INF I take-ST-INF come-AC-PST
   'Some money was lying over there, I picked it up and brought it here.'

(15) *atsuko: huNdama gara   du   <u>ut-i:.</u>*
   Atsuko veranda from FOC fall-ST-INF
   'atsuko has fallen down from the veranda.'
   The hearer would think that she is in hospital or at least in bed.

The Grammar of Ishigaki Miyara Dialect in Luchuan

(16) wa: b-i: dur-u ?   gusji ba du   num-i ?
     you drunk-ST-INF AX   sake AP FOC drink-ST-INF
     'You are drunk?' 'Have you drunk sake?'

In response to these kinds of questions, the listener will not repeat the same verb form by itself. That is to say, the answer is not a single-word sentence consisting of this form, like "*kak-i.* " or "*ar-i.* " etc. The existential verb can not be independently used as in answer without other elements of the question sentence as shown above. This phenomenon stands out especially with the verbs whose agents are not human.

  A: *kazji Ndu huk-i:?*   B: *huk-i-da.*   /   *kazji Ndu huk-i:.*

In the examples from (1) to (11), the persons concerned perceive that the action arose. Every one turns his attention to the focused word.

Examples (3), (4), (5) and (6) show the confirmation of action that has arisen.

(7) can be differently translated in common Japanese according to the listener. Their concern is only "where" because every one knows that the action "go" did arise. In (8), the concern is "you, too" because the action took place already.

(9), (10) & (11) are examples of existential verbs. Since the speaker sees a lot of people searching for something or milling about, he knows something "happened". For him, "what or where" is needed.

In (12), as the result of action "coming", the speaker is now in front of the hearer.

The exceptions are (14) & (15). These are the verbs of Group 2. The attention of the speaker is concentrated on the moment that the action arises. Such an example is difficult to find because in instantaneous verbs the start and the end of the action are almost at the same time. Therefore, the verb indicates usually the whole action. In (14), *ut-i* can not be replaced with another form. If one were to say "*uti-da*", the money would already be

109

on the ground. In (15), if one said *"ut-i-da"*, Atsuko would still be on the ground at that time. Another form <u>*uti-Ta*</u> indicates that the subject "just now fell down". I will explain *-Ta* form later on.

Also in the verbs of Group 1, the arising of action can be indicated by the stative-infinitive.

(17) *m-i: m-ir-i   Nma Nga hana Ndu   <u>sak-i:.</u>*
look-ST-INF look-IMP there in flower NOM-FFOC bloom-ST-INF
'Look! There flowers are in bloom.'

(18) The farmers have to cross-fertilize pumpkin flowers right after blooming. So they go around their field every day.

Monologue walking in the field :

Nma NgaN hana nu <u>sak-i:.</u>   kuma NgaN hana nu <u>sak-i:.</u>
there-in-also flower NOM bloom-ST-INF here in-also flower NOM bloom-ST-INF

'Flowers are blooming over there. Here, too.'

hana du a:h-u:
flower FOC cross-CON

'We cross-fertilize.

(19) monologue in the field :   *hana nu <u>saki.</u>*
                                        flower NOM bloom-ST-INF
                                        'Flowers are blooming / have bloomed.'

Since the farmer is waiting for flowers and looking around everyday, this infinitive form can not be continuative (durative). It is not the perfection of action (*sakiTa*) because the farmer has to begin working with these flowers. The farmer need not report that he took a look at flowers (*sakida*) in this case.

These examples show that the action arises independently of the speaker's recognition. That is why this form is used generally as infinitive for the dialect speakers.

(20) *auda nu nak-i.*
 frog NOM croak-ST-INF
 'Frog croaks.'

When one of speakers gave me a word "frog" she continued to make a sentence with that word. It seems that this infinitive form is suitable for the action by non-human agent in expressing it in an abstract way. "Frog" is the agent of the verb "croak".

The speaker continued as follows.

(21) *auda nu nak-ir-u* .
 frog NOM croak-EPS-CON
 'Frog is croaking.' It means that someone (including the speaker) is listening to a frog.

The stative-infinitive indicates the state where the action arises independently of the speaker. The speaker takes a look at it or hears it and he knows that the action has arisen. That is why we can translate this infinitive with *N* into durative ; Miyara "*kakiN*" will be translated into CJ "*kaite-iru* (be writing)". The action has arisen. The speaker takes a look at it and he says "*kakiN*". At the point when he takes a look at the action, it has arisen and still is in progress. Otherwise the speaker could not take a look at it.

The stative-infinitive form without *N* can be translated into the past tense. In the moment when people have a conversation the action must have arisen. The moment when it arose is objectively the past for people looking at that state of action arisen.

It seems that the stative-infinitive has a role of neutral basic form for the verbs whose agents are not human. The dialect speakers often mention this form as a being equivalent to the conclusive *-ru* form of Common Japanese verbs. Since the verbs of Group 2 do not have the active, the stative-infinitive is the most basic and important infinitive form.

We have to add that this form can not be said as continuative because it does not mean continuation when it is suffixed with rational *ki* (corresponding approximately to English "because ~"). This suffix is not added to active-infinitive.

> *ba:* <u>*kak-i-ki*</u> *wa: kak-a-na:r-ja.* ×*kak-<u>I</u>-ki*
> I write-ST-INF-*ki* you write-NEG-IMP
> 'I will write. So (you) do not write.'

> *ba:* <u>*kak-i-ki*</u> *muc-i har-ja:.* ×*kak-<u>I</u>-ki*
> I write-ST-INF-ki take-ST-INF go-IMP
> 'I write (a letter or something), and you take it.'

7. 5. 2. Speaker and stative-infinitive

The speaker's morpheme *N* is added to the stative-infinitive and it is translated as if continuative. However, the continuation is not its distinctive feature. We have to note that morphemes *N, so:* and *ru* are here mutually exclusive.

As mentioned above, *ar-*(be), *ur-*(be) and *jar-*(copula) do not have the stative-infinitive.

The form with *N* is restricted in where it can occur; it is important whether the action is in sight of the speaker and hearer or not.

Examples

(1) On the road: (It is natural that they are not taking a look at the writing action.)

> A: *ba: taraN-da-ru muno:* *wa:* <u>*kaki-N*</u>?
> I ask-AC-PST-ATT thing-TOP you write-ST-INF-*N*
> 'Are you writing what I asked you to?'

> B: <u>*kak-i-N.*</u> / *me:da* <u>*kaka-nu*</u> .
> write-ST-INF-*N* yet write-NEG
> 'I am writing.' 'Not yet.'

(2) The person who has come to get some documents to be written is calling out of the house. He is not in sight of the speaker.

> *ba : nama* <u>*kak-i-N.*</u>　　　*mac-a:.*
> I　now　write-ST-INF-*N*　wait-IMP
> 'I am writing now.　Wait.'

(2') In the case that he is in sight of the speaker : (e.g. when he came into the room or when the door was opened :)

> *nama du* <u>*kak-i-ru.*</u>　　*mac-a:.*　× *nama* <u>*kak-i-N.*</u>
> now　FOC　write-ST-CON　wait-IMP
> 'I am now writing.　Wait.'

(3) An old man has a hard time writing without his glasses, and he asks a small child :

> A :　　*wa:　zI:*　<u>*kak-i-N*</u> ?　*ba: ka:rI*　<u>*kak-i*</u>　　*h-ir-u-N?*
> 　　　　you　character　write-ST-INF-*N*　my　in-place-of　write-ST-INF　give-EP-CON-*N*
> 　　　　'Do you write characters?　Could you write this instead of me?'

Child : <u>*kak-i-N.*</u>
　　　　　write-ST-INF-*N*
　　　　　'(I) am writing.' ('I can write.')

(4) Atsuko's son must be writing a letter in the next room.　She asked his brother to see whether he is working hard at writing.　His brother went to see him and came back.

> Mother : *ure:*　<u>*kak-i-N*</u>?　　　Brother:　<u>*kak-i-N*</u>
> 　　　　　He-TOP　write-ST-INF-*N*　　　　　　write-ST-INF-*N*
> 　　　　　'Is he writing?'　　　　　　　　　　'(He) is writing.

(5) A mother is holding a small child.　He looks about 1 year old.

> A :　　*ure:*　<u>*arag-i-N*</u>?　　(*arag*-'walk' Group 1)
> 　　　　he-TOP　walk-ST-INF-*N*
> 　　　　'Is he walking?'

Mother : <u>*arag-i-N.*</u>
　　　　　walk-ST-INF-*N*
　　　　　'He is walking.'

(6) *ut-* (fall Group 2)

kɪnu   kazi   nu   hukɪ-da-ra: ki: nu ha: nu   <u>ut-i-N.</u>   so:zɪ   h-i:.

yesterday wind NOM blow-AC-PST-CAU tree GEN leaf NOM fall-ST-INF-*N* sweep do-IMP

'Since the wind blew yesterday, the leaves of the trees have fallen (on the ground). Sweep them up!'

(6') Conversation on the road in the fall season

baNca Nga: ki: nu   ha: nu   <u>ut-i-N.</u>   waQca Nga N   <u>ut-i-N</u>?

my-house-in tree GEN leaf NOM fall-ST-INF-*N* your-house-in also fall-ST-INF-*N*

'The leaves are falling off the trees at my house. Are they falling at your house, too?'

(7) Toshio's friend visited him early in the morning and he asked to his mother.

    Friend : *tosjio <u>uk-i-N</u>?*

        Toshio rise-   ST-INF-*N*

        'Has Toshio gotten up?'

She shouted to Toshio whose room is upstairs

      wa: <u>uk-i-N</u>?   Toshio : *<u>uk-i-N.</u>*

      you rise-   ST-INF-*N*   rise- ST-INF-*N*

      'Are you awake?'   'I am awake.'

His mother <u>can not say to her son directly in her sight.</u>   × *wa: uk-i-N*?

(8) Since an old man is not wearing his glasses, so he can not see well and asks to someone.

     A : *ure:tigami <u>kak-i-N</u>?*   B : *<u>kak-i-N.</u>*

       he-TOP letter write-ST-INF-*N*   write-ST-INF-*N*

       'Is he writing a letter?'   '(He) is writing.'

(8') To the person writing a letter :

    wa: tigami   du   <u>kak-iru</u> ?   × *wa: tigami   <u>kak-i-N</u>?*

    you letter FOC write-EP-CON   write-ST-INF-*N*

    'You are writing a letter, aren't you?'

(9) A mother asked her friend to baby-sit and went out. On the way back, she met the baby-sitter's son near to their house. He said to her:
   wa: hwa: ja   nak-i-N.
   your child TOP cry-ST-INF-N
   'Your child is crying.'

(10) Then she went to the baby-sitter's house in a hurry.
   Mother: ba: hwa: ja nak-u-N ?   × ba: hwa: ja nak-i-N?
              my child TOP cry-AC-CON-N   cry-ST-INF-N
              'Does my child cry? (Is my child crying?)'
   Baby-sitter : nak-i-da-soNga   nama   nak-a-nu.
              cry-ST-PST-but   now   cry-NEG
              'He was crying before but now he isn't.'

(11) From a distance, we saw a neighbor's child who looks to crying.
   A: ure: nak-i-N ?   B : nak-i-N.
       she-TOP cry-ST-INF-N   cry-ST-INF-N
       'Is she crying?'   '(she) is crying.'
   Then going near to her
   A: no: di du   nak-ir-u ?   × wa: naki-N?
       why FOC cry-ST-CON   you cry-ST-INF-N
       'Why are you crying?'

(12) To a mother who is going back in a hurry because she left her baby in her house.
   wa: hwa: nak-u-N kaja:.   × wa: hwa: naki-N?
   your baby cry-AC-CON-N FP   your baby cry-ST-INF-N
   'I wonder whether your baby is crying.' 'Your baby is crying?'

"wa: hwa: nak-i-N?" does not mean 'Your baby is crying? (Go back in a hurry)'. This sentence scarcely appears but if pressed to say so, it might express the question of sentence meaning that your weak baby, who is not even strong enough to cry, is actually crying.

It seems that there is a co-occurrence restriction with the third person ;

but as shown in the next example, there is in fact no such restriction .
(13) The daughter, a juvenile delinquent, came back when her mother died. Her neighbors talked to each other :

    A :   *ure:*   *nak-i-<u>N</u>*?   B :   *nak-i-<u>N</u>*.
         she-TOP cry-ST-INF-*N*   cry-ST-INF-*N*
         'Is she crying?'   '(She) is crying.'

This conversation means that the daughter, who wouldn't normally cry even in the case of her mother's death, is in fact crying.

The conversation among the neighbors attending the funeral :

ure: *nak-i-<u>N</u>*.   *nak-i-<u>N</u>*?   *nak-i-<u>N</u>*.
she-TOP cry-ST-INF-*N*   cry-ST-INF-*N*   cry-ST-INF-*N*
'She is crying'   'Is she crying?'   'She is crying'

(14) The mother who is waiting to have a grandchild asks her daughter repeatedly :

    Mother :   *wa: haram-i-<u>N</u>*?   (Her daughter does not have any sign.)
                you conceive-ST-INF-*N*
                'Are you pregnant?'
    Daughter : *me:da <u>haram-a-nu</u>*. / *me:da <u>haram-i</u> <u>ura-nu.</u>*
                yet conceive-NEG   / yet conceive-ST-INF AX-NEG
                '(I) have not conceive yet.'

The stative-infinitive indicates 'arising of action', and is not dependent on the speaker's recognition or judgment. The action arises without the speaker, and the speaker experiences as things as they stand now. The speaker takes a look at it or listen to it, has a direct experience of that state and then he recognizes that state as a whole. This is the meaning of -*N* added form.

This *N*-form appears often in question sentences in the beginning of conversation. However, it can not fill the role of confirming the listener's action in <u>his sight</u> because everyone (including the speaker) can see it, so it is not necessary to question the obvious fact. As far as N-form is concerned, it appears in questions when the persons concerned do not know how the things go. The action of the listener in his sight can be confirmed by taking a look at it.

When the hearer is not in sight, the situation is as same as the third person ; so the *N*-form can appear. On the other hand, the both speaker and hearer use the conclusive form in their sight.

Since this form indicates the arising of action, it is curious to ask whether the human action arises in general. There is no person who never cries. The sentence "*wa: naki-N?*" is not acceptable. If the meaning of this category is continuative, say 'be crying', the reason of the unacceptability has to be explained.

In this *N*-form, the action is usually desirable for the speaker. It might be expected.

(15)   ?   *wa: nak-i-N?*
         'you cry/are crying?'

The speakers always laugh on hearing the above sentence. According to them, this sentence suggests that crying is nice. The word *sjin-i-N* (*sɪn-* 'die') is another example, which is hardly used in conversation. To die is not nice, not desirable. Using this *N*-form, people have a concern about arising of the action. If it is not desirable, people do not need to talk of it. One more example is added here.

(16) When a rat is found lying down on the ground after eating a drug, someone wants to make sure whether it dies or not. In this case, dying is desirable.

   unu ujaNco: sjin-i-N ?   sjin-i   ur-a-nu ?
   this rat-TOP   die-ST-INF-*N*   die-ST-INF be-NEG
   'Is this rat dead?   It hasn't yet died?'

7. 6. Conclusive
7. 6. 1. Attributive usage

The conclusive form is called *rentaikei* (attributive) in traditional grammar and it is considered that its main function is to modify nouns. There is no doubt that it modifies the nouns that follow it, but its usage is rather limited in comparison with common Japanese as follows.

 kak-u <u>*pɪtu,*</u> <u>*munu,*</u> <u>*basju,*</u>   <u>*hazɪ*</u>
 write-AC-CON person, thing, occasion, certainty

'the person who writes, what someone writes, when someone writes, someone must write

It can not be used to make long phrases such as "the person who goes to the next room and writes a letter with a pencil..." (its Common Japanese equivalent, *tonari no heya ni itte enpitsu de kaku hito*, would not sound unusual). In Miyara dialect, though, the sentence "<u>*kuma: ba: tigami kaku za:*</u> (This is the room <u>where I write a letter</u>.)", for example, is not acceptable.

In fact, the word "attributive" is not really appropriate for this form. Its main usage is not attributive but predicative. Since the attributive usage is based on general recognition, it is not contradictory with the independent predicative usage.

The word *hazɪ* (certainty) is exceptional. It can be followed with *-N* added conclusive form like <u>*kak-u-N*</u> *hazɪ*.

I will leave this topic here.

7. 6. 2. Conclusive in predicate

In the contemporary research,[38] {the conclusive form + *N*} is considered the most basic form as predicative. It is said that this form denotes the future for one group which indicates the action and the present for the other group which indicates the state.

---

(38) Karimata (1992, p.868)

In Miyara Dialect, the form with N is always accompanied with some elements of modality, that is, the speaker's recognition or judgment. We have to examine sentences with N-forms and non-N-forms of the conclusive.

(1) The focus particle *du* influences on the N-forms. Generally speaking, when there is a word accompanied with *du* the verb form of the predicate does not accompany N. This phenomenon is similar to *kakari-musubi* in old Japanese. It is interesting that for the dialect speaker their *du* corresponds to *ga* (the nominative marker) in the common Japanese.

(2) The N-form has an occurrence restriction with the person as stated. The conclusive form without N has the same kind of restriction. The question "*wa: du kaku?* (Do you write?)" is acceptable but answering with "*wa: du kaku.* (You write.)" is not acceptable.

(3) In wh-question, the interrogative words are usually followed with du and the verb does not take the N-form.

(4) There are some cases that the verb takes forms without N even if there is not any word accompanied with *du*.

(5) It is important to note that there is a special tense–aspectual phase concerning to the <u>instantaneous recognition</u> of the action before one's eyes.

Examples for (1), (2), (3)

Group 1 (the active-conclusive often denoted with simple CON instead AC-CON.)

(a) Two persons have to write something. They are deciding who will do what.

A : *ba: uri kak-u-N*.   *wa: kuri kak-ja*.
    I that write-AC-CON-N   you this write-IMP
    'I will write that.'   '(You) write this.'

B : *wa: uri kak-u-N*? *aNzu-Ka ba : kuri kak-u-N*. × *wa: uri kak-u-N*.
    you this write-CON-N then I this write-CON-N   you that write-CON-N
    'Will you write that? Then I will write this.'   'You write that.

119

A : *atsuko:*   <u>*kak-u-N*</u>   <u>*kaja:*</u>.
Atsuko-TOP write-AC-CON-*N* FP
'I wonder whether Atsuko writes or not.'

(b) Two persons are talking in front of a tree.

A : *unu ki: ja   hana <u>sak-u-N</u>*?   B : <u>*sak-u-N*</u>.
this tree TOP flower blossom-AC-CON-*N*   blossom-AC-CON-*N*
'Does this tree blossom?'   '(It) blossoms.'

(c) Four people have to decide who will write some documents.

A : (*ure:*) *ta: du <u>kak-u</u>*.   B : *ba: du <u>kak-u</u>*.
(that-TOP) who FOC write-AC-CON   I FOC write-AC-CON
'Who will write (this)?'   'I will write it.'

C : *wa: du <u>kak-u</u>?*.   × <u>*wa:*</u>   *du <u>kak-u</u>*.
you FOC write-AC-CON   you FOC write-AC-CON
'Will you write?'   'You (will) write.'

D : *atsuko   N (/ nu) du <u>kak-u</u>*.
Atsuko NOM-FOC write-AC-CON
'Atsuko will write.'

(d) They have papers to write on.

A : *wa: no: du <u>kak-u</u>*.   B : *unu   zI: du <u>kak-u</u>*.
you what FOC write-AC-CON   this letter FOC write-AC-CON
'What will you write?'   'I will write this letter.'

(e) *ba: mainitsI   sjiNbuN   <u>jum-u-N</u>*.
I every day newspaper read-AC-CON-*N*
'I read a newspaper every day.'

Group 2 (the epistemic-conclusive often denoted with simple CON instead of EP-CON.)

(a) A child is about to fall from the veranda.

Mother :   <u>*ut-i-ru-N*</u>!   cf. (e)
                fall-EP-CON-*N*
                '(He's) falling!'

(b) *kazji nu huk-ja: du ki: nu ha: ja ut-ir-u*.
wind NOM blow-REA FOC tree GEN leaf TOP fall-EP-CON
'Since the wind blows leaves fall from the tree.'

(c) *kazi nu huk-ir-i du ki: nu ha: nu ut-ir-u*
wind NOM blow-EP-INF FOC tree GEN leaf NOM fall-EO-CON
'The wind is blowing and leaves are falling off the tree.' (The speaker is looking at it.)

(d) *kazji nu huk-I-da-ra: du ki: nu ha: nu ut-ir-u*.
wind NOM blow-AC-PST-CND FOC tree GEN leaf NOM fall-EP-CON
'Since the wind blew, the leaves have fallen off the tree.' (The leaves are on the ground.)

(e) At night in bed, hearing leaves fall because of the wind :
kazji coho:-ri-ki ki: nu ha: nu ut-ir-u-N. cf. (a)
wind strong-RAT tree GEN leaf NOM fall-EP-CON-*N*
'Since the wind is strong, leaves are falling off the tree.' (The speaker is hearing it.)

(f) Discovery (f-1) when a lost wallet was found : *ar-u-N*!
be-CON-*N*
'Here it is!'

(f-2) when a lost child was found : *ur-u-N*!
be-CON-*N*
'Here he is!'

The speaker need not judge in wh-questions as shown in (c) and (d) of Group 1. The people concerned must know all about the action in common ; therefore, *N*-form is not necessary. The important word is only focused one. On the contrary, the speaker judges it in an instant when he discovers something. That is why *N*-form appears in the case of discovery.

Now we will examine above (4) ; there are some cases that the verb takes the form without *N* even if there is not any word accompanied with *du*.

The following examples show that the conclusive form (without *N*) is used with the action coming out, repeating as usual or being in view of the persons concerned.

(A) In the question with interrogative adverb and in its answer

The action itself has been recognized in common among the people concerned. Only the answer to the focused interrogative word is indispensable.

(a) <u>no: di</u>   (*du*)   <u>kak-u</u>.
why   (FOC) write-AC-CON
'Why do you write?'

(b) A: <u>no: sa:ri</u> (*du*) <u>kak-u</u>.   B: <u>hudi   sa:ri   kak-u</u>.
what with (FOC) write-AC-CON   writing brush with write-AC-CON
'What do you write with?'   'I write with a writing brush.'

(c) A: <u>zINga</u> (*du*) <u>kak-u.</u>   B: <u>kaNga   kak-u.</u>
where-in (FOC) write-AC-CON   over-there-in   write-AC-CON
'Where do you write?'   'I write over there.'

(d) A: <u>no: sI-na:</u>   (*du*) <u>har-u.</u>   B: <u>mai kai-na: har-u.</u>
what do-to (FOC) go-AC-CON   rice buy-to go-AC-CON
'For what purpose are you going?'   'I am going to buy rice.'

(e) A: <u>zINge</u> <u>du</u> <u>har-u.</u>   Cf. <u>zINge</u> <u>har-u.</u>
where-to FOC go-CON   where-to go-CON
'Where are you going?'   'Where are you going?' (A fixed greeting)

(B) When there is an adverbial phrase and the action is in view of the people concerned, the conclusive form appears without *N*. In this case, the persons concerned can perceive the action.

(a) *ba:*   <u>hudi   sa:ri   zI: kak-u.</u>
I   writing brush with letter write-AC-CON
'I am going to write with a writing brush.'

(b) *ba:*   <u>nikkirI sa:ri</u> <u>ki:</u>   <u>kIs-u.</u>
I   saw   with   tree cut-AC-CON
'I am going to cut the tree with a saw.'

(c) *ba: hatsɪ sa:ri NboN hwo:.*
I chopsticks with rice eat-AC-CON
'I will eat rice with chopsticks.'

(d) *ma:su kaina: haru.*
salt buy-for go-AC-CON
'I am going out to buy salt.'

In all cases, the action itself is perceived and everyone knows it. The speaker's concern is what the adverbial phrase indicates. Without the adverbial phrase, the conclusive form without *N* may not appear in these cases.

(C) The conclusive form without *N* often appears to indicate the actions in sight of the speaker and hearer without adverbial phrase. The action is recognized among the persons concerned.

Serving some cakes in a dish :

A : *zɪri du tur-u?*   B : *ba: kuri tur-u.*
which FOC take-AC-CON   I this take-AC-CON
'Which one are you taking?'   'I'll take this one.'

C : *ba: saQta: tur-u.*
I sugar take-AC-CON
'I'm taking a piece of sugar.'

(D) The conclusive without *N* appears when talking about a habitual action which is understood in common among the persons concerned.

The child says to his mother when he goes to school.

nama gaQko: ge: har-u.
now school to go-AC-CON
'I am now going to school.'

Now we will examine (5) ; the conclusive form may indicate the action being taken when the speaker recognizes it in an instant.

(A) A friend came to go somewhere together with Atsuko, who was still washing dishes.

(a) *ba: makarı <u>a:ro:-N.</u> maǫc-a.* / *ba: makarı <u>du</u> <u>a:ro:.</u> maǫc-a.*
   I dish wash-AC-CON-*N* wait-IMP / I dish FOC wash-AC-CON wait-IMP
   'I am washing dishes. Wait.'   'I wash the dishes. Wait'

She can say to her friend either in sight or not in sight (just hearing her voice).

(a') Her mother will answer in place of Atsuko.
   atsuko: makarı <u>a:rai-so:.</u> maǫca. / *atsuko: makarı <u>du</u> <u>a:ra-ir-u.</u> maǫc-a.*
atsuko-TOP dish wash-ST-INF-*so*: wait-IMP/ atsuko-TOP dish FOC wash-EP-CON wait-IMP

   'Atsuko is washing dishes. Wait.' 'Atsuko is washing dishes. Wait.'

   It is impossible for the mother to say this with active-conclusive ; the epistemic-conclusive is expected or {stative-infinitive +*so*:} is preferable.

(B) At the appointed time, I found that my friend was reading newspapers without getting ready.
   I (irritated) :   *wa: no: du <u>h-u:</u>* (/ *h-ja:*). *har-a-nu*?
                     you what FOC do-AC-CON (/do-ST-REA) go-NEG
                     'What are you doing? Aren't you going?'
   Friend (being upset) :   <u>*har-u-N*.</u>
                            go-AC-CON-*N*
                            'I'll go.'

(B') A mother asks loudly to her daughter in the next room, planning to go shopping with her.
   Mother :   *wa: no: du <u>h-i: r-u.</u>*   ×<u>*h-u:*</u>
              you what FOC do-EP-CON   do-AC-CON
              'What are you doing?'
   Daughter : *sjiNbuN <u>du</u> <u>jum-ir-u.</u>*   ×<u>*jum-u*</u>
               newspaper FOC read-EP-CON   read-AC-CON
               'I am reading a newspaper.'

124

In the similar cases, the active-conclusive does not appear even if the speaker hears suddenly a loud noise, because the speaker already knows there is someone in the next room. It is not classified into actions recognized in an instant.

(C) People are surrounding a computer and talking ; their friend who has never seen one before came to visit ; and, wondering what it is he asked :

    wa: no: du   h-u: ?   mizɪraha-so: na:. (hi:-ru is also acceptable.)
    you   what FOC do-AC-CON   curious-so: FP (do-EP-CON)
    'What on earth are you doing? It is new for me.' ('What are you doing?')

(C') In the same situation, he can say to their daughter in the next room.

    uQta: no: du   h-u: .   (h-i:-r-u is also acceptable.)
    They-TOP what FOC do-AC-CON   (do-EP-CON)
    'What on earth are they doing?   ('What are they doing?')

(D) The following examples are not included into the category of future. Some of them have N and others do not have N.

(a) The husband who is reading the articles about sumo (Japanese wrestling) says to his wife, who is just entering :

    sɪmo: nu kutu sɪsɪ-Taha-ri-ki   du   sjiNbuN jum-u.
    wrestling GEN matter know-eager-INF-RAT FOC newspaper read-AC-CON
    'I am reading the newspaper to see the results of the sumo match.'

(b) There is a house which is famous for its cherry tree. Two people came to see it and told the house master.

(b-1) hana   mi:-na: (du)   k-u:.[39]
         blossom see-ST-INF-to (FOC) come-AC-CON
         'I have come to see the blossoms.

(b-2) atsuko N hana   mi:-na: (du)   k-u:.
         Atsuko also blossom see-ST-INF-to (FOC) come-AC-CON
         'Atsuko has come also to see the blossoms.'

---

(39) This is changeable for kɪ-ta (Past), ki : (ST-INF)

(c) Someone is working hard.
A: *wa: ju: hatarag-i-so: na:.*
   you well work-ST-INF-*so*: FP
   'You are working hard, aren't you?'
B: *du: gaNzjoho: nar-u   tami   Nga du   sjigutu   h-u:* .
   body healthy become-AC-ATT purpose in FOC work do-AC-CON
   'I work for the sake of my health.'

(d) A mother holds a baby in her arms. The baby looks about one year old.
A: *ure: arag-i-N?*
        he-TOP walk-ST-INF-*N*
        'Is he walking?'
Mother: *arag-u-N.*   / *arag-i-N.*
        walk-AC-CON-*N*   walk-ST-INF-*N*
        '(He) walks.'   'He is walking.'

The above examples (a), (b) & (c) do not indicate the future. People are looking the action. The example (b) indicates the state of result. The example (d) pairs the active-infinitive with the stative-infinitive. The former is the mother's judgment at that moment. By the latter she explains that he is in the state of walking.

The speaker may indicate his recognition by the conclusive. He can recognize the action at any stage : it is either going to occur or on the way to occurring ; it occurs repeatedly or usually ; the occurrence of action remains. However, the action must be also recognizable by all the people concerned.

Since the persons concerned recognize the action while speaking, it must not have completely disappeared. As far as the instantaneous verbs like *ut-*(fall) are concerned, it is not necessarily required to have seen the exact moment in which something fell. We could thus define the conclusive as "non-past".

Since the conclusive does not have the speaker's morpheme *N* and indicates recognition in common among the people concerned, it must imply some objectivity in a sense as its category.

7. 6. 3. Epistemic-conclusive

The epistemic-conclusive usually takes *N* when the verb comes from Group 2. In the Group 1, the conclusive form takes *N* depending on the meaning and aspect of the verb.

Even though the forms of this category are translated as continuative (*te -iru* in common Japanese), strictly speaking, there is not any verbal category to which this continuation of action is assigned.

We are going to examine two forms corresponding to Japanese *te-iru*. One is Epistemic-conclusive and the other is collocation of the auxiliary ; e.g. stative-infinitive + (*d*) *uru*.

The former (-*ir-u*) is confirmation of the state where the action is arising by the persons concerned. In this point, it is close to *te-iru* of the instantaneous verb in common Japanese. On the other hand, by means of (*d*) *ur-u*, the speaker confirms objectively the state of action which arose and still now is in progress (as words are spoken).

(A) Group 1

(1) Someone was writing a letter. His friend saw him <u>writing</u> and approached him.

  wa: tigami du   <u>*kak-ir-u*</u>?
  you letter FOC write-EP-CON
  'You are writing a letter, aren't you?'

(2) It seemed they were having a party. He saw them drinking something, and approached.

  gusji du <u>*num-iru*</u> ?
  sake FOC drink-EP-CON
  'You are drinking sake, aren't you?' (I would like to join. / If it's not

sake, is it tea or juice?)

(3) There is a child in distance. He seems to be crying. I approach and talk to him.

? *wa:du nak-iru* ?

you FOC nak-EP-CON

'You are crying, aren't you?'

This sentence is acceptable only if the speaker heard child crying and wanted make sure it.

? *wa:nak-i duru*?

you nak-ST-INF duru

'you are crying, aren't you?'

This sentence means that you are crying even though you do not need to cry.

The acceptable sentence is only following.

wa: *no:di du nak-iru*?

you why FOC nak-EP-CON

'Why are you crying?'

The form *nak-ir-u* itself means that the persons concerned recognize it. It is contradictory to ask again, but asking why is reasonable.

This example implies that there is no question sentence to confirm the continuation of action in sight. That is to say, the epistemic conclusive form does not mean the continuation of action, even though it is usually translated into common Japanese as the continuative.

(B) Group 2

This Group has only one conclusive form, that is, epistemic-conclusive. The transitive verb can indicate the continuation of action by adding an accompanying particle (*ba*). The intransitive verbs do not have the formal distinction between the result and the continuation (repetition) of action as stated earlier.

(1) Atsuko is ready to take a bath. She has her towel and soap in her hand.

The Grammar of Ishigaki Miyara Dialect in Luchuan

    A :   *mizɪ du am-iru*?   (CJ *mizu o abiru no*?)
             water FOC bathe-EP-CON
             'Are you going to take a (cold) bath?'

(2) Someone visited Atsuko. He heard the water running in the bathroom.
    A :   *atsuko: mizɪ ba du am-ir-u*?   (CJ *mizu o abi-teiru no*?)
             Atsuko water AP FOC bathe-EP-CON
             'Atsuko! Are you bathing?'
    Atsuko: (Answering loudly in the bathroom.)
             ba: nama mizɪ ba du am-ir-u. me:ma mac-ir-ja.
             I now water AP FOC bathe-EP-CON a-moment wait-EP-IMP
             'I am taking a bath. Keep waiting a little while.'

(3) Atsuko has a cold. Even so, she is taking a cold bath.
    A :   *mizɪ ami duru*?   *amuNtiN misja:ru munu*.
             (CJ *mizu o abiteiru no*? *abinakutemo ii mono o*)
             water bathe-INF *dur-u*   ami-NEG-even good Fm-N
             'Taking a cold bath? You should have not taken a bath.'

(4) *atsuko: jadu ba du ak-ir-u*.
    (CJ *atsuko wa to o aketeiru*.)
    atsuko-TOP sliding-door AP FOC open-EP-CON
    'Atsuko is opening the sliding doors.'

(4') *jadu du ak-ir-u*   (CJ *to o aketeiru*)
    sliding-door FOC open-   EP-CON
    '(I) am going to open the sliding doors.'

(5) A typhoon blew down a light for crime prevention in the field. Someone reported it to the electrical company.
    bo:haNto: Ndu baNca nu hatagi Nga ut-ir-u. (CJ *ociteiru*)
    light NOM-FOC our-house GEN field in   fall-EP-CON
    'The light has been blown down and is now laid on the ground.'

(6) *kama Nga no:Ngasa Ndu ut-ir-u.*   (CJ *ociteiru*)
    over-there in something NOM-FOC fall-EP-CON

129

'Over there, something fell down and still is there.'

(6') *kazji   nu   hukja*: <u>*du*</u>   *ki: nu   ha: ja   <u>ut-ir-u.</u>* (CJ <u>ociru</u> / <u>ociteiru</u>)
wind   GEN   blow-ST-REA   FOC   tree   GEN   leaf   FOC   fall-EP-CON

'Since the wind is blowing, the leaves of tree are falling.' (Taking a look at it :)

As well as the active-conclusive, the epistemic-conclusive may appear without preceding *du*, as follows.

(7) Atsuko's son reads news papers every morning before going to school. She frowns at him.

Mother :   *wa: sjiNbuN   <u>jum-iru</u>* ?   (CJ <u>yomu</u> no? / <u>yonde iru</u> no?)
you   newspaper   jum-EP-CON

'Are you reading newspapers?'

(8) *auda nu   <u>nak-iru</u>.*   (CJ <u>naiteiru</u> / <u>naku</u>)
frog NOM nak-EP-CON   'Frogs are croaking.' (The persons concerned are listening.)

7. 6. 4. Epistemic-conclusive form with *N* in Group 1.

Not all verbs of Group 1 have this form. It is acceptable only with human agent and his intention. The following are the examples.

×*<u>sak-iru</u>-N*   × *<u>hwu-iru</u>-N*
bloom-EP-CON-*N*   rain-EP-CON-*N*

Only if a flower could talk could it say "*ba:* <u>*sakiruN*</u>" ("I'm blossoming") ; the same applies to rain and "*ba:* <u>*huiruN*</u>." ("I'm raining.")

×*<u>sjin-iru</u>-N*   (*sIn-*)

die-EP-CON-*N*   This form could only be said by a dead person from the next world.

This form is translated into CJ as continuative *te-iru*, but it does not indicate a simple objective continuation of action. It has an intention of going on. The persons concerned recognize the action arisen and the speaker intend to go on.

Its usage is limited, as in the following examples. They show a striking contrast to the conclusive form which does not accompany N.

(1) ba: <u>kak-ir-u-N</u>   keN   wa: ik-i-te   k-u:
    I   write-EP-CON-N while   you   go-ST-INF-and come-IMP
    '(You) go and come back. I'll go on writing the whole time.'

(2) ba: ik-i-te kuN   keN   wa: <u>kak-ir-u-N</u> ?
    I   go-and-back-N while you   write-EP-CON-N
    'I will go out and come back. Will you be writing the whole time?'

(3) She is dressing up to attend a party. Her friend helping her has to go out a little while.

   baN-taNga: <u>kisj-i-ru-N</u>.   wa: hajamari ik-i-te k-u:.
   I -alone   wear-EP-CON-N   you in-a-hurry go-ST-INF-and come-IMP
   'I'll go on getting dressing by myself. Go and come back in a hurry.'

7. 7. Realis

The independent realis form appears in wh-question. It does not necessarily accompany particle *du* in a preceding word. However, this form does not appear in its answering sentence. In the answering sentence, {realis + N} form usually appears even if there is a particle *du* in preceding part, and the conclusive form may appear instead of it. That is to say, the independent realis form appears only in wh-question.

The conclusive indicates that the action is taken. The realis indicates that the action is at the level of arising.

The realis does not have any attributive function. This is a big difference between the conclusive and the realis.

7. 7. 1. Speaker and realis

The {realis +N} does not occur with rising intonation in a question. It indicates the speaker's recognition that the action arises certainly in due time or his new recognition of the state where the action already arisen.

Examples:

(1) When I am recommended to do so
  (a) (*ba:*) *atugani kak-ja-N*.   × *wa: atugani kak-ja-N*./?
     (I) later write-REA-*N*   you later write-REA-*N*
     'I certainly write later.'   'Will you certainly write later?'
  (b) (*ba:*) *atugani hwai-ja-N*.   × *wa: atugani hwai-ja-N*./?
     (I) later eat-REA-*N*   you later eat-REA-*N*
     'I certainly eat later.'   'Will you certainly eat later?'

(2) The person said to his friend who had come to ask him to go together.
   ba: har-ar-a-nu.   *atsuko*   Ndu   *har-ja-N.*
   I go-POT-NEG   atsuko NOM-FOC go-REA-*N*
   'I can not go; Atsuko is going.'

(3) The trees are budding.
   jagati sak-ja-N.
   soon bloom-REA-*N*
   'Soon they will bloom.'

(4) The sky is filled with dark clouds.
   jagati ami hwui-ja-N.
   soon rain fall-REA-*N*
   'It is going to rain soon.'

(5) I was surprised looking at the small child writing characters.
   zI: kak-ja-N   /   *kak-ir-ja-N* .
   character write-ST-REA-*N* / write-EP-REA-*N*
   '(He) writes characters.' / '(He) is writing characters.'

(6) Offering: *ba: kak-ja-N ju:.*   (*ju:* a particle of politeness)
            I write-REA-*N* PLP
            'I will write for you.'

(7) A: *unu hwa: ja nak-a-nu?*   B: *nak-ja-N.*
      This baby TOP cry-NEG   cry-REA-*N*
      'Does this baby cry?'   '(He) cries (often).'

(8) One person has to get up because someone came in the middle of the night.
 wa: *uk-una:-ка*: *ba*: *uk-ir-ja-N*.
 you uk-NEG-CND I rise-EP-REA-*N*
 'If you won't get up, I'll get up.'

(9) A : *uk-ir-i*. *uk-ir-i*. B : *uk-ir-ja-N*.
   rise-IMP rise-IMP   rise-EP-REA-*N*
   'Get up! Get up!'   '(I) have been woken up.'

(10) Mother called to her daughter at the door of her room. (The door was closed.)
 Mother : *atsuko*: *uk-i-N*?
    Atsuko rise-ST-INF-*N*
    'Atsuko! Have you woken up?'
 Atsuko : *uk-ir-ja-N*.
    rise-EP-REA-*N*
    '(I) have woken up.' '(I am) awake.'

(11) Discovery : Someone who was looking for what he had lost on the road found it at last.
 (a)   *Nga du ut-ir-ja-N na*:
     here-in FOC fall-EP-REA-*N* FP
     'It dropped and lay here.'
 (b)   For the second searching, someone found what he had lost.
     ar-ja-N !
     be-ST-REA-*N*
     'Here it is.'

(When I looked for it in this place for the first time, it must have been there.)

 The forms of examples from (7) to (10) are exchangeable with the conclusive (*-u-N*). The latter is the recognition of doing, however the former is the recognition of the action arising.

7. 7. 2. Realis and wh-question

In the answer to wh-question, the realis form is remarkably different from the conclusive form. The realis form indicates the action which has been decided, but has not yet started.

Examples :

(1) They have decided who would write documents in a meeting. Then one person who did not know the decision (because he was late) asked to them.

(1-a) A : *ta*: *du* *kak-ja*.   (*kak-u*. acceptable.)
        who FOC write-ST-REA   (write-AC-CON)
        'Who is going to write?'   ('Who writes?')

(1-b) B : *atsuko* *Ndu* *kak-ja-N*. (*Ndu kaku* also acceptable, but not ... *Ndu kak-ja*.)
        atsuko NOM-FOC write-ST-REA-N (NOM-FOC write-AC-CON)
        'Atsuko is going to write.'   (Atsuko writes.)

(2) *unu ki: ja   no: sa:ri du kis-ja:* .
    this tree TOP what with FOC cut-ST-REA

'As far as this tree (which you are going to cut) is concerned, what will you cut it with?'

        Cf. *ki: ja no: sa:ri du   kIsu*
            tree TOP what with FOC cut-AC-CON
            'Speaking the tree in general, what will you cut it with?'

(3) *mana haN-na-ca: no:di har-ja*.   (At the door, or on the way out)
    Never go-PR but why go-ST-REA
    'I tolled you not to go. Why are you going out?'

(4) When I was requested to write something, I took the pencil and asked :
    no: du   kak-ja.
    what FOC write-ST-REA
    'What shall I write?'

(5) When I ask how to do something :

　　　　no: ba hi　　du　h-ja:　　(*no: ba hi　du　hu:*　acceptable)
　　　what AP do-ST-INF FOC do-ST-REA　(what AP do-ST-INF FOC do-AC-CON)
　　　'How shall we/I do it?'　　　　(How do we/I do it?)

(6) *no: ba h-i　du　h-u:　ju　nara-h-o:-r-i*.　×*no ba hi du hja: ju naraho:ri*
　　what AP do-ST-INF FOC do-AC-CON AP teach-HO-IMP
　　'Please tell me how to do it.'

(7) Casual greetings.　　On the road :

(7-a) *zINge　du　har-ja:*
　　　where-to FOC go-ST-REA
　　　'Where are you going?'

(7-b) *zINge　jar-ja:*　　　× *zINge　jar-u*
　　　where-to COP-REA　　where-to COP-CON
　　　'Where to?'

7. 8. Perfect

The perfect is indicated by two forms which are not paired by *N*. One is {stative-infinitive ＋ *Ta*}. The other is {stative-infinitive ＋ *caN*}. However, they are paired in usage.

7. 8. 1. Confirmation of completion of actions

(1) The action has finished in the speaker's sight. Generally speaking, its agent is not mentioned.

　(a) I was writing for a long time and at the moment when I finished it.
　　　kak-i-Ta !　　　×*kak-I-da*　　×*kak-i-da*
　　　write-ST-INF-PF　write-AC-INF-PST　write-ST-INF-PST
　　　'I finished!'

　(b) A child suddenly fell down from the veranda, or a fruit fell down unexpectedly. The person who was watching cried :
　　　ut-i-Ta !　　× *ut-i-da*
　　　fall-ST-INF-PF　fall-ST-INF-PST
　　　'(He/It) fell down.'

(2) Confirmation of having finished the action.
   (a) People are taking turns writing.
   A : wa: kak-i-Ta?   × kak-I-da   × kak-i-da
        you   write-ST-INF-POT write-AC-INF-PST   write-ST-INF-PST
        'Did you finish writing?'
   B : kak-i-Ta.
        write-ST-INF-POT
        '(I) finished writing.'
   A : atsko: kak-i-Ta?   B : me:da kak-a-nu.
        atsuko-TOP write-ST-INF-POT   yet   write-NEG
        'Atsuko, did she finish writing?' 'Not yet finished.'
   (b) My brother was writing a letter to our friends a little while ago. I suddenly thought of something to add to that letter. I asked him whether he finished it or not.
   kak-i-Ta   me:?   ×kak-I-da me:?
   write-ST-INF-POT yet   write-AC-INF-PST
   'Did you finish writing?'
   (c) Toshio's mother calls him at the door. (The door is closed.)
   Mother : wa: uk-i-Ta?   Toshio : uk-i-Ta.   × uk-i-da
             you rise-ST-INF-PF   rise-ST-INF-PF rise-ST-INF-PST
             'Have you gotten up?'   'I have gotten up.'
(3) In the next room, two persons were writing letters. One of them came out of the room.
   A : wa: tigami kak-i-Ta ?   ×kak-I-da   ×kak-i-da
        you letter write-ST-INF-PF write-AC-INF-PST write-ST-INF-PST
        'Did you finish (writing a letter)?'
(4) I suggested John to eat it, but he said no, and later he ate it anyway. I complained about it.
   hwa:-nu di aN-te: hwai-Ta.   ×hwo:da   ×hwaida
   eat-NEG AP say-AC-INF-and   eat-ST-INF-PF eat-AC-INF-PST eat-ST-INF-PST

'(He) said "I won't eat it", and then he ate it.'
(5) Mother finds that her daughter is pregnant. She is delighted and tells to her husband.

 atsuko haram-i-ᴛa ! ×haraɴ-da ×haram-i-da
 atsuko conceive-ST-INF-PF conceive-AC-INF-POT conceive-ST-INF-PST
 'Atsuko has got pregnant.'

7. 8. 2. Completion of action and speaker's intentions

The perfect form stated above follows a second person pronoun taking rising intonation in a question. The form suffixed with -caɴ, however, can neither follow a second person pronoun nor appear in question. That is to say, these two are paired in the perfect aspect.

 A : wa: kak-i-ᴛa ? B : kak-i-ᴛa. × wa: kak-i-ca-ɴ./?
  you write-ST-INF-PF write-ST-INF-PF
  'Did you finish writing?' '(I) did.'

The form suffixed with -caɴ indicates that the speaker confirms the action has been completed, against his intention. Accordingly it indicates the action undesirable for the speaker.

Examples :

(1) My baby fell asleep at last. I began to work and then suddenly he cried again.

 agaja: uk-i-ca-ɴ.
 Interjection wake-ST-INF-PF-ɴ
 'Oh! Dear! (He) woke (again).'
  Cf. In the case that I am waiting for him to wake up : uk-i-ᴛa.
              wake-ST-INF-PF
              '(He) woke up.'

(2) A drunken man left at last after a party. Then he came back again.
 kunu bi:ca: ja mata k-i:-ca-ɴ.

      this   drunk TOP again come-ST-INF-PF-*N*

      'This drunk has come again.'

        Cf. In the case of waiting for someone. *atsuko*   *k-i:-Ta*.

                                         atsuko come-ST-INF-PF

                                       'Atsuko has come.'

(3) I thought that fruit would ripen tomorrow for picking, but then a bird ate it.

     pju:sI nu   hwai-Ca-N.   /   *pju:sI   nu   mata   k-i:-Ca-N*.

     bird's name NOM eat-ST-INF-PF-*N* bird's name NOM again come-ST-INF-PF-*N*

     'A bird has eaten (it).'   /   'A bird has come again.'

(4) The fruit, which should have ripened a few days later, fell down on the ground because of typhoon.   *agaja: ut-i-Ca-N*.

                              oh dear fall-ST-INF-PF-*N*

                            'Oh. Dear! It has fallen.'

  This form may have a same usage as the perfect-*Ta* form. In the answer to a negative question, the speaker can emphasize by this form that the action was completed, because the hearer is very much anxious whether it finished or not.

(5) A: *wa: me:da kak-a-nu*? (They are taking turns writing.)

           you yet write-NEG

           'You don't write yet?'

    B: *kak-i-Ca-N*

           Write-ST-INF-PF-*N*

           'I have witten.'

(6) A: *ba: kak-i-Ca-N*.   *wa: me:da kak-a-nu*?

           I Write-ST-INF-PF-*N*   you yet write-NEG

           'I have written. You haven't written yet?'

(7) A: *ba: hwai-Ca-N* .   *wanu N hwai-ja:*

           I eat-ST-INF-PF-*N*   you also eat-IMP

           'I have eaten. You eat too.'

(8) Mother had to give a meal to her child.
>Father : NboN atsuko ge: hwa:h-ja: Mother : atsuko hwai-ca-N
>   meal atsuko to eat-CAS-IMP   Atsuko eat-ST-INF-PF-N
>   'Make Atsuko eat the meal.'   'Atsuko has eaten.'

7. 9. Past and speaker

"The past" does not refer to an unlimited amount of past time ; rather, it only means the past <u>within</u> the speaker's experience. It indicates that the speaker has an experience to have seen, heard, touched etc. in his life.

Examples :

(1) ba: tigami kak-I-da.
>I letter Write-AC-INF-PST
>'I wrote a letter.'

(2) When I forgot whether I wrote it or not.
>ba: tigami kak-I-da kaja:.
>I letter Write-AC-INF-PST FP
>'I am wondering whether I wrote a letter.'

(3) The response for the above question.
>wa: tigami kak-I-da (so:).
>you letter write-AC-INF-PST (so:)
>'You wrote a letter.'
>Since the speaker saw the questioner writing a letter, he can answer with "<u>kak-I-da</u>"

(4) In the case that he did not see him writing but he saw the letter written by the questioner.
>wa: tigami kak-e: so:
>you letter write-CSC-so:
>'(I know that) you have certainly written a letter.'

(5) When the person wants to tell the action or event which he did not experienced.

ba: *mar-i-da-keN   ja   kazji Ndu   huk-i-da co:*
I be-born-ST-INF-PST-while TOP wind NOM-FOC blow-ST-INF-PST AP
'It is said that the wind was blowing the day when I was born.'
We do not know how the day was when we were born. We only heard about that. That is why we have to add "*co:*" which marks the auditive like in a next sentence.

(5') *ami nu hui-r-i-ki   muka-i na: k-u-N co:*
rain NOM fall-EP-INF-RAT meet-ST-INFto come-AC-CON-N FP
'Someone said that he was coming to pick up you because it was raining.'

(6) The speaker told his life in the old days :

mukasa: *jamaNgarasI sa:ri tamunu putso:-da*
old time-TOP hatchet with firewood get-AC-CON-PST
'(I/We) used to get firewood with a hatchet in the old days.

(7) When the author writes this talk in a leaflet called "the old life in Miyara" in dialect, she has to add "*co:*" in final position.

(7') *mukasa*: *jamaNgarasI sa:ri tamunu putso:-da co:*
'It is said...'

(8) The historical incidents are told in the same way.
The story of Tsunami wave in the period of Meiwa (in 1771) :

mukasI takarabe:kIN di aNz-u pItu nu ta: Nga sjigutu h-i: o:r-u-N keN
old time takarabekIN AP say-ATT person NOM field in work do-ST-INF be-HON-while

'Long ago, there lived a person called Takarabe:kIN and he was working in the field.

du naN nu   kI-ta-ra: du takaha-ru kata ge: nubur-u-N di:
FOC wave NOM come-PST-CND FOC high side to   climb-CON-N AP

Then, a wave came, so he climbed up to the high place, and then

o:r-u-NkeN   du haN ba a:ra-i   unu naN ja haQ-ta   <u>co:</u>
be-CON-*N*-while FOC foot AP wash-ST-INF this wave TOP go-AC-INF-PST it is said
the wave washed his feet and went out. We / I heard so.'

7. 9. 1. Active past

The active past is formed with the active infinitive + *da*. The speaker confirms with his experience that the action occurred in the past time. Active past phrases are often accompanied by words indicating the past time. The action is grasped as a whole, even if it was repeated.

The past form of the existential verbs *ur-* & *ar-* appears in the discovery. It indicates the sudden confirmation that the speaker saw the action or state a moment ago.

Examples :

(1) *mukasa: tigami ju: <u>kak-I-da</u>.   nama: kak-a-nu.*
    old times letter well write-AC-PST now write-NEG
    'I/We used to often write letters in the old days but now we don't.
    (Speaking about the speaker himself or people he knows well.)

(2) A : *tigami nu kak-ar-i   aQ-soNga   ta: du <u>kak-I-dakaja</u>:*
        letter NOM write-PSS-INF be-AC-INF-but who FOC write-AC-INF-PST FP
        'Here is a letter written ; and I wonder who wrote it.'
    B : (a) *ba: <u>kak-I-da</u>-so:.   basjik-i   dur-u?*
            I write-AC-INF-PST-*so*: forget-ST-INF AX-CON
            'I wrote (it). Did you forget?'
        (b) *wa: <u>kak-I-da</u>-so: basjik-i dur-u?*
            you write-AC-INF-PST-*so*: forget-ST-INF AX-CON
            'You certainly wrote. Did you forget?' (The speaker looked at the listener writing.)
        (c) *atsuko: <u>kak-I-da</u>-so: basjik-i dur-u?*
            atsuko write-AC-INF-PST-*so*: forget-ST-INF AX-CON
            'Atsuko wrote it. Did you forget?' (The speaker took a look at Atsuko writing.)

(3) The speaker forgot whether he wrote a letter or not.
   A : *ba: tigami kak-ɪ-da kaja:*
   I letter write-AC-INF-PST FP
   'I am wondering whether I wrote a letter or not.'
   B : *wa: kak-ɪ-da so:*
   you write-AC-INF-PST-*so:*
   'You certainly wrote it.' (The speaker once looked at Mr. A writing a letter.)
(4) A sent B a letter in which he wrote ill of me. B told me about it, and then I said to A :
   wa: anzji aznzji tigami ba kak-ɪ-da?
   you such and such letter AP write-AC-INF-PST
   'Did you write such and such a letter to B?'
(5) Finding scribbling on the wall, I have got mad and said :
   kure: ta: du kak-ɪ-da ?
   this-TOP who FOC write-AC-INF-PST
   'Who wrote this?!' cf. *kure: ta: du kak-i:* ? (Mild and normal usage)
   this-TOP who FOC write-ST-INF
   'Who wrote this?'
(6) *kunu oNta: kuzo: hara-N-da. hwa: nasɪ-ta.*
   this pig last-year conceive-AC-INF-PST child deliver-AC-PST
   'This pig conceived last year. It gave birth to piglets.'
(7) The doctor asked to his patient who was having a stomachache.
   Doctor : *wa: no: du hwo:-da*? Patient: *ba: izu du hwo:-da.*
   you what FOC eat-AC-PST I fish FOC eat-AC-PST
   'What did you eat?' 'I ate fish.'
(8) *Nma-ha-ri-ri taka:ni hwo:-da.*
   delicious-and a-great-deal eat-AC-PST
   'It was delicious and I ate a great deal.'

(9) *ki:pai   ja   nama   ne:nu-soNga   mukasa*: *aǫ-ta*.
   Wooden-plow TOP now be-not-but old times-TOP be-AC-PST
   'There aren't any wooden plows these days but there were in the old days.'

(9') At the moment when you find what you are looking for.

                                aǫ-ta!
                                be-AC-PST
                                'Here it is.'

(10) A : *wa: kIno: ja: Nga (du) uǫ-ta*?   B : *N: uǫ-ta*.
        you yesterday house in (FOC) be-AC-PST   yes be-AC-PST
        'Were you at home yesterday?'   'Yes, I was.'

(10') When I visited B, his house was so quiet that I thought nobody was home, but in fact B was there.

   A : *ura-nu   ju: di   umu-i ja: jaNga   du   uǫ-ta*?
      be-NEG AP AP think-ST-INF AP house-in FOC be-AC-PST
      'I thought you were not at home but you're here?!'

   B : *N: jaNga du ur-u*.
      yes house-in FOC be-AC-CON
      'Yes, I am home.'

(11) The following examples are not predicative but rather elements of dependent clauses. However, it is interesting in comparison with stative-past which is explained in the next chapter.

  (a) *wa*: *kak-I-da-ǃa:*   *ba: kak-a-na:ra i*?   ×*kak-i-da-ǃa:*
     cf. kak-u-ǃa: ×*kak-i-ǃa:*
     you write-AC-PST-CND I write-NEG-IREA Q
     'You wrote so I will not write. O. k.?'

  (b) *kak-I-da   hazI*.   *kak-ir-u   hazI*   × *kak-i-da   hazI*
     write-AC-PST certainty write-EP-ATT certainty write-ST-PST certainty
     'I think he did indeed write.' 'I think (he/they) is certainly writing.'

(c) *banu ge: aNze-:-r-u-Ka:* <u>*kak-I-daru*</u>⁽⁴⁰⁾ *munu*   × *kak-i-dar-u munu*
    I to say-CSC-CON-CND write-AC-PST-ATT Fm-N
    'If you asked me to, I would have written.' (As a matter of fact, I did not write.)

7. 9. 2. Stative past

It is usually translated in CJ as *te-ita* (progressive or resultative). It indicates, however, that the speaker recognized the action arising by means of his direct experience. The action itself is not now in sight of the speaker, so accordingly, if it is the speaker's action, it must belong to the past. Other people's actions, however, do not necessarily belong to the past. If the time when the speaker experienced it is a little while ago, both the speaker and the listener will think that the action is still in progress. The existential verbs do not have this form. (×*ar-i-da*, ×*ur-i-da*)

(1) A : *ba: zI:* <u>*kak-i-da*</u> *kaja:.* (The speaker forgot whether he wrote it or not.)
    I letter write-ST-INF-PST FP
    'I am wondering whether I wrote letters or not.'

   B : *wa:* <u>*kak-i-daso:.*</u> *ba:* <u>*mi:-da*</u>. (The speaker took a look at him writing.)
    you write-ST-PST-*so*: I see-ST-INF-PST
    'You were writing them. I saw it.'

(2) Yoko and Atsuko were writing in the next room. The door was closed. Yoko came out of the room, and their mother asked her :
    Mother (a) : *atsuko:tigami* <u>*kak-i-da*</u>? (Mother thinks that she <u>is still writing</u>)
        atsuko letter write-ST-INF-PST
        'Is Atsuko writing a letter?'

---

(40) *kakIdaru* is a special attributive form.

The Grammar of Ishigaki Miyara Dialect in Luchuan

    (b)   *atsuko: tigami   kak-i-Ta*? (Mother thinks that she <u>finished writing</u>.)
            atsuko   letter write-ST-INF-PF
            'Did Atsuko finish writing a letter?'

Yoko (a) :   *kak-i-da*.
            write-ST-INF-PST
            '(She) was writing.' (= She is writing. 'When I left, she was writing. I saw it.')
    (a')   *nama du   kak-i-ru*.
          now FOC write-EP-CON
          '(She) is writing now.'
    (b)   *kak-i-Ta*.
          write-ST-INF-PF
          '(She) finished writing.'

These examples show that "*kakida*" and "*nama du kakiru*" indicate almost the same fact.

(3) Then Atsuko came out of the room.
    Mother :   (*wa:*) *kak-i-da*?   Atsuko :   *kak-i-da*.
                (you) write-ST-INF-PST   write-ST-INF-PST
                'Were you writing?'   '(I) was writing'

(4) It begins to rain lightly outside. I enter in the house and say :
    A :   *ame:ma   Ndu   hwui-da*.
          drizzle NOM-FOC rain-ST-PST
          'It was drizzling.' (=It is raining.)
          Someone in the house, upon hearing this, would then hurry outside and bring the laundry in.
    A' : *ame:ma   Ndu (/ba du)   hwui-ru*.
          drizzle NOM-FOC (/AP FOC) rain-EP-CON
          'It is drizzling.'
          A and A' indicate the same fact. The former is that it was raining

and the speaker experienced it. The latter is that the speaker recognizes the state of raining.

(5) Their dog is kept on the leash at the door. Mother told her child to feed the dog. After a little while, her friend came in through the door.

    Mother :   *unu hwa: ja iN ge: munu <u>hwa:-h-i(:)-da</u>* ?
                 that child TOP dog to food   eat-CAS-ST-INF-PST
                 'Is that child feeding the dog?' (= making the dog eat?)
    Friend :   <u>*hwa-:h-i(:)-da*</u>
                 eat-CAS-ST-INF-PST
                 '(He) was. (I saw him giving foods to the dog.)'

This does not mean continuation of the action. The mother thinks that her child is now feeding the dog, and in her question, she wonders whether or not her friend saw that happening. Her friend answers that she saw the state in which the child was giving food to the dog. Both of them think that the child is still doing this.

In the case that she wants to confirm whether or not the child finished it, she would ask :

    unu hwa: ja iN ge: munu <u>hwa:sɪ-ta</u>?
    that child TOP dog to food   eat-CAS-AC-INF-PST
    'Did that child finished giving foods to the dog?'

(6) When Mother came back home, her child told her :
  (a) *ujaNco: <u>kama</u> Nga du   <u>sjin-i-da</u>*.
      rat-TOP over-there in   FOC die-ST-INF-PST
      'A rat is dead over there'

He saw the rat dead over there. He thought that the rat still lay dead on the ground.

  (b) In the case that the child tells :
      ujaNco: <u>umaNga</u> du <u>sjin-i-da</u>.
      rat-TOP here in   FOC die-ST-INF-PST
      'A rat died here.'   (The dead rat is put it away.)

Cf. In the case that the dead rat still is there.

(b') *ujaNco: uma Nga du sjin-iru.*
    rat-TOP here in FOC die-EP-CON
    'A rat is dead here.' (Anybody can look at the rat dead.)

The conjugational form of this past has an attributive usage. It might be a form suffixed with the auxiliary **du + *aru > dar-u*

    Ex. *ba: kak-i-da-ru   tigami muc-i   haQ-ta?*
        I write-ST-PST-ATT letter bring-ST-INF go-AC-INF-PST
        'Did you bring the letter I wrote?'

7. 9. 3. Past followed with -ra:/-ro:

This category is rarely used by younger speakers, and in fact even older speakers are using it less frequently than they once did. Both the active and the stative infinitives accompany *dara:* and *daro:*. The former appears in question and the latter in declarative sentence. The speaker confirms afresh the act in the past which has brought some phenomenon that can now be perceived.

(1) A child has a stomach ache.

    Mother : *wa: no: du hwo:-da-ra:*   × *hwo:-da-ro:*
                you what FOC eat-AC-INF-PST-*ra:*
                'What did you eat?'

    Child : *naba du hwo:-da-ro:* .   × *hwo:-da-ra:*
             toadstool FOC eat-AC-INF-PST-*ro:*
             'I ate a toadstool.'

(2) His mother told him to go to buy salt. After a while she found him still at home.

    Mother : *no: di hara-na:-da-ra:* (/ *no:di hara-na:-da*).
                why go-NEG-PST-*ra:* (/ why go-NEG-PST)
              'Why didn't you go?' (/ 'Why didn't you go?')

Child : *ami* Ndu *hwo:-da-ro:* .
rain NOM-FOC fall-AC-PST-*ro*:
'Because it was raining.'

(3) The person came back from the field all wet with rain, but around his house it was not raining.

A : *wa: no:di* *zo:r-ir-u:* ?   B : *ami* Ndu *hwo:-da-ro:* .
you why be-wet-EP-CON   rain nom-FOC fall-AC-PST-*ro*:
'Why did you get wet?'   'Because it was raining.'

(4) Mother came back home. She could not find cake that had been in the cupboard.

Mother : *unu kwa:sa*: *no: du h-i:*?
That cake-TOP what FOC do-ST-INF
'That cake, what happened to it ?'

Child : *ja:ha-da-ra:*   *ba*: *hwo:-da-ro:* .
hungry-PST-CAU   I   eat-AC-PST-*ro:*
'I was hungry so I ate it.'

(5) In the same situation as above :

Mother : *wa: du unu kwa:sa: kam-i*?
you FOC that cake-TOP eat-ST-INF
'Is it you that ate the cake?'

Child : *ba:kam-ana:-da atsuko* Ndu *kaN-da-ro:* .
I eat-NEG-PST atsuko NOM-FOC eat-ACT-PST-*ro*:
'It wasn't me ; Atsuko ate the cake.'

(6) When the adjective is followed with auxiliary *ar-*, it can be suffixed to it.

A : *no:di ikkoNbaN kIN ba kisj-i-rja* .
Why that-much clothes AP wear-EP-REA
'Why do you have so many clothes on?'

B : *pi:sja du aQ-ta-ro:* .
cold FOC be-PST-*ro*:
'(I) felt it was cold.'

(7) A :   wa: no:di   ka-i   *k-u:-na:da-ra:* .
          you why   buy-ST-INF come-NEG-PST-*ra*:
          'Why didn't you buy (something and come back)?'
    B :   takaha du *aQ-ta-ro:* .
          high FOC be-PST-*ro:*
          'It was too expensive (the price was too high).'

7. 10. Stative-infinitive followed with auxiliaries

Since the stative-infinitive form does not include the speaker's recognition it is easy to make collocations with other forms.

7. 10. 1. *duru*

This form is historically considered as *du uru* > *duru*. Since it has the same inflections as *ur-*, the dialect speakers feel intuitively that *du uru* > *duru*. Unlike *te-iru* in CJ, the existential verbs *ar-* and *ur-* can accompany it. It can be certainly translated as progressive *te-iru*. However, it does not indicate the continuation of action. It indicates that the action or state the speaker can see can probably be confirmed by both the speaker and anyone else in the same place. The following are examples :

(1) At a store   Customer :   *mai   ar-u- N*?
                              rice be-AC-CON-*N*
                              'Is there rice?' ('Do you have rice?')
                 Storekeeper : *ar-i   d-ur-u* .   (CJ *aru*.)
                               be-ST-INF FOC-AX-CON
                               'There certainly is.' (He knows that the rice is at his store.)

(2) Someone thought that there was no salt on the table and was going to go get some. Another person found the salt and say :
    A :   *ar-i   d-ur-u.*   (CJ *aru yo*.)
                be-ST-INF FOC-AX-CON
                'There it is.'

149

(3) I visited my friend. His house was so quiet that I thought nobody was there, but in fact he was home.

 ja: *Nga ur-a-nu ju: di umu-i ja ur-i d-ur-u*. (CJ *iru no?/ ita no?*)
 house in be-NEG AP AP think-ST-INF AP be-ST-INF AX-CON
 'I thought that you weren't home, but here you are.'
 (This sentence might be better to be uttered towards the third person.)

(4) *ba*: *mainitsI nikki kak-i d-ur-u*. (CJ *kaite-iru*)
 I every-day diary write-ST-INF FOC-AX
 'I write a diary every day.'

(5) *mainitsI sjiNbuN jum-i d-ur-u*. (CJ yonde-iru)
 every-day newspaper read-ST-INF FOC-AX
 'I read a newspaper every day.'

(5') I want to know what someone is doing. (He may or may not be in the speaker's sight.)

 A: *wa: no: du hi-ir-u*.? ×*hi: duru* (CJ *shi-teiru*)
   you what FOC do-EP-CON
   'What are you doing?'

 B: *sjiNbuN du jum-ir-u*. ×*jum-i duru* (CJ *yonde-iru*)
   Newspaper FOC read-EP-CON
   '(I) am reading a newspaper.'

(6) *su: ja pisj-i d-ur-u*.
 tide TOP go-out-ST-INF *d-ur-u*
 'The tide is low.' (It is the low tide now.)

(6') *pisj-i du har-u*.
 go-out-ST-INF FOC go-AC-CON
 'The tide is going out'

(7) *su: ja Nc-i d-ur-u*.
 tide TOP rise-ST-INF *d-ur-u*
 'The tide is high.' (It is the high tide now.)

(7') *Nc-i   du k-u:*
rise-ST-INF FOC come-AC-CON
'The tide is coming in.'

(8) A small child stayed up late at night
　Father :　　*naN* (/ *nama*) *ma: di   uk-i d-ur-u*?
　　　　　　now (/ now) up to rise-ST-INF *d-ur-u*
　　　　　　'Are you still up now?'

(9) We didn't have the key to the house and thought that we couldn't get in, but when we walked   around the house, we found the door unlocked.
　　　jadu   ak-i d-ur-u.   *Nga ak-i   d-ur-u.* (CJ. *aite-iru*)
　　　sliding door open-ST-INF *d-ur-u*　here open- ST-INF *d-ur-u*
　　　　'The sliding door is open.   Here it is unlocked.'

(10) Our bird is flying out of the cage. Looking at it :
　　ping-i   d-ur-u! (CJ. ? *nigete-iru*. In this case, *nigete iku* is acceptable.)
　　escape-ST-INF *d-ur-u*
　　'(Our bird) is flying away.'

(11) I was going out, and then my friend came in with her wet umbrella.
　　ami   hwu-i d-ur-u ?   (CJ. *ame hutte-iru no*?)
　　rain fall-ST-INF *d-ur-u*
　　'Is it raining?'
　In this case, I would like to continue :
　　hwo:-N-tiN   misja:-ru   munu
　　rain-NEG-though better-ATT Fm-N
　　'I wish it were not raining'

(11') I had been home all day long. My friend came in with a wet umbrella.
　　ami   Ndu   hwu-iru?   (CJ *ame hutte-iru (no)* ?)
　　rain NOM-FOC fall-EP-CON
　　'Is it raining?'

151

(12) I asked to my sister who looks pregnant.
    wa: <u>haram-i   d-ur-u</u>?   (CJ <u>ninshin shite-iru</u> no?)
    you conceive-ST-INF d-ur-u
    'Are you pregnant? (I suppose so.)'

(12') Mother, who wants to have a grandchild, often asks her daughter (who does not have any sign of pregnancy):
        wa: <u>haram-i-N</u>?   (CJ <u>ninshin shite-iru</u> (no)?)
        you conceive-ST-INF-N
        'Are you pregnant?'

(13) I heard Atsuko crying in the next room. Its door was closed. I asked loudly to her:
        atsuko: <u>nak-i d-ur-u</u>?   (CJ <u>naite-iru</u> no?)
        atsuko cry-ST-INF duru
        'Atsuko, are you crying?'
    In the case that she is in my sight:
        ×atsuko: wa: <u>nak-i d-ur-u</u>? ×wa: <u>nak-i ur-u-N</u>?
        'Atsuko, are you crying?'   'Are you crying?'

(14) I heard someone reading a newspaper.
        wa: sjiNbuN <u>jum-i d-ur-u</u>? (CJ yonde-<u>iru</u> no?)
        you newspaper read-ST-INF duru
        'Are you reading a newspaper?'

(15) Atsuko's father told her to write a letter. Now Atsuko must be writing in the next room. Her father wants to confirm it, but since he can not see her writing in his vantage point, he asked his wife (who has a clear view of Atsuko):
    Father: ure: <u>kak-i-N</u>? (CJ <u>kaite-iru</u>?)
                                    she-TOP write-ST-INF-N
                                    'Is she writing?'
    Mother (taking a look at her):   <u>kak-i-N</u>. / <u>kak-i duru</u>. (CJ. <u>kaite-iru</u>)
                                    '(She) is writing. / (She) is writing.'

The above examples show that the auxiliary d-ur-u puts emphasis on the confirmation of action which the speaker takes a look at. That is why it gives a nuance of 'unnecessary' action ; the speaker feels that the listener doesn't need to do the action. Consider the following example :
(16) The speaker found some money on the ground which must have dropped from someone's pocket :

    kama Nga zjiN nudu ut-iru.
    over there in money NOM-FOC drop-EP-CON
    'There's some money on the ground over there.'
    ? *kama Nga zjiN nu ut-i d-ur-u.*
    over there in money NOM fall-ST-INF duru

In this situation, the last sentence is hardly acceptable because it is unreasonable to emphasize the action "drop".

Examples of inflectional forms of this auxiliary :
(1) I visited my friend. His house was so quiet that I thought there was nobody at home, I looked in thorough the window. He was there!
    ura-nu ju: di umu-i ja: ur-i d-ur-ja-N. (Discovery)
    be-NEG AP AP think-ST-INF AP be-ST-INF d-ur-REA-N
    'I thought you were not here, but here you are!
(1') In the same situation, after I found him I report it to my companion :
    ur-a-nu ju: di umu-i ja: ur-i du uQ-ta.
    be-NEG AP AP think-ST-INF AP be-ST-INF FOC be-AC-PST
    'I thought he was not there, but he was.'
(2) Talking about the village in the old days.
    na: na: ja: Nga Nma nu ja: N usI nu ja: N ar-i du uQ-ta.
    each house in horse GEN house also cattle GEN house also be-ST-INF FOC be-AC-PST
    'There used to be a cowshed and a stable in each house.'

(3) I was surprised to see a small child writing kanji (Dhinese characters).
   ure: zi: kak-i d-ur-ja-N.
   he-TOP letter write-ST-INF d-ur-REA-N
   'He is writing *kanji*!'
(4) kak-i   d-ur-i-ki   kak-a-ba   muc-i   har-ja.
   Write-ST-INF dur-RAT write-IREA-CND bring-ST-INF go-IMP
   'Since I am writing the letter now, you take it (somewhere) when I finish.'

7. 10. 2. *du(:)*

As with the auxiliary duru, the form *du(:)* does not occur with the similar-sounding focus particle du. Although there is not an independent usage of the verbal stem in the contemporary dialect, this *du* can be considered *du(:)* < *du-*u*-(stem of *ur*-).

The speaker wants to confirm the action which, having left some evidence behind, must have arisen at some point. The action is usually unexpected for the speaker, who is not now experiencing it directly; contrast this with the -*da* form in which the speaker sees the action directly.

If the speaker begins with a sentence including this *du* as the predicate and if it is a declarative sentence (not question), it sounds like a monologue.

Examples:

(1) A child came out with tear-stained eyes.
   A: *nak-i du*?   (CJ *nai-ta* (*no*)?)
         cry-ST-INF *du*
         'Did you cry?'
   Child: *naki du*.   (CJ *nai-ta*.)
         cry-ST-INF *du*
         '(I) did.'
(2) A: *ami hwui du:* ?   B: *hwui du*.
        rain fall-ST-INF *du*   fall-ST-INF *du*
        'Did it rain?'   'It rained.'

154

This conversation is opened in the following cases:
(a) A farmer came back from the field, wet with rain. But around his house, it was not raining. Then his wife asks him:
(b) I came back home and brought the laundry in, but it was still wet. I asked the neighbors:
(c) I was at home and my friend came in with a wet umbrella. I did not know it was raining:

(3) A child says that he has a stomachache. He seems to have eaten something bad.
Mother: *wa*:   *uri*   *hwai du:*?
                   you   that   eat-ST-INF *du*:
                   'Did you eat it? (I was thinking to throw it away.)'

(3') Mother can not find the cake which she had put on a dish. She asks her child.
Mother: *wa*:   *du*   *hwai*?
                   you   FOC   eat-ST-INF
                   'Is it you who ate it?'

(4) Someone looks very busy. Then I ask him:
         unu   *sjigutu*   *uki du*?
         that   work   receive-ST-INF *du*
         'Did you take that job on yourself?'

(5) I visited my friend after a while. I did not see his dog, so I asked:
A: *unu iN ja ur-anu-soNga sjin-i du:*?
      that dog TOP be-NEG-but die-ST-INF *du*:
      ' The dog is not here. I wonder if it died.'
B: *sIN du sI-ta*.   /   *sjin-i-Ta*.
      die-AC-INF FOC do-AC-INF-PST   die-ST-INF-PF
      'It died.'   'It died at last.'

(6) I didn't see any salt on the table, and as my friend was about to go buy some, I suddenly found it. My friend asks :
>ne:nu di umui-da-songa <u>ar-i du</u>?
>exist-NEG AP think-ST-INF-PST-but be-ST-INF *du*
>'(We) thought there was not table salt but then you found it?'

(7) A : waQca Nga kIno: ju:zji Ndu aQ-ta ? (The room was messy ;)
>>your house in yesterday meeting NOM be-AC-PST
>>'Was there a meeting in your house yesterday?'
>B : ju:zji nu <u>ar-i du</u>.
>>meeting NOM be-ST-INF *du*
>>'There certainly was a meeting.'

(8) I did not ask him to do my job but it has been done.
>A : unu sjigutu <u>h-i: du</u> ?
>>that job do-ST-INF *du*
>>'Did you do that job?' (You didn't have to do it.)
>B : sI-tu sI-ta.
>>do-AC-INF-FOC do-AC-INF-PST
>>'I certainly did it.'

(9) Someone came in but he was not glad to see him.
>ku-N-ti-N misja:-ru munu <u>k-i: du</u> ?
>come-NEG-even better-ATT Fm-N come-ST-INF *du*
>'Did you come? You should not have come.'

(10) A friend said she could not come to the meeting, but she came in time.
>A : wa: k-u-:nu di anzj-i-da-soNga <u>k-i: du?</u>
>>you come-NEG AP say-ST-INF-PST-but come-ST-INF *du*
>>'You've come, even though you said that you wouldn't?'
>B : <u>k-i: du</u> uQ-ta.
>>come-ST-INF FOC be-AC-INF-PST
>>'I have.'

(11) My daughter caught cold. I found her hair wet after taking a bath.

mizI am-i du?   amu-N-ti-N   misja:-ru munu.
water bathe-ST-INF *du*   bathe-NEG-even better-ATT Fm-N
'Did you take a bath?   You should not have taken a bath.'

(12) I visited my old friend after a long while. He could not recognize me.

ba: maNtaNga k-e:-N jo   wa: basjik-i du?
I before in come-CSC-N FP you forget-ST-INF *du*
'I once came here. Did you forget ?'

(13) Monologue

kju: ja ba: taNzjo:bi ju-N.   ba: basjik-i du.
today TOP my birthday COP-CON-N   I forget-ST-INF *du*
'Today is my birthday. I had forgotten.'

7. 10. 3. *ur*-

The stative does not have its conclusive form. Instead, the form accompanying this auxiliary can be used as the conclusive.

This form is translated into CJ *te-iru* and the difference between CJ and dialect is almost ignored. In Miyara dialect, auxiliary *ur*- does not mean 'be/exist' but it means that the speaker takes a good look at the action and confirms it. Accordingly, it mainly indicates the action of third person.

The verbs belonging to Group 2 are classified into two groups by the function in collocation of this auxiliary. The verbs corresponding to *shimo-2dan* do not accompany it, but if one were to use *ur*- anyway, it would indicate only existence. For instance, *ak*- (open) taking *ur*- has its form *aki uruN* which means that (someone) opened the door and is still there next to the opened door.
Examples :

(1) The breakfast was ready but the child did not come to the dining room. Mother went to his bedroom door, which was closed, and called out :

uk-i   ur-u-N ?   daNdi NboN hwa-i
rise-ST-INF ur-CON-N   in-a-hurry meal eat-IMP
'Are you up? Hurry up and eat breakfast!'

(2) After the child went to bed his father told his wife to check and see if he was sleeping or not. Mother went to see him in the bedroom and said to her husband :

<u>nimi ur-a-nu</u>.　　<u>uk-i d-ur-u</u>.

sleep-ST-INF *ur*-NEG rise-ST-INF *d-ur-u*

'(He) is not asleep ; he's still awake.'

(3) *ure: du: nu i*N *ge: du munu ba* <u>hwa:-h-i ur-u</u>. (*hwa:hiru* acceptable)

he-TOP his-own GENdog to FOC food AP eat-CAS-ST-INF *ur*-CON (eat-CAS-EP-CON)

'He is feeding his own dog.' (The speaker is looking at it.)

(4) His mother asked her friend, who came in after seeing him feed the dog.

Mother : *unu hwa: ja i*N*ge: munu* <u>hwa:-h-i ur-u-</u>N ?

that child TOP dog to food eat-CAS-ST-INF *ur*-CON-*N*

'Was he feeding his dog?' ×*hwa:-h-ir-u-*N? (<u>hwa:-h-i-</u>N? acceptable)

Friend : <u>hwa:-h-i　d-ur-u</u>　/　<u>hwa:-h-i　ur-u-</u>N. × *hwa:-h-ir-u-*N

eat-CAS-ST-INF *du-r*-CON / eat-CAS-ST-INF *ur*-CON-*N* eat-CAS-EP-CON-*N*

'(He) is feeding his dog.　(He) is feeding his dog.'

(4') The child said to his mother while feeding his dog.

ba: *i*N *ge: munu* <u>hwa:-h-ir-u-</u>N.

I　dog　to　food eat-CAS-EP-CON-*N*

'I am feeding my dog .'

(5) *unu hwa: ja mainits*I *i*N *ge: munu ba du* <u>hwa:-h-i u-ru</u>. / <u>hwa:-h-i:r-u</u>.

that child TOP every day dog to food AP FOC eat- CAS-ST-INF *ur*-CON / CAS-EP-CON

'That child feeds his dog every day.

The former mentions the state of the action after the speaker confirmed it. (We can compare it with Jap. *no da*.) The latter is the statement of the speaker's recognition.

(6) *niN niN sjigutu*   *uk-i u-ru-N*
    year year job undertake-ST-INF *ur*-CON-N
    '(I) undertake the job every year. (It does not mean the result.)

(7) *ak-i*   *ur-u-N*.   (This is an unusual sentence.)
    open-ST-INF *ur*-CON-N
    '(I) opened the door and (I) am still there.'

(7)'Looking at Atsuko opening the sliding doors :
    atsuko jadu ba ak-i-N.   / *jadu ba ak-i so:* .
    Atsuko sliding-doors AP open-ST-INF-*N* / sliding-doors AP open-ST-INF-*so*:
    'Atsuko is opening the sliding doors.' / 'Atsuko is opening the sliding doors.'

(8) *ping-i*   *ur-u-N*   =   *unu tura: piNg-i   kama Nga ur-u-N*.
    escape-ST-INF ur-CON-N   that bird-TOP-ST-INF-and over-there-in ur-CON-*N*
    'That bird flew away and it is over there. = That bird flew away and it is over there.'

This sentence is unusual but understandable.

(9) *ba: mainitsI nikki   kak-i   ur-u-N*
    I everyday diary   write-ST-INF *ur*-CON-*N*
    'I write (in my) diary every day.

(10) Atsuko's friend found Atsuko standing up in the meeting while other people were sitting.
     kaNga atsuko Ndu tac-i   ur-u. bir-u kata Ndu ne:nu kaja:.
     over there-in atsuko NOM-FOC stand-ST-INF *ur*-CON sit-AC-ATT place NOM-FOC not-FP
     'Atsuko is over there standing up. Maybe she can not find a chair to sit on.'
                              (Instead of *tac-i ur-u*, *tac-ir-u* is acceptable.)

(11) While her friend was saying that, Atsuko came over and said.
     ba: biru kata ne:na:-ki na:i tac-i ur-u-N. (*tac-ir-u-N* is acceptable.)
     I sit-AC-ATT place not-RAT all-the-time stand-ST-INF *ur*-CON-*N*
     'I keep standing up because there is no chair to sit on.'

(12) A child seems to be looking for something.
>A: wa:no: du h-i:r-u ?
>you what FOC do-EP-CON
>'What are you doing?'
>
>Child: ba zjiN ba ut-a-hi-te: du tum-ir-u.
>I money AP drop-CAS-ST-INF-and FOC seek-EP-CON
>'I am looking for the money I have lost.'
>
>A: Ms. A explained his situation to her friends looking at him.
>unu hwa: ja zjiN ba ut-a-hi-te: tum-i ur-u-N
>that child TOP money AP drop-CAS-ST-INF-after seek-ST-INF ur-CON-N
>'That child is looking for his lost money.'

(13) They began to look for his lost money all together.
>B: Nga ut-i uQ-so:.
>Here fall-ST-INF ur-AC-INF-so:
>'here it was on the ground.' (Ms. B hands it to him saying so.)

(14) When Ms. B found it on walking with him, she said:
>Nga du ut-i u-ru.
>there FOC drop-ST-INF ur-CON
>There, it was on the ground.'

(15) Atsuko's friend came early in the morning.
>Friend: atsuko: me: da uk-u-nu ?
>atsuko yet rise-NEG
>'Atsuko did not get up yet, did she?'
>
>Mother (She confirmed that Atsuko is awake already): uk-i ur-u-N.
>rise-ST-INF ur-CON-N
>'(She) is awake.'

(16) They found a rat lying on the ground. It might have eaten poison.
>A: sjin-i-N?
>die-ST-INF-N
>'Is it dead?'

B :   *sjin-i ur-a-nu*.   (He took a good look and confirmed it.)
       die-ST-INF *ur*-NEG
       '(It) is not dead.'

C :   *sjin-i-so:*.   /   *sjin-i   d-ur-u*.
       die-ST-INF-*so*:   die-ST-INF *dur*-CON
       '(It) is dead.'   '(It) is certainly dead.'

       (*sjin-i ur-u-N* is acceptable but not preferable in this case.)

(17) After a little while, they were there again and saw the rat.

A : *me:da sɪn-a-nu kaja*:
    yet die-NEG FP
    'I wonder whether it died or not.'

B : (confirming its death he was expecting)   *sjin-i   ur-u-N*.
                                                die-ST-INF *ur*-CON-*N*
                                                '(It) is certainly dead.'

(18) This form is often used when talking on the telephone. Since the speaker can not see the listener, they always need confirmation.

A (on telephone) :   *wa: nama: no: du   h-i: ur-u* ?   /   *hi:ru*?
                     you now what FOC do-ST-INF *ur*-CON do-EP-CON
                     'What are you doing now?'

B (on telephone) :   *ba nama: NboN du   bagah-i: ur-u*. / *bagah-iru*.
                     I now rice FOC cook-ST-INF *ur*-CON / cook-EP-CON
                     'I am cooking rice now.   I am cooking rice now.'

(19) A conversation on the telephone :

A :   *ba: taraN-da-ru   muno: kak-i ur-u-N*?
       I ask-AC-PST-ATT thing-TOP write-ST-INF *ur*-CON-*N*
       'Are you writing what I asked ?'

B :   *nama kak-i-N*.   /   *kak-i ur-u-N*.   /   *kak-i d-ur-u*.
       now write-ST-INF-*N* /write-ST-INF *ur*-CON-*N* / write-ST-INF *dur*-CON
       'I am writing now. / 'I am writing now.' / 'I am writing now.'

(19') A conversation on the road

A :   *ba:taraN-da-ru muno: <u>kak-i-N</u>?*
       I ask-AC-PST-ATT thing-TOP write-ST-INF-*N*
       'Are you writing what I asked?'

B :   <u>*kak-i-N*</u>.   × <u>*kak-i   ur-u*-N</u>   × <u>*kak-i d-ur-u*</u>
       write-ST-INF-*N*   write-ST-INF *ur*-CON-*N*   write-ST-INF *dur*-CON
       'I am writing.'

(20) Mother told her son Haruo to write something, and after a while she wanted to confirm whether he was writing or not. Since she couldn't see him from where she was, she asked to her husband (who could see their son from where he was sitting) :

Mother : *haruo <u>kak-i   ur-u-N</u>?   × <u>kak-i-N</u>?*
         haruo write-ST-INF *ur*-CON-*N*   write-ST-INF-*N*
         'Is Haruo writing?'

Husband (having taken a good look at him) :
         <u>*kak-i ur-u-N*</u>   /   <u>*kak-i d-ur-u*</u>   /   <u>*kak-i-so:*</u>
         write-ST-INF *ur*-CON-*N* / write-ST-INF *d-ur*-CON / write-ST-INF-*so*:
         '(He) is certainly writing.' / '(He) is certainly writing.' / 'He is writing.'

(20') His mother can ask her son in a loud voice as follows, when he is not in her sight :

Mother : *Haruo: <u>kaki   uruN</u> ?*
          haruo write-ST-INF *ur*-CON-*N*
          'Haruo, are you writing?'

Haruo :   <u>*kak-i ur-u-N*</u>   /   <u>*kak-i d-ur-u*</u>   /   <u>*kak-i-so:*</u>
          write-ST-INF *ur*-CON-*N* write-ST-INF *dur*-CON write-ST-INF-*so*:
          'I am certainly writing. 'I am writing.'   I am writing.'

(21) I see someone who walks for exercise every day. Looking at him, I explain to someone next to me:
     ure: mainitsI uma nu mitsI du <u>arag-i ur-u</u>. (/arag-u / arag-i:ru)
     he-TOP everyday here GEN route FOC walk-ST-INF *ur*-CON walk-AC-CON/-EP-CON
     'He walks this same route every day.'

(22) Atsuko's father told her to write some documents. She must be writing them now, but her father can not see her from where he is. He asked her mother, who can see Atsuko.

    Father :   *nama atsuko <u>kak-i-N</u>?*
                 now atsuko write-ST-INF-*N*
                 'Is Atsuko writing now?'
    Mother (taking a look at her) :   *<u>kaki ur-a-n</u>u.*
                                    write-ST-INF *ur*-NEG
                                    '(She) is not writing.'

(22') On the road :
    A : *<u>kak-i-N</u>?*
          write- ST-INF-*N*
          'Are you writing?'
    B : *me:da <u>kak-a-nu</u>* ×*<u>kaki uranu</u>* (This is acceptable only in looking at it.)
          yet write-NEG
          'I haven't done it yet. / I have not yet written.'

(23) Getting angry, father cried loudly
    Father :   *atsuko*: *<u>kak-i ur-a-nu</u>?*
                                 atsuko write-ST-INF *ur*-NEG
                               'You were not writing, were you?'
    Atsuko (in a flurry) :   *nama du <u>kak-ir-u</u>.*   × *<u>kak-i ur-u-N</u>*
                                   now FOC write-EP-CON
                                 'I'm doing it now!' ("I'm writing now!") '

(24) I told Atusko to do some jobs and I wondered whether or not she was doing them, so I asked someone to look at Atsuko and tell me about it. These are his answers after confirming what she was doing.

    (a) When she is doing the job :
      atsuko: sjigutu <u>h-i: dur-u</u> / <u>h-i:-N</u> / <u>h-i:-da</u> / <u>h-i: uQ-ta</u> / <u>h-i: du uQ-ta</u>. (<u>hi: uru-N</u> acceptable)

      The last one (*hi: du uQ-ta*) is most preferable.

(b) When she is not doing :

 atsuko: sjigutu <u>h-i: ur-a-nu</u> /<u>h-i: ur-ana:-da</u> / me:da <u>ha:-nu</u>.

In the case of reporting, the past forms are preferable. They indicate the speaker's confirmation of having taken a good look.

(25) In the case of (23) (Atsuko is out of her father's sight.)

 Father (in a loud voice) : *atsuko*: <u>*h-i: ur-a-nu*</u> ?

         atsuko do-ST-INF *ur*-NEG

         'Atsuko, you are not doing it, aren't you?'

 Atsuko (in a loud voice) : <u>*h-i: ur-u-N*</u>.

         do-ST-INF *ur*-CON-*N*

         '(I) am writing.'

(25') In the case that her father asked her the same question again :

 Atsuko (in a loud voice) : *katsɪma-ha-nu* <u>*h-i: d-ur-u*</u>.

         noisy-*nu* do-ST-INF d-*ur*-CON

         'Don't bother me. I am really doing it.'

 Cf. saying quietly   *nama* <u>*du h-i:r-u*</u>.

         now FOC do-EP-INF-CON

         'I am now writing.'

(26) On the road near the house, a neighbor asked.

 A : *zɪNga du har-i*?

    where-in FOC go-ST-INF

    'Where were you?'

 B : *sɪka Nga du* <u>*har-i-da*</u>. × <u>*har-i uQ-ta*</u>

    sɪka in FOC go-ST-INF-PST go-ST-INF *ur*-AC-PST

    'I was in the center of town'

The forms accompanied with such auxiliaries indicate that the speaker confirms that the action occurred by his own experience (mostly watching). It seems similar to the continuity or result of action ; however, they are not distinctive features.

 It is important to note that the verbs corresponding to those of *shimo-1 dan* take this *ur*- collocation with a different meaning and that this *ur*-collocation form does not precisely mean the result of action even in momentary verbs.

The following are examples of conjugational forms of this auxiliary.
(1) The husband came to the meeting by himself, so someone asked him how your wife was.

    Husband :   *ba*: *kI-ta-keN*   *ja*   *atsuko*: *mizI*   *du*   <u>*am-i*   *uQ-ta*.</u>

    I come-AC-PST-time TOP atsuko-TOP water FOC bathe-ST-INF *ur*-AC-PST

    'When I left our house, Atuko was taking a shower.'

In this case, two sentences will be acceptable.

    mizI du <u>*am-i uQ-ta*</u>.   /   *mizI (ba)* <u>*du am-i-da*</u>.

    water FOC bathe-ST-INF *ur*-AC-PST / water (AP)FOC bathe-ST-INF-PST

(2) Someone has an appointment.

    atsuko nu   k-u-N-keN   ja <u>uk-i ur-a-ba</u>   du   ja-ru

    atsuko NOM come-AC-CON-*N*-time TOP rise-ST-INF *ur*-IREA-COD FOC COP-CON

    'Since Atusko will come, I have to get up in time.'

(3) His friend came in time for the appointment, but he was still in bed.

    Mother :   <u>*uki urja:*</u>   *misja:-ru munu naNma:di* <u>*nim-i d-ur-u*</u>

    rise-ST-INF *ur*-REA better-ATT Fm-N   now-up to sleep-ST-INF *dur*-CON

    'You should have gotten up ; you have been sleeping all this time!'

(4) *gaNzju: ni* <u>*h-i:r-i ur-i*</u> *jo*:

    healthy AP do-EP-INF *ur*-IMP AP

    'I wish you a good health!'

7. 11. Consecutive

This category is well known as the characteristics of the Luchuan dialects. Its main feature, it is said, is the result or trace of the action. Some researchers have discussed this, along with evidentiality (i.e., the speaker's witnessing of events), which is something that must be considered when examining the whole structure of the Miyara dialect verbal system. The followings are to be noted in general.

(1) The conjugation of this category is parallel to that of the adjective, as stated before. Just like the adjective the stem is followed with the speaker's morpheme N. That is to say the form without N does not have independent predicative function.

(2) N can appear in this category, but with a certain restriction. The condition is that the speaker should have recognized the whole action, that is, both the action's result and its origin.

(3) The morpheme so:, with which the speaker describes something external, is opposed to N (with which the speaker expresses his own judgment about something), is suffixed also to the stem just like adjective. These two morphemes are mutually exclusive.

(4) In the predicate, the stem suffixed da form appears with its conjugational form. It has almost the same conjugation as the adjective; e. g. takaha-da -ru (high) kak-e:- da-ru (write).

(5) Three morphemes which are suffixed to the stem {N, so:, ru} are mutually exclusive. They are incompatible.

(6) Not a few contemporary researchers assert that this form originates in old Japanese {*kaki (write-adverbial) +*ari (be-conclusive)}; its meaning corresponds with CJ te-aru. However, this is not acceptable for the following reasons.

    (a)   In CJ, te-aru form can co-occur with nominative ga as follows:

        tegami ga   kai-te   aru.

        letter NOM write-te be-CON

        'Here is a letter which someone wrote (for later use).'

    In Miyara, it is impossible to accompany a nominative particle.

        × tigami nu kak-e:-N.   × tigami Ndu kak-e:-ru.

        letter NOM write-CSC-N   letter NOM-FOC write-CSC-CON

    (b)   In CJ, the intransitive verb does not have this form.

× *oki-te   aru*   × *nai-te   aru*
get-up-*te* be-CON   weep-*te* be-CON

In Miyara, it may have this form.

(c)　In CJ, the speaker takes a look at the result of the action. The example which is mentioned above can be uttered by the speaker who takes a look at only the result.

tegami ga   kai-te aru.
letter NOM write-suspensive be-CON
'Here is a letter someone wrote.'

The person who saw the letter can say an above sentence. However, in Miyara *e:-N* form, the speaker must take a good look at the action-writing. This is a big difference.

7. 11. 1. Action, result and recognition.

Let us examine following examples.

(1) I asked someone to write some documents and later I went to his house to get them.

A :　　*ba: taraN-da-ru   muno: kak-e:-N*?
　　　　I ask-AC-INF-PST-ATT thing-TOP kak-CSC-N
　　　　'Have you written the documents I asked you for?'

B :　　*kak-e:-N.*
　　　　kak-CSC-N
　　　　'I have written them.'

(1') When I went to his house to get the documents, he wasn't home. His daughter was there.

A :　　*ba: taraN-da-ru   muno: kak-e:-N   kaja:.*
　　　　I ask-AC-INF-PST-ATT thing-TOP kak-CSC-N　FP
　　　　'I wonder whether he wrote the documents and left them for me.'

C :　　× *kak-e:-N.*

Since the listener is not the person whom I asked I can not say "*kake:*

_N_?" I have to add the particle of doubt. The listener can not answer "*kake: N*" even if she knows that these documents are on the desk, unless she saw her father writing them and knew everything about them.

If his wife, who had a good look at him writing the documents (and knows about the affairs), answered me, she could say "*kake:N*" (if her husband had told her to hand me them when I came to their house to get them), but otherwise only the person who wrote them can answer by means of this form -*e:N*.

His daughter may answer

aQsoNga...
be but
'There is but...'

(2) Some people grow a special kind of spinach in their field. Their spinach is so good that all neighbors know about it. A person in next village who heard about the special spinach wants to have its seeds and came to the grower's house. At that time they were not at home and had asked me to stay at their house.

A stranger : *waQcaNga ho:reNso*: *ibe:-N*?
your-house-in spnach   plant-CSC-N
'Did you plant spinach and are you still growing it?'

Since he does not know who I am, he would say "*ibe:N*?" He thought that I was a member of the family. And in fact I know that spinach well, having seen it many times. However, I can not say "*ibe:N*". Only those who planted it and are growing it can answer that way. That is to say, those who know <u>whole action</u>—arising and process and result—can answer in this verbal form. This is why only the speaker can use this form without restriction ; the speaker must certainly know his own actions completely.

The consecutive form without *N* is free in comparison with the form with *N*.

7. 11. 2. The speaker's recognition

The "past" of this dialect, as stated before, indicates the past within the speaker's experience. It implies that the speaker looked at it, listened to it or touched it etc. In the consecutive, however, the speaker recognizes the whole action which arose and finished by means of looking at something belonging to the action. The speaker sometimes recognizes, by looking at its results or traces which belong to the action as a whole, that the action arose in the past.

Since it indicates that the action arose (and finished) even though the speaker is looking at the present state, something belonging to the action must be still left and recognizable to the speaker. Sometimes it causes the speaker to recall something he has forgotten. The speaker looks back on the past and recognizes a past action anew. In any case, this category makes it possible to mention a past action which the speaker can no longer look at directly.

We have to distinguish the action taken by the speaker from the action taken by the others because the memory is entirely different between the actions which the speaker did by himself and those which he objectively looked at or listen to.

As far as the speaker's action is concerned, the role of memory is greater than that in the case of the others' action. That is why the speaker can talk about his own experiences, making his own confirmation of an action or state in the past.

Concerning the others' action, however, the phenomena accompanied with the action and watched by the speaker, not the agent or agents of the action being discussed, are used to tell that the action arose. On that occasion, the speaker needs some memory or knowledge to judge or recognize the action having arisen on the bases of the accompanied phenomena.

The action indicated by the intransitive verb requires more memory or knowledge than that by the transitive because the former usually left its trace less than the latter.

This category does not indicate the speaker's direct recognition of the act itself but indicates the phenomenon where action arose. That is why, like the subjunctive in English, it can indicate the action which arose in imagination, not in reality,

Looking only at the phenomena left behind by a completed action, the speaker can not use the *N*-form to ask a question to confirm whether or not the listener did something. It is impossible to ask "*wa: kake:N*? (You wrote it?)" in front of the listener's letter. It is parallel with the idea that the speaker can not ask the listener in his sight whether he is doing something or not by using the *N*-added stative-infinitive form; as explained earlier, it is impossible to ask "*kakiN*?" in looking at the listener writing.

In daily conversation, when answering a question of the form with *N*, the agent usually isn't explicitly stated. That is to say:

A: *wa: kake:N*?

B: (*ba:*) *kake:N.*

The conclusive form indicates that anybody can now recognize something left by the action and so anyone would agree that the action has once occurred.

The suffix -*ki* which indicates the reason, is suffixed to the consecutive -infinitive. It is not suffixed to the past morpheme -*da*. This phenomenon also indicates this -*da* does not simply indicate the tense.

Examples:

(1) When I forgot whether I wrote the letter or not:

    A: *ba: tigami kak-I-da Kaja:.*
           I   letter   write-AC-INF-PST FP
           'I wonder whether I wrote the letter or not.'

    B: *wa: kak-I-da-so:.*
           you write-AC-INF-PST *so:*
           'You wrote the letter. I saw it.'

C : *kak-e:-so:* .
write-CSC-*so*:
'You must have written it.' (I did not see you writing but I saw the letter you wrote.)
(The state which I'm recalling indicates that your action of writing must have arisen.)
We can paraphrase as follows : I can judge, based on my memory, that your action arose. We can judge that the action arose in past on the bases of the present state. The action as a whole is important in this case. The result (a written letter) is only a means to recognize the action that has arisen. In this example, the listener's memory is also a means of recognition of the action. The listener states the scene objectively by the particle *so:*.
(2) When I opened the door in the morning, the ground was wet.

ami hui-e:-N! cf. *ami Ndu hui-e:-r-u na:*.
rain fall-CSC-N   rain NOM-FOC fall-CSC-CON FP
'It has been raining!'   'It looks like it's been raining.'

(3) I thought that tree was too old to blossom, but one day I found some petals on the ground. I could not find them on the tree.

ure: hana sak-e:-N! Cf. *hana Ndu sak-e:-r-u na:*
this-TOP flower blossome-CSC-N
'It has blossomed!'

(4) At an exhibition of calligraphy, they are talking while looking at the works.

A : *ta: du kak-i kaja:*.
who FOC write-AC-INF   FP
'I wonder who wrote it.'

B : *na: nu ar-i-ki atsuko Ndu kak-e:-ru na:*.
name NOM be-ST-INF-RAT atsuko NOM-FOC write-CSC-CON FP
Since (her) name is there, it must be Atsuko who wrote it.

(5) A teacher asks his pupils, holding up a work which does not have a name:

    Teacher: *kure: ta: du   kak-e:-r-u:* ?
               this-TOP who FOC write-CSC-CON
               'Who wrote this?'
    Pupil: *ba: du   kak-e:-r-u* .
               I FOC write-CSC-CON
               'I wrote it.'

Everyone can see the work and knows that it was written by someone; the teacher just wants to know who that someone is.

(6) Looking at the letter on the table:

    tigami nu aQ-soNga   wa: du kak-e:-r-u?   × *wa: kak-e:-N*?
    letter NOM be-AC-INF-but you FOC write-CSC-CON   you write-CSC-N
    'There is a letter. Is it you that wrote it?'

The speaker thought the listener might have written it because of the writing style or of the place where it was.)

(7) I went to his house to get the documents which I asked him to write.

    A: *ba: taraN-da-ru   muno: wa: kak-e:-N* ?
         I ask-AC-INF-PST-ATT thing-TOP you write-CSC-N
         'Have you written the documents I asked you for?'
    B: *kake:-N*.
         write-CSC-N
         'I have written them.' ('The writing that I was asked to do is completed.')

(8) I told my child who was playing outside to open the house door before I came back. When I came back he was still outside. I asked him:

    Mother: *ja: ja ak-e:-N* ?   Child: *ak-e:-N*.
             house TOP open-CSC-N   open-CSC-N

'Is the house door open?(Have you opened the door?)' 'It is open' (I have opened it.)

(9-1) *hatagi ka:h-i: di aN-ta-soNga <u>ka:h-e:-Nkaja:</u>.*
　　field cultivate-IMP AP tell-AC-INF-PST-but cultivate-CSC-N FP
　　'I told him to cultivate the field. I wonder whether he has cultivated it or not.'
　　Here the state of the field is important. It is a kind of result of his action. Instead of <u>*ka:h-e:-N kaja:*</u>, *ka:sI-ta kaja:* would be all right. This active past indicates the person's action, and the main point is whether or not he did it. In the consecutive, it is important for the speaker how the field is. For the speaker it is not necessary to look at him cultivating the field but the field must have been cultivated.

(9-2) *sjigutu h-i: di aN-ta-soNga <u>h-e:-N kaja:</u>.*
　　job do-IMP AP tell-AC-INF-PST-but do-CSC-N FP
　　'I told him to do the job. I wonder whither he has done it or not.'

(10) In the case of intransitive verb

　(a) When we came back, we found a gift from Atsuko. She must have brought it to our house.
　　ku:-nu di aN-ta-soNga <u>ke:N</u>.
　　come-NEG AP say-AC-INF-but come-CSC-N
　　'She said that she would not come but (she) must have come.'

　(b) While we were looking for the lost child, we found something that belonged to him.
　　ure: <u>k-e:-N</u>.
　　he-TOP come-CSC-N
　　'He must have come here.'

　(c) *uQta Nga cibisjike: nu puts-ar-i-so:. hwa: Ndu <u>mar-e:-r-u</u> na:.*
　　They in diaper NOM dry-PSS-INF-*so:* baby NOM-FOC be-born-CSC-CON FP
　　'Diapers were drying in the sun at their house. A baby might have been born.'

　　The speaker knows that a young couple lives there, and that diapers are used only for a baby etc.

　(d) Since we heard that a thief stole some money in our neighborhood, we inspected around our house and I found strange footprints.

    nusuturI   Ndu   <u>arag-e:-r-u</u>.
    thief   NOM-FOC walk-CSC-CON
    'It is certain that the thief was walking around.'

(e) When the verandah marked with dirty slacks :

  A : *taniNgasa: nu   <u>bir-e:-N</u>.*
     someone NOM sit-CSC-N

'It is certain that someone was sitting there.' ('Someone must have been sitting there.')

  B : *ta: du <u>bir-i</u>?*
     who FOC sit-ST-INF
     'Who was sitting?'

  C : *ta: du <u>bir-i-da</u> ?*
     who FOC sit-ST-PST
     'Who sat there?' ('Do you know who was sitting there?')

  D : *ta: du   <u>bir-e:-ru</u> ?*
     who FOC sit-CSC-CON
     'Who was supposed to be sitting there?'

  E : (reminded that Atsuko was playing a little while ago and got muddy.)
     atsuko   Ndu   <u>bir-e:-ru</u> na:.
     Atsuko NOM-FOC sit-CSC-CON FP
     'Atsuko must have been sitting there.'

(11) Collocation form

    I met a mailman at the corner of my house.

  A :   *wa: tigami <u>muc-i</u>   <u>k-e(:)-N</u> ?*
         you letter bring-ST-INF come-CSC-N
         'Have you brought a letter for me?'

  Mailman : *<u>muc-i</u>   <u>k-e:-N</u>.*
          bring-ST-INF come-CSC-N
          '(I) have brought it.'

(11') A :　　　　wa: tigami　muc-i　　kɪ-ta ?
　　　　　　　　you　letter　bring-ST-INF AC-INF-PST
　　　　　　　　　　　'Did you bring a letter for me?'
　　Mailman :　muc-i　　kɪ-ta.
　　　　　　　　bring-ST-INF AC-INF-PST
　　　　　　　　　　　'(I) brought it.'

(12) Flash back

The speaker takes a good look at something to remind himself that he has experienced it before.

(a) I thought this was my first time coming here, but, looking at stores and houses on the street, I remembered that I had been here before.
　　　　　ba: maNta Nga　k-e:-N　jo:.
　　　　　I　before in　come-CSC-N FP
　　　　　'I have come here before.'

(b) Two old persons are talking about the old days.
　　　　　baga hutara: kama ge:　har-e:-N jo:.　basjik-i d-ur-u?
　　　　　we-SG two-TOP over-there to go-CSC-N FP　forget-ST-INF AX-CON
　　　　　'We have been there. Have you forgetten?'

(c) While looking at a person I say to my friend.
　　maina Nga mi:-da　　ubui　nu　ar-u-N.　a: ure: me:N　jo.
　　before in see-ST-INF-PST-ATT memory NOM be-CON-N INT he-TOP see-CSC-N FP
　　'I remember seeing him before. Ah! I have certainly seen him.'

(d) I was sorting out some old documents and I found a piece of paper.
　　　　　kure:　ba: zɪ:.　ba: du　kak-e:-ru.
　　　　　this-TOP my letter　I FOC write-CSC-CON
　　　　　'This is my writing. It is me who wrote this.'

(d') kure: atsuko nu zɪ:.　atusko Ndu　kake:ru na:.
　　　　　this-TOP atsuko GEN letter atsuko NOM-FOC write-CSC-CON FP
　　　　　'This is Atsuko's writing. It must be Atsuko who wrote this.'

(13) Hypothetical :

The action arose not in reality, but in the speaker's imagination based on the real situation.

(a) After Looking at a person who nearly fell down from the roof.

   ure:jagati   *ut-e:-N*.
   he-TOP in a few minutes fall-CSC-N
   'He nearly fell.' (The fact is that he did not fall.)

(b) I was taken seriously ill. My sister attended me all the while.

unu pItu nu mi: hu:-na:-ka: jagati sjin-e:-N na:
that person NOM look-ST-INF give-IREA-NEG-CND soon-after die-CSC-N FP
If she did not attend me, I might have died. (I nearly died.)

(c) *me:sItu kazji nu huk-e: -ru-Ka: muru ut-e:-N.*
a little wind NOM blow-CSC-CON-CND all fall-CSC-N
'If the wind blew a little longer, all (the fruits) might have fallen down.'

(14) The experience

The experience is usually denoted by the auxiliary *m-e:-N* (*m-ir*-'see' CSC -*N* 'have seen') added to the stative-infinitive. That means originally 'I have seen so and so.' There are some actions which can not be seen even if the agent is the speaker himself. The verb *haram*-'conceive' is one of those verbs. This might be why the consecutive can indicate the experience.

  ba: mi: musI haram-e:-N.
  I three times conceive-CSC-N
  'I have been pregnant three times.'

(15) The juvenile delinquent who had run away from home came back for her mother's funeral.

(a) People talked to each other in whispers looking at her tear-stained face at the funeral.

 A : *ure: nak-e:-N*. B : *nake:N*? × *wa: nake:N*./?
   she-TOP cry-CSC-N cry-CSC-N   you cry-CSC-N
  'She has certainly cried.' 'Has she certainly cried?' 'You have cried./?'

(Everyone does not think she will cry but it is certain that she has cried *finely*.)

(b) Later on another person, who did not attend the funeral, asked to them:

C : *unu hwa: ja nak-ana:-da* ?
That child TOP cry-NEG-PST
'That child did not cry, did she?'

A : *nake:N*.
cry-CSC-*N*
'(She) did cry.'
(I did not see her crying but I saw her tear-stained face. So I recognized that she had cried.)

This is a special case and it is a good example to explain this category. The form *nake*: *N* hardly appear in daily conversation. If we do not have such a special situation, *nake: N* is ridiculous because it can not indicate the experience. Even if he is not now crying any more, anyone must have the experience of crying.

As stated before, it is impossible to say "*wa: kake:N*? (Have you written it?)" while pointing at another person's writing. Similarly we can not say "*wa: nake:N*?(Have you cried?)" when the listener's face is stained with tears. The speaker can not say *ba: nake:N* with a tear-stained face.

This phenomenon reminds us the stative-constative : *kak-i-N*, *nak-i-N*. It is impossible to ask a question with them about the listener's action in the speaker's sight.

(16) Existential verb

The speaker has a good memory of having seen it, but at present he can see nothing of it.

(a) *nama ne:nu-soNga mukasa: ar-e:-N*.
now not-exist-but old time-TOP exist-CSC-*N*
'There is not such and such thing now but it was certainly there in the

old times.'

(b) kju: ja ura-nu-soNga kInu madi *ur-e:-N*.

today TOP not-exist-but yesterday till exist-CSC-N

'(He/She/They) is/are not here today but (He/She/They) was / were here till yesterday.'

(c) A :   kIno: atsuko ur-ana:-da?   B: *ur-e:-N*.

yesterday atsuko exist-NEG-PST   exist-CSC-N

'Atsuko was here yesterday, wasn't she?'   '(She) was here.' (Now she isn't.)

(d) kIQsa   baNca Nga du   *ar-e:-r-u*.

old times our-house in FOC exist-CSC-CON

'It was once in our house.' (Now it is not in our house ; only in others' houses.)

(17) The usages of realis

They are parallel with stative and epistemic realis.

(a) I repeated to my son : "Write it." He never said yes. One day I found unexpectedly a letter.

kak-e: r-ja-N!

write-CSC-REA-N

'(He) has written it.'

(b) I repeated to my husband to write the document which someone asked him for but he would not write. One day the person who asked him to write it came to get it. Surprisingly, he brought it from his room and handed it over! I said to myself.

kak-e:-dar-ja-N !

write-CSC-PST-REA-N

'(He) had written it.'

(c) I am looking for my glasses. I had looked for them on the table and could not find them there. Looking again, to my surprise, they were there! I found them when I looked for them for the second time.

<u>ar-eːr-ja-N</u> !
exist-CSC-REA-N
'It had been there.'

(d) Two people are looking at a letter.

A: taː du <u>kak-eːr-jaː</u> .　B: atusko Ndu <u>kak-eːr-u</u>.
who FOC write-CSC-REA　　　atsuko NOM-FOC write-CSC-CON
'Who wrote it?'　　　　　　'It is Atsuko that wrote it.'

(e) Suddenly someone heard a loud noise.

A: noː Ndu <u>ut-eːr-jaː</u> .　B: noː Ndu <u>ut-eːr-u</u>.
what NOM-FOC fall-CSC-REA　　what NOM-FOC fall-CSC-CON
'What did fall down?'　　　　'What fell down?'

7. 11. 3. da

The morpheme *da* can be added to the stem like the morpheme *N* and *soː*. This form has its conjugational form *daru*. We may treat it as an auxiliary. It is considered to originate in *du + *ar-u, that is *daru* < *du + *ar -u. The sentence which has this form does not include another *du* any more. This morpheme can be added also to the adjective stem as stated.

It is used as a confirmative statement. The speaker confirms the state where the action has arisen. The following examples show the difference between the confirmative and the constative.

Examples :

(1) Mr. A went to Mr. B's house to take the document which he had asked for.

A: baː taraN-d-ar-u munoː waː <u>kak-eː-N</u> ?
I ask-AC-AX -ATT thing-TOP you write-CSC-N
'Have you written the document I asked you for?'

B: <u>kak-eː-N</u>.
write-CSC-N
'(I) have written it.' (Said while handing it to Mr. A.)

179

B': *kak-e:-d-ar-u.*   *sjiwa sɪ-na.*
    Write-CSC-AX-CON   anxiety do-PR
    'It' been written. Don't worry.'
    (He went to his room to get the document and then handed it to Mr. A.)

(2) Mr. A brought a bag of sugar to his uncle's house.

    A (at the door) : *ba: saQta: muc-i   <u>k-e:-N</u>.*
                        I sugar bring-ST-INF come-CSC-N
                        'I have brought (a bag of) sugar.'

And he put his bag at the door and went into the house. His uncle was in the kitchen.

    A :   *ba: saQta: muc-i   <u>k-e:-da-ru</u>.*
          I sugar bring-ST-INF come-CSC-AX-CON
          I have brought (a bag of) sugar.

Both form and usage of this category are entirely similar with the adjective. In the case of the form with daru anyone can recognize that the state where the action has arisen.

(3) A :   *ba:nak-a-na:-da.*
              I cry-NEG-PST
              'I did not cry.'

    B :   *wa: <u>nak-e:-daru</u>   mi: Ndu   akam-iru.*
              you cry-CSC-AX-CON eye NOM-FOC get-red-EP-CON
              'You must have been crying. Your eyes have gotten red.'

(4) When I came back home I found letters there. After a few minutes, I met the mailman at the corner of my house.

    A :   *wa: baNca ge: tigami <u>muci   k-e:-da</u> ?*
              you our-house to letter bring-ST-INF come-CSC-PST
              'Did you bring letters to my house?'

    Mailman :   <u>*muci   ke:da.*</u>   /   <u>*muci   ke:N.*</u>
              bring-ST-INF come-CSC-PST   bring-ST-INF come-CSC-N
              'I bought them.   I have brought them.

(5) The difference depending on -*da*.

   A: *ure: me:da kak-a-nu* ?
                      this-TOP yet write-NEG
                      'You haven't written that yet?'

   B: *kak-e:-N*.
                      write-CSC*N*
                      'I have written it' (But he hasn't mailed it yet.)

   B':   *kak-e:-da*.   kak-e:-da ≅ kak-I-da
                      write-CSC-PST   AC-INF-PST
                      'I wrote it.' (… and have already posted it.)

(6) The veranda is stained with mud. I remembered that Toshio had been playing in the mud.

        tosjio bir-e:-da-ru.
        toshio sit-CSC-AX-CON
        'Toshio must have been sitting there.'

(7) I thought that I put the letter I had written on the desk, but I could not find it.

        ba: Nga tigami kak-e:-da-so:. muc-i haQ-ta ?
        I there letter write-CSC-PST-*so*: take-ST-INF go-AC-INF-PST
        'It is certain that I wrote a letter there (and left it there). Did you take it?'

(8) I found a letter on the table. I guessed that my sister had written it. After a while, I came into the room again with her, and noticed that the letter was not on the table.

        Nga tigami nu aQ-ta-soNga wa: kak-e:-da?
        there letter NOM be-AC-PST-but you write-CSC-PST
        'There was a letter here. Did you write it?'

(9) I arrived at Ishigaki from an island where we had a long spell of dry weather. I found that it must have rained because it was wet everywhere.

(a) *ami hwui-e:-N!*
rain fall-CSC-N
'It must have rained!'

(b) I said to my companion
ami ba du hwui-e:-ru na.
rain AP FOC fall-CSC-CON FP
'We know that that it must have been raining here.'

(c) I told to my family when I went back to our island.
kama Nga ami (N) du hwui-e:-da.
over-there in rain (NOM) FOC fall-CSC-PST

'It must have been raining over there.' (I did not see it raining, but I know that it rained.)

(10) Her baby looks about 14 months old.

A :   *tanka: ma:di Nga tac-e:-da?*
      birthday till in stand-CSC-PST
      'Had he stood up before his (first) birthday?'

Mother : *tac-i-da / tac-e:-da.*
         stand-ST-INF-PST stand-CSC-PST
         '(He) was standing.'   '(He) had stood up.'

(10') *tanka: ma:di Nga tac-e:-da soNga nama: me:da arag-a-nu.*
birthday till in stand-CSC-PST but now-TOP yet walk-NEG
'He had stood before his birthday but he does not walk yet.'

8. Copula

The copula is one of the characteristics of the Luchuan dialects. It does not have a corresponding form in Japanese

8. 1. The copula in Shuri dialect

CJ.	tense	declarative	question	negation	negative-question
da	present	'jaN	'jami/'jaga	'araN	'arani/'araNga
daQta	past	'jataN		'araNtaN	

According to Uemura (1992, p.809) it has a predicative function as follows :

    'jaN.   It is so.
    'jami, 'arani.   Is it so? Or not?
    'jasa.   Ofcourse, it is.

According to *Okinawago jiten*, it has other forms.

    nuu-ga 'ja-ra.   *bjooci 'ja-i-(gisaN).*
    'What is it?'   '(He) looks sick.'
    'aN 'ja-kutu.   *'ja-ru tuui 'ee.*
    As it is so   it is like say-IMP 'Say as it is.'
    'aN 'ja-ree.   *taruu 'ja-rawaN 'jaraci kwiree.*
    If it is so   Taroo even it is let go please 'please let Taroo go.'

The conjugational forms in traditional frame work

Irealis	Adverbial	Conclusive	Attributive	Realis	Question
ja-ra	ja-i-	ja-N	ja-ru	ja-ree	ja-mi

8. 2. The copula in Miyara dialect

In Miyara dialect, there is no sentence which corresponds to Shuri *"kure'e isji 'ja'N."* (This is a stone.)
The following is the comparison Shuri copula with Miyara copula.

---

(41) Following Hattori (1955, pp.328-329) and *Okinawago jiten* (pp.84-85)

Shuri	Miyara
'jaN	jaruN
kuree 'isi 'jaN.	kure: isji.
This is a stone	This is a stone.
kuree 'isi 'jami	kure: isji?
Is this a stone?	Is this a stone?
kuree 'isee 'araN	kure: isji aranu.
This is not a stone.	This is not a stone.
kuree nuu 'jaga.	kure: no:. / kure:no: jarja. / kure:no:rja.
What is this?	What is this? / What is this? / What is this?

The conjugation of copula in Miyara

		infinitive	conclusive	Realis	Irealis
Group 1	Active	j-aQ- (*j-arI)	j-u(:)/j-ar-u	---	j-ar-a-
	Stative	j-ar-i	---	j-ar-ja	---
	Consecutive	j-ar-e:r-i	j-ar-e:r-u	j-ar-e:r-ja	j-ar-e:r-a-

It has a special form *ju:* whose vowel *u* is to be noted. It is important for the history of verbal conjugation. The morpheme boundary must be *j-ar-u-N* because of *j-u-N*.

The following is the paradigm of *ar-*. We can compare these two verbs.

	infinitive	conclusive	Realis	Irealis
Active	arI(aQ)⁽⁴²⁾	ar-u	---	ar-a
Stative	ar-i	---	ar-ja	---
Epismetic	ar-ir-i	---	---	---
Consecutive	ar-e:r-i	ar-e:r-u	ar-e:r-ja	ar-e:r-a-

The other forms to be compared:

---

(42) ara: (*arI + ja) sIsoNga

	jar-	ar-
Conditional	j-a-r-a-ba	ar-a-ba
Negation	(a-r-a-nu)	(ne:nu)
Infinitive (-so: added)	ja-Q-so:	a-Q-so:
Conclusive (-N added)	j-u-N	(ur-u-N)
	j-ar-u-N	ar-u-N
Imperative	---	ar-i
Perfect	---	ari-Ta
Realis (-N added)	j-ar-ja-N	ar-ja-N
Past	ja-Qta	a-Qta

The negation form *ar-a-nu* means 'it is not'. It must be a negative form of *jar-* in meaning. The negation of ar- is ne: *nu* which is a special form.

Irealis form of *jar-* can not be independent. It is always suffixed with some morphemes ; e.g. *-nu, -ba*.

The stative-infinitive of *jar-* is not accompanied with the speaker's morpheme N. That is to say, *jariN* is impossible. It is not suffixed with the past *-da*. That is, there is no *jarida*.

It is important that there is an active-conclusive form accompanied with N (*ju-N*) for stating the speaker's judgment at the moment.

Examples :
(1) The speaker's recognition
  (a) Seeing a person coming to you, you talk about whether she is Atsuko or not,
    A :   *ure*: *atsuko:*.
           that-TOP Atsuko
           'That is Atsuko.'
    B : (*ure:*) *atsuko*: *ar-a-nu*.
           that-TOP atsuko be-NEG
           'No, she is not Atsuko.'

A : (*ure*:)   *atsuko*:   <u>*jar-u-N*</u>.
    that-TOP atsuko COP-AC-CON-*N*
    'Yes, she must be Atsuko.'
  Cf. (*ure*:)   *atsuko*:   *dara*:.
    that-TOP atsuko FP
    That is Atsuko.

(b) As she approaches, you find that she is indeed Atsuko.

  A : (*atsuko*:)   <u>*jar-u-N*</u>.
     (atsuko) COP-AC-CON-*N*
     Yes, she is Atsuko.
  A' : (*atsuko*:)   <u>*jar-ja-N*</u>.
     (atusko) COP-ST-REA-*N*
     'She is Atsuko (as I expected.)'
  B : *atsuko*:   <u>*jar-e:-rja-N*</u>.
    atusko COP-CSC-REA-*N*
    'She happened to be Atsuko (unexpectedly).'

(c) Looking for a tea-container, you open it accidentally without knowing that there was tea insede.

  ca: <u>*jar-e:-N*</u>.
  tea COP-CSC-*N*
  'This happened to be tea.' (I didn't think it was.)

(d-1) I forgot that today was my birthday. Now I found it and said to my sister.

  a: *kju*:   *ba*:   *taNzjo:bi*   <u>*jar-e:-r-ja-N*</u>.   *basjik-i*   *du*   *u-Q-ta*.
  INT today my birthday COP-CSC-REA-*N* forget-ST-INF FOC *ur*-PST.
  'Well, today happens to be my birthday. I had forgotten it.'

(d-2) When I took noticed it I said.

  kju: *ja*   *tanzjo:b*   <u>*ju-N*</u>.
  today TOP birthday COP-ACT-CON-*N*
  'Today is my birthday.'

(d-3) kju: ja ba: taNzjo:bi <u>jaQ-ta</u>. basjik-i du.
today TOP my birthday COP-AC-PST forget-ST-INF du
'I forgot today was my birthday ; I had forgotten.' (This might be a monologue.)

(e) Someone was walking noisily. I guessed it would be Atsuko, and then she showed up. I told my husband at my side.

    atsuko du <u>jar-e:-r-u</u>.
    atsuko FOC COP-CSC-CON
'It was Atsuko as I guessed.' (...from listening to her footsteps).

(2) The idiomatic expressions and various forms

(a)   zIma ge (/zINge)   <u>jar-ja:</u> ?   (Greeting on the road)
    where to (/ where to) COP-ST-REA
    'Where are you heading?'

(b)   A :   gaNzju:?   B :   gaNzju: do
           healthy   healthy FP
           'Are you fine?'   'Yes, I am fine.'

     A :   uri N   gaNzju: (<u>jar-u</u>) hazI do:
           he also   healthy COP-ATT certainty FP
           'He must be fine.'

(c) gaNzju: <u>jar-a-ba</u>   du no: nu kutu N   nar-u.
    healthy COP-IREA-CND FOC what GEN affair also become-AC-CON
'Health should make everything successful.' (I am healthy therefore I can do anything.)

(d) gaNzju: <u>jar-a-ba</u>   du   <u>jar-u</u>.
    healthy COP-IREA-CND FOC COP-CON
'(You / We) should be good in health.'

(e) kImugakari sI-soNga   gaNzju: <u>jaQ-so:</u> .
    anxiety   do-AC-INF-but healthy   COP-AC-INF-so:
'Though I'd been worrying about you, I found you are all right.'

(f) gusji   <u>jar-i-ki</u>   nuN-na

    liquor COP-ST-INF-RAT drink-AC-INF-PR
    'As this is sake (alcohol), don't drink it.'
 (g) *a*N-*tu*   *jar-i* (*i*)?
    say-so COP-ST-INF (Q)
    'Is that so?'
(3) Active-conclusive *ju*N and *jaru*N
 (a) Two people are looking at a package whose contents they don't know
   A :   *no*: *kaja*:
        what FP
        'I wonder what (is in the package)'.
   B (touching it) : *makarI* *j-u-*N.
        bowl COP-AC-CON-*N*
        'It must be a bowl.'
 (b) Opening it, they find a bowl.
   A : *jar-u-*N!   B : *ja*Q*-ta*!
     COP-AC-CON-*N*   COP-AC-PST
     It is (a bowl)!   So it is!
 (c) You don't know what is in a bottle. You open it expecting it is sake.
    ure:gusji *ar-a-nu* *sItadi* *j-u-*N.
    this-TOP sake be-NEG soy-sauce COP-AC-CON
    'This is not sake. It is soy sauce.'
 (d) When you think a person coming towards you is Atsuko :
    atsuko: *jar-u-*N *kis-ja-*N.
    atsuko COP-AC-CON-*N* seem-to-be-*N*
    'She looks like (to be) Atsuko.'
 (e) And you finally find that she is Atsuko,
    atsuko *j-u-*N.
    atsuko COP-AC-CON-*N*
    'She is sure to be Atsuko.'
 (f) When you meet a person you haven't seen for a long time :

A :   gaNzju: j-u-N   na:.
        healthy   COP-AC-CON-N   FP
        'You have been fine, haven't you?
B :   gaNzju: do:.
        healthy   FP
        '(Yes, I've been) fine.'
C :   jam-i   d-ur-u?
        be-sick-ST-INF d-ur-CON
        'Are you sick?'
D :   a:i   gaNzju: juN.
        No   healthy   COP-AC-CON-N
        'No. I have been fine. / I am fine.'
        cf.   gaNzju: do: 'I am in good health.'

(g) Entering a sunny room :

        nuku nuko: hi   zjo:to: j-u-N   na:.
        warm warm do-ST-INF   fine   COP-AC-CON-N   FP
        'This room is warm and fine.'
        cf. ure: zjo:to: (do:)   'This is fine.'

(h) When you ask a person to do a job, you praise his job :

        zjo:to: j-u-N.
        fine   COP-AC-CON-N
        'You've done a good job.' 'It's a good job.'

(i) When you happen to know a person makes a net skillfully :

        wa: zjo:zI   j-u-N   na.
        you   skillful   COP-AC-CON-N   FP
        'You are good at making a net.'

As shown above, *juN* indicates the speaker's judgment at the instant when he takes a look at the state of things. Therefore, it does not have any other form. In short, neither *juru* nor *juQta* exists. We will compare it to

Group 1 verbs as follows:

j-u-N	kak-u-N	'write'
*j-a	kak-a	(irealis)
*j-I- >*i /ji	kak-I	(active)
*j-i >*ji>*i	kak-i	(stative)
*j-(j) a>*j-a	kak-ja	(realis)

(4) The difference between two conclusive forms.

The active-conclusive *juN* can not occur independently even when answering questions. On the other hand, another active-conclusive form *jaruN* can be independent as a sentence.

(a) A: ko:ice: aNsIkI zjo:zI j-u-N.
ko:ici-TOP net-making skillful COP-AC-CON-N
'Koichi is good at making a net.'

B: jar-u-N. ure: zjo:zI. (B knows that he is good at it.)
COP-AC-CON-N he-TOP skillful
'Yes. He sure is good.'

(b) When B doesn't know he is good,

(b-1) B: aNzji? zjo:zI (jar-u-N)?
so-do-ST-INF skillful (COP-AC-CON-N)
'Right?' (Is it so?) Isn't he good?'

(b-2) B: zjo:zI j-u-N?
skillful COP-AC-CON-N
'Is he good?' ('Did you find he is good at it?')

(c) When you see someone doing a job differently from the traditional way, you might correct him, saying:

(c-1) uri du huNto: j-u-N.
this FOC true COP-AC-CON-N
'This is the right way.'

(c-2) Watching it, a person nearby who thinks that is correct says:
jar-u-N.

COP-AC-CON-*N*

'You are right.'

(d) When talking about lyrics of old songs which you don't know well, a person who is familiar with them comes and says,

    a*N*zji   *j-u-N*.
    so-say-ST-INF COP-AC-CON-*N*

    'You say like this.'

Then each person says according to his confidence in his memory in the following way.

    ja-r-u-N.   *ja-r-ja-N*.   *ja-r-e:-r-ja-N*.
    COP-AC-CON-*N*   ST-REA-*N*   CSC-REA-*N*

    That's right. I remember that's right. Now I've remember that's right.

When the speaker agrees with the listner, he says *jaruN*.

(5) *j-u-N* is only one special form, but there exists a form without *N*. The speakers of Miyara understand intuitively that these two forms come from the same word.

(a-1) Finding liquid in a bottle,

    gusji   *j-u:*   bagar-a-nu.
    sake COP-AC-CON know-NEG

    'I don't know whether it is sake (or not).'

(a-2) After drinking it,

    gusji *j-u-N*. / gusi du *jar-ja-N*.
    sake CON-AC-CON-*N*   sake FOC COP-ST-REA-*N*

    'This is sake.'   'This happened to be sake.'

(b) Talking about a sick person you haven't met for a long time,

(b-1) ga*N*zju: *j-u:*   bagar-a-nu.
       healthy COP-AC-CON know-NEG

       'I don't know whether he is doing well or not.'

(b-2)   Wondering if he might have died, you call his house ; and surprisingly he answers the phone himself. After hunging up, you might think:

gaNzju: du jar-e:-r-ja-N.
healthy FOC COP-CSC-REA-N
'Now I know he has been fine.'

(c) Nga   ar-u muno: no: j-u: di umui ja: uri   j-u-N. .
here be-ATT thing-TOP what COP-AC-CON AP think ST-INF-TOP that COP-AC-CON-N

'I wondered what that thing was, and it (turned out to be what I had been thinking of)."

(d) The honorific word which is considered as a particle could be included in this category.

mi:hai   ju: cf. mi:hai
Thank you very much.   Thanks. (to the speaker's inferior)

(e) The question particle i might have the same origin with this copula.

ba: kaka i ? (Offering that the speaker writes it for the hearer and asking his agreement.)

It is important to note that *jaruN* and *juN* exist but *jaN* and *juruN* do not exist. It must be connected with the historical formation of the verb system. Miyara has *jaruN* instead of *jaN* in other dialects and it has *aruN* instead of *aN* in other dialects. We have to compare various dialects to understand the history of Luchuan and Japanese.

9. Compound sentences

9. 1. The durative usage of infinitive
Stative-infinitive

(1) kIno: ju:zji   nu   ar-i   du kir-ar-a-na:-da.

192

yesterday meeting NOM exist-INF FOC come-POT-NEG-PST

'I had a meeting yesterday and so I could not come.'

(2) *juːzji nu   ar-i   du   poːri sjik-eː-ru.*

party NOM exist-ST-INF FOC mess-up-CSC-CON

'I had a party and that's why this room is messy.'

(3) *Nge   kiː   maːzoN terebi   mir-ja.*

here-to come-INF together television watch-IMP

'Come here and watch TV together.'

(4) *gaNzjuː   nar-i   hwuː   Ndu   ar-eː-ru na.*

healthy   become-INF good-luck NOM-FOC exist-CSC-CON FP

'You are lucky to have gotten over your illness.'

(5) *uri   kisj-i har-a naː.*

this wear-INF go-SUG FP

'Let's go out wearing these clothes .'

(6) *waː   haː-naː-ri   baː   sI-ta-soː.*

you do-NEG-INF I do-AC-INF-PST-*so*:

'You didn't do this, and so I did.'

Epistemic-infinitive

(1) *nama nu   juː ja   suidoː nu ar-ir-i   raku ba   hiːri   mizI N sIka iru.*

now GEN age TOP running-water GEN exist-INF comfort AP do-INF water use-POT-CON

'At present we have running water, so we can use water easily.'

(2) *kuma Nga   ur-ir-i   maːzoN NboN hwaː naː.*

here in   be-EP-INF together meal eat-IREA FP

'Let's stay here and eat a meal together.'

(3) *uri   tur-ir-i uma Nga ur-ja.*

that take-EP-INF here in   be-IMP

'Take this and stay here.'

(4) *ureː   zIː   kak-ir-i   zjama   sI-na.*

he-TOP character write-EP-INF disturbance do-PR
'Don't disturb him as he is writing characters.'

(5) *uta* *sjik-ir-i* *kak-i* *jo:.*
song hear-EP-INF write-IMP FP
'Listen to the song and write it.' (Write the song while listening to it.)

(6) *saki* *num-ir-i* *hanasI* *ha:*
sake drink-EP-INF speech do-SUG
'Let's talk over sake.'

(7) *tigami* *kak-ir-i* *du* *ki-rar-a-na:-da.*
letter write-EP-INF FOC come-POT-NEG-PST
'I could not come because I was writing a letter.'

(8) *NboN ba* *hwair-ir-i* *terebi* *mi:da.(/mir-u-N.)*
meal AP eat-EP-INF television watch-ST-INF-PST (EP-CON-*N*)
'I was watching TV while eating.'(I watch TV...)

(9) *hana* *nu* *sak-ir-ir-i* *kaihe:-dar-a:* *du* *bur-i* *hi:-da.*
flower NOM blossom-EP-INF beautiful-PST-CND FOC break-ST-INF give-ST-INF-PST
'The blossoms were in beautiful bloom and so I cut them to give him.

(10) *ma:* *nu* *mar-ir-i* *sanehe:-r-ir-i* *joi* *sI-ta.*
grandchild NOM be-born-EP-INF happy-DR celebration do-AC-INF-PST
'We had a grandchild and we were so happy that we had a party for the celebration.

(11) *narI* *nu* *ut-ir-i* *tuN-na:* *haQ-ta.*
nut NOM fall-EP-INF take-AC-INF to go-AC-INF-PST
The nuts fell down on the ground and so we went to collect them.

(12) *munu* *nu* *ut-e:-ri* *du* *tuN-na:* *har-u.*
something NOM fall-CSC-INF FOC take-AC-INF-to go-AC-CON
'I had dropped something and so I go to pick it up.'

(13) *munu* *nu* *ut-i* *uri* *(/ur-ir-i)* *du* *tuNna:* *haru.*
Something NOM fall-ST-INF *ur*-ST-INF (/*ur*-EP-INF) FOC take-AC-INF-to go-AC-

CON
'I'm going to pick up the thing which has fallen (and is still on the ground).'

(14) NboN ba <u>hwai-ri</u> du sjiNbuN jum-u.
rice AP eat-INF FOC newspaper read-AC-CON
'I read a newspaper while eating breakfast.'

(14') NboN <u>hwai-TaNna:</u> sjiNbuN jum-u-N.
meal eat-ST-INF-while newspaper read-AC-CON-N
I read a newspaper while eating breakfast.

Consecutive-infinitive + *ri*

The independent form of this infinitive does not appear. Instead, the form suffixed can occur. It rarely appears in the daily conversation, though, and is acceptable but not preferable.

(1) hwa: nu tigami <u>kak-e:-r-i-ri</u> ba: muc-i haQta.
child NOM letter write-CSC-INF-*ri* I bring-ST-INF go-AC-PST
'I took the letter which the child had written.'

(2) kuzo: hana nu <u>sak-e:r-i-r</u>i mi:-na: har-i-da.
last-year-TOP flower NOM open-CSC-INF-*ri* look to go-ST-INF-PST
'Last year I went to see the blossoms. They were in full bloom.'

(3) kuzo: hana nu <u>sake:-r-i-ri</u> kaihe:-da.
last-year-TOP flower NOM bloom-CSC INF-*ri* beautiful-CNF
'Last year the flowers were blooming and they were beautiful.'

-te ; It may be considered the infinitive form of perfect -Ta ; e.g. *kak-*(write), *kakiTa*, <u>*kakite*</u>

(1) <u>uk-i-te</u> uboN hwai-ja:.
rise-ST-INF-*te* meal eat-IMP
'Wake up and eat breakfast.'

(2) <u>ki:te</u> ur-a-nu di <u>umu-i-te</u> mudur-i haQ-ta-songa wa: ur-i du ?

come-ST-INF-*te* *ur*-NEG AP think-ST-INF-*te* return-ST-INF go-AC-PST-but you be-ST-INF *du*

'I came here and went back because it looked like you were out. Were you at home?

(3) *tigami* <u>*kak-i-te:*</u>   *du*   *k-u:*.
    letter write-ST-INF-*te* FOC come-AC-CON
    I will come after I finish writing a letter.

(4) *uboN   hwai-te: du   sjiNbuN   jum-u*.
    rice eat-ST-INF-*te* FOC newspaper read-AC-CON
    'I eat breakfast and then read a newspaper.'

(4)' *uboN*   <u>*hwaite:gara*</u>   *du*   *sjiNbuN jum-u*.
    rice eat-ST-INF-*te*-after FOC newspaper read- AC-CON
    'I read a newspaper after I eat breakfast.'

(5) *gaNzju*: <u>*ar-i-te*</u>   *hatarag-ar-ir-u*. (He was ill. Now he recovered.)
    healthy be-ST-INF-*te* work-POT-CON
    You can work, since you have gotten well.

   cf. *gaNzju*: <u>*ar-ir-i*</u>   *hatarag-i jo:*.
       healthy be-EP-INF work-IMP FP
       'Work in good health.'

9. 2. Suffixes forming compound sentences
(A) -*ki*

This suffix is attached to rational clauses and carries the meaning "because ~". It is suffixed to the infinitives of the stative, epistemic and consecutive.

(1) *ki*: *nu* <u>*ut-i-ki*</u>   *madag-ir-i*. (in a construction site)
    wood NOM fall-ST-INF-*ki* leave-IMP
    'Leave here, because the trees will be falling .

(2) *ba*: <u>*uk-i-ki*</u>   *sIkai*   *hir-ja:*. (A sick person says :)

196

I rise-ST-INF-*ki* support give-IMP
'Support me as I want to get up.'

(3) *ba*: *kak-i-ki*   *wa*:   *kak-ana:-r-ja*.
I write-ST-INF-*ki* you write-NEG-IMP
'Don't write it as I write it.'

(4) *tigami*   *kak-i-ki*   *hudi*   *tur-i*   *k-u:*.
Letter write–ST-INF-*ki* writing brush take-ST-INF come-IMP
'Bring me a brush because I'm going to write a letter.'

(5) *ba*: *hwai-ki*   *patsɪ*   *muc-i*   *ku:*.
I eat-ST-INF-ki chopsticks bring-ST-INF come-IMP
'Bring me chopsticks, because I'm going to eat.'

(6) A : *me:da*   *kak-a-nu*?
       yet   write-NEG
   Haven't you finished writing it?

   B : *ba*: *nama* *kak-ir-i-ki*   *me:ma*   *ma(c)-c-a*.
   I now write-EP-INF-*ki* a little while wait-IMP
   'Wait as I'm writing it.'

(7) *ba*: *uk-ir-i-ki*   *sɪka-i*   *ukah-i*   cf. (2)
   I rise-EP-INF-*ki* support-ST-INF set-up-IMP
   'Help me get up as I'm getting up.'

(8) *ba*: *uk-ir-i-ki*   *NboN* *tur-i*   *k-u:*.   cf. (2)
   I rise- EP-INF-*ki* meal take-ST-INF-ki come-IMP
   'Bring me something to eat as I have gotten up.'

(9) *hwa: nu*   *uk-ir-i-ki*   *NboN*   *hwa:-h-ja:*.
   child NOM wake-EP-INF-*ki* meal feed-IMP
   'The child is awake and you must feed him.'

(9') *hwa*: *nu*   *uk-ir-i-ki* *NboN*   *hwa:hi-Ta*.
   child NOM wake-EP-INF-*ki* meal feed-ST-INF-PF
   I fed the child already because he was awake.

(10) *kama* Nga *zjiN* *nu*   *ut-ir-i-ki*   *tur-i*   *k-i:*   *nusɪ* *ge: h-ir-i*.

197

overthere in money NOM fall-EP-INF-*ki* take-ST-INF come-ST-INF owner to give-IMP

'There's some money (that someone dropped) over there ; pick it up and hand it to the owner.'

(11) *ba*: *tigami* <u>*kak-ir-i-ki*</u> *zjama sI: na.*
I letter write-EP-INF-*ki* disturbance do-PR
'Don't disturb me while I'm writing a letter.'

(12) *nama ami nu* <u>*hwu-ir-i-ki*</u> *Nkai-na: k-u:-N* ? (talking by telephone)
now rain NOM fall-EP-INF-*ki* pick-up-ST-INF to come-AC-CON-*N*
'As it is raining, shall I go pick you up?'

(13) *atsuko*: <u>*kak-ir-i-ki*</u> (/<u>*kak-i d-ur-i-ki*</u>) *ba: kak-a-nu.*
atsuko write-EP-INF-*ki* (/ ST-INF*dur* : -ST-INF-*ki*) I write-NEG
'I won't write it as Atsuko is writing it.'

(14) *ba: nama* <u>*kak-i d-ur-i-ki*</u> *wa: m-ir-u-N?.*
I now write-ST-INF AX-ST-INF-*ki* you see-EP-CON-*N*
'I'm writing this. So do you want to see it?'

(15) *atsuko* <u>*kaki ur-i-ki*</u> *ba: kak-a-nu.*
atsuko write-ST-INF *ur*-ST-INF-*ki* I write-NEG
'I won't write it as Atsuko is (/was) writing.' (The speaker saw Atsuko writing.)

(16) <u>*sjikaraha-r-i-ki*</u> *asabI-na: har-u-N.*
feel-lonely-RAT play-AC-INF-to go-AC-CON-*N*
'I'm feeling lonely, so I'll go out and have fun.'

(17) *atsuko:* <u>*kak-e:-r-i-ki*</u> *ba: kak-a-nu.*
Atsuko write-CSC-INF-*ki* I write-NEG
'I won't write it as Atsuko has written it.' (The speaker saw the letter Atsuko wrote.)

(18) *kuzo*: <u>*sak-e:-r-i-ki*</u> *kuNduN sak-u hazI.*
last-year-TOP blossom-CSC-INF-*ki* this-year-also blossom-AC-ATT inference
As the flowers blossomed last year, they ought to blossom this year, too.

198

(19) *ba: joi   sɪ-na   har-e:-r-i-ki   wa: har-ana:-ti-N   misha-N.*
   I congratulation do-AC-INF to go-CSC-INF-*ki* you go-NEG-though good-*N*
   'I went to offer congratulate him, so you don't have to.'
(20) *ba: kak-e:d-ari-ki   wa: kak-a-na:-rja.*   [Note : (22) is preferable to (20).]
   I write-CSC-AX-*ki* you write-NEG-IMP
   'Don't write it because I've written it.'
(21) *kak-i   du   ar-e:-r-i-ki (/ ur-e:-ri-ki)   muc-i   har-ja.*
   write-ST-INF FOC *ar*-CSC-INF-*ki* (/*ur*-CSC-INF-*ki*) bring-ST-INF go-IMP
   'Take this with you as it has been written already.'
(22) *ba: kak-i   du   ar-e:-ri-ki   wa: kak-a-NtiN   misha-N.*
   I write-ST-INF FOC *ar*-CSC-INF-*ki* you write-NEG-though good-*N*
   'You don't need to write because I have written it.'

(B) *soNga* 'but'

This is an important conjunctive word. It follows the same form as *so:*. That is to say, it dose not follow the conclusive forms (kak-u / kak-ir-u / kak-e:-r-u).

It does not necessarily mean the reverse but it looks like a kind of suspension.

The examples of form

kakanu-soNga   *kakɪ-soNga*   *kaki-soNga*   *kakɪda-soNga*
I don't write but   I write but   I am writing but   I have written but
kakida-soNga   *kakana:da-soNga*   *kaki uQ-soNga*   *kaki uQta-soNga*
I was writing but   I didn't write but   I have been writing but   I had been writing but

Examples :

(1) *ba: kak-a-nu-soNga.*   (When you are told that you wrote it, you assert yourself)
   I write-NEG-
   I did not write it, yet (you blame me ...)

(2) NboN   hwo:- soNga   ma:zoN   hwo:-N?
    meal   eat-AC-INF-   together   eat-AC-CON-N
    'I'll eat now and can you join me?'

(3) ba: NboN   hwo:- soNga   hatsI   N du   ne:nu.
    I   meal   eat-AC-INF-   chopsticks   NOM-FOC   exist-not
    'I'll eat now but there are no chopsticks.'

(4) ami   nu   hwo:-Ka: na:.   jasai   ib-i-soNga.
    rain   NOM   fall-AC-CND   FP   vegetables   plant-ST-INF-
    'I wish it would rain. I could grow vegetables.'

(5) kazji   nu   huk-I-da-soNga   ki: nu   ha: ja   ut-i-N?
    wind   NOM   blow-AC-PST-   tree   GEN   leaf   TOP   fall-ST-INF-N
    'Did leaves fall after the wind blew?'

(6) ba: ki:-da-soNga   wa: uk-i   ur-a-na:r-i   du   mudur-i haQ-ta.
    I come-ST-PST-   you get-up-ST-INF   ur-NEG-INF   FOC   return-ST-INF go-AC-PST
    'I came to you but I went back because you hadn't been awake.'

(7) jam-i-da-soNga   gaNzju: nar-i-te   hatarag-I-da.
    be-ill-ST-PST-   healthy become-ST-INF-te   work-AC-PST
    'Though I had been ill, I got well again and worked.'

(8) kaNga   pItu nu   nim-i   uQ-soNga   no:N   h-a:na: misja-N   kaja:
    overthere-in person NOM sleep-ST-INF ur-AC-INF- nothing do-NEG-TOP
    good-N FP

    'There is a man lying over there; but I wonder if I could do anything for him.'

(C) -TarI (Repetition)

(1) uta   izI-TarI   budurI   sI-TarI   asab-I-da. /asab-u-N.
    song sing-AC-INF- dance do-AC-INF- play-AC-PST/ -AC-CON-N
    'I sing songs, dance, and enjoy myself.'

(2) kak-I-TarI   juN-TarI   h-u-N.
    weite-AC-INF- read-AC-INF- do-AC-CON-N
    'I write and read books.'

10. Conditional expressions

There are two kinds of conditional. One has the form {irrealis + ba} and the other has the same form as the realis with the final vowel lengthened. In this dialect, the vowel may be lengthened at the end of a word or sentence ; the extra length might be phonologically meaningless.

The forms to be examined are listed below :

kak- 'write'	(a) irrealis+ba	(b) realis (long vowel)
active	ka-ka-ba	kak-ja:
epistemic	kak-ir-a-ba	kak-ir-ja:

In addition to these verbal conjugational forms, the suffixes can form the conditional clause. They are -ki and -ka: {infinitive + ki} and {conclusive + ka:}

10. 1. Idiomatic phrases

(a-1) *kak-a-ba*   du   jar-u.
write-IREA-ba FOC COP-CON
'You have to write it.'

(a-2) *kak-a-ba* N   misja-N?
write-IREA-ba even better-N
'Can I write it?' (Is it O.K. if I write it?) (The speaker asks for permission.)

(a-3) wa: *kak-a-baN*   misja-d-ar-u
you write-IREA-ba even better-dar-
It's O.K. if you write it. (Urging the listener who hesitates to write)

(a-4) *kakabaN*   misja: ru   munu
write-IREA-ba even better-CON Fm-N
It's O.K. if you write it. (Don't hesitate to write it.)

(b-1) *kak-ja:*   misja:-ru   munu.
write-REA better-CON Fm-N
'You should write it.' (In fact, the listener doesn't write it.)

201

10. 2. The optative

Both irrealis form suffixed -*ba* suffixed and realis form can express the desire accompanying the final particle *na:*. The form suffixed with -*ka* also functions as the optative.

    ar- 'exist / be'   *kak*- 'write'

(a) *ca: nu <u>ar-a-ba</u> na:.* *atusko nu <u>kak-a-ba na:</u>*(CJ *kakeba na*)
  tea NOM exist-IREA-*ba* FP atsuko NOM write-IREA-*ba* FP
  'I wish we/I had tea.' 'I wish Atsuko wrote it.'

(b) *ca: nu <u>a-rja:</u> na:.* *atsuko nu <u>kak-ja</u>: na:* (CJ *kaitara na*)
  tea NOM exist-ST-REA FP atsuko NOM write-REA FP
  'I wish we/I had tea.' 'I wish Atsuko would write it.'

(c) *ca: nu <u>aru-ka</u> na:.* *atsuko nu <u>kak-u-ka</u> na:*(CJ *kaku nara na*)
  tea NOM exist-CON-*ka* FP atsuko NOM write-CON FP
  'I wish we/I had tea. 'I wish Atsuko would write it.'

10. 3. Condition "Irrealis + *ba*" and "reales"

Examples :

(A) Existential verb *ar*-

"irrealis + *ba*" is used only for the assumption which uses the focus particle *du*. On the other hand "realis" form without *du* can indicate the anaphoric assumption in which the existence is fixed. If it accompanies the focus particle *du*, it can express the assumption.

Examples : Irrealis forms are illustrated in (a) and realis forms in (b).

(a–1) Said to a person who comes to borrow something :

 <u>*ar-a-ba*</u> *du sɪka-:r-ir-u*.
 exist-IREA-*ba* FOC use-PT-CON
 'If I had it, you could use it. (But I don't have it.)'

(a–2) *zjiN nu <u>ar-a-ba</u> du asab-ɪ-na: har-ar-ir-u*.
 money NOM exist-IREA-*ba* FOC play-AC-INF-to go-PT-EP-CON
 'If I/we had money, I/we could go and have fun. (But I/we don't have

money.)'

(b-1) Said to a person who comes to borrow something:
ar-ja: sıkai-ja: ×*ar-a-ba*
exist-REA use-IMP
'I have it, so use it.'

(b-2) *zjiN   nu   ar-ja: asab-I-na: har-a.*
money NOM exist-REA play-AC-INF-to go-IREA
'We have money, so let's go and have fun. (We do have money.)

(B) The other verbs:

The two forms are hardly distinguished in usages where they indicate actions which are going to be taken. They do not indicate assumptions.

Examples:

(1) *kak-* 'write'

I'm going to write a letter and have it sent

(a) (*ba:*) *tigami kak-a-ba* (*wa:*) *muc-i   har-ja.*
I   letter write-IREA-*ba* (you) bring-ST-INF go-IMP
'I'm going to write a letter; please deliver it.'

(b) *ba: tigami kak-ja:* (*wa:*) *muc-i   ha-rja.*
I   letter weite-REA (you) bring-ST-INF go-IMP
I'm going to write a letter; please deliver it.

(2) *h-* 'do' (Irregular verb)

To a person who is about to clean:

(a) *ba: h-a:-ba   wa: h-a:-na:r-ja.*
I do-IREA-*ba* you do-NEG-IMP
'Don't clean up; I will do it.'

(b) *ba: h-ja: wa: h-a:-na:r-ja.*
I do-REA you do-NEG-IMP
'Don't clean up; I will do it.'

(3) kak- 'write'

(a) (*ba:*) *tigami* <u>*ka-ka-ba*</u> (*wa:*) *kak-a-na:r-ja.*
   'Don't write a letter; I will do it.'
(b) (*ba:*) *tigami* <u>*kak-ja:*</u> (*wa:*) *kak-a-na:r-ja*
   'Don't write a letter; I will do it.'

10. 3. 1. The aspectual difference between realis and irrealis with *ba*

The realis indicates the condition that the action arises. On the other hand, the irrealis with *ba* grasps the action as a whole which does not have any break; and its realization is the condition .

(1) Group 1   *hwo-* 'eat'   (a) *hwa:-ba* (active-irrealis-) (b) *hwai-ja:* (realis)
  (a–1) To the speaker's daughter when the speaker is about to eat:
       ba: NboN <u>*hwa:ba*</u> *makarI sjizjim-ir-i*   (× <u>*hwai-ja:*</u>)
       I meal eat-IREA-*ba* dish clear-away-EP-IMP
       After I eat clean up the dishes.
  (b–1) To a child who is in this seat that the speaker should be in:
       ba: NboN <u>*hwai-ja:*</u>   *madagir-i.*   (× <u>*hwa:-ba*</u>)
       I meal eat-ST-REA go-away-IMP
       'I'm going to eat, so go away.'
  (a–2) To the person who came to invite the speaker:
       ba: NboN <u>*hwa:-ba*</u> *ma:zoN har-a na:*   (× <u>*hwai-ja:*</u>)
       I meal eat-IREA-*ba* together go-IREA FP
       'After I eat, we will go together.'
  (b–2) To the person who came to invite the speaker:
       ba: NboN <u>*hwai-ja:*</u> *ma:zoN hwo:N?*   (× <u>*hwa:-ba*</u>)
       I meal eat-REA together eat-AC-CON-*N*
       'I'm going to eat. Would you join me?'
  (a–3) Taking turns eating or when eating something for the first time:
       ba: <u>*hwa:-ba*</u> *wa*: *hwai-ja.*   (× <u>*hwai-ja:*</u>)
       I eat-IREA-*ba* you eat-IMP
       'If I eat, you eat too.' ('I will eat and then you eat, too')

(a-4) Eating in turn, I hesitate to eat ahead
    wa: *hwa:ba*   *du*   *banu* N   *hwo:*
    you eat-IREA-*ba*   FOC   I also   eat-AC-CON
    When you eat I will eat, too.

(b-3) To the person who is about to going to clean up the table :
    ba: *hwai-ja:*   *na:i*   *sjikir-i*.   (× *hwa:-ba*)
    I eat-REA   just   leave-IMP
    'I'm going to eat ; just leave them alone.'

(c-1) *ba*: NboN *hwai-ki* *a:N-na*.   (≅ *hwai-ja:*)
    I   meal   eat-RAT   make-noise-PR
    'I'm going to eat so don't make noise.'
    To express clearly the reason, the suffix   *-ki* is preferable.

(c-2) NboN *hwai-ki* NboN   *ir-i*   *k-u:*.
    rice dat-RAT   meal   put-in-ST-INF   come-IMP
    I' m going to eat so you get rice for me and come.

(2) Group 2 *ut-* 'fall'   (a) *ut-u-ba* (stative-irrealis-)   (b) *ut-ir-ja*: (epistemic-realis)

    The examples of group (a) need the realization of whole action and those of group (b) need the arising (beginning) of the action.

(a) *ki*: *nu nara*: *ut-u-ba*   *putsu-i*.   (× *ut-ir-ja:*)
    tree GEN fruit-TOP fall-IREA-ba pick-IMP
    'If a nut falls from the tree, pick it up.'

(a'-1) *ki*: *nu hwa: nu* *ut-u-ba*   *po:gɪ h-ja:*.
    tree GEN leaf GEN fall-IREA-*ba*   broom do-IMP
    'If leaves fall, clean them up.'

(b) To a person standing under a roof that is under construction.
    ki: *nu* *ut-ir-ja:*   *madagir-i* (× *ut-u-ba*)
    tree GEN fall-EP-REA   go-away-IMP
    wood might fall, so get out of the way.

(b'-1) *unu iN ja ui gara ut-ir-ja:* sIN *du h-u:.* (× *ut-u-ba*)
   this dog TOP top from fall-EP-REA die-AC-INF FOC do-AC-CON
   'This dog has fallen from the top and will die.'
(b'-2) *ki: nu ha: nu ut-ir-ja: po:gI h-ja:.*
   tree GEN leaf GEN fall-EP-REA broom do-IMP
   'Leaves are falling from the tree (and piled up on the ground,) so clean them up.'
(c) *ui gara ut-ir-u-Ka:* sIn-*u-N dara* (× *ut-ir-ja:* × *ut-u-ba*)
   top from fall-EP-CON-*Ka* die-CON-*N* FP
   'If you fall from the top, you will die.'

10. 3. 2. The modal difference between realis and irrealis with *ba*

The difference is whether the condition is desirable for the speaker or it is the simple acknowledgement of the fact.
(a-1) *hana sak-a-ba m-i:-na: har-a na:*
   flower bloom-AC-IREA-*ba* see-ST-to go-AC-IREA FP
   'When the flowers bloom, let's go to see them.'
(b-1) *hana sak-ja: m-i:-na: har-a.*
   flower bloom-REA see-ST-INF-to go-IREA
   'The flowers are going to bloom ; let's go to see them.'
(a-2) The farmers have a long dry weather ; they are waiting for raining.
   ami nu hwo-:ba: yasai du ib-ir-u (× *hwuija:,* × *hwo:Ka:*)
   rain NOM fall-AC-IREA-ba vegetable FOC plant-EP-CON
   'If it would rain, I would plant vegetables.'
(b-2) *ami nu hwu-i-ja: hate:ge: haN-na* (× *hwo:ba*)
   rain NOM fall-ST-REA field to go-PR
   'It's raining, so don't go to the field.'
(b-3) *ami nu hwu-i-ja: jasai du ib-ir-u* (× *hwo:ba*)
   rain NOM fall-ST-REA vegetable FOC plant-EP-CON
   'It's raining, so I'm going to plant vegetables.'

The Grammar of Ishigaki Miyara Dialect in Luchuan

After a long spell of dry weather, farmers want it to rain so they can plant vegetables. The rainy condition is desired by them. Series-(a) express the speaker's modal elements. To express general neutral condition :

(c-1) *ami nu <u>hwo:-ka:</u> yasai du ib-ir-u* (× <u>hwuija:</u> , × <u>hwo:ba</u>)
 rain NOM fall-AC-CON-CND vegetable FOC plant-EP-CON
 'If it's raining, we plant vegetables.'

We will choose the verbs which imply undesirable conditions to examine the above hypothesis.

(1) *kazji huk-* 'wind blow = typhoon blow' *huk-a-ba* (irrealis-) *huk-ja:* (realis)

× (a) *kazji nu huk-a-ba*

 (b) *kazji nu <u>huk-ja:</u> hate:ge: haN-na*
  wind NOM blw-REA field to go-AC-INF-PR
  'We are having a typhoon, so don't go to the field.'

 (c) *kazji nu <u>huku-ka:</u> huni Nd-u-nu.*
  wind NOM blwAC-CON-CND ship start-NEG
  If we are having a typhoon, the boat won't depart.

The form with *-ka:* expresses a simple fact. In Okinawa, a typhoon does not bring anything to be desired.

(2) *sIn-* 'die' *sIn-a-ba* (irrealis-) *sjin-ja:* (realis)

× (a) *ba: <u>sIn-a-ba</u> ure: wa: kisj-i.*
  I die-IREA-*ba* this-TOP you wear-IMP
  'I'm going to die, so you shall wear this.'

The hearer must be surprised wondering the speaker might kill himself.

? (b) *ba: <u>sjin-ja:</u> ure: wa: kis-ja: jo:.*
  I die-REA this-TOP you wear-IMP FP
  'When I die, you wear this.'

It means that the speaker has decided to die. This sentence can not be uttered.

In a will, "*ba: <u>sInu-ka:</u>*" would be acceptable.

207

10. 3. 3. Epistemic form of conditional

The following are the examples of Group 1 epistemic form in conditional and Group 2 epistemic-irrealis

(1) *wanu* N <u>*hwa-ir-ja:*</u>   *banu* N *hwa-i du h-u*:
   you also eat-EP-REA   I also eat-ST-INF FOC do-AC-CON
   'You're eating ; that's why I will eat too.'
      cf. active-realis :   *wanu* N <u>*hwai-ja:*</u>   *banu* N *hwa-i du h-u:*.
                             you also eat-REA   I also eat-ST-INF FOC do-AC-CON
                             'Since you eat, I will eat too.'

(2) Recommending eating a new food :
   ba: <u>*hwa-ir-ja*</u>   *wanu* N   *hwa-:r-i*   *du*   *h-u*:
   I eat-EP-REA   you also   eat-POT-INF- FOC do-AC-CON
   'I always eat it ; so can you.'

(3) *ki: nu hwa: nu* <u>*ut-ir-ja:*</u>   *po:gɪ h-ja:*
   tree GEN leaf NOM fall-EP-REA   broom do-IMP
   'The leaves have piled up, so clean them up.'

Group 1 epistemic-irrealis

(1) *ba:* <u>*hwa-ir-a-ba*</u>   *wa:*   *ik-i-te*   *ku-ba*:
   I eat-EP-IREA-*ba*   you go-ST-INF-and come-IMP
   'While I'm eating, you go and come back.'

(2) *ba:* <u>*hwa-ir-a-ba*</u>   *wa: atugani hwai-ja*:
   I eat-EP-IREA-*ba* you later eat-IMP
   'I'm eating, so you eat later.'

×(3) <u>*wa: hwa-ir-a-ba*</u>

(4) *ma:zon NboN hwa: na:. wa:* <u>*uk-ir-a-ba*</u>   *na:*   (×*ukuba*)
   together meal eat-IREA FP   you rise-EP-IREA-ba FP
   'Let's eat together when you can get up.(The hearer is keeping his bed.)

(5) *ma:zon NboN hwa: na:. wa:* <u>*uk-u-ba*</u>   *na:*
   together meal eat-IREA FP   you rise-ST-IREA   FP
   'Let's eat together when you get up.'   (in daily life : he is not sick.)

11. Sample of Miyara dialect

(1) *ur-* 'exist'

When Mr. A found a missing child :

A : <u>*ur-u-N*</u>!
    exist-AC-CON-*N*
    'Here she is! (I found her.)'

Then he shouted to the people who were looking for the child with him.

Nga du <u>*u-ru*</u>.   /   *Nga* <u>*uQ-so:*</u>
here FOC exist-AC-CON   here exist-AC-INF-*so*:
'She is here.'   'I found she is here.'

B (to A): <u>*uQ-ta*</u>?
    exist-AC-INF-PST
    'Was she there?' 'Have you found her?'

A little while later :

C : *unu hwa: ja   zIma Nga   du* <u>*uQ-ta*</u>?
    that child TOP where in   FOC exist-AC-INF-PST
    'Where has she been?'

A : *gaQko: nu maNta Nga du* <u>*uQ-ta.*</u>
    school GEN front in FOC exist-AC-INF-PST
    'She was in front of the school.'

C : *gaQko: nu maNta Nga du* <u>*ur-i*</u>?
    school GEN front in FOC exist-ST-INF
    'Was she in front of the school?'

A : *anzj-i, Nga du* <u>*ur-i*</u>.
    so-do-ST-INF there FOC exist-ST-INF
    'Yes, she was there.'

(2) *ar-* 'exist'

(a) In the shop between a customer and a shopkeeper :

Customer :   *mai ar-u-N*?
                rice exist-AC-CON-N
                Do you have rice? (Is there any rice in this shop?)
Shopkeeper : *ne:nu*.   /   *ar-i duru*
                exist-not   exist-AX-CON
                No, we don't. (No, there isn't.) 'Yes, we have.'(There is certainly.)
Customer :   (Looking around herself)   *ar-i dur-ja-N*!
                                                exist-AX-REA-N
                                                 You've got rice. (Rice is here)
                (to a shopkeeper) : *wa: ne:nu di aN-ta-soNga ar-ja-N*.
                                  you be-not AP say-ac-PST-but exist-REA-N
                                'Though you said you didn't, you have rice.'

(b) Lost and found

  There are several forms to utter in finding a lost article.

     ar-u-N.   *aQ-ta*.
     AC-CON-N   AC-PST

  These two forms are usually uttered in finding a lost article.

     ar-i-Ta.   The speaker wasn't expecting to find it.
     ST-INF-PF

     ar-ja-N
     REA-N   The speaker did not think it was there.

     ar-i dur-ja-N.
     ST-INF AX-REA-N

        Though the speaker did not think it was there, he looked around there to make sure it wasn't. Then he found it unexpectedly.

     ar-e:-r-ja-N.
     CSC-REA-N   'It was not here but I've found it now.'

He once looked for it there but he could not find it. This time, unexpectedly he found it.

     ne:na:-da-soNga nama mir-u-NkeN Nga du ar-e:-r-jaN.

be-not-PST-but　　now see-EP-CON-while here FOC exist-CSC-REA-*N*

'I thought it was not here but I looked for it here again and now I've found it here.

(I could not find it here a little while ago)'

(c) Carrying things, you walked backward and stumbled over a stone.

isji　nu　Ndu　ar-e:-r-ja-N.

stone NOM FOC exist-CSC-REA-*N*

'There's a stone here! I didn't notice there was a stone.'

(d) *ar-e:-N*.　　　There used to be certainly but now not...

exist-CSC-STM-*N*

'It was certainly here, I know.'

(d-1) *kju: ja ne:nu-soNga　kIno: ar-e:-N*.

today TOP exist-NEG-but yesterday exist-CSC-*N*

'It is not here today, but it was here yesterday.'

(d-2) Arguing whether something was here or not,

A: *ne:na:da　ar-a-nu*?　　　B: *ar-e:-N*.

exist-NEG-PST ar-NEG　　　　exist-CSC-*N*

'It was not here, was it?'　　　Yes, it was certainly here.'

(d-3) When you see a rare vase used for a ceremony in your friend's house,

kazaru kubiN ja　waQca Nga　aQ-soNga　mukasa: baNca NgaN　ar-e:-N.

display vase TOP your-house in exist-AC-INF-but old-time-TOP our-house in exist-CSC-*N*

'I found a display vase in your house ; there used to be one in my house.'

(e) *ar-e:-d-ar-ja-N*!

When cleaning your room, you happened to find something which you thought was missing and which you didn't search for. For example, when something very old, which you weren't expecting to see, came out of a warehouse, you might say this.

Cf. *baNcaNga N   ar-e:d-ar-u*.
our-house-in-also exist-CSC-ST-dar-CON
'We used to have one.' (The speaker reported it to someone)

(f)   *ar-i   du   ar-e:-r-ja-N*.
exist-ST-INF FOC AX-CSC-REA-N
ne:nu   di   umu-ir-u-NkeN   ari   du   ar-e:r-j-aN.
exist-NEG AP think-EPCON-N-while exist-ST-INF FOC AX-CSC-REA-N
'I thought it was missing, but I found it.'

(g) *ar-i   du   ur-e:-r-ja-N*.   (This is almost same as (f))
exist-ST-INF FOC *ur*-CSC-REA-N
'Though I thought it was missing, I found it after searching all over.'

(3) *kIs*- 'wear / put on'

(a) When you are putting on your clothes, someone visits you.
mac-i jo:. nama kIN ba du kis-ji-ru.
wait-IMP FP now clothes AP FOC wear-EP-CON
'Wait. I am putting on my clothes.'

(b) Seeing you in the beautiful clothes :
wa: kaihe:-ru   kIN   (ba)   kis-ji-so: na:.
you beautiful-CON clothes (AP) wear-ST-INF-*so:* FP
'You wear a pretty kimono.'

(c) It takes time to wear the formal dress and the person helping you ought to have something to do.
baN taNga: kis-jir-u-N.   wa: hajamar-i   ik-i-te   k-u:.
I alone wear-EP-CON-N you hurry-ST-INF go-ST-INF-te come-IMP
'I 'll keep putting this on by myself, so you may go right now and hurry back .'

(d) Your favorite kimono becomes dirty. To a person who suggest you throw it away :
ba: unu kIN ja (mainitsI)   kis-ji   d-ur-u.   sjitir-ar-a-nu.

> I this kimono TOP (everyday) wear-ST-INF AX-CON throw-POT-NEG
> 'I wear this every day. I cannot throw it away.'

(e) When you don't know if a person in the next room is dressed yet:

A: wa: kIN kis-ji-N?
you clothes wear-ST-INF-N
'Are you dressed?' (naked or not?)

B: me:da kIs-a-nu. hadaga du nar-ir-u.
yet wear-NEG naked FOC become-EP-CON
'No, I'm not dressed. I am naked.'

(f) Looking at a piece of kimono,

A: wa: unu kIN ja kis-ji-N?
you this kimono TOP wear-ST-INF-N
'Do you wear this kimono?'

B: kis-ji-N. / kis-ji ur-a-nu.
wear-ST-INF-N wear- ST-INF AX-NEG
'I (always) wear it. / 'I don't wear it.' (I haven't worn it.)

A: banu ge: h-ir-u-N?
I to give-EP-CON-N
'Can I have it?' (Do you give me it?)

(f') Looking at a new kimono hanging,

A: wa: unu kIN du kis-ji?
you this kimono FOC wear-ST-INF
'Did you wear this kimono?'

B: me:da kIs-a-nu. / me:da kis-ji m-u:-nu.
yet wear-NEG / yet wear-ST-INF-see-NEG
'I didn't wear it.' / 'I haven't tried it on.'

(g) Pointing at the kimono I don't wear,

unu kIN ja ba: kis-ji-te hurum-i-soNga wa: kIs-u-N?
this kimono TOP I wear-PF-and get-old-ST-INF-but you wear-AC-CON-N
'I have worn this and it looks old. Can you wear this?

213

(g') *unu k<small>IN</small> ja ba*: *kis-je:-r-u* k<small>IN</small>   *ja<small>Q</small>-so<small>N</small>ga   wa*: *k<small>IS</small>-u-<small>N</small>*?
    this kimono T<small>OP</small> I wear-C<small>SC</small>-C<small>ON</small> kimono C<small>OP</small>-A<small>C</small>-I<small>NF</small>-but you wear-A<small>C</small>-C<small>ON</small>-*N*
    'This is the kimono I used to wear. Can you wear this?'

(h) *ba*: *kis-jir-u*   k<small>IN</small>   *wa*:   *k<small>IS</small>-u-<small>N</small>*?
    I wear-E<small>P</small>-C<small>ON</small> kimono you wear-A<small>C</small>-C<small>ON</small>-*N*
    'Would you wear the kimono I am wearing?' (...if I gave it to you?)

(4) *har-* 'go / leave'

(a-1) Grandmother heard her grandchild's car. She came out of the next room, asking :

Grandmother :   *ka<small>N</small>ge du   har-i*?   / *ha<small>Q</small>-ta* ?   ×*har-i-da*
                 overthere-to F<small>OC</small> go-S<small>T</small>-I<small>NF</small>/ go-A<small>C</small>-P<small>ST</small>   go-S<small>T</small>-P<small>ST</small>
                 'Did he go that way?' (though there are many routes)

(a-2) Grandmother :   *kange   du   haru* ?
                       over-there-to F<small>OC</small> go-A<small>C</small>-C<small>ON</small>
                       'Is he going that way?'

   Though he was not in her sight, the conclusive is acceptable.

Grandfather (He looked at him going away) : *ka<small>N</small>ge   du   ha<small>Q</small>ta* .
                                            over-there-to F<small>OC</small> go-A<small>C</small>-P<small>ST</small>
                                            'He has gone that way.'

(5) *s<small>IN</small>-* 'die'

(a) A rat lies eating a rat-bane,

   A : *sjin-i-<small>N</small>*?
        die-S<small>T</small>-I<small>NF</small>-*N*
        'Is it dead?'

   B : *sjin-i ur-a-nu.* (He is looking at it to confirm its death.)
        die-S<small>T</small>-I<small>NF</small> ur-N<small>EG</small>
        '(I'm afraid) it was not dead.'

   C : *sjin-i-so:* .   D : *sjin-i dur-u* .

　　　　　　 die-ST-INF-*so*:　　　　　　　　 die-ST-INF AX-CON
　　　　　　 'It died.'　　　　　　　　　　　　 'It is dead.'
　E :　*sjini duru?*　　　*sjin-i-Ta?*
　　　　 die-ST-INF AX-CON　die-ST-INF PF
　　　　 'Is it dead?'　　　　 'Did it die?'
After a short time, they come again.
　A :　*me:da*　*sIn-a-nukaja*: .
　　　　 yet　die-NEG　FP
　　　　 'Hasn't it died yet?'
B (Confirming its death) :　　*sjin-i ur-u-N*
　　　　　　　　　　　　　　　 die-ST-CON ur-AC-CON-*N*
　　　　　　　　　　　　　　　 'I'm sure it is dead.'
C (Looking at the rat) :　　*sjiniN?*　　　*sjin-i　ur-a-nu?*
　　　　　　　　　　　　　　 die-ST-INF-*N*　 die-ST-INF AX-NEG
　　　　　　　　　　　　　　 Is it dead?　　　It isn't dead?
(Poking the rat to confirm its death) :　*sjin-i dur-ja-N*.
　　　　　　　　　　　　　　　　　　　　　 die-ST-INF AX-REA-*N*
　　　　　　　　　　　　　　　　　　　　　 It has died!
(b) A caretaker says to her master when he comes.
　(b-1)　*ujaNco: kama Nga du sjin-i-da*.
　　　　　 rat-TOP over-theer in FOC die-ST-INF-PST
　　　　　 'A rat is dead over there.'
　　　 It means that she saw the rat dead over there and she thinks that the dead rat is still there.
　(b-2) The other day, it happens that she says as follows
　　　　 ujaNco: uma Nga du sjin-i-da.
　　　　 rat-TOP here in FOC die- ST-INF-PST
　　　　 'A rat died here.'　(It means that the dead rat is cleared away.)
　　　　 Cf.　*ujaNco: uma Nga du sjin-ir-u*.
　　　　　　　 rat-TOP here in　FOC die-EP-CON

215

A rat is dead here. (It means that anybody here can see the dead rat.)

(c) You visit your friend and don't see her dog.

    A: *unu iN ja ur-a-nu-soNga sjin-i du:* ?
        that dog TOP exist-NEG-but die-ST-INF *du*:
        'I don't see the dog. Did it die? I guess.'

    B: *sIN du sI-ta*. / *sjin-i-Ta*.
        die-AC-INF FOC do-AC-PST / die-ST-INF-PF
        'It did die.' / 'It died.'

(d) People say a number of persons are going to attend a funeral. (In this case, because they have information about the age of the person who died they are not using honorific words.)

(d-1)   A: *ta*: *du sjin-ir-u* ?
            who FOC die-EP-CON
            'Who died?'

(d-2)   B: *atsuko du sjin-ir-u*.
            atsuko FOC die- EP-CON
            'Atsuko died.'

            atsuko ja araja: *ba du sIkur-i-te*: *du sjin-iru*.
            atsuko TOP new-house AP FOC make-ST-INF-and FOC die-EP-CON
            'Atsuko died after she built a new house.'

(e) A dog was run over by a car.

(e-1) *kuruma Nga sIk-ar-i-Ca*: *sIN du hu: me*:.
        car in run-over-PSS-INF-CND die-AC-INF-FOC do-AC-CON soon
        'Run over by a car, the dog is dying.'

(e-2) A little while later they are talking of that topic.

    A: *kuruma Nga sIkar-i-da-soNga sI-Ndu sI-ta kaja* :
        car in run-PSS-INF-PST-but die-AC-INF-FOC do-AC-INF-PST FP
        'As a car ran over the dog, I guess it died.'

    B: *unu iN ja sjin-i-Ca-N*?

that dog TOP die-ST-INF-PF-*N*
'Has that dog died?'
C: *sjin-i-ca-N*.   *nama ur-a-nu*.
die-ST-INF-PF-*N*   now exist-NEG
'It has been dead. It is gone now'

(f) The Subjunctive

(f-1) *kunu iN ja huciri ba hwa-i-te jagati sjin-e:-N*.
this dog TOP poison AP eat-ST-INF-PF-and soon die-CSC-*N*
This dog ate a poison and it might have died. (But the dog did not die.)

(f-2) *unu pɪtu nu mi: hu:-na:-ka: jagati sjin-e:-N na:*.
this person NOM see-ST-INF give-NEG-CND soon die-CSC-N FP
If he hadn't taken care of me, I would have been dead.

(f-3) *ui gara ut-e:-ra-ba sjin-i du ar-e: -ru*.
top from fall-CSC-IREA-ba die-ST-INF FOC AX-CSC-CON
'If I had fallen down from the top, I would have died.'

(f-4) *hwu: ba ar-i du ut-u-na:r-e:-ru*.
luck AP be-INF FOC fall-NEG-CSC-CON
'I was lucky not to have fallen.'

(6) haram-   'conceive'

(a) Breeding a pig,

kana sɪ-ta-soNga hram-i-N? / haram-u-N?
mating-do-AC-INF but conceive-ST-INF-N   conceive-AC-CON-*N*
The pig finished mating. Has it become pregnant?   Is it get pregnant?

(b) A professional person presumes that it may be pregnant without knowing its mating.

A: *waQca nu onta haram-i-N?*   × *haram-i-da*
your-house GEN pig conceive-ST-INF-*N*   conceive-ST-PST
'The pig in your house is pregnant, isn't it?'

B: *haram-i dur-u.*

conceive-ST-INF AX-CON
'It is certainly pregnant.'

(c) *ba*N*ca   nu   o*N*ta   haram-i-*T*a*.
our-house GEN pig conceive-ST-INF-PF
'The pig has just become pregnant.'
The situation is right after finishing mating. The pig is not now perceived to be pregnant.

(d) *kunu o*N*ta   hram-i dur-u*.
this pig conceive-ST-INF AX-CON
'This pig is certainly pregnant.' (After the speaker saw the pig looking pregnant)

(e) *hara*N*-da*

This active past form is hardly used for the human beings. It does not mean the state after giving birth but right after mating.

*kunu   o*N*ta*: *kuzo*:   *hara*N*-da.hwa*: *nas*I*-ta*.
this pig last-year conceive-AC-PST child give-birth-AC-PST
'This pig was pregnant last year and bred baby pigs.'

(e-1) The doctor examining a woman who consults with him about the pregnancy can say.

*hara*N*-da* ?
conceive-AC-PST
'Do you think you have become pregnant?'

(e-2) After examining her, he will say

wa: *haram-i dur-u*
you conceive-ST-INF AX-CON
'You are certainly pregnant.'

(f) *kana*: *s*I*-ta-so*N*ga   hara*N*-da*? / *haram-i-*N*?*
mating-do-AC-INF-but conceive-AC-PST / conceive-ST-INF-*N*
The pig finished mating. Has it got pregnant? / Is it pregnant?
(The speaker wants to make sure of its success.)

218

(g) *unu usa: kana: hi:-ca:* <u>*haraN du hu:*</u> .
this cow mate-do-ST-INF-PF-CND conceive-AC-INF-FOC do-AC-CON
'As this pig finished mating, it must have become pregnant.'

(h) *kana: he:-ri-ki* <u>*haraN-du h-u:*</u> ?
mate do-CSC-RT conceive-AC-INF-FOC do-AC-CON
As (this pig) has been mated, is it pregnant?

(i) The stative-past is hardly used ; no one, except doctors and nurses, can see the pregnancy. It is only used in the case that the pregnancy ends in a failure.

(i-1) A daughter tells her mother about pregnancy.
<u>*haram-i-da*</u>-*soNga du hwa: na:h-ana:-te sjin-i ne:nu.*
conceive-ST-PST-but FOC child give-birth-NEG-te die-ST-INF end-in
'Though I was pregnant, I could not give birth to him. The baby had died.'

(i-2) <u>*haram-i-da*</u>-*soNga urah-i du sI-ta.*
conceive-ST-PST-but abort-ST-INF FOC do-AC-CON
'I was pregnant but I had an abortion.'

(i-3) The patient can not say *urahida* (stative-past) 'had an abortion' but *urasIta* (active past). Only the doctors and nurses can say so because they can see it.

Nurse (who took care of her): *atsuko:isja nu ja:naNga hwa:ba* <u>*urah-i-da*</u>.
atsuko doctor GEN house in child AP abort-ST-PST
'Atsuko had an abortion at the hospital.'

(j)The forms which can be translated into CJ *te-iru*

(j-1) *wa:* <u>*haram-i-N*</u>? 'Are you pregnant?' CJ *ninshin* <u>*shite-iru*</u>?
Without any signs of pregnancy, mother asks as usual her daughter whether she expects to have a grandchild or not.

(j-2) *wa:* <u>*haram-i duru*</u>? 'Are you pregnant?' Jap. *ninshin* <u>*shite-iruno*</u>?
A close friend asks a girl with a big stomach.

(j-3) A : *wa:* <u>*haram-i-N*</u>?

219

   'Are you pregnant?'   C J *ninshin <u>shite-iru</u>*?
  B : *me:da <u>haram-i u-ra-nu</u>* / *me:da harm-a-nu*.
   'I haven't become pregnant yet.' / I am not pregnant.
   C j *mada ninshin <u>shite-inai.</u>* / C J *mada ninshin <u>shinai</u>*.
(k-1) *sɪkɪ nu munu ɴdu tumar-iru*. <u>*harami duru*</u> *kaja*:
   month GEN thing NOM-FOC stop-EP-CON conceive-ST-INF *dur*-CON FP
   'My periods stopped. I wonder if I'm pregnant.' (And she goes to
   see the doctor.)
(k-2) The next day, after visiting the doctor, her mother asked her as
   usual.
  Mother : <u>*haram-i-ɴ*</u> ? 'Are you pregnant?'
  daughter : <u>*haram-i-ɴ.*</u> 'I am pregnant.'
    kɪnu isjana:ge haruɴkeɴ <u>haram-i dur-u</u> di aɴzjio:ta.
   yesterday hospital to go-when conceive-ST-INF AX-CON AP say-HO-PST
  'Yesterday I went to the hospital and the doctor told me I was certainly
pregnant.'
 (k-3) Coming back, mother was very pleased to announce
   atsuko ja <u>haram-i-ᴛa</u> co:.
   atsuko TOP conceive-ST-INF-PF QT
   'Atsuko said that she was pregnant.'
 (l-1) They planned to go on a trip to Okinawa , but Atsuko is several
   months pregnant.
   atsuko ja <u>haram-i du ur-i-ki</u> kuruma nusji-rar-a-nu. × <u>*haram-ir-i-ki*</u>
   atsuko TOP conceive-ST-INF AX-RAT car take-in-POT-NEG
   'Atsuko is pregnant. She cannot go in a car.'
 (l-2) There is no epistemic conclusive +ɴ (*haram-ir-u-ɴ*) but its realis
   form appears.
   wa: <u>*haram-ir-ja:*</u> *muri ha:na:rja:*.
   you conceive-EP-REA overwork-do-NEG-IMP
   'You are pregnant. Don't overwork yourself.'

(m) ba: mi:musɪ   haram-e:-N.
I   three-times conceive-CSC-N
'I have been pregnant three times.'

(n) atsuko haram-u-ka: ja: ge: sa:r-i   k-u-ba.   ×haram-a-ba ×haram-ja:
atsuko conceive-AC-CON-CND house to bring-ST-INF come-IMP
When Atsuko becomes pregnant, we'd better bring her home.

Acknowledgments

In completing this research and presentation regarding the grammar of Miyara dialect, I would like to warmly thank Prof. Osahito Miyaoka of Osaka Gakuin University and Prof. Shinji Sanada of Osaka University. Also, I would like to thank University of Tokyo graduate student Mark Rosa for his great contributions to the translation in English ; he is a great reader and also gave me some suggestions for the manuscript. Many people have helped me with my research for over a decade, and I offer heartfelt thanks to the speakers from all over Yaeyama. I extend my gratitude especially to the Miyara dialect speakers named below.

Speaker's name and year of birth

Tamori, Uzura. (1911-2003)   Tamori, Haru. (1914-)
Higashinarisoko, Mitsuhide. (1913-) Moriyama, Shinhachi. (1928-)
Moriyama, Shizu. (1930-)   Moriyama, Mantu. (1905-)
Takehara, Chiyo. (1917-1998)

Reference

Chamberlain, Basil Hall (1895) *Essay in aid of a grammar and dictionary of the Luchuan language*. Tokyo : Z. P. Maruya & Co., Ltd.

Hattori, Shiro (1955) *Ryukyugo (Luchuan)* . In : *Sekai gengo gaistu* (Language of the world). (Part 2 of 2) Kenkyusha

Iwakura, Ichiro (1941) *Kikai-jima hogen-shu* (Word book of Kikai-jima). Chu-o-koron

Izuyama, Atsuko (1992) *Ryukyu-hogen no 1-ninsho daimeishi* (A study of personal pronouns in Luchuan dialects). Kokugogaku (Studies in the Japanese Language) 171

────── (1996) *Ryukyu-hogen no boin chowa-teki keiko* (A kind of vowel harmony in Luchuan dialects). The Dokkyo University Bulletin of Liberal Arts 31-1

────── (1997a) *Ryukyu · Ishigaki Miyara hogen no doshi-gokei-henka* (A study on the conjugation of Luchuan verbs). The Dokkyo University Bulletin of Liberal Arts 31-2

────── (1997b) *Ryukyu-hogen keiyoshi seiritsu no shiteki kenkyu* (A historical study on the adjectives in Lhchuan dialects). Journal of Asia & African Studies 54. ILCAA

────── (1998) *Ryukyu-hogen hojo-doshi (Copula) no kigen* (A historical study on the copula in Luchuan dialects). The Dokkyo University Bulletin of Liberal Arts 1-2

──────(2000) *Ryukyu · Yaeyama (Ishigaki Miyara) hogen jyoken hyogen no aspect to modality* (Conditional expressions in Miyara dialect). Mathesis Universalis 2-2. Dokkyo University

────── (2001) *Ryukyu · Yaeyama Ishigaki (Miyara) hogen no doshi iikiri no katachi.* Asia & African Linguistics. 29 ILCAA

──────2002. *Ryukyu · Yaeyama (Ishigaki-Miyara) hogen no bunpou* (Grammar of Miyara dealect in Yaeyama of Okinawa). In: Grammatical Aspects of Endangered Dialects in Japan (1). ELPR publications Series (Osaka Gauin University) A4-004

Jodai-go jiten henshu iinkai (1967) *Jidai betsu kokugo dai-jiten* (Dictionary of acient Japanise). Sanseido

Kamei, Takashi et al. (1992) *Gengogaku dai jiten* (The Sanseido encyclopaedia of linguistics. vol. 4. Language of the world, part 3) Sanseido

Karimata, Shigehisa (1992) *Yaeyama hogen* (Dialect of Yaeyama). 848-873

Shimabukuro, Sachiko (1992) *Okinawa hokubu hogen* (Dialect of northern part in main island of Okinawa). 814-829

Takahashi, Shunzo (1992) *Yonaguni hogen* (Dialect of Yonaguni). 873-882

Uemura, Yukio (1992) *Ryukyu retto no gengo* (Introduction). 771-814

Miyara mura shi henshu iinkai (1986) *Miyara son shi* (History of Miyara). Miyara kominkan

Nakamatsu, Takeo (1987) *Ryukyu hogen jiten* (A Dictionary of Lucuan dialects). Naha shuppan

Nohara, Mitsuyoshi (1986) *Ryukyu-hogen joshi no kenkyu* (Studies on particles in Luchuan dialects). Musashino-shoin

Suzuki, Shigeyuki (1960) *Shuri hogen no doshi no iikiri no katachi.* Kokugogaku. 41

Suzuki, Karimata et al. (2001) *Ryukyu Yaeyama hogen no doshi no kenkyu.* Kakenhi report

The national Institute for Japanese Language (1963) *Okinawa-go jiten* (Dictionary of Okinawa language).

Yaeyama rekishi henshu iinkai (1953) *Yaeyama rekishi (History of Yaeyama)* .

琉球・宮古（平良）方言の文法基礎研究

1．平良市の概要

　琉球列島のほぼ中間にある宮古島は、沖縄本島から南西約290kmの位置にある。平良市はその中心地で、面積64.60平方km 人口35,241人である。[1]

　平良市というのは、旧市街地の他、狩俣・西原など宮古島北西部のみならず、大神島・池間島（架橋がある）など島嶼をも含み、広範囲にわたっている。それらの地域は各々異なる方言を持っている。

宮古島の位置

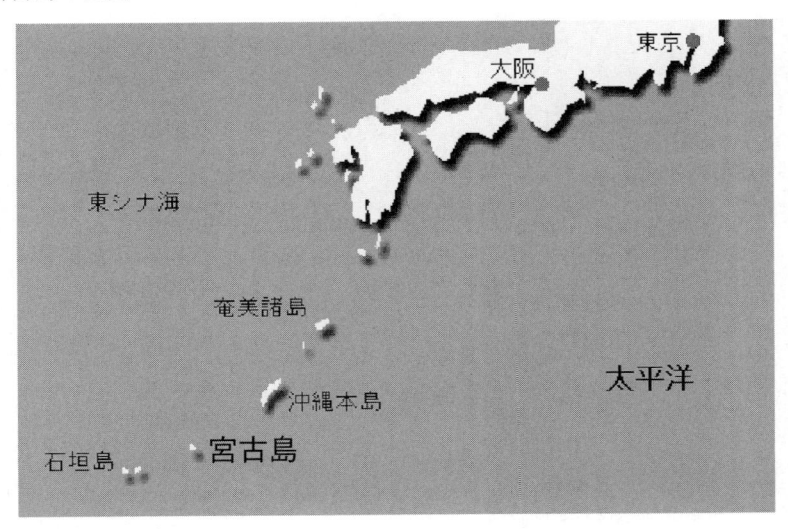

---

(1) 平良市ホームページ（平成14年5月31日現在の統計）、位置図は宮古島オンライン、西仲宗根位置図はマピオタウン情報による。

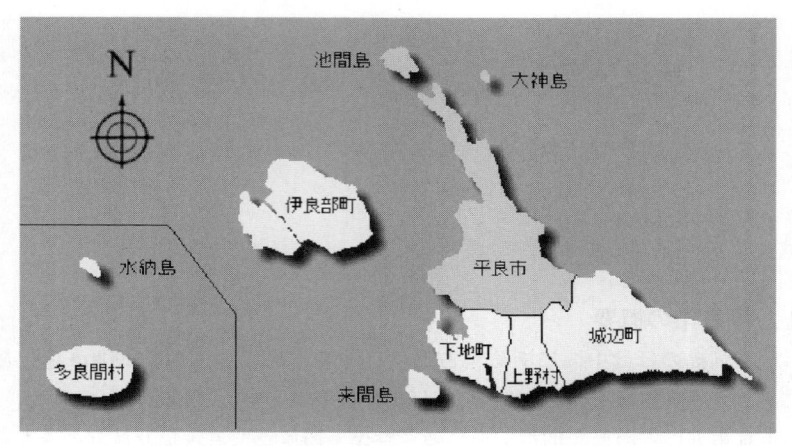

宮古の名が初めて記録に現れたのは1317年「元史」で、密牙古の人が中国温州に漂着した記録だという。(2)宮古は、14世紀後半から全島統一に向かった。平良（ぴぃさら）はその中心地であった。
　ここで報告するのは、平良市旧市街地(3)の中でも、歴史的遺跡に囲まれてい

るので、最も古い地域の一つだと考えられている西仲宗根（西仲）の方言である。ここは古くから港に向かって開け、また、古くからの住民が変わらず住み、老人と暮らしを共にする習慣があったため、比較的よく方言が保たれたと言える。

特に、satu という小地域単位の、縦子供縦組織があり、小学生くらいから15歳くらいまでの子供達はこのグループ内で育てられた。遊びも、泳ぎも、魚取りも、生活も、年上の子供が年下の子供を指導した。彼等は島の童名（jarabi na:）で呼び合い、方言を日常用語としていた。この組織は、現在60代の人々までは経験したが、その後消滅した。子供達の方言使用機会もなくなっていった。童名も、次の世代の子供達（40代前後）は持っていない。

先にあげた平良市の人口統計は、拡大した市の人口である。旧市街地の人口を、市統計の自治会別人口[4]でみると、方言的に同じだとされている西仲宗根と東仲宗根の合計人口は、4,899人である。このうち方言話者と考えられる60歳以上を知るために、平良市の年齢別人口1995年推移統計表を使うと、平良市全人口33,095人中の60歳以上が約20％である。東洋経済新報社のHP（都市データパック2002年版）では、人口34,896人中65歳以上が16.2％である。それ等に比例して考えると西仲宗根と東仲宗根の方言を話す人の数は794～960人である。正確ではないが大体のイメージは掴めるであろう。都市部のことであるから、他地域からの流入人口も多いと思われる。従って方言話者数はこれより多くはないだろう。

琉球方言は変化に富んでいる。その例に漏れず、平良市の旧市街地でさえ、南と北では少し異なるところもある。同じ平良市でも出身区域の違うご夫婦が、細かい点では「エーッ！そう言うの！？」と驚くこともある。普段は意識していないので気付かないのである。

そのような方言も今では、消滅寸前なのである。次の世代（話者世代の子供達）では、最早、方言による生活は失われた。

（2）平良市史（1979, p. 1 ）
（3）五箇と呼ばれる五つの集落（東仲宗根、西仲宗根、下里、西里、荷川取）。
（4）平良市役所HPによる。東仲宗根（仲屋・旭・高阿良）、西仲宗根（仲保屋・保里一区・二区・添道）の統計による。

最近、平良市久松出身の青年（30歳前後）が方言で作詞作曲して、コンサートを開き大好評である。CDも忽ち売り切れである。彼はお年寄りと同居していたので方言が使える。そして略完全に方言でお爺さんお婆さんの生活を歌いあげ、弾き語りをしながら多くの聴衆をひきつけている。しかしその歌詞は、彼と同世代の人々には翻訳しないと解らない。

　方言大会も大人気だという。それは逆に、方言が日常から消えてしまったことを意味している。現在は、方言の文法が調査研究できる最後のチャンスかもしれない。そして「方言にも規則があるんですか？！」という驚きを、方言話者皆が共有し、その美しさを慈しんで貰いたい。

２．表記

　宮古方言は、本島方言と大きく異なるが、同じ先島(さきしま)といわれている八重山の人々からも「解らない」と言われるほど異なる。そう言われる一つの原因は、これら二つの方言より、音節の形成が複雑なことである。もう一つはいわゆる中舌母音の存在である。

　例えば、最も新しい狩俣（1992, pp. 849-851）は、「宮古本島を代表する、平良方言に基づいて」（平良市のどの地域の方言であるか明記していない）記述しているが、「短母音/a, i, u, I/長母音/a:, i:, u:, (e:), o:, I:/」(5)である。そして、更に説明し、「平安時代の古代日本語の /i/ に対応する /I/, /I:/ は宮古方言に特徴的な音で、唇の丸めをともなわず、舌縁が上の歯茎に近づき、摩擦音のzやsを調音するときのような狭めをつくっている。そして、同時に、舌尖から中舌にかけて持ち上がっていて、呼気が強いと、Iの音色とともに、zのような摩擦音がきこえてくる。単独、あるいは、有声破裂音b, gの後ろでは、有声の摩擦音zをともなって発音され、無声破裂音p, kの後ろでは摩擦音sをともなって発音される。（中略）また、この母音は、語頭においては摩擦が強く、語尾、特にaI, uI, iIのような母音連続に

---

(5) 狩俣（1992）では特殊な記号（[ɿ] に似ている）が用いられているが、ここでは、印刷の都合でこのように転写した。

なって語尾あるいは文末に現れる場合、摩擦が弱くなる。」

問題となるのはこの特殊な文字を用いて表されている母音（[I] で転写した）である。上掲書の語例（p.849）を見ると、

　　/ɪ/:[maɪ] 米、[ɪzu] 魚　　　/ɪ:/:[ɪ:] 飯、[bɪ:] 亥

さらに（p.853）に短母音の例として sadzɪ（手拭い）、kabɪ（紙）等がある。これら全部を同じ母音とするのは賛成できない。

この同じ母音が bɪ, kɪ, sɪ などの音節をつくっているのだろうか疑問である。

この [I] で記されている母音は、宮古方言の特徴として挙げられるが、八重山にも同様な母音がある。しかし宮古にはその他に、<u>もう一つ別の音があるのである</u>。

上掲書母音連続の後部要素母音に対応する、平良西仲の音は、音声的にも母音ではない。この常に [I] で記されている音は、方言により変種がある。数年前に狩俣方言を調査した時、この母音に対応する音は、[I] だか、あるいは [L] と同じ舌の位置で、歯茎に舌尖がつかない反り舌気味の接近音であるか解らなかった。意識的にこの二つの音を作り話者に聞いて貰ったが話者はどちらも「いい」と言ってくれた。狩俣も行政的には平良市に属しているのであるが、ここで述べる平良西仲方言とは全く異なる。

もし、狩俣（1992）が平良市の旧市街地の方言を記しているのなら、2種類の異なる音を同じだと認定しているのだと思われる。

同書における単独あるいは2重母音要素の I に対応する平良西仲の音は、張唇反り舌[注6]の有声摩擦音である。弱まると騒音が無くなり接近音ないし母音に近づく。音韻論的には、他の成節子音同様、成節的子音とした方がよい。この論文では [Z] で記す。

子音と共に音節を形成するもう一つの母音 [I] は、八重山と極めて近い張唇前舌狭母音である。この記号で表される母音は、前舌の緊張度の高い張唇狭母音なのである。そして、その直前の子音は口蓋化しない。無声閉鎖音の直後では渡り音 s が、有声閉鎖音の直後では渡り音 z が聞こえる。

（6）反り舌の程度は低く、舌の裏が調音に与るというより、前舌面が持ち上がり摩擦は舌先及び前舌面と（後部）歯茎で行なわれる。

要するに、平良西仲方言の2種の音が、多くの先行研究で混同されていた[7]のである。しかし、柴田（1972, pp. 36-37）は、平良市西里を扱っているが、以下のように狩俣（1992）とは異なる。「/i/は [ɯ] 乃至その前寄りの母音で、cï, zï は [tsï], [dzï] のような破擦音である。ż[8]は有声摩擦音で破擦音の z とは区別される。」語例は以下。

　　　　　'agaż　東　　'iż　西

柴田（1988, pp. 155-162）に、宮古平良市の音声と仮名表記がある。片仮名の「ス」に半濁点がついている「これだけで、一つのシラブルを表す（成節的な）摩擦音」とする考えに、筆者は賛成である。この論文では印刷の都合上、大文字 [Z] で表した。

つまり、狩俣（1992）他の研究書が採用している [I] は、少なくとも平良旧市街地では、2つの異なる音なのである。[9]

表記は、簡略音声表記によるが、印刷の都合で以下のように書き換える。

　　ɡ→g, dz〜z→z, dʒ〜ʒ→zj, tʃ→c, ʃ→sj, β〜v→v, ŋ→G

成節的な鼻音に関しても音韻的解釈が決定されているわけではない。この方言では [m], [n] が単独で音節を成す。しかしそればかりではなく、例えば動詞否定形の語末音の成節鼻音は、[p] の直前では、[m] に変わる。

　　例　kakaṇ（書かない）→kakam̩ pazɪ（書かない筈）。

ところが、be: ja（かな）の直前では変わらない。kakaN be: ja（書かないかな）

この語は、語末でも [n] でなく前寄り [ŋ] で発音されることが多い。更に語中には、[aŋga]（姉さん）のように軟口蓋閉鎖音直前の軟口蓋鼻音がある。ban（私）は、baŋkaɪ（私に）と発音される。また、摩擦音の直前の鼻音は [n] である時も、[ŋ] らしい時もあり観察が難しい。

単独では bikidum（男）だが、karja : bikidun na？と、質問辞 na の前では n に変わることもある。gazam（蚊）・num（蚤）などは質問辞 na の直前でも m である。音節数が多いと不安定なのかも知れない。[10]

---

(7) 古くは、平山（1967, p. 86）
(8) 柴田（1972）では、z の下に黒点をつけているが印刷の都合で上につけた。
(9) 筆者は、[I] を中舌母音だとは考えていない。詳しくは伊豆山（2002）参照

琉球・宮古（平良）方言の文法基礎研究

そのような事情で、音韻的には［N］を立てる必要がありそうなので、いささか曖昧なのだが、研究が進むまで暫定的に、この論文ではNも適宜採用した。(11) 従って語中では曖昧になった。恣意的だが、単語形を保つ為にNを用いない場合もある。

成節的子音は、上記zの他v, fがあり、pもありそうでsもある。b, g, zなどもそう解釈できるのもあるかもしれない。しかし個々の語については、語中、語末で母音が聞こえることもあり、まだ十分調査していない。

音声学的考察と音韻論的解釈は更に研究観察して、次の機会に改善する。

3．名詞（附助詞）
3.1　語末音と語形変化
3.1.1　主題表示（「名詞＋は」相当の形）

共通語の「（名詞）＋は」に相当する方言形は、名詞語末音による語形変化を示す。これは琉球諸方言に広くある特徴で、首里その他主要方言でも見られる。

語末音　　　　　　　　「は」対応形語例

①長母音　V:→＋ja　　sjinsji: ja(sjinsji: 先生), nuzzju: ja(nuzzju: 糸)

②短母音　a→a:　　　 pana:（pana 花）, musa:（musa 人名）

　　　　　u→o:　　　 fumo:（fumu 雲）, kamado:（kamadu 人名）

　　　　　i→ja:　　　 amja:（ami 雨）, keizja:（keizji 人名）

③子音　　m→mma　 numma（num 蚤）, gazamma（gazam 蚊）

　　　　　n→nna　　 inna（in 犬）

　　　　　v→vva　　 pavva（pav ハブ）

④長子音　m: →m:ma　　m:ma（m: 芋）

⑤短母音　I　に関しては次のように上記の他母音とは異なる。

―――――――――
(10) これらの現象は年代的相違の可能性もある。古い世代の発音は未観察。
(11) 柴田（1988, p.160）の平良方言の音韻仮名表には、「ん（N）」は無いが例文中には出て来る。狩俣（1992, p.850）はnだけでNは無い。平山（1967, pp.136-142）はNを用いている。

231

語末音節	語例
－bɪ ＋ -za	kabɪza（kabɪ 紙）
-gɪ ＋ -za	mugɪza（mugɪ 麦）
-kɪ ＋ -za	kakɪza（kakɪ 垣）
{-kɪ ＋ -sa	iskak(ɪ) sa（iskak(ɪ)[12] 石垣)}
[13] -sɪ → -ssa	junussa（junusɪ 人名）, missa（misɪ 白い飯）
-tsɪ → -ttsa	mattsa（matsɪ 人名）, nnuttsa（nnutsɪ 命）
-dzɪ → -ttsa	tuttsa(tudzɪ 妻), pittsa(pidzɪ 肘), bo:ttsa(bo:dzɪ 坊主)

上記諸例から、語末音が、sɪ, tsɪ, dzɪ の形は、成節子音語末の名詞と同じ型に属すことがわかる。そして、bɪ, gɪ, kɪ では、渡り音が音韻としての位置を獲得したことを除けば、基本的には -a 後接であろう。特に -kɪ の場合、kakɪ（垣）と isɪkakɪ（石垣）の違いは興味深い。これは、琉球方言音韻変化の歴史的研究の際、極めて重要な事例である。

　無声摩擦音と破擦音に、この母音 ɪ が後接した場合は、成節子音末音の名詞と同じ型である。実際、これらの音節では、母音が屡無声化しているのである。[14]

　有声破擦音音節 dzɪ は、音声的には弱まり破擦音で、破裂音は殆ど聞こえないが、摩擦性は弱い。音韻的にはこのように解釈される。このタイプが語形変化の際、無声破擦音で現れるのは興味深い。

⑥　成節子音　z[15]

語例	「は」対応形
maz 米	mazza
piz 針	pizza
iz 西	izza

---

(12) iskakɪ は母音が無声化している
(13) 共通語の影響の可能性も考え、もっと詳細に観察すれば、これらも成節的子音なのかもしれない。今の所単独では母音が聞こえるので、一応このように扱った。尚調査を要する。柴田（1988）は狭母音の直後の語末成節母音をあげている。例　nis（北）
(14) 共通語の影響の可能性も考え、もっと詳細に観察すれば、これらも成節的子音なのかもしれない。今の所単独では母音が聞こえるので、一応このように扱った。
(15) 狩俣（1992）で「2重母音の後部母音」と言われている音の対応音

琉球・宮古（平良）方言の文法基礎研究

juz　夕飯　　juzza
tuz　鳥／鶏　tuzza
a:z　蟻　　　a:zza

この型は、語末音が他の成節子音の場合と全く同様なのである。即ちその語末音を重ねて+aなのである。この重なった子音の調音位置は正確には既述できないが、自然な発音では摩擦音の[z]であるらしい。ゆっくり発音されると前述の子音zが現れ舌が[z]へと動きながら調音されるようである。前述のように、語中の[zɪ]は基本的に破擦音[dzɪ]であるらしく[16]、摩擦性が極く弱いのが普通で、弱い破裂音を伴う事もある。しかし、今問題にしているこの成節子音の語形変化形は、摩擦性が明瞭であるという点で区別される。

3.1.2　対格表示（「名詞＋を」相当の形）

語形変化は、対格表示に際しても現れる。基本的には、助詞「を」相当のjuが名詞に後接する。しかし前項同様に名詞語末音により語形が変化する。

① 長母音　V:　→　+ju　sjinsji:ju(sjinsji: 先生)，nuzzju:ju(nuzzju: 糸)
② 短母音　a　→　o:　pano:(pana 花)，muso:(musa 人名)
　　　　　u　→　u:　fumu:(fumu 雲)，kamadu:(kamadu 人名)
　　　　　i　→　ju:　keizju:(keizji 人名)
③ 子音　　m　→　mmu　nummu(num 蚤)，gazammu(gazam 蚊)
　　　　　n　→　nnu　innu(in 犬)，zjinnu(zjin 銭)
　　　　　v　→　vvu　pavvu(pav ハブ)
　　　　　z　→　zzu　mazzu(maz 米)
④ 長子音　m:　→　　　m:mu　m:mu(m: 芋)
⑤ 短母音　ɪ

　語末音節　　　　語例
　-bɪ　+　-zu　kabɪzu（kabɪ 紙）

---

(16) 柴田（1972, p.36）にも同じ観察がある。

233

-gɪ ＋ -zu　　mugɪzu　(mugɪ 麦)
-kɪ ＋ -za　　kakɪza　(kakɪ 垣)
{-kɪ ＋ -su　　iskak(ɪ)su　(iskak(ɪ)[17] 石垣)}
-sɪ → -ssu　junussu (junusɪ 人名), missu (misɪ 白い飯)
-tsɪ → -ttsu　mattsu (matsɪ 人名), nnuttsu (nnutsɪ 命)
-dzɪ → -ttsu　tuttsu (tudzɪ 妻), pittsu (pidzɪ 肘), bo:ttsu (bo:dzɪ 坊主)

例文

sjinsji: ju tumo:sji ku:.
先生を　お連れしろ

pano:　kai ku:.
花を　　買って来い

kamadu: sa: ri ku:.
かまどを　連れて来い

gazammu kurusji:
蚊　　を　殺せ

pavvu kurusji.
蛇を　　殺せ

kabɪzu kai ku:.
紙　を　買って来い

bo:ttsu tumo:sji ku:.
坊さんを　連れて　来い

mattsu sa: ri iki.
松を連れて行け

jonezo: ju sa: ri piri.
米三　　を　連れて　行け

ke: zju: sa: ri piri.
恵二を　　連れて　行け

mtsu:　kai ku:.
味噌を　買って来い

innu sa: ri iki.
犬　を　連れて　行け

mazzu kai ku:.
米を　買って来い

mugɪzu kai ku:.
麦を　買って来い

junussu sa: ri iki.
ゆぬすを連れて行け

tuttsu sa: ri iki.
妻を　連れて　行け

3.2　助詞の共存関係

　動作主体を表す nu は、ja（主題、取り立て、対比を表す）と共存することはないが、対格表示の ju は、助詞 ba（取り立て対比）と共存できる。従

---

(17) iskakɪ は母音が無声化している

って否定の場合に現れる。例えば命令形は普通 ba を伴わないが、否定命令では ba を伴う。また、ただ眼前の事象を述べるときは現れないが、話題となった時は現れる。眼前の事象を述べる時も、もし対比する事情があれば、ba も出現し得る。

(a) kunu pavvu kurusji.（ba は入らない）
　　この　蛇を　殺せ
(b) kunu pavvu ba kurusɪ na（片目蛇は神様だから殺してはいけないと言われるから）
　　この蛇　を　ば　殺す　な
(c) jonezo: ju ba sa: ri ikan na？（ba が必要）
　　米三　をば　連れて　行かないの
(d) junussu ba sa: ri ikɪ na.
　　ゆぬす　は　連れていくな
(e) mugɪzu du maki uz.（ba は無い）(18)
　　麦　を　蒔いている　（その動作を見ながら言う）
(f) mugɪzu ba maki nu ukɪ？
　　麦　を　ば　蒔いた　か（蒔いてあるか）（意訳：麦は蒔いてあるか）

　この順序は、他の係り助詞「も」相当の mai についても同様で、名詞対格表示の後に mai が続くのである。

(g) junussu mai sa: ri iki.
　　ゆぬす　をも　連れて行け

---

(18) もし、麦と粟と両方蒔くと知っている時なら、ba を用いて「麦は」と対比することもある。

4．代名詞
4.1　人称代名詞

	1人称	2人称	3人称	疑問代名詞
単数 敬称	ban～ba:～ba-	vva unzju	kai～kar-	ta:/to:
複数	banta	vvata	kaita	ta: da:/to: do:

　1人称単数形は、不規則な形を持っている。主格及び所有格（+ga）は、ba-gaと母音が短い（baという形は単独では現れない）。3人称代名詞（文脈指示）がある。これと、同形の指示代名詞は、共に、2形を持っている。後述の指示代名詞 kui～kur-, ui～ur- は、人に対して用いることもできるが、その場に居ない人を指すことはできない。kai～kar- が現場指示に用いられる場合は、発話当時者に無関係の遠い存在として捉えられる人を指す。[19]

　疑問代名詞は2形ある。全く同様に用いられると報告されたが、自然には ta: が多い。話者は、子供の頃から用いて to: の方が多いという感じをもっている。古い世代は ta: だった気がするという報告もある。ta: の方が「いい言葉」という印象があるらしいが、詳細は未調査である。複数形の語尾は、t̲o̲ d̲o̲:/ta: da:と、母音調和をなしている。

　主題語形変化（+ja）や対格語形変化は、不規則語形以外は、名詞に準じる。

(1)　1人称単数形について
　① 電話の相手などに、声で自分が誰であるかを知らせる時
　　　ban.　　私
　② 夜遅く戸を叩く人が居る
　　A：ta: jarja　答えて声で解らせる　　B：ban.　または　ban do:ja.
　　　誰　か　　　　　　　　　　　　　　　私　　　　　　私　です
　③ 道で見知らぬ人に呼びかける

---

(19) 敬意を持つ人に対して用いることは避ける傾向がある。特に ku は避けられる。

琉球・宮古(平良)方言の文法基礎研究

  A：hai hai   B：<u>ban</u> na？
   もしもし   私　か

④ <u>ban</u> tu　<u>vva</u>　tu　kanu ju: gami ma:tsɪki ikadi.
 私　と　あなたと　あの世　まで　一緒に　行こう

⑤ A：<u>ta:</u> ga ikacca？   B：<u>ba</u>ga　ikadi.
   誰　が　行くの   私が　行く

 A：<u>ta:</u> ga　(ga)　kakɪga mata B：<u>ba</u>ga du kakɪga mata.
   誰が　　書くか   私が　書く

⑥ kurja:　<u>ba</u>ga　munu.　<u>vva</u> ga　munu araN.
 これは　私の　もの　あんたの　物　ではない

⑦ ja が後接する形。 <u>ba:</u> ja ja:sɪ: jasɪ.
        私　は　ひもじい

⑧ <u>ban</u>　ju:samai
 私　よりも

⑨ 対格表示と係り助詞
 (a) <u>banu</u>:　sa: ri iki.
   私を　連れて　行け
 (b) <u>banu</u>:　ba sa: ri ikɪna.
   私を　ば　連れて　行くな
 (c) <u>banu</u>:　mai sa: ri piri.
   私を　も　連れて　行け
 (d) ban kai (／banunkai)　fi:ru.
   私に　　　　　　　　くれ

(2) 代名詞も名詞に準じる変化形を持つ。
 ① <u>vvo:</u>　　sa: ri ikadi.
   あなたを　連れて　行こう
 ② <u>vvo:</u>　<u>mai</u>　sa: ri ikadi.
   あんたをも　連れて　行こう
 ③ karju(:)　<u>mai</u>　sa: ri ikadi.
   彼を　　　も　連れて行こう

④ **kurju** mai sa:ri piri.
　　この人　も　　連れて行け
⑤ **ta:** ga　（ga）　kakɪga mata ?　/　**ta:** ga: kakɪga mata ?
　　誰　が　　　　　書くか
　　kai ga du kakɪga mata.
　　彼が　　　書く
⑥ **ta:** **ga** munu ja ?　　答えて **urja:** **kaiga** munu.
　　誰の　　物　か　　　　　　　　　それは　彼の　物
⑦ **vvata:** piri.　　　　　Cf. vvata **mai** piri.
　　あんた達は　行け　　　　　　あんた達も　　行け
⑧ **vva** **Nkai** tura
　　あんたにあげる
⑨ **kaita** **mai** ikɪ du sɪ.
　　彼等　も　行くのだ
⑩ **kaito:**（/kuito:/uito:）**mai** sa: ri piri.
　　彼等を（これら/あれら）　も　連れて　行け
⑪ **kaita:** pukarasɪki munu ja.
　　彼等は　嬉しそう　だ　ね
⑫ **ta:** **mai** ikadja:N na ?　答えて **baga** ikadi.　/　**ta: mai** ikaN.
　　誰　も行かないのか　　　　　　　　私が　行く　/　誰も　行かない

(3)　2人称敬称について

　同輩（同年齢）ないし目下・親しい友には vva が普通だが、同僚はともかく、二つ三つ年下の人から vva と言われる場合は、いささか不愉快な感じがする。二つ三つ年下からは unzju と呼ぶのが望ましいことになる。親しい人や、子供の時から親しんできた目上には、aza（兄さん）、aGga（姉さん）、を童名に加えて呼ぶ。例えば年上の男性で親しい童名カーミの人には　**ka: mi aza:**（カーミ兄さん）のように言う。[20] unzju は、男女の区別なく用いられ

---

[20] 呼称の場合は語末母音が長くなる

る。この語は、成人してから知り合った目上に対する、いささか他人行儀の敬称らしい。目上というのは、先ず年齢が高いということである。

(4)　1人称複数形について
　①　自己称（彼等に対する我等）[21]は無い。他の宮古方言（池間・来間等）で自己称として機能している、du:ta （自分達）と言う言葉は使わない。父親世代が酒酌み交わし親しい人たちと言い合っていた。お互い同士という意味だと理解している[22]。
　　　敵味方に分かれているとき　bantaga bo: ru　　kama nu bo: ru
　　　　　　　　　　　　　　　　我等　　ボール　　あっち　の　ボール
　du: ta は「あの人たちと違って親しい人」と言う感じだという。
　②　banta: ma:tsɪki kaka　(ja:).
　　　私達は　一緒に　書こう（ね）
　③　A：uvata: ma: tsɪki nu kakadi？　別々に書くか一緒に書くかの質問
　　　　　　あんた達は　一緒に　質問辞　書こうか
　　　B：banta: ma: tsɪki kakadi.
　　　　　私たちは一緒に書く
　　　C：mba ju: ma: tsɪkja: kakadja:N.　du: na: sji kakɪ du masɪ.
　　　　　嫌だ　一緒には　書かない　　自分　銘々　で　書く　が　良い
　　　　　　　　　　　　　　　　　　　unaga: buN buN sji kakɪ du masɪ
　　　　　　　　　　　　　　　　　　　各人　それぞれ　で　書くが　いい
　　　D：mba banta:　kakadja:N.
　　　　　嫌　私たちは　書かない
　④　banta mai kaka
　　　私たちも書こう
　　　　　×banta: kakɪga mata.　　私達は書く（べきだ／に決まった状態だ）
　　　　　×banta: du kakɪ.　　　　私達は書く
　⑤　自己称はないが次のような例にはその名残がある。

―――――――――
(21) inclusive と言われることもある。伊豆山（1992）参照
(22) 比嘉夫人はこの語を全く知らなかったという。

239

「私の家」「あなたの家」は、bantaga ja:(私達の家)、vvataga ja:(あなた達の家)

 bantaga jaNkai ku:. vvataga jaNkai ikadi.
 我 家 に 来い あんたの家に 行こう
 但し独身者なら baga ja:(私の家)という

ところが、初めて、他村からやって来た孫に baNtaga ja:(私達の家)とは言いたくない。そう言ったのでは、孫が他人のように感じられる。孫は身内で他所の人ではない。こういう時、孫には、ja: Nkai ikadi.(家に行こう)のように bantaga を付さずに言う。

この方言が、かつては、banta と異なる「彼等に対する私達」を持っていたであろうことが推測できる。これに限って言うなら、banta は exclusive と言えそうである。

(5)「自分」について
① du: ga du: mutsImja:.
 自分 の 体 救え （格言 他を頼るな）
② 遊んでいる大勢の子供達にもう夕方だから、
 unaga jaNkai piri.
 各自の家に 行け これは古い言い方で、現在は次の方が好まれる。
 du: ga jaNkai piri.
 自分の 家に 行け
③ du: sji sji:ti sIsan huz du sji: uz.
 自分 で して 知らぬ 振りを して いる
④「自然に」と言う意味に用いられるのも琉球諸方言に共通である。
 na:ra⁽²³⁾ sji du ui uz. 古い言い方
 du: sji du ui uz. 普通の言い方
 自分 で 生えている （自然に、種を蒔いたわけでなく）
⑤ 貸した物を持ち帰って行く人を見て、その事情を知らず、盗った人が

---

(23) na:ra は再帰代名詞（3人称）として用いられることも稀にある。古い言い方。

居ると言うと、
　　urja:　du: ga munu　(/kaiga munu)　jaru munu.
　　それは　自分の　物　(/彼の　物)　だ　もの
持って行った本人に「何故取って行った」と咎めたなら
　　urja:　du: ga munu　(/　baga munu)
　　あれは　自分の　物　　(/私の　物)

(6) 3人称代名詞　人を指す場合は複数形もあるが、物には用いられない。眼前に居ない人を指すことができる。居る人を指す場合もある。男女の別は無い。
　① kai ga du kakɪ pazɪ
　　　彼　が　書く　筈
　② karja: anci nu kutu su:ca ?
　　　彼は　そういうこと　するか（しない）。（するものか）
　③ kaita: kaki uz suga baNta mai kakɪtsɪka no: ba: sji: ga ?
　　　彼らは　書いている　けど　私たちも　書いたら　何　を　するか（どうか）
　④　3人称複数形が、彼のうち（家族）を意味する場合があるのも琉球諸方言共通である。
　　　urja: kaita ga munu
　　　あれは　彼等　の　もの　彼の家（族）に属する物。例えば鍋、釜等

(7) 疑問代名詞（不定代名詞）　ta: は　to: で置き換え可
　① ta: ga ikacca ?　　　baga ikadi.
　　　誰　が　行くの　　　私が　行く
　② ta: ga munu ja ?　　 kai ga munu.
　　　誰　の　ものか　　　彼　の　物
　③ ta: ga (ga) uki uz ? / ta: ga (du) ukitarja ?
　　　誰　が　起きてる　　誰　が　　　起きた
　④ ta: mai numaN.
　　　誰も　飲まない

241

⑤ sju: tu mma gadu ta:ju:samai pukarasɪkaz
   祖父さんと　祖母さんが　誰よりも　喜んでいる
⑥ ta: da: ga ikadi ?
   誰々　が　行くか

4.2　指示代名詞　等

　人称代名詞と同形語もあるが、物を指示する場合は複数形を用いない。ui, kui などが人を指示する場合は、現場指示であり、敬意度は高くない。

	こ	そ	あ	疑問詞
物	kui～kur-	ui～ur-	kai～kar-	no:
場所	kuma	uma	kama	nza
連体修飾	kunu	unu	kanu	nzji

　琉球諸方言の常で、「こ、そ、あ」は本土方言と必ずしも対応しない[24]。この件の詳細は未調査である。平山（1967, p. 142）にみえる izji（どれ）は、この方言には無い。

　「どの」に相当する nzji は人に対しては用いられず、代わりに ta:(誰) が現れる。

　　　　ta:　ga　vva　ga　anna　rja ?
　　　　どの人が　あんたの　お母さん　か

　尚、表示しなかったが、kanci（こう）anci（そう）はあるが、kunci や unci は無い。

(1)　指示代名詞の例文
　①　例えばたくさんある名前の中から、求める名前を探しあてた時、指さしながら
　　　kui !　　と言って人に知らせる。
　　　これ！

---

(24) 柴田（1988, pp. 220-226）参照

　　　　　　　　　　　　　　　琉球・宮古（平良）方言の文法基礎研究

　　大勢の中から、例えば泥棒の顔を探しだした時なども指して　kui！
② <u>ui</u>　tu　<u>kui</u>　　対にする場合は、このような対で用いられる
　　それ　と　これ
　　<u>ui</u>　tu　<u>kui</u> tu　Nzji ga masɪ ?
　　それ　と　これ　と　どっち　が　いいか
③ <u>ui</u> du masɪ. ／ <u>kui</u> du masɪ. ／ <u>kai</u> du masɪ.⁽²⁵⁾
　　これが　いい　これが　いい　　あれが　いい
④ <u>ui</u>　ga munu.
　　この人の　もの　　（そこに居る人を指す）
⑤ <u>urju</u> mai sa: ri piri.
　　この人　も　つれて　行け
　　<u>urju</u> mai fai.
　　これ　も　食べろ
⑥ <u>kurja:</u>　baga munu.
　　これは　私の　もの
⑦ <u>nzji</u> ga ga ／ <u>nzji</u> ga: takakarja: ?
　　どれ　が　どれ　が　高いか
⑧ <u>kui</u> ga du takakaz.
　　これ　が　　高い
⑨ <u>ui</u> ga du jasɪkaz
　　それ　が　　安い
⑩ <u>kurja: no:</u> jarja ?　　答えて　　m:nuz do.
　　これは　何　だ　　　　　　薩摩芋飯　だ
⑪ <u>urja:</u> saki dara:.
　　これは　酒　だね
⑫ どの実が落ちるか収穫を迷っていると農業をよく知っている人が
　　<u>karja</u> utiN.
　　あれは　落ちない

―――――――
(25) 注19参照、自分ではまだ詳しく検討していない、手元にあるものを指してはコ、ソ共に可

⑬　nza Nkai （ja）rja？　　　道で出会った時の挨拶言葉
　　どちらへ　　　　答えて　　kama Nkai.
　　　　　　　　　　　　　　　あっちへ
この場合 uma は近くて、見えているところなので使えない。kama なら遠いから良い。一寸そこまでと言いたいなら　　umata Nkai.
　　　　　　　　　　　　　　　　　　　　そこらへ
⑭　no: nu ga atarja　?　答えて　o:hai du jataz.
　　何　が　あったの　　　　　　火事　だ
⑮　uito: mai / kuito: mai sa: ri piri. （対格形に係り助詞が後置）
　　　彼等をも　　　連れて行け
⑰　kunu pambinna mmamunu.
　　この　天ぷらは　美味しい
⑱　unu ka: ja hukamunu ja:.
　　この　井戸　は　深い　ね
⑲　kanu ffa: zo: gi （ja:）.
　　あの　子は　美しい（ね）

(2) 関連して副詞的な語をあげておく。
　①　ance: naraN.
　　　そうはできない。（借金の利息を）決める時借方の申し出に対して
　②　kance: naraN.　同上
　③　kanci du ssI　やって見せている。模範を示している。
　　　こういう風にする　（見えるとき）
　④　ふすまに落書きしそうな孫に
　　　ance: naran do:　　×kance:
　　　そうしたら　ダメ！　悪いことを咎めるとき
　⑤　no: sjiga su: cca:.
　　　どういう風にするのか　（指導を頼む時）
　⑥　no: tiga ikja:
　　　何故　行くのか

5．話し手の優位性　（モダリティー的側面）

　この方言も他の琉球諸方言同様、話し手中心である。そのため、動詞の形を、本土方言に倣って終止形等とすることはできないのである。命令、意思などのようなモーダルな要素の強い文のみならず、叙述文からも話し手のムード的要素を除くことはできない。特に宮古では、動詞の形そのものに話し手のムード的要素のあるのが目立つ。動詞・形容詞の全体系は、この話し手優位の上に成立している。本土共通語と基本的に異なるこの点は、注目しなければならない。この論文では動詞全体に関する詳細な報告はできないが、基本的なモダリティー的要素への認識を得るために、少しだけ説明する。

5．1　動詞語形変化の検討

　動詞の語形変化を簡単に記す。本土共通語と比較すれば、基本的語形変化形は少ない。解り易いように、伝統的な枠組みに従って表示する。

語形	終止	志向	接続	已然[26]	命令
書く　kak-	kak-ɪ	kak-a	kak-i	kak-ja	kak-i
起きる　uk-i-	uk-i-（z）	uk-i	uk-i	uk-i-rja	uk-i-ru

　上記の形に接辞・助詞などが後接・後置する。見られるように、連用形・連体形の形がない。それらは、終止形と同じなのである。否定形は志向形と同形＋N（kak-a-N）である。志向形というのは、意思・勧誘を意味する。終止形の括弧は後に説明する。伝統的活用形の体系から見れば、いかにも不規則的である。

　問題になるのは、この接続形である[27]。この形は頻出し且つ重要である。u-が後置される構文ではこの形が現れる。

　過去は kakɪ-ta-z, uk-i-ta-z （終止形＋taz）だが、kaki u-ta-z, のように kaki＋u- の連語があり、「ている」だとされて、継続相といわれている[28]。しかし

---

(26) 平山（1967）と狩俣（1992, p.858）にはない。前者には kaki（接続形）もない。
(27) 狩俣（1992, p.857）では「標準語の第2中止形に意味・機能的に対応する」。p.855に，継続相 numi:uɪ とあるのは、この中止形だと考えるのであろうが機能が違いすぎる。
(28) 狩俣（1992, p.855）

以下の例で見るように必ずしも継続ではない。その行為が既に出現したのを、話し手が確認するのである。従って、目にしていない3人称主体の行為とは共起し難い。

否定は kak-a-N 否定過去は kak-a-tta-N である。否定形には2種あるが、過去否定形は1種だけである。

kak-i（継続形）の独立性を示す事項はいくつかある。その一つ、構文上重要で、一般言語学的にも興味深い事実がある。質問文とその答えにおいて、この形 kaki に後置される助詞が異なるのである。これはその行為の出現か否かを問うもので、話し手の認識判断に関わる。この形は、その行為の出現を示すいわば不定形的な用法だと考えられる。以下にこの形をまず、検討する。

眼前に行為が無い場合
(1) 道で出会って書くことになっている書類の話をする。(眼前に行為はない)
kaki umma?[29]
（今）書いているか（現在書きつつあるか）
(2) 応答は次のようであろう
（2-1） kaki du uz.
書いている（執筆中）
（2-2） Nnama du kaki uz.
今　　　書いて　いる（現在執筆中）
（2-3） kaki du ukI.
書いて　おく（書いてある。書き終わった）
（2-4） Nnada kakaN.
まだ書かない。
(3) 友人に花の種をあげたがちゃんと咲いたかどうか尋ねる。(花の時期)
saki umma ?　　答えて　saki du uz.
咲いて　いるか　　　　　　咲いて　いる

---

(29) 正式には、uzmma だという。

眼前に行為が見える場合
(4) 今目前で行なわれている行為を確かめる為
　　(4-1)　vva　kaki ummma？　　　　　　　答えて　kaki du uz.
　　　　　あんた　書いているよね（書いていることの確認）書いて　いる
　　(4-2)　vva　uki u:mma？　（尋ねる人はそうだと思っている）
　　　　　あんた　起きているよね（起きていることの確認）
　　　　　　　　　　　　　　　　　　　　　答えて　uki du uz.
　　　　　　　　　　　　　　　　　　　　　　　　　起きている

　このように uz は話し手の確認に出現する。そしていわゆる接続形が示すのは、その行為が既に出現していることなのである。眼前にその動作がある時とそうでない時の違いを見れば明らかであろう。質問と答えとの呼応関係からも同様なことが解る。
(5) 今居ない人の事を尋ねる。
　　atsuko: kaki umma？
　　敦子　　書いて　いるか　（敦子のことを必ず知っている人に尋ねている）
(6) atsuko: kaki uz be:ja？
　　敦子　　書いているかしら（知っているかどうか解らない人に）

独立的用法
　あまり見られない。(6)が普通だが（6-1）もあり得る。
(6) 黒板に悪いことがかいてあるので咎めて
　　ta: ga kaki　ukja:？
　　誰　が　書いて　あるのか（誰が書いておいたのか）
　　　　　　Cf. ta: ga kakɪtarja　　この場合は過去も可
　　　　　　　　誰　が　書いたか
　（6-1）子供などの用法（あまり正しくないのではないかというが）
　　ta: ga kaki:？
　　誰　が　書いた

247

質問辞 nu と、du の挿入呼応

　例外的にせよ単独でも出現し得るのに、接続という名は相応しくない。更に、質問の場合、質問辞として infix のように nu が現れ、答えでは du と交代する現象がある。構文上極めて重要である。

(7)　頼んだ物を書いてくれたかまだかを尋ねる

　　（7-1）　baga tanumtaz muno: kaki nu ukɪ ?
　　　　　　　私が　頼んだ　ものは　書いて　おくか（あるか）
　　（7-2）　ɴ：kaki du ukɪ.
　　　　　　　うん　書いて　おく（ある）

質問のポイントは書いたかどうかにあり、その対象が nu によって示されるのである。答えはそれを du で明示する。

＋nja:ɴ（無い）

　琉球諸方言に、「とうとう……しちゃった」と期待に反した動作・状態が現れたのを意味する形式がある。「無い」を後置する連語である。この方言にもそれがあり、5段対応動詞では、接続形＋nja: ɴ＝kaki nja: ɴ（書いちゃった）がそれにあたり、1段動詞でも同様　uti nja:ɴ（落ちちゃった）がある。kak-a-ɴ（書かない），uk-i-ɴ（起きない）が否定であるのに反し、kak-i-nja: ɴ，uk-i-nja: ɴ では、その行為が既に出現している。その出現状態を話し手は否定したいのである。

　①　pavvu　du　kurusji nja: ɴ.
　　　蛇　を　殺し　ちゃった（殺す積りで無かったけど）

　②　ja: nu　du　jaki nja: ɴ.
　　　家　が　　焼けちゃった

　③　kaci nja: ɴ.
　　　勝って　しまった（弱いから、自分も人も勝つと思わなかったのに）

　④　sɪni nja: ɴ.
　　　死んでしまった

⑤　uki nja: N.
　　起きちゃった（赤ちゃんをせっかく寝かせたのに）
⑥　uti nja: N.
　　落ちちゃった（収穫を楽しみにしていた木の実が台風で）

以上の事実を踏まえて、ここでは語形変化の基本だけ記す。動詞体系の詳細は後に譲る。括弧内は、先行研究の伝統的用語である。下は伊豆山の仮称である。語幹末音が、音韻的に［I］後接の音節を作らないものは、語幹末音が成節子音となる。Ex. num-（飲む）

基本的な5段対応動詞と1段対応動詞をあげる。（不規則変化は今考慮外にする）

意味	語幹	（終止形）[30] 不定（非過去）	（継続形） 出現（未完了）	（志向形） 未然（未来性）	（なし） 已然	（命令） 命令
書く	kak-	kak-I	kak-i	kak-a	kak-ja	kak-i
起きる	uk-	uk-i-（z）	uk-i	uk-i	uk-ir-ja	uk-ir-u

過去形　　不定形＋ta-z　ex. kak-I-ta-z, uk-i-ta-z　（書いた、起きた）
連体修飾　不定形＋名詞　ex. kak-I-pazI, ukiz-pazI　（書く筈、起きる筈）
否定形　　未然形＋N　　ex. kakaN, ukiN　（書かない，起きない）

1段対応動詞の過去形形成と連体修飾形形成の相違は注目すべきである。形態素-zが話し手の認識を示すと理解される。

1段対応動詞 uk-（起きる）の変化形は注目に値す。5段対応動詞が母音を変えているのに、1段対応動詞は語幹＋iの形を持ち、あたかもそれが新たな語幹を形成したかのようなのである。そして出現形と未然形以外は、話し手の出現確認形態素が加わっているかのごとくである。表に見るように、1段対応動詞の終止形は、5段対応動詞と並行的でない。後章で説明する。これら動詞の全体系は後に改めて報告する予定である。

---

(30) 狩俣（1992, p. 858）は ukiI を終止形としているが kakI と同じ環境出現するのは -ki で kakIm：ukizm がむしろ例外である。

5.2 話し手の認識と動詞の形
5.2.1 言い切りの形への考察（1）

　伝統的に終止形とされている形の用法の概要を見る。平山（1967, pp. 138-139）、狩俣（1992, p. 855）などが、終止形～いいきりのすぎさらずとしてあげている形を検討してみる。また、1段対応動詞の終止形に関する問題点も見る。

　　　4段対応型動詞　　　kak-I　　　　1段対応型動詞　　　uki-(z)
　　　　　　　　　　　　書く　　　　　　　　　　　　　　起きる

終止形

(1) 5段対応動詞

　例えば書く人を決める時

　① ta: ga du kakɪ gamata？
　　　誰　が　書く　か（書くべきか、書くと決まる状態か）

　② 上に答えて A：baga kaka-di.　　×　vvaga kakadi　×kaiga kakadi
　　　　　　　　　私が　書く　　　　あんたが書く　　彼が　書く

　　　　　　　　B：ba: ja kaka-dja: N.[31]
　　　　　　　　　私は　書かない

　　　　　　　　C：kaiga du kakɪ pazɪ
　　　　　　　　　彼が　書く　筈

　　　　　　　　D：karja: kaka-N.　×　karja: kakadja: N.
　　　　　　　　　彼は　書かない　　　　彼は　書かない

　　　　　　　　　karja: kaka-N pazɪ
　　　　　　　　　彼は　書かない筈
　　　　　　　　　他人のことだから言い切れないので pazɪ）

　　　　　　　　E：vva　　kaki.
　　　　　　　　　あんた　書け

　　　　　　　　F：vva　kakadi？　　×　vva　kakadi.
　　　　　　　　　あんた 書く？

---

(31) kakamba（書かない）が、kakadja:Nと全く同様に用いられる。kakambaの詳細は未調査。

話し手の意思を含む形は、話し手以外には用いられない。更に否定の形も2形あり、話し手自身の行為には、話し手の意思を含む形式が現れる。動作主体が話し手以外なら、話し手の判断・推測・希望・等等、話し手のムード的要素が入るのである。上の会話に続けて

  G：atsuko ga du <u>kakɪ gamata</u>.
    敦子　が　書く（べきだ）（書くと決まっている）
  H：araN atsuko: kakaN.
    いや　敦子は　書かない（と私は判断する）

(2)　1段対応動詞
 ① atsa: naNzjiN ga <u>uki gamata</u>.
  明日　何時に　起きるか（起きるべきか、起きると決まるか）
 ② sjicizjiN du <u>uki gamata</u>.
  7時に　起きる　　　（起きるべき、起きると決まっている）
    Cf. sjicizji Ndu　ukiti　　umui　　uz.
      7時頃　に　起きようと　思って　いる
 ③ sjicizjiN du <u>ukidi</u>.
  7時に　起きる（そういう積りである）

この最も多く用いられる形 <u>uki gamata</u> には <u>-z</u> が現れないのである。この形が連体修飾形であると見るなら、以下のように z が現れる筈なのである。

 ④ <u>ukiz</u>　<u>pazɪ</u>
  起きる　筈

この ukiz 形は禁止の形にも現れる。

 ⑤ kak<u>ɪ</u>na.　　書くな
  uki<u>z</u>na.⁽³²⁾　起きるな

以上のように、この -z 形には話し手の認識が入っていると考えられる。

---

(32) 同化した形 uki<u>nn</u>a（起きるな）もある。

251

現在の習慣的行為

　平山（1967）が終止形としてあげている na'a'ju'u kakɪ （名前を書く）は、単語としてはあるが、実際の文として、このままでは現れない。狩俣（1992）では文例が無い。[33]

① mainitsɪ tigabɪ ju kakɪ　　動作主体は1人称でも3人称でも可。2人称不可。
　　毎日　　手紙　を　書く　　　（現在の習慣的事実）
　　mainitsɪ sjicijiɴ ukiz.
　　毎日　　7時　に　起きる　　（現在の習慣的事実）

② ɴkjanna guzjiɴ du ukitaz.　　ɴnama uipɪtu ɴ nari hacizjiɴ ukiz.
　　昔は　5時に　　起きた　　　今　老人　に　なり　8時　に　起きる

③ karja:(／ba; ja)　itsɪɴmai rukuzjiɴ du ukiz.
　　彼は　（／私は）　何時も　　六時　に　起きる

　3人称主体の文は、話し手がその事実を、はっきり知っていることを意味するのである。

duのある文（行為出現が決まっている）

① 書く人がいなくて、誰か書く人が居ないかと求められている時。
　　　　nnzji nnzji.　baga du kakɪ.
　　　　どれ　どれ　　私が　　書く　　（書くことになる）

② 書く人を決める会議に遅刻したので、決まったのに自分だけが知らないので尋ねる。
　　　　ta: ga ga (／du)　kakja？　／　ta: ga du kakɪ gamata rja？
　　　　誰　が　　　　　書くの　　　誰　が　　書くのだ
　　　　atsuko ga du kakɪ (ga mata). ／ baga du kakɪ (ga mata).
　　　　敦子　が　書く　　　　　　　　私が　　書く
　　　　atsuko ga du kakɪ？　　　　　×　vva ga du kakɪ？
　　　　敦子が　　書くの

---

(33) 狩俣（1992, p.855）は、「すぎさらずは基本的には、動作動詞の場合には<u>未来</u>を（<u>下線筆者</u>、中略）表す」としている。

③　kakɪ suga du zɪ: ja pita.
　　書く　けど　字　は　下手　（書く能力はあるが、常々書いているが）
④　unaga buNbuN　sji kakɪ du masɪ.
　　各人　それぞれ　　で　書くの　が　いい
⑤　kakɪ guffanjaN.
　　書きそうもない
　　uki gu: fu du az.
　　起きそうである
⑥　１人称複数形とは共起しない。
　　×banta: du kakɪ（ga mata）.
　　　私達は　書く　　　代わりに
　　baNta:　kaka.
　　私達　書こう
　　banta:　ma: tsɪki kakadi.
　　私たちは　一緒に　　書こう
　　ma: tsɪki　uki.
　　一緒に　起きよう

　以上のように、終止形と言われてきた形は、現在の習慣的行為、出現が決まっている行為、能力、などを表すので、「未来」で括ることはできない。また、③④は名詞的であり、⑤は派生語を形成している。このような理由で、一種の不定形と考えた方がいいと思われる。この形が banta や vva と共起しないことも注目しなければならない。このような理由で、１段対応動詞の終止形 -iz は、話し手の認識を表す形態素 -z が後接されたと考える。

5.2.2　言い切りの形への考察（２）

　平山（1967, pp. 138-139）は、kakɪm という形を終止形の項であげている。狩俣（1992, p. 855）では、いいきりのすぎさらずの形に、kakɪm「書く」という形をあげ、「この形はあまり用いられない」としている。しかし西仲では次のようである。平山（1967）も述べているように、常に do を伴う。

4段対応型動詞　　　kak-I-m do　　　1段対応型動詞　　　uki-Z-m do[34]
　　　　　　　　　　　　書く　　　　　　　　　　　　　　　　起きる
　do は、名詞、形容詞（語幹、その他）、否定形、動詞不定形など色々な形式に後置され、そうだと断定し、話し相手に教える気持ちを表す。例文をあげる。

① urja: ca: do.
　それは　茶　だよ
② ance: naran do.
　そうしては　ダメ　だ！　　（悪いことを咎めるとき）
③ baka: baka do.
　若いん　だよ
④ pIkarasI ki do.
　嬉しそうだよ
⑤ sINkja: patarakI du sI do　　（主体は1・3人称とも可）
　死ぬまで　　働く　　よ

次にこの do を伴う終止形とされている -m do 形式の例文をあげる。
① kai ga kakIm do:.　　vva pu:ci iki kaki.
　彼　が　書く　よ　　あんた　早く　行って　書け
（彼が書こうとしているから、自分が書かせたい人に、だからあんた早く行って書け。）

　kakIm do.
　書く　ぞ　　これから書く（　動作主体、1人称）
② 雲や潮の状態で天気の具合を判断することができる人が
　atsa: kazji　nu　hukIm do:.
　明日は　　風　が　吹く　よ　（台風だよ）
　atsa:ami　nu　huzm do.
　明日は雨　が　降るよ

---

(34) このZの摩擦は極めて弱く殆ど無く聞こえないこともあるくらいで、母音に近い。

③　月下美人を育て良く知っている人が
　　kunu pana:　　kju: ga ju:　sakɪm do:.
　　この　　花は　　今日　の　夜　咲くよ
④　子供が大切なものにいたずら書きしそうなとき、気付いた人が傍の人に教える。
　　kakɪm do:！
　　書くよ　　（とめなさいと続けたい）
⑤　A：ukizm do.　　（自分からすすんで起きる）
　　　　起きるぞ！　　　　答えて
　　B：ukibusɪkatsɪka: ukiru.
　　　　起きたいなら　　起きろ
　　A：kai mai ukizm do
　　　　彼　も　起きるよ　（起きそうに動いている人を見て）
⑥　anci ɴɡjamasɪ: ɴɡjamasɪ sji uztsɪka: jarabi nu ukizm do:.
　　そんなに　　喧しく　　　していると　子供　が　起きる　よ

　この形式は、2人称代名詞とは共起しない。「しようとしている」「まさにする」などと訳される。話し相手のことは、その人自身の方が話し手よりよく知っているのだから、相手の行為については用いることがない。これは、話し手の行為では意思を表し、話し手以外についてはその行為がなされようとしているとの話し手の判断なのである。

5.2.3　言い切りの形へ考察（3）

　この方言では、話し手の意思に関わる形が複数ある[35]。これらは、話し手のモーダルな要素と動作主体がどのように関わるかを示して興味深い。特に1人称複数主体は注目すべきである。共通語では「書こう」「起きよう」などと翻訳される。

---

(35) 平山（1967, p.138）は志向形として、4段対応動詞 kaka（書こう）、kakaQtii（書こうと）、kakadi（書こう）、1段対応動詞 uki（起きよう）をあげている。

255

4段対応型動詞	① kak-a	1段対応型動詞	uk-i
	② kak-a-di		uk-i-di
	③ kak-a-tto		uk-i-tto
	④ kak-a-cca		uk-i-cca
	⑤ kak-a-cu		uk-i-cu
	⑥ kak-a-ttsai		uk-i-ttsai

翻訳は「書こう」だが、<u>独り言にはならない</u>。自分の気持ちを相手に言っているのである。以下に説明する。

① kak-a 動作主体は1人称である。質問文には現れない。1人称複数 baNta と共起するときは、いわば <u>inclusive</u>（全員）である。
  (a) kaita: kakja: uraN suga baNta: zi: <u>kaka</u> / <u>kakadi</u>.
      彼らは　書きは　してない　けど　私達は　字　書こう
  (b) 向こうのグループを見て自分達もと思い
      baNtamai ma:tsIki <u>kaka</u>.
      私達　も　一緒に　書こう
  (c) baNta: kama Nkai bIza ja:
      私達は　あそこに　座ろう　ね
  (d) baga ika.
      私が　行こう
  (e) da: da: baga <u>kaka</u>.
      さあ　さあ　私が　書こう
      nzji baga <u>kaka</u>.
      どれ　私が　書こう
  (f) baga <u>kaka</u> ja:.
      私が　書きましょう　ね　（同意を求めている）
② kak-a-di 動作主体は1人称。質問文では2人称及び疑問代名詞も可。
  (a) <u>ta: ga kakadi</u>？
      誰　が　書くの　　答えは（b）のようになる。

(b) baga kakadi
 私が　　書こう
 kijo ga du kakI.　　×　kijo ga du kakadi
 清　　が　書く
(c) baga kakadi na?　（書き難そうにしている人に）
 私が　書きましょう　か
(d) vva kakadi?　答えて　mba kakadjaN.　×　kakaN
 あんた　書く　　　　　いや　書かない
 vva　　ukidi?
 あんた　起きる
(e) ke:zja: kakadi be:ja?　×　ke:zja: kakadi?
 恵二は　　書く　　かね
(f) atsuko: kakadja: N　ti du uzu.
 敦子は　書かない　とて　いる（のを私は認めている。書かないと言っている。）
 atsuko: kakadja: N　tsa.
 敦子は　書かない　ってさ
(g) 自分が行きたいと思って仲間に
 m: na ma: tsIki ikadi na?　/　banta: ma: tsIki ikadi.
 皆　一緒に　　行こうか　　私達　一緒に　　行こう.
(h) 向こうに行く人（々）が見えたので
 bantamai ma: tsIki ikadi na?
 私達　も　一緒に　行こうか？（私が言い出して皆の意見を聞いている）
(i) 答えて、賛成なら　　ikadi.　　ikadi.　（二回繰り返してもいい）
 　　　　　　反対なら　　banta: ikadja: N.
 　　　　　　　　　　　　私達は　行かない
(j) vva　kaki uz suga ba:ja kakaN / kakadja: N.
 あんた　書いてる　けど　私　は　書かない／書かない（この場合は双方可）

③ kak-a-tto

動作主体は1人称単数だけで2人称・3人称にはない。2人称への質問文も無い。1人称が動作主体の質問文は、申し出の意味で相手に念をおす時に現れる。

(a) baga <u>kakatto</u>.　　　　×　vva ga <u>kakatto</u>　　×atsuko ga <u>kakatto</u>
　　私が　書くよ

(b) baga <u>kakatto</u>？　　　×vva ga <u>kakatto</u>？
　　私が　書きましょうか？　　Cf. baga kakadi？　穏やかな尋ね方

(c) 出かけ際に、「出かけるよ」と子供に声をかけるとき
　　<u>ikatto</u>.
　　行くよ

(d) 挨拶の「さようなら」
　　<u>piratto</u>.
　　去るよ

(e) <u>ukitto</u>？　　　　　　vva:　zjo: bun　nuvvi uri.
　　(私) 起きるよね。　あんたは　よく　寝ていなさい

(f) 隣の人のお酒があまっているから勿体無いと思って
　　baga　numatto？
　　私が　飲みましょうか (いいですか)

(g) A：zjo: bun vva ga izjiru.　　B：izjitto？　　A：N: izjiru.
　　いいよ あんたが 貰いなさい　貰っていいの？　うん 貰いなさい

④ kak-a-cca

前項より話し手の意思が積極的である。

(a) 宴会で、自分は酒を飲まないから、誰か飲む人いないかと探している
　　　A：ta: mai numadjan na？　B：baga numacca.（／numadi.）
　　　　誰か　　飲まないか　　　私が　　飲む　　　飲む
前項(f)の代わりに、「隣の人のお酒があまっているから勿体無いと思って」いきなり baga <u>numacca</u>. と言っては失礼になる。

-tto は、他にする人が（居なかったら）のような気持ちで、他の誰かがし

琉球・宮古（平良）方言の文法基礎研究

てもいいような気持ちがある。
　-cca は、他にしたい人がいても、私がするというような意図がある。
- (b) 　×　vva ga kakacca?　　　代わりに　vva ga kakadi?
　　　　　あんた　が　書くか　　　　　　　あんた　が　書く
　　　　　×atsuko ga kakacca?　　代わりに atsuko ga du kakɪ?
- (c) 　A：no: ju ga kakacca?
　　　　　何　を　書くの？（書く人に決まった。では、何を書くのかと尋ねている）
　　　　B：tigabɪ ju（sai）．丁寧に言えば　tigabɪ ju du kakɪ gamata sai.
　　　　　手紙　を　だ　　　　　　　　　　手紙　を　　書く　のだ
- (d) 　A：ta: ga su: cca?　　　B：baga sudi. ／baga su: cca.
　　　　　誰　が　する　のか　　　私が　する　私が　するのだ
- (e) 　baga su: ca?
　　　　　私が　しようか

この形式は本来の意味の他に、イントネーションを変えて反語的に用いられる。

- (f) 　希望者を募る時
　　　　ta: ga　ikacca:?
　　　　①誰　が　行くのか？　②誰が行くものか（誰も行かない）二通りの意味がある
- (g) 　ta: ga　numacca?!
　　　　誰　が　飲むか！　（例えば人の飲み残しを誰がのむものか！）
　　　　taga　ukicca!
　　　　誰が　起きるか　（起きるものか、起きはしない）
- (h) 　ke:zja:　kakacca?!
　　　　恵二は　書くか　（書くものか、書きはしない）

⑤　kak-a-ccu と ⑥　kak-a-ttsai

　この形は１人称主体にだけ現れ得る。質問文にはならない。複数形主体では、exclusive（話し相手を含まない）であると思われる。

259

(a) ba: ja <u>kakaccu</u>.　　×vva <u>kakaccu</u>. / ?　　×atsuko: <u>kakaccu</u>. / ?
　　　私　は　書く　　あんた　　　　　　敦子

(b) 何度も起きろ起きろと言われた時や、起きるか起きないのかと問い詰められた時
　　<u>ukiccu</u>.
　　起きるよ　　ちょっと反抗的

(c) 1人称複数が動作主体の時は <u>exclusive</u>（話し相手が入らない）である。
　　相手に向かって　　<u>vvataga</u>　<u>kakadakara</u>:　　<u>bantaga</u>　<u>kakaccu</u>.
　　　　　　　　　　あんた達が　書かないから　私達が　　書く

(d) 薬など飲み難いものを飲めといわれて
　　　<u>numattsai</u>.
　　　飲むよゥ　（強いて飲んでみせる）

(d) 何度も書け書けと言われ
　　　<u>kakattsai</u>.
　　　書くよゥ　（しつこく言うから書くよ）　　　Cf. <u>kakadi</u> は素直

(e) 1人称複数動作主体の時は相手が同じことをすると解っていて自分達も進んでする。
　　<u>banta</u> mai <u>ikattsai</u>.
　　私達　も　行く
　　　　　　Cf. <u>banta</u>:　<u>ikaccu</u>.　　相手は行かない。

単数の意味するのは、「自分だけでは、いやいや仕方なくする」のだが、複数では、はっきり「する」意思表示を意味するところが面白い。自己称は無いが代わりに動詞では区別があるところも興味深い。

5.3　話し手の直接経験

　平良方言も他の琉球諸方言と同様、話し手の直接経験（話し手の見聞）が重要である。自分以外が動作主体である時は、話し手がそれを<u>直接経験（見聞）</u>しているのである。即ち話し手自身の認識・判断が含まれている。
　例をあげる。

琉球・宮古（平良）方言の文法基礎研究

① ba: ja kakattaN.⁽³⁶⁾
　　私　は　書かなかった

② atsuko: kakattaN.
　　敦子　は　書かなかった．（敦子が書かなかったことを見聞して知っている）

　自分以外が動作主体の場合は、その行為を<u>直接経験</u>していることが必要である。もし<u>直接見聞した</u>のではなく、噂や伝聞で知ったのなら、<u>tsa</u>を付さなければならない。

②' atsuko: kakattaN tsa.
　　敦子は　書かなかった　って

　全ては、話し手の目を通しているのであるから、過去以外の方が複雑になってくる。

③ ba: ja kakadja: N.
　　私　は　書かない

× atsuko: kakadja:N.

　前述のように、この形式は話し手の意図に関わるから２・３人称主体では不可である。自分以外の人の気持ちは、判定できないのだ。その場合は次のようである。

④ atsuko: kakadja: N ti du uzu.
　　敦子は　書かない　と言っている（のを私は認めている。書かないと言っている。）

⑤ atsuko: kakadja:N tsa.
　　敦子は　書かない　ってさ

　以上のことは、あまり知られていないが、琉球諸方言の重要な特色である。宮古平良方言もかつて「書かれる」ことは無かった。「書く」ことは、話者の選択肢の中に無い。姿の無い話し手などはいないのである。ちなみに、最近地元でも記録が計画されているが、仮名を用いるためには、常に発

---

(36) １人称動作主体に出現する kakadja: N（書かない）の過去は無い。

261

音と表記の問題があり、なかなか難しい。

　方言では、常に具体的な話し手が存在するのである。動詞・形容詞などに対して、本土共通語同様に終止形という枠組みをあたえるのでは、誤解を招くようになる。文を言い切る形にには、なんらかの意味で、話し手のモーダルな要素が含まれるのだから。

　過去というのは、抽象的な、現在に対する過去ではない。話し手が過去に経験したことなのである。

　例えば、明和津波という歴史的事実を述べる時、誰も230年前のことは経験していないのだから、いわゆる「過去」で語ることはできない。

⑥　meiwa nu tukjanna husaciNmi gami su: nu du agaz taz tsa:
　　明和 の 時には ふさちん まで 潮 が あがった とさ（明和大津波の話）
必ず tsa を必要とする。

　このような歴史的事実でなくても、自分の経験したことを語った次のような場合

⑦　jarabi pada: agata nu uriga:Nkai tago: katami mizi hum ga kaju: taz
　　子供 頃は 向こうの 降り井戸に 桶 担いで 水 汲み に 通った
これは、話し手自身の経験なのである。例えばこの話者の夫人が、何度もこの話を聞き、その頃の状況も良く知っていて、この uriga: のことも見て知っているとしても、karja:(彼は) を加えて、この通りに言うことはできない。最後に tsa を付さなければならない。

　まして例えば筆者が方言で「平良の昔の生活」と言う話をするなら、当然 tsa が必要である。

　更に面白い例がある。自分で実際経験しもしないのに知った振りしてあれこれ言う人に

⑧　vva mi: nu sItarja？
　　あんた 見 た のか
のように言うと、返すことばもないので、仕方ないから次のように言う。

　　tsa.
　　だってさ
例をあげると

⑨　A：kɪno takanohana makidu sɪtaz.
　　　昨日　貴乃花　負けた　んだよ　これは実際（テレビを含む）見たの意味。
　　昨日その時間には他のところで仕事をしていた筈なのにと思い、
　　B：vva ma: nti mi: nu sɪtarja？
　　　あんた　本当に　見（質問辞）たのか
　　A：tsa:. /anci: tsa　　　　（実は聞いたか読んだかしただけだった）
　　　だとさ。そうだってよ
⑩　この事情は、共通語との兼ね合い次第で、現代生活では誤解を招きかねない。
　　kanu ko: hosja zjinna fi: du to: sen sɪtaz.
　　　あの　候補者　銭　くれて　当選　した
　　これは、共通語の翻訳と違い、そのことを実際に見て知っていることになってしまう。tsa がなければ名誉毀損になりかねない。
　　動詞・形容詞などの体系は、全てこの基本の上にある。

6．形容詞

　宮古方言の形容詞は、同一規則により、かなり自由に形成される。動詞語幹との共通性も高いし、性質を表す名詞からの形成も生産的のようにみえる。
　形容詞は大きく2類に別けられる。一つを描写形容詞と名付け、もう一つを気分形容詞と呼んでおく。形の上で違いがある。気分形容詞語幹末音は基本的に-sɪ である。[37]
　もう一つの違いは、話し手内部表現の気分形容詞語幹には、ki が後接する。そして、他者の内部認識表現を可能にさせる。描写形容詞では ki の代わりに gi が現れる。そして、容態描写表現の形容詞語幹に対して、話し手の認識・判断を追加する。

---

(37) 逆は真でなく、sɪda:sɪ（涼しい）のような例もある。また、-sɪ 以外もあると思われる。

6.1　形容詞の修飾的用法と叙述的用法
(1) 語幹による修飾用法（描写形容詞）
気分形容詞に、この用法は無い。
- (a) taka-gi: 高い木　Cf. ki: 木
  taka-gi ɴkai du kazja: ataz.
  高木　に　風は　あたる　（＝出る釘は打たれる）
- (b) kagi pana　美しい花
  maitusɪ kunu kinna kagi pana nu du sakɪ.
  毎年　この　木には　美しい花　が　咲く
- (c) kagi kɪmu　美しい心
  美しい心（心の綺麗な人に言う）
- (d) aparagi ffa　綺麗な子
  kanu ffa: aparagi ffa.
  あの子は　綺麗な子
- (e) sɪda:sɪ tukara
  涼しい　所
- (f) tsu: kazji,　tsu: pɪtu
  強風　　　　強い人
- (g) pɪguru ca:(38)
  冷えた茶
- (h) ×pukarasɪ sju:,　×uka: sɪ pɪtu
  嬉しい　お祖父さん、　恐ろしい　人

話し手以外の人が、嬉しいか、恐いか、ひもじいか等、その人の内部状態は、見た様子からは、解らない。だから、このような語幹用法はないのである。代わりに後述の
- (h') pukarasɪ ki sju:,　　uka: sɪ ki pɪtu,　ja: sɪ ki ffa
  嬉しい様子をした祖父さん、恐い様子をした人　ひもじい様子をした子
  （嬉しそうな祖父さん、　恐そうな人、　ひもじそうな子）

---

(38) しかし pɪguri pɪtu（冷たい人）

琉球・宮古（平良）方言の文法基礎研究

(2) 語幹の繰り返しによる叙述的用法

　語幹の繰り返しによる、叙述的用法と修飾的用法がある。語幹の語末音は、普通長音化する。その際母音が次のように変化することが多い。a→a:, i→e:, u→o:。母音 I は変わらず長音化する。語幹末が ki/gi では、変化しないのが原則のようにみえる(39)。繰り返しの場合は、語によっては強調的な意味になることもある。例　imi: imi (40)（とても小さい）、uka: sI ukasI（とても恐い）。

(a) <u>taka: taka</u> ja:.　　（高いものを見て）
　　高い　　　　ね　　　（相手に同意を求める。ja が無ければ独り言）
(b) kurja: <u>upo: upu</u> ja:.
　　これは　　大きい　ね
(c) <u>pukarasI: pukarsI</u>.
　　嬉しい　　　（独り言）
(d) uma: <u>sIda:sI sIdasI</u> na ?
　　そこは　　涼しい　　か
(e) unu ka: ja <u>asa: asa</u> ja.
　　その 井戸 は 浅い　ね
(f) urja: <u>aka: aka</u> (/sso: ssu / ffo: ffu) ja:.
　　それは　赤い　　（白い　　黒い　）　ね
(g) kju: ja <u>pisje: pisji</u> ja.
　　今日 は 寒い　ね
(h) ba: <u>ja ja:sI ja:sI</u>.
　　私 は 　ひもじい
(i) 以下単語の形のみあげる。
　　<u>kaZ: kaZ</u> 軽い, <u>kagi: kagi</u> 綺麗, <u>apragi: aparagi</u> 綺麗,
　　<u>zo:gi: zo:gi</u> 綺麗, <u>atsI: atsI</u> 暑い, <u>psI: psI</u> 薄い, <u>ffa: ffa</u> 暗い

---

(39) おそらく歴史的には派生であろう。
(40) この母音 i は変わらない

(3) 語幹の繰り返しによる修飾用法
　　副詞的用法
- (a) <u>taka: taka:</u> vvi:.
　　　高く　　売れ　　（値下げしないで売れ）
- (b) <u>upo: upu</u> nasji.
　　　大きく　なせ　（収穫する芋など、まだ小さいから畑にもう少し置いて大きくしろ）
- (c) <u>tsu: tsu</u> du huki uz.
　　　強く　　吹いている　（台風の話）
- (d) <u>tsu: tsu:</u> du pakaz.
　　　強く　　計る　（竿秤で、厳しく計る）
- (e) <u>taka: taka</u> tubi.
　　　高く　　飛べ
- (f) <u>taka: taka</u> du utaz.
　　　（値段）高く　だった　（高い値段がついていた）
- (g) 　ba: ja <u>ja:sɪ ja:sɪ</u> du uz.
　　　私は　ひもじくしていた　（ひもじかった）
- (h) <u>pisje: pisji</u> du uz.
　　　寒く　している　（寒いといっている／寒くしている）

この du uz との連語は多用され、本来の副詞的修飾とはいい難いが、ここにあげた。

　　名詞修飾用法　nu（の）を伴う
- (a) <u>upo: upu</u> <u>nu</u> pɪtu ja:.　　　　（<u>upo: pu</u> とも）
　　　大きい　の　人　だね
- (b) <u>taka: taka</u> <u>nu</u> pɪtu
　　　（背の）高い　の　人
- (c) <u>taka: taka</u> <u>nu</u> ki: ja:.
　　　高い　の　木　だね

266

琉球・宮古（平良）方言の文法基礎研究

(d) ko: ko nu pɪtu ja:.
　　貧しい　　の　人　だね
(e) ujaki: ujaki nu pɪtu ja:.　　　　×ujaki nu pɪtu は無い
　　富んでいる　　の　人　だね
　　(ujaki pɪtu 富んでいる人　　karja: ujaki 彼は金持ちだ)

気分形容詞語幹の繰り返し形は、原則、名詞的修飾にはならない。
(f) ×ja: sɪ ja: sɪ nu ffa:. 代わりに前項であげたのと同様 ki 後置の形を用いる。
(f') ja: sɪ ki⁽⁴¹⁾ ffa ja:.
　　ひもじそうな　子　だね

(4) 語幹＋munu による叙述的用法
多用される。叙述的用法としては、先ず最初に思い出される形式である。
(a) mma munu ja　　　　　（二人で食べながら言い合う）
　　美味しいね
(b) お茶の熱いのがいいか冷たいのがいいか尋ねる。
　　atsɪ munu na: ?　　pɪguru munu na: ?
　　熱いの　　か　　冷たいの　　か
(c) hantagi munu ja:
　　忙しい　　ね　　（挨拶言葉）
(d) unu ka: ja huka munu ja:.
　　この井戸　は　深い　ね
(e) kurja: upu munu ja:.
　　これは　　大きい　ね
(f) ffu munu ja:.
　　黒い　ね
(g) 欲しがっていたものをあげた時

---

(41) ja: sɪ ki のように ki の付いた形は2回繰り返されることは無い

267

　　　　A： pukarasɪ: pukarasɪ na？　　B： N:(ba: ja) pukarasɪ munu.
　　　　　　嬉しい　　　　か　　　　　　　うん（私　は）　嬉しい
(h)　工事の音がして喧しいところで奥さんに話し掛ける。
　　　　Jagamasɪ munu ja:
　　　　うるさいねー
(i)　A： vva kasamaffanjaN？　　B： ban mai kasamasɪ munu.
　　　　あんた　腹立たない　　　　　　　私も　　腹立たしい
　　　　A： kai mai kasamasɪ munu be:ja:.　(42)
　　　　　　彼　も　腹立たしい　　かなー
(j)　kju: ja pisji munu.
　　　今日　は　寒い
　　　uva pisji munu na:？　　　　ban mai pisjimunu.
　　　あんた　寒い　　か　　　　　　私も　寒い
(k)　高いビルの下で見上げながら「高いね」と言う時は
　　　taka: taka du uZ　　　より　　taka munu ja:.　の方がいい
　　　高いんだ　　　　　　　　　　高いね
(l)　kagi munu jataZ.　(43)　　　kagi munu jataN do.
　　　綺麗だったよ　　　　　　　　綺麗だったんだよ

6.2　独り言の言い切る形

話し手が感じたことであり、相槌を求めるわけではない。全ての語幹に sa: が後置されて出現する。基本的な形の一つである。気分形容詞では、当然話し手の気持ちを表し、他人のことに言及するのではない。

(a)　taka-sa:　　　　　　　高い
(b)　pukaras(ɪ)-sa:　(44)　嬉しい
(c)　mma-sa:　　　　　　　美味しい
(d)　pisji-sa:　　　　　　　寒い

---

(42) 話し手以外の人の気持ちは解らないから be: ja が必要。
(43) 現在形は無い。つまり kagi munu jaz のような形は無い。

琉球・宮古（平良）方言の文法基礎研究

(e)　atsɪ-sa:　　　　　　　暑い
(f)　tsu:-sa:　　　　　　　強いな
(g)　gabjo:-sa:　　　　　　痩せてるな
(h)　zo: gi-sa:　　　　　　綺麗だ（普通自分に対しては言わない）
(i)　ja: s(ɪ)-sa:　　　　　ひもじいな　3人称に言う
(j)　pɪguru-sa:　　　　　　冷たいな（氷など触って）
(k)　imi-sa:　　　　　　　 小さいな
(l)　psɪ-sa:　　　　　　　 薄い
(m)　ŋgjamas(ɪ)-sa:　　　　やかましい
(n)　kasamas(ɪ)-sa:　　　　腹がが立つ　腹立たしいな
(o)　sukara-sa:　　　　　　塩辛いな
(p)　vuda-sa:　　　　　　　太っているな

6.3　描写形容詞と気分形容詞

　人の気持ちを表す気分形容詞と、人が物や様子などについて認め表現する描写形容詞は、厳しく区別されている。前述のように、基本的に、話し手優位なのだから、そのような別があるのは当然なのである。自分の気持ちは解るが、他人の気持ちはわからない。他人の気持ちはその様子から見てとるか、そう言っているのを認めるかである。

　気分形容詞として「嬉しい」に当たる pukarasɪ で例示する。一方、描写形容詞の形は（'）で対比させる。

(a)　a:　pukarassa.　　　　(a')　takasa:.
　　 あー　嬉しいな　　　　　　　 高いな
　これは独り言的で、ba: ja（私は）も出現しない。話し手の気持ちに決まっのている
　他人から何か貰った時などは　ba: ja pukarasɪ munu.（私は嬉しい）
(b)　欲しかったものを貰って喜んでいる人に

---

(44) これらは pukarassa: のように発音される。

269

（vva）pukarasɪ: pukarasɪ na？　　答えて　　N: pukarasɪ munu.
　　　（あんた）　嬉しい？　　　　　　　　　　うん　嬉しい
　　　pukaraffanja:N.　　　　　　（b'）　takaffanja:N.
　　　嬉しくない　　　　　　　　　　　　　　　高くない
(c)　3人称が主体の時
　　客から、土産を子供に貰ったので、他室の子供に渡してきた。そこで、その客が言う。
　　　pukarassa: sji nu uz？　　答えて　pukarassa: sji du utaz.(45)
　　　嬉しく して いる（喜んでいる）　　嬉しく して いた（喜んでいた）
　それから、二人で隣室の子供の様子をそっと見に行って、
　　　pukarassa: sji du uzzja.
　　　嬉しく して いる（喜んでいる）ね　　（と互いにいい合う）
　この場合、共通語なら、「嬉しいんだね」も可だが、この方言では、このように-sa:の形式に動詞の s (I) sI（する）を添えて、「喜ぶ」のような動詞形だけが可なのである。
　この動詞形は自由度が高く、次のように1・3人称ともに可となる。2人称には質問文だけに出現する。
　嬉しそうな様子の人に
　　　A： pukarassa: sji nu uz？　　　B： ba:ja pukarassa: sji du uz.
　　　　　嬉しくして（質問辞）いるの？　　私は　嬉しく して いる
　　　　　atsuko: pukarassa: sji du uz.
　　　　　敦子は　嬉しく して いる
つまり話し手以外が主体の時は、「嬉しい気持ちが表れる動作を行なっていると判断する」という形式だけが可になる。一方描写形容詞には、この形式は無い。
　×（c'）takasa: sji du uz.
　　　　　　高く して いる
　塀などを高く造る時、このように言うことはできない。塀は自分から変化

---

(45) 今子供を見てきたから uz（でいる）より、utaz（でいた）。共通語の「いる」とは異なる。

270

することはできないのだから、塀が自分でする行為ではなく、人間の行為だとする表現をとる。

(c-1) taka fu du nasji uz.
　　　高　く　　なしている

また、本来の動詞形をもつものには、この形は無い。

(c-2) vudai du uz　　×vudasa: sji du uz.
　　　太っている　　　動詞　vuda-iz（太る）がある。

この形式をとらない語幹を例示する。

　　×asasa: sji:uz.　　×bakasa: sji: uz　　×gabasa: sji: uz[46]
　　　浅い　　　　　　　若い　　　　　　　老けて

6.3.1　気分形容詞語幹＋ki[47]

ここにもう一つ、話し手以外が主体となる場合の重要な形式がある。これは、殆ど報告されることがなかった。気分形容詞は、話し手の気持ちを表すものだのに、話し手主体には用いられない形がある。気持ちの現れ（様子）を見て「そうである」と判断する形である。従って話し手とは共起しない。

(a) 喜んでいる様子を遠くから見ている二人が話し合う。
　　karasɿ ki ja:.
　　嬉しくしている　ね　　（嬉しそうだね）

(b) 試合に勝って喜んでいるチームを見て、
　　kaita:　karasɿ ki munu ja.
　　彼等は　　嬉しそう　　だね

(c) unu sju: ja karasɿ ki ja:.
　　あの　祖父さんは　嬉しくしているね　（嬉しそうだね）

(d) karasɿ ki sju: 　　ja:.
　　嬉しくしている　祖父さん　だね　（嬉しそうな祖父さんだね）

(e) vva karasɿ ki ja:　（そわそわしている人に）
　　あんた　嬉しそう　だね

---

(46) 代わりに gabari du uz.（老けている）
(47) この形が日本語上代の形容詞シク活用の語尾シキと対応するのは偶然とは考え難い。

271

上述のように形容詞語幹と同様に、修飾用法と叙述用法とがあるが、繰り返しの形 pukarasɪki: pukarasɪki は無い。前述したように、
  unu sju: ja pukarasa: sji du uz.（嬉しくしている）はある
  ×unu sju: ja pukarasɪ ki du uz.（嬉しい様子をしている）
代わりに
(f) pukarasɪ ki nari du uz.（嬉しい様子になっている）である。例えば負けそうな試合が逆転すれば、応援団について、このように言う。

この ki 形は、話し手（ba:）とは共起せず、話し手以外（3人称）にのみ可である。外観・様子から判断する形なのだから当然のことである。

6.3.2　描写形容詞語幹＋gi の形式

上述の気分形容詞語幹末音は sɪ だった。語幹末音が広母音の描写形容詞では、ki の代わりに対応の有声音 gi 後置の語が形成される[48]。taka gi sa sji:uz は不可だから、機能的には描写形容詞と同じである。

(a) 洞窟の前に立って、入りかけで、
  kamaɴkai paztsɪka ffa-gi ja
  あそこに　入ったら　暗い（気配だ）よね
(b) 灯台のそばに行って
  umu: taz ju: zsa taka-gi ja:
  思った　より　高い（様子だ）よね
(c) 宮古の空港に着いて、涼しい機内から外を見て、
  atsɪ-gi ja:.　（atsɪgi sa:.／atsɪgi munu. などと交換可）
  暑い（気配だ）ね
(d) kunu ja: ja ujaki-gi ja:.
  この　家　は　金持ちそうだね
(e) 初めて入った海なら、その色から判断して
  huka-gi ja:. と言い huka-gi du aiba……（気をつけろと続ける）

---

(48) fufa-kaiba はあるが、fufa-gaiba は無い。

琉球・宮古（平良）方言の文法基礎研究

深い（よう）よ。　　　深そうだから……
実際入ってみて　hukaffanja: N.
　　　　　　　　深くない
(f)　火にかけた鍋を取ろうとして、atsɪ-gi ja:. 応えて　atsɪffanja: N.
　　　　　　　　　　　　　　　熱そう　　　　　　　熱くないよ
(g)　huka-gi ka ja:.
　　　深い　井戸　（深いと思われる井戸、深そうな井戸）
(h)　taka-gi sa.
　　　高そうだ

この gi は、多くの描写形容詞語幹に現れるが、語幹によって共起しないものもある。(49) そして、かなり自由度が高い。動詞にも後置され、似た意味を付け加えることができる。
(i)　Nivvi du uz gi （munu）ja.
　　　眠って　いる　気配だ　ね
(j)　kaki uz gi ja.
　　　書いている様子だね
(k)　kakati: uz　gi ja.
　　　書こうとしている　様子だね

次のような例を見ると、gi～ki は、音韻的な規制によるものかもしれない。気分形容詞は、原則、語幹末音が -sɪ であるが、次のような例もある。
(l)　paNta gi ja:
　　　忙しそうだ
更に　karja: pantagi munu ja:.（彼は忙しいね）の他に、気分形容詞と同様に
(m)　karja:　panta sji: du uz.
　　　彼は　　忙しがっている

---

(49) ×gabjo:gi（痩せている）

273

(n) karja: paNtakaztsıka:　ikaiN.　　×　paNtakaiba
　　彼は　　忙しければ　　行かれない
(o) ba:　ja paNtakaiba ikadja: N.
　　私は　忙しいので　　行かない

(m)(n)(o)の用法から見ると、後述するように気分形容詞であると解る。しかし paNta gi なのだから、ki～gi の選択は語幹末音の無声化によるものかもしれない。今後語彙を増やして観察する。

6.3.3　語幹＋fu の形式

ki は、話し手以外が主体である。では、話し手主体ではどうなるか。前述のように、pukarassa: sji du uz は、1・3人称に可であった。そのように、1・3人称に可の形が -ki の系列にもあるだろうか。

fu は、1・3人称と共起する。その性質状態を認めるという、話し手の判断を表している。そして、du az（ある）が後置されることが多く、naz（なる）が後置されることもある。文を終える形として頻出するから、琉球形容詞の歴史的解釈として「ク＋アリ」説[50]などが唱えられることにもなるのである。

例示のように　fu du az ～ fu du naz　のような連語で出現する。文末に独立で出現することはない。1・3人称と共起する。常に話し手の認識である。

(a) ba: ja pukaras (ı) fu du az.[51]　≅　ba: ja pukarassa: sji du uz.
　　私は　嬉しいと認める状態なのだ　　私は　嬉しく　して　いる
(b) そろそろお乳をあげる時間に赤ちゃんが泣いていたら
　　urja: ja: s(ı) fu du az.　　×ja: sı mmunu
　　あれは（私が）ひもじい（と認める）状態にあるのだ
(c) kai ga pukarasıfu du az.　≅　kai ga pukarassa: sji du uz.
　　彼が　嬉しい（と認められる）状態である　　彼が　嬉しく　して　いる

---

(50) 平山（1967, p.141）
(51) 殆ど ja: ffu du az. のような発音である。

琉球・宮古（平良）方言の文法基礎研究

(d) gabjo: fu nazjijo: n nigai.
痩せ（と認める）状態に なるように 願え　　（gabjo:gi は無い）

(e) urja: takafu du az.
これは 高い　　　　　（正札を見て高いと解った）

(f) 子供の服を買おうとして見て、大きいと思った時
unu ffanna upugi ja:.
この 子には 大きそう だね　　　そして着せてみて
upu fu du az.　　大きい（と認められる）状態なのである。

(g) karja: kasamasɿ fu du az.
彼は 腹立たしい（と認められる状態）なのである
ba: ja kasamasɿ fu du az.
私は 腹立たしいのである

(h) kagi fu du ataz do
美しく あったんだよ （相手は見ていない）

6.4　語幹十kam do

　この形式は質問文にならない。常に do:を伴う。共通語には「そうなる」とでも訳せる場合が多い。恒常的な状態を表すのではなく、変化して「そうなのである」という、話し手の認識を表している。動詞的である。質問文にはならない。

　平山（1967, p.141）によるこの形の歴史的解釈は、音韻対応から見ても、意味用法から見ても受け入れ難い。また、狩俣（1992, p.860）は「takakaɪ と takakam の ɪ 語尾と m 語尾の違いは、動詞のいいおわる形の kakɪ「書く」と kakɪm の違いに、パラレルに対応する」としている。しかし、同書 p.855 の動詞説明では、kakɪm「書く」という語形があるが、「この形は平良方言ではあまり用いられない」としているので、どういう「パラレル」なのか解らない。

　恒常的状態性質の語幹では、この形式は起こり難く、-fu naz（なる）が現れる。

(a) bata mutsɪkja hwa:dakara:　ja:sɪ kam do.
　　おなか　満ちるまで　食べないと　ひもじくなるよ
(b) お使いに行かせる。
　　kama nu ja:Nkai ikɪtsɪkara:　ffa kam do.
　　向こうの　家　に　行ったら　暗くなる　よ
　　応えて　ffa fu du az na？
　　　　　暗くなるの？
(c) jamatu Nkai ikɪtsɪkara: pisji kam do:
　　内地　に　行くと　寒いよ
(d) mja:ku Nkai ikɪtsɪkara; atsɪ kam do:
　　宮古　に　行くと　暑いよ　　答えて
　　mja:ku Nkai ikɪtsɪkara:atsɪ fu du az na？
　　宮古　に　行ったら　暑い　の　か？（atsɪkam の質問形は無い。）
(e) kasamasɪkam.
　　腹立たしくなる
(f) 高い（taka-）のような恒常的な意味の単語は、この形になりにくい。
　　例えばスーパーなどで、安売りの時間制限があるから早く行かないと……のような時、
　　takakam do:. は不可とは言えないが takafu nazm do:. の方が好ましい。
　　　　　　　　　　　　　　　　　　　高く　なる

6.5 語幹＋kaz

平山（1967, p.141）では終止形としてあげられている。[52] しかし、その終止形に複数の形があり、終止形の意味がわからない。先に述べた形容詞の2大類別の特徴が、この形に現れるから、その意味でも重要である。この形は言い切りではあるが、ある物を見てその性質状態を述べるのではない。以下のように質問文への答えであることが多い。そのせいか、話者達は、共通語終止形の対応形として求められても、思い出せないくらいである。つまり、

---

(52) 平山は、takakaZ を「高くあり」に対応する (p.141) としているが、takafu も高くなのである。

琉球・宮古（平良）方言の文法基礎研究

その性質状態が存在していることは、話し手に関わりなく決まっている。話し手は「何がそうであるか」を選ぶだけなのである。この形はさらに語形変化する。

以下に実例を示す

(a) nzji ga ga (/ga:/ nu ga) taka karja: ?
どれ が 高いのか
kui ga du taka kaz.
これ が 高いのだ
taka kaiba du ka:n
高いので 買わない

(b) nzji ga ga (/ga:/nu ga) jasɪ karja ?
どれ が 安いのか
kui ga du jasɪ kaz.
これ が 安いのだ
jasɪ kaiba kai.　　　　jasɪ kaiba du kai kɪtaz.
安いから 買え　　　　安いから 買って来た
jasɪ kaztsɪka ka:di.　/　kai ku:.　/　ka:tto.
（もし）安かったら 買おう　買って来い　　買おうね

(c) nzji ga ga zo: kaz ?
どれが 良いのか
kui ga du zo: kaz.
これが 良いのだ

(d) ta: ga (du) vuda karja ?
誰 が 太っているか
kaiga du vuda kaz.
彼 が 太っているか

(e) ta: ga (du) pukarasɪ karja ?
誰が 嬉しいのか （喜んでいるのか）
(e-1) kai ga du pukarasɪ kaz.
彼 が 嬉しいのだ

277

(e-2) baga du <u>pukarasɪ kaz</u>.
私　が　　嬉しいのだ
(e-3) baNta ga du <u>pukarasɪ kaz</u>.
私達　が　　嬉しいのだ
(e-4) N: na ga du <u>pukarasɪ kaz</u>.
皆　　が　　嬉しいのだ
(e-5) sju: tu mma ga du ta: ju: samai <u>pukarasɪ kaz</u>.
祖父さんと祖母さんが誰よりも　嬉しいのだ

以上のように終止形といわれている形は、述べたてる文には出現せず、その主体「何が」の選択判断を必要とする文に現れる。だから、du を伴うのである。

提題の文、つまり ja を伴う文に出現することはない。例えば、

× 　<u>karja: pukarasɪ kaz</u>. と会話の初めに、言い出すことはないのである。
　　彼は　　嬉しいのだ

○ 　<u>karja: pukarasɪ fu　du az</u>

他人の気持ちは解らないのだから、こう言い切らず、次のように言うのもいい。

karja: <u>pukarasɪ ki ja:</u>. 　　彼は嬉しい様子だね（嬉しそうだね）
karja: <u>pukarasɪ kaz pazɪ</u>. 　　彼は嬉しい筈

性質状態の主体が判断主体（話し手）と同じであるか異なるかは、-k- の系列に共通して、反映される。自分のことは、話し手が自分で確認できる。他人のことは、確認できないのである。条件を表すのにも同様なことがある。kaiba は、話し手と共起するが、それ以外は kaztsɪka: と共起する。

(f) <u>pukarasɪ kaiba　buduradi</u>.
　　嬉しい　　ので（から）踊ろう　　（話し手）

(g) vva ga <u>pɪkarasɪ kaztsɪka:　buduri fi:ru</u>
　　あんたが　嬉し　ければ　　踊ってください

(h) karja: <u>pɪkarasɪ kaztsɪka:　buduri uz</u>.
　　彼は　　嬉しいから　　踊っている

(i) (ba:) ja:sɪ kaiba munu hwadi.
   (私)　ひもじいので　食べ物　食べる

(j) (unu ffa) ja:sɪ kaztsɪka: tsɪsɪ numasji.
   （あの子）ひもじい（と認められる）から　乳　飲ませろ

(k) upu kaiba du ka:ttaɴ.
   大きい　ので　買わなかった（見て大きいと解った）

(l) upu kaztsɪka: ka:ɴ.
   （もし）大きかったら　買わない　（まだ見ていない）

(m) atsa: paɴta kaiba du ikaiɴ.
   明日は　忙しいから　行かれない（話し手）

(n) karja: paɴta kaztsɪka: ikaiɴ.
   彼は　忙しいかったら　行かれない

(o) pukarasɪ kaiba buduztaz.
   嬉しく　してるので　踊った（話し手）

(p) karja: pukarasɪ kaiba du buduztaz.
   彼は　嬉しくしているので　踊った

過去では、du が入る事により karja: が pukarasɪ kaiba に構文的には直接関係しなくなる。pukarasɪ kaiba が非人称的になるのだと考えられる。

ところで、描写形容詞の方にも確認の差が見られる。疑問詞のある質問文の言い切りの形として -karja: という形が出現する。条件と併記する

(q) taka karja: ka:djaɴ.
   高いから　買わない　（高いと既に決まっている）

(r) jasɪ karja: kai.
   安いから　買え

(s) ta:ga pukarasɪ karja:?　（嬉しいことは決まっている）
   誰が　嬉しいのか

(t) ɴzji nu ga taka karja ?　（高いことは決まっている）
   どれ　が　高いのか

6.6 特殊な形

(1) -kari

次のような形が現れるのは、特別の場合（決り文句）だけのようである。しかし同じ形が副詞的に現れることがある。

(a) kɪnna jo:kari nussa tsu:kari.
着物は 弱くあれ 主 は 強くあれ （願いの言葉 [53] 着物に負けるなよ）

(b) gaNzu:kari ura:ci.
頑丈 で いらっしゃるように （元気でいてください）

(c) A：vva zo:kari umma？ B：zo:fu du az.
　　　 元気　　　 か　　　 元気　　 だ

(d) A：vvataga sju:ja zo:kari umma？
　　お宅の　祖父さんは　元気です　か？
B：o:zo:fu du az.　／　zo:zo du uz.
　はい 元気　　です 元気　　　です

(e) pja:kari ku:.　　（＝pja:pja ku:）　pja:kari ukiru.
　早く　来い　　　　　　　　　　　　早く　起きろ
cf. pja:fu du az （早い）、pjakaiba （早いので）

以上の用例を見ると狩俣（1992, p.860）のいう命令形とするより、中止法に近い。出現確認の不定形なのではなかろうか。

6.7 形容詞と動詞の共通性

6.7.1 形容詞と動詞化

気分形容詞では、3人称がその主体である時、sji:du uz（している）を後置して動詞形で表現する。このことは既に述べた。この連語は動詞として機能する。次例のような特別な表現の例を見ると、この「する」の意味が良く解る。

(a) ujakja: sji: uri.
金持ちでは いなさい （ずっと金持ちでいなさい）

---

(53) 新しい着物を身に着ける前に、柱に着せる真似をして、こう願ってから着ていた。

(b)　taka:　taka sji: uri.
　　　　高く　していなさい　　（高い地位を保ちなさい）
これは、塀を高くするなどと物に対しては不可。塀は高さが決まっている。
自分の努力で変わらない。こういうと、塀が自分で高くする感じだという。
　(c)　悪い子なので、罰にご飯上げないよという場合
　　　vva　ja: ssa: sji: uri.
　　　あんたひもじい状態でいろ　（ひもじくなっていろ）
これらは、次のような表現と同じである。次例は形容詞ではない。
　(d)　o: mbja:rja:　　sji du uz.　　no: fu ka arja:.
　　　青い顔は　　　している　　　どうしたのか
「青い顔をしている」は共通語にもあるから気持ちがわかるであろう。
動詞としての機能を果たす例を付け加える。
　(e)　takassa ssu:　jo:.
　　　可愛く　しろ　（可愛がれよ）
　(f)　kanu ffa:　ukassa:　sji du uz.
　　　あの子　恐く　している　（恐がっている）
　(g)　ukassa:　suminna
　　　恐く　させるな（恐がらすな）
ついでに気分形容詞の形と意味の理解のために数例付け加える。
　(h)　uka: sɪ ki pɪtu
　　　恐い　人　（包丁など振り回す人）
　(i)　包丁を振り回す人を見ている人が言う。
　　　uka: sɪ ki munu ja:/　uka: sɪ: uka: sɪ　ja:
　　　恐そうだ　ね　／　恐い　ね
　(j)　傍でそれを見て震えている子供に気付いて既述の（f）のように言う。
　　　kanu ffa:　ukassa:　sji du uz.
　　　あの子　恐く　している　（恐がっている）

6.7.2　形容詞語幹の自由度

語幹が単語としての独立性をもつとは言えないが、形態素よりは自由度が

高いことは既に見た。ここでは、改めて動詞語幹と形容詞語幹の類似性と名詞的類似性の例をあげる。

(a) takakaiba ka: dja: N. ≅ taka: taka: jaiba du ka: dja:N.
　　高いので　買わない　　高いの　であるので　買わない（名詞的）

(b) vuda wa:　　　　　　　　太り豚
　　vuda: vuda ja:.　　　　　太っているね
　　vudafu du az　　　　　（痩せてるか？）太っている
　　vudakaiba　　　　　　　太っているので
　　ta: ga du vudakaz?　　　誰が太っているのか
　×vudasa: sji: uz　　　　　代わりに動詞が現れる。
　　vudaiz
　　太る
　　mmamunu faiba du vudaiz. （vuda kam は殆ど使われない）
　　美味しいもの食べれば太る
　　bantaga wa: ja budai du uz.
　　我が家の　豚　は　太って　いる
　　vva nnapi vudairu.
　　あんた もっと　太れ
　　vudai du masɪ.
　　太（っている）がいい
　　vudakaiba du du mutsɪ kani uz.
　　太っているから体　もちかねている

(c) gabjo: wa:　　　　　　　　痩せ豚
　　gabjo: sa:　　　　　　　　痩せてる（独り言）
　　kai ga du gabjo: kaz　　　彼が痩せている
　　gabjo: fu nari　　　　　　細くなれ
　×gabjo: sa sji: uz　×gabjo:gi　代わりに動詞が現れる
　　gabjo: du sji: uz　　　　1・3人称に可
　　　やせ　　している

琉球・宮古（平良）方言の文法基礎研究

```
gabjo:   s(I) su:.
痩せ     しろ      （痩せろ）
fa:dakara:   gabjo:   s(I) sIm do:.      ×gabjo:kam
食べないと    痩せ     するよ
```

6.8　語形の纏めと語形変化

　平山（1967, p.141）の平良方言動詞活用表をあげる。語例は「高い」である。表記は簡略化した。非常に不均整である。

		未然	連用	終止	連体	条件	過去	命令
k	takak-	-ara	×	-aI	-aI	-aiba	-ataI	-arisiQti
f	takaf-	×	-u	×	×	×	-uduataI	×

　語幹をkとfに分けている。「クアリ」とか「カリ活用(54)」とか言われる由縁である。
　この活用表は、足りない形（takak-arja）もあり、また、f 語幹過去形として連語（taka-fu du ataz）まで活用表にあげているので賛成できない。

　語形の整理をする。
(1)　描写形容詞も気分形容詞も、①語幹＋s-のグループと　②語幹＋k-のグループとに分けられる。①はその対象とする物がそのように「なっている」状態を示し、②は話し手がそのような状態であることを「認めている」のである。
(2)　気分形容詞は、当然ながら制限が多い。話し手自身の内部状態なのか、他人なのかによって、取り得る形に制限がある。
(3)　描写形容詞は、常に話し手の認識の対象に向けられるから、気分形容詞のように、話し手と無関係に「そうなっている」を意味する形は無い。
```
        karja: pukarassa: sji du uz.        ×takasa: sji du uz
        彼は   嬉しくしていると（私は）認める
```

---

(54)　狩俣（1992, p.861）

(4) 語幹は、munu に前接する他、繰り返しにより、単語として独立し、叙述機能（taka: taka ja）を持つ。副詞的修飾機能（taka: taka vvi）や、名詞的修飾機能（taka: taka nu ki:）も持ち得る。

(5) 全ての形容詞語幹には、sa:が後接する。それは、<u>話し手の感じ</u>の表現である。

    taka sa:（高い）   pukaras(ɪ)sa:（嬉しい）

(6) gi（/ki）は、形容詞の示す状態性質の<u>出現様子</u>を、話し手が<u>見て認めて</u>いるのである。

    taka-gi. pukarasɪ-ki

(7) 形容詞語幹は自由度が高い。動詞語幹と共通だったり、形容詞的名詞だったりし得る。

(8) 形容詞は、語形変化を含めて動詞との類似性が高い。

形容詞語形

描写形容詞   taka- 高い

気分形容詞   pukarasɪ 嬉しい　（語幹末が -sɪ であることが多い。）

  pɪkaras(ɪ) -sa: taka-sa:

  pɪkaras(ɪ) -sa:sji（du uz） ×taka-sa:sji

  pɪkaras(ɪ) -ki   taka- gi

   s(ɪ) -kam   taka- kam (55) (atsɪ-kam)

   s(ɪ) -kaiba   taka- kaiba

   s(ɪ) -karja: taka- karja:

   s(ɪ) -katsɪka: taka- katsɪka:

   s(ɪ) -fu ～ffu   taka- fu

   s(ɪ) fanja: N～ffanja: N taka- ffanja: N

① S－型

 <u>描写形容詞</u> 話し手に属す話者形（語幹＋sa:）だけがある。一般形はない。語幹用法がカバーする。

---

(55) この形は、既述のように、taka（高）では、現れにくい。

<u>気分形容詞</u>　話し手に属す話者形（語幹＋sa:）の他に、話し手に無関係な一般形（話者形＋sji）があり、後者は動詞 ssɪ の変化形 sji:du uz と連語で現れ、更に語形変化をする。pukarassa:sji du utaz.（過去）

語形	話者形	一般形（動詞形成）	(sji du uz)
taka-	taka-sa:	×	
pukarasɪ-	pukarasɪ-sa:	pukaras(ɪ)sa:	sji du uz

② K－型

描写形容詞では、その意味によっては、容態形と予断形が現れにくい。気分形容詞では、話し手が直接は見聞感知できない他者の内部情感を、その表出（態度・表情・動作・言葉等）により、描写形容詞同様に認識判断するのである。

言い切りの形

容態	予断	確認	判断（＋du a-/na-）	否定
-s(ɪ)-k-i-	-s(ɪ)-k-a-m	-sɪ-kaz	-s(ɪ)- fu ～ ffu	s(ɪ)-fanja:N～ffanja:N
-gi	-k-a-m	-kaz	-fu	-ffanja:N

判断形は、du az/du naz（である／になる）との連語で現れる。そして az は更に、その語形変化をする。

　例　karja:　kasamasɪ fu du aiba du…（彼は腹たてているので）
　　　karja:　kasamasɪ fu du ataz.（腹をたてていた）
　　　karja:　kasamasɪ fu du aztsɪka:(腹をたてているならば)

他人のことへの判断ならば、ja: sɪfu du arambe:ja.（ひもじいのではないかね）のような控えめな表現にする方が好ましい。

　この語形変化を見れば、気分形容詞は、本土上代シク活用を彷彿とさせ、描写形容詞は、本土ク活用を思い出ださせる。歴史的研究にとっても、共時的な詳しい研究が求められるのである。消滅の危機にある言語に対して、我々は、現在の為にも、過去の為にも研究調査を行い、できるだけの保持を

図りたい。

【付記】
　琉球諸方言の研究と発表に関して、宮岡伯人大阪学院大学教授と真田信治大阪大学教授に深く感謝したい。国立国語研究所主任研究員大西拓一郎氏及びそのグループの方々との学問的交流は支えとなり常に感謝している。そして、面倒な質問を受けて考えてくださる話者の方々のお名前を記して深い感謝を表したい。

【話者のお名前と生年（敬称略、順不同）】
　比嘉米三　昭和11年　　　　　平良恵二　昭和3年

【参照文献】
伊豆山敦子（1992）　「琉球方言の1人称代名詞」　国語学　171
伊豆山敦子（1997）「琉球方言形容詞成立の史的研究」『アジア・アフリカ言語文化研究54』東京外語大 AA 研
伊豆山敦子（1998）「琉球方言補助動詞（コプラ）の起源」『独協大学諸学研究』1-2
伊豆山敦子（2001）「琉球・八重山（石垣宮良）方言条件表現のアスペクト・モダリティー的側面」『マテシス・ウニウェルサリス』2-2　獨協大学外国語学部言語文化学科
伊豆山敦子（2002）「琉球・宮古（平良西仲）方言の名詞語末音と語形変化」『マテシス・ウニウェルサリス』3-2
伊豆山敦子（2002）「琉球・八重山（石垣宮良）方言の文法」文部省科学研究費補助金「特定領域研究（A）『環太平洋の「消滅に瀕した言語」にかんする緊急調査研究』成果報告書 A4-004
奥平博尚（1996）『宮古方言散歩道』麻姑山書房
狩俣繁久（1992）「宮古方言」『言語学大辞典』4巻　pp.848-863
柴田武　（1972）　全国方言資料第11巻　琉球編Ⅱ　　日本放送協会
柴田武　（1988）『語彙論の方法』三省堂
中松竹雄（1987）『琉球方言辞典』那覇出版社
平山輝男 et al.（1967）『琉球先島方言の総合的研究』明治書院
平良市史編さん委員会（1979）『平良市史』第1巻　平良市役所

A Study on the Formation of Luchuan (Ryukyuan) Adjective Endings

Phonological change   To do   Evidentiality   Descriptive   Emotive

Abstract : The formation of Luchuan (Ryukyuan) adjective endings is historically based on the affixation of the verb *$k(i)$- "to do", not on *sa* (noun formation affix) + *ari* "to be". The phonetic correspondence of adjective endings in Yaeyama dialects (Miyara, Kuroshima, and Yonaguni) shows that *k changed to *s* before *i* and to *h* before other vowels. The adjectives in Luchuan are divided into two classes on the basis of evidentiality, that is, the descriptive adjective and the emotive adjective. The latter has to be followed by the verb meaning "to do" in order to describe the internal feelings, such as "happy, sad, delicious, etc.", of another person.

1. The established theory on the formation of Luchuan adjectives

Since Chamberlain published his famous book "Essay in aid of a grammar and dictionary of the Luchuan language (1895 : 117)", it has been established that the Shuri adjective was historically derived from "adjective stem + *sa* (abstract noun formation) + *a-N* (to be)". This has been applied to explain the adjective formation in other dialects. The bases of this theory are as follows :

---

(1) gengogaku dai-jiten

(A) The adjectives are divided into two classes by their conjugational type. One has -sa- in its *shūshi* (conclusive) form, and -ku in its *ren'yō* (adverbial) and negative form ; the other has -sja- in its *shūshi* form, and -siku in its *ren'yō* and negative form.

(B) The -sja-/-siku-type words likely correspond to those of the Japanese -shiku conjugational type, with some exceptions.

(C) The endings attached to -s- stem have the same forms of the verb "to be", with some exceptions.

(D) It happens that -sa/sja forms can be used as a kind of noun.

2. Differences in the adjective forms between Shuri and Yaeyama Miyara

Yaeyama-Miyara adjectives do not have any of those four features. They do not have any conjugational differences corresponding to the -ku- and -siku- type. They have, however, a syntactical difference which divides them into two classes, that is, the descriptive adjective and the emotive adjective.

As below, the endings attached to the -h- stem do not have the same forms of the verb "to be". Their -ha forms can not be used as a kind of noun.

Conjugation

	Shūshi Conclusive	Ren'yō Adverbial	Hitei Negative	Shūshi Conclusive	Ren'yō Adverbial	Hitei Negative
	high	highly	not high	happy	happily	not happy
Shuri	taka-sa-N	taka-ku	taka-koo neeN	ʔuQ-sja-N	(ʔuQ-siku)	ʔuQ-sikoo neeN
Miyara	taka-ha-N	taka-ha	taka-ha ne:nu	sane-he-N	sane-he	sane-he ne:nu

Note: Miyara has a kind of vowel harmony like -ka-ha-N/-ne-he-N. (See Izuyama 1996)

A Study on the Formation of Luchuan (Ryukyuan) Adjective Endings

Example of predicative :

Descriptive Adjective

(1) *takaha-N*. The speaker takes a look at it and judges that it is high.

(2) *takaha ja:*. The speaker takes a look at it and is wondering about it.

(3) *takaha daru*. The speaker describes it as a state generally recognized.

Emotive Adjective

(4) *baa sanehe-N* The speaker has a direct experience of happiness, and states this.

I happy

*(5a) *wa: sanehe-N*. You are happy.

you happy

(5b) *wa: sanehe-N?* Are you happy? (Only the question sentence is acceptable.)

*(5c) *ure: sanehe-N./?* He/She is happy. / ?

Since we cannot directly experience another person's feeling, we have to express it in the indirect way by looking at his attitude. By the rule of evidentiality, the verb phrase (an objective expression) has to be used :

(5d) *ure: sanehe hu-N*. He is happy. He looks happy. (He has a happy attitude.)

he happy do

The endings attached to the -s- stem in Shuri have the same forms of the verb "to be", with some exceptions. In Miyara, however, they have different forms from *aruN*.

	Shuri		Miyara	
	to be	high	to be	high
Shūshi (Conclusive)	ʔa-ɴ	taka-s-a-ɴ	a-ru-ɴ	taka-h-a-ɴ
Question	ʔa-mi	taka-s-a-mi	a-ru-ɴ?	taka-h-a-ɴ?
Past	ʔa-taɴ	taka-s-a-ta-ɴ	atta	taka-h-a:da
Past Question	ʔa-tii	taka-s-a-tii	atta?	taka-h-a:da?
Rentai (adjectival)	ʔa-ru	taka-s-a-ru	a-ru	taka-h-a-ru
+nu	×	taka-s-a-nu	×	taka-h-a-nu

Note : Shuri and Miyara -nu forms are often used to express personal feelings at the end of the sentence.

Miyara : (6) ure: *takaha-nu*. This is expensive.(I wouldn't buy it.)

(7) ure: *ɴmaha-nu*. This is delicious.(Recommending to eat it.)

It is said that the *-sa/sja* form can be used as a noun in Shuri ; they can be used as a predicate, but when it is used at the end of the sentence, it expresses an exclamation. (Examples in *Okinawago-jiten* p.84)

(8) waɴne: ʔukaasja du　　ʔuhusa-ru　　I am in a dangerous condition.
　　I-TOP　danger　part　have a lot of　(about the condition of a disease.)

(9) ʔanu　muinu　takasa.　　That hill is high!
　　that　hill　be high

For the sake of convenience, the author adopted the *-ɴ* form as *Shūshi* (conclusive) ; in Yaeyama, however, the *Shūshi*-form includes the speaker's recognition or judgment. This will be explained in the section about evidentiality.

The *ren'yō* (adverbial) form is not so free as in common Japanese. In common Japanese, *ure-shi-ku* (happy-*ren'yō*) *naru* (become) /*omou* (think) is possible, in Yaeyama, however, it is not possible. The verb which means "to do" can widely co-occur with adjectives. The form which co-occurs with the verb "to do" is here adopted as the *ren'yō* (adverbial) form.

taka-ha hu-N (literally "to make high") means to make something (e.g. a fence) high, in addition, to insist that it is high. *Sane-he hu-N* (literally : to make happy) means to be pleased or happy in describing any person (1st, 2nd, and 3rd person), because it is not permissible to describe anyone other than the speaker using the *-N* form of emotive adjectives. We can feel and recognize directly our own feelings such as "sad, happy, lonely, etc", but as far as another person is concerned, we cannot directly experience their feelings ; we can only guess them by watching their attitudes. That is why, in Yonaguni, they use an expression containing the verb "to do" which expresses the speaker's estimation of another person's feelings. This frame is a kind of grammatical evidentiality. Shuri dialect also has the same kind of verb phrase : *ʔuǫsja sju-N* (happy do).

Miyara dialect does not have the nominal usage of the adjective. It does not have a single word corresponding to "the height" in something like "measure the height of ~", or the like. The expressions corresponding to that of Shuri are *takaha:* or *takaha ja:* (*ja:* is a particle for exclamation). They are used to talk to oneself and cannot have the question intonation ; they can not appear in a question sentence. Miyara dialect does not have any specialized form for the question ; rather, the assertive forms change into questions by changing their intonation. The question sentence means "Do you recognize / feel it?". An affirmative answer means "I (the speaker) recognize / feel it." The usages of the *shūshi* form in Yaeyama are different from those in CJ.

3. Evidentiality and personal restriction in the Miyara adjective

Miyara adjectives do not have any morphological differences corresponding to the Japanese *-ku / -shiku* conjugational patterns, but they are syntactically divided into two classes : descriptive adjective and emotive adjective. This distinction is based on the personal restriction by the evidentiality.

(10) *ba:* sanehe<u>N</u>.   *wa:* sanehe<u>N</u>?   **wa:* saneheN.   **ure:* saneheN./?
     I happy   you happy   you happy   he/she happy
     I am happy.   You are happy? *You are happy. *He/She is happy

The speaker knows his own feelings and can recognize them. We can not, however, directly experience the feelings of other persons. We can ask the 2nd person about his feelings; we cannot, however, experience directly his feelings, much less those of the 3rd person. We can only guess other persons' feelings by observing their attitudes; in Miyara, by adding the verb hu - "to do", the others' feelings are expressed as they seem to be. Those verb phrases can objectively describe any person's feelings including the 1st person's.

(11) *ure: sanehe du hi: ru.*/?   *ba: sanehe du hi: ru.*   *wa: sanehe du hi: ru.*/?
     He is happy./?   I am happy.   You are happy./?

As far as the personal restriction is concerned, Yonaguni (another Yaeyama dialect) has the same rules; for the second person, the emotive adjective is permissible only in the question sentences, and it should be followed by "*k(i)*-" (to do) to indicate the 3rd person:

(12) ○*(anu) sjana-<u>N</u>.*   ○*<u>N</u>da sjana na?*   ○*u ja sjana kiru-<u>N</u>*   **u~<u>N</u>da (ja) sjana-<u>N</u>.*

I happy   you happy Q   he TOP happy do   he~you (TOP) happy
(I) am happy Do you happy? He/She looks happy. He/She~You is~are happy.

4. Adjective forms of two dialects in Yaeyama

Adjective endings: Shuri *-sa-N/-sja-N*, Miyara *ha-N*, Kuroshima *ha-N / -ja-N*, Yonaguni *ø-N*. Miyara dialect uses adjective stem reduplication.

A Study on the Formation of Luchuan (Ryukyuan) Adjective Endings

	Miyara	Kuroshima		Miyara	Kuroshima
red	akahaN	akahaN	delicious	NmahaN	ma:haN
bad	janahaN	janahaN	black	ɸuɸohoN	vo:hoN
weak	jo:hoN	jo:hoN	wide	pɪsohoN	pisohoN
hard	ko:hoN	ko:hoN	itchy	bjo:hoN	bju:waN
strong	co:hoN	su:waN	far	to:hoN	tu:waN
blue	auhoN	auhaN	big	maiheN	ubohoN
cool	pirigeheN	pi:rakeheN	cute	ap(p)areheN	abareheN
bitter	NgahaN	NgeheN	dirty	janeheN	janijaN
beautiful	kaiheN	haijaN	happy	saneheN	sanijaN
cold	pi:sjaN	pi:jaN	sour	sɪ:saN	si:jaN
heavy	iɸɸa(ha)N	guɸɸaN	ticklish	ko:hoN	hauwaN
hot	ats(ɪ)saN	attsaN	light	karuhoN	harraN
thin	pɪs(ɪ)saN	pisjaN	to be thinned	pɪsa: pɪsa(h)iN	pisiheN

Note : Miyara uses reduplication of stems ; e.g. kɪN-kɪ-i yellow, in adjectives. As seen above, Miyara and Kuroshima have a kind of <u>vowel harmony</u> : the vowels of endings of adjectives correspond to those of the stems.

Table of correspondence between final vowels of stems and those of endings.

Miyara						
Vowels of stem final	a	u/o	i/e	ɪ	i:
Endings	-haN	-hoN	-heN	-saN	-sjaN

Kuroshima						
Vowels of stem final	a/a:	o/o:	e	i/i:	(u:)
Endings	-haN	-hoN	-heN	-jaN	(-waN)

293

(a) Kuroshima -*u:* stems corresponding to Miyara -*o:* are affixed with -*wa*, not -*ho*. So far, all words belonging to that category are one-syllable words. As in the case of affixation of the particle *ha* (direction "to –"), they might not be harmonized with their stems. They might lose the -*h*- in *-*haN* after the rounded vowels, except *auhaN* (blue) which is rarely used.

(b) *guΦΦaN* (heavy) and *karraN* (light) do not have -*ha*, probably because of assimilation.(2)

(c) -*he* is affixed to -e- stems, most of which have derived forms.

(d) -*sa* is exceptional; it can be affixed instead of -*wa*, or to derived or compound words.

(e) the words which have [u] or [e:] at the end of the stem are not found.

(f) -*ja* in the endings should be special in Kuroshima. They can be found in -*i:* stem in one syllable words or *i*-stem words.

(g) It is significant that Kuroshima has -*ja*, which we can find in neither Shuri nor Miyara. -*i*-stem and one-syllable -*i:* stem have it.

The Kuroshima adjective ending -*jaN* is an exceptional form. In addition, it is not harmonized with its stem vowels. It is expected to have -*heN*/-*haN* ; for one-syllable stem words, we can infer that [h] in -*ha* is lost after *i* and instead that morpheme has a glide [j], that is *-*i-ha* → -*i-ja*. Two syllable words, however, are difficult to explain, for they do not have -*heN* or -*jeN*.

The Kuroshima particles "*ha* ~ *he* ~ *ho* (direction "to") and "*hara* ~ *hera* ~ *hora* (from)" have initial /h/, and a phonological change *k > *h* is reasonably considered for those particles.

---

(2) Two forms for "fearful": nahaburahaN and nahaburaN, but no nahaburraN

A Study on the Formation of Luchuan (Ryukyuan) Adjective Endings

5. Discussion about a phonological change *s→h in adjective endings

In order to verify the theory that the phonological change *s→h caused the change *-sa- → -ha- in adjective endings, we have to examine the list of the correspondences among the dialects which have the ending -ha-N. Hentona is situated in the northern part of mainland Okinawa ; examples fom this dialect are added for reference :

Noun

	liquor	soba	island	nest	sweat	woven hat	navel	mortar	stone
Shuri	sa_ki_	su_ba_	si_ma_	sii	a_si_	ka_sa_	hu_su_	ʔuu_si_	ʔi_si_
Miyara	sa_ki_	su_ba_	sI_ma_	sI:	a_sji_	kuba:_sa_	pu_tsu_	u_sI_	i_sji_
Kuroshima	sa_ki_	su_ba_	si_ma_	si:	a_si_	ka_sa_	pu_tsu_	u_si_	i_si_
Hentona	sa_ki_	su_ba_:	si_ma_	sI:	a_si_:	huba_ga_sa	pu_su_	ʔu_su_	ʔi_si_

Verb

	bloom	scrub	not push	do	awake	make sb. write
Shuri	sa_cu_N	si_ju_N	ʔu_sa_N	s_ju_N	ʔuku_sju_N	kaka_sju_N
Miyara	sa_ku_N	sI_su_N	usanu	hu_N	uka_hu_N	kaka_hu_N
Kuroshima	sa_ku_N	zu :N (3)	usanuN	si:ruN	huka_su_N	haka_su_N
Hentona	sa_ki_N	unknown	unknown	s_u_N	ʔuku_su_N	unknow

Adjective

	shallow	sour
Shuri	ʔasa-_sa_N	sii-_sa_N
Miyara	asa-_ha_N	sI:-_sa_N
Kuroshima	asa-_ha_N	si:-_ja_N
Hentona	ʔasa-_ha_N	unknown

---

(3) Kuroshima z is expected. E.g. _za_:nuN "not grind", _za_nuN "not know", _zo_:h- "white", _za_N lice.

295

Explanation of the above list :
(a) Correspondence of *s*

   Noun   Shuri *s* : Yaeyama *s*
   Verb and adjective   In adj. stems   Shuri *s* : Yaeyama *s*
                               In adj. endings   Shuri *s*- : Yaeyama *h*-

In the words corresponding to "shallow", we can find s : s in their stems ; the endings, however, show the corresponding -<u>sa</u>N : -<u>ha</u>N, which is very striking and atracts our attention.

The initial consonants of "sour" are the same *s*, their endings, however, are s in Miyara and *j* in Kuroshima.

We have to pay attention to Miyara *huN* (to do) ; it has *h* corresponding to the *s* in Shuri. On the other hand, Miyara *sIsu-N* (to scrub) has *s* just like Shuri *siju-N*.

In all dialects, the verbs meaning "to push" keep *s*. In Miyara, its conjugational forms always keep *s*.

In Miyara, the morphemes to make a verb transitive (e.g. *uka-hu-N*) and the causative verbs (*haka-hu-N*) have *h* corresponding to Shuri s.

We can show them as follows :

(b) We do not have any examples of *s* (Shuri) : *h* (Miyara) in the stems of nouns, adjectives, or verbs.

(c) The morphemes of adjective formation generally have the correspondence *s* (Shuri): *h* (Miyara and Kuroshima) with some exceptions *s : s* in Miyara and *s : j* in Kuroshima.

(d) In Miyara, only the initial sound of the verb *hu*- (to do) and a causative affix *hu*- correspond to *s*.

If the established opinion were acceptable, we could have answered the questions as follows :

(1) Only the affix to form abstract nouns, which were bases of the adjective, changed from *s* to *h*.

(2) Only the affixes to form adjectives were weakened and became *j* (Kuro-

A Study on the Formation of Luchuan (Ryukyuan) Adjective Endings

shima), and not weakened but kept *s* in other places (e.g. Miyara).
(3) Only the initial sound of the important verb "to do" was weakened into *h* in Miyara.
(4) Some morphemes were weakened but others were not.

To answer the above questions, the theory that phonological change **s →h* caused the change **-sa-* → -ha- in adjective endings should be denied.

6. Miyara verb *hu-N* "to do"
Conjugation of main verbs :

	to do	to come	to write	to get up
Conclusive (*shūshi*)	hu-N	ku-N	kaku-N	ukiru-N
Volitional (*ishi*)	ha:	ku:	kaka	uku
Negative (*hitei*)	ha:nu	ku:nu	kakanu	ukunu
Adverbial (*ren'yō*)	sɪ(:)	kɪ(:)	kakɪ	uki
Prohibitive (*kinshi*)	sɪna	kɪna	kakɪna	ukina
Additive (*rentai*)	hu:	ku:	kaku	ukiru
Perfect (*kanryō*)	hja(-N)	kja(-N)	kakja(-N)	ukirja(-N)
Imperative (*meirei*)	hi:	ku:	kaki	ukiri
Conjunctive (*keizoku*)	hi	ki:	kaki	uki
Past (*kako*)	sɪ-ta	kɪ-ta	kakɪ-da	uki-da
Completion (*shuryō*)	hi:-Ta	ki:-Ta	kaki-Ta	uki-Ta
Resultive (*kekka*)	he:(-N)	ke:(-N)	kake:(-N)	uke:(-N)
Continuative (*keizoku*)	hi:(-N)	ki:(-N)	kaki(-N)	uki(-N)

We can not conclude that this dialect has undergone the change **s→h*.

Table of correspondence of Miyara *h* :

	shoulder	liver	cloth	mouth	cloud	hair	hips	hear	wear
Shuri	kata	cimu	ciN	kuci	kumu	kii	kusi	cic-uN	cijuN
Miyara	kata	kɪmu	kɪN	hutsɪ	humu	ki:	kutsɪ	sɪk-uN	kɪsuN
Kuroshima	hata	kimu	kiN	huci	humu	ki:	kusi	sik-uN	kisuN
Hentona	hata	cimu	k'iN	k'uci	khumu	hi:	husi	cik-iN	k'i:N

In Miyara and Kuroshima, we found a phonological change *$k \rightarrow h$ right before the vowel *u* ; this is a wide-spread phonological change in Luchuan dialects (*$k \rightarrow \chi \rightarrow h$). Kuroshima also has the same *$k \rightarrow h$ change right before the vowel a. In Miyara, "kɪmu" and "kɪN" retain *k* before the vowel *ɪ* , in the case of sɪk-uN, however, the initial consonant is *s*, counter to our expectation. We must then refer to the other dialects.[4]

	Shiraho	Hateruma	Kabira	Komi	Iriomote-sonai	Iriomote-uehara
To hear	sɪkuN	sɪ(~u)kung	sɪkun	sɪki	sjiki	sjiku
Liver	sɪ(~ji)mu	sjimu	kɪmu	kimu	kimu	kimu
Cloth	sɪnu	sɪnu	kɪN	kɪnu	kinu	kiN

The phonological enviroment where the initial *k corresponds to *s* seems to be that the narrow vowel [ɪ] is followed by the voiceless consonants. The 1st syllable is completely devoiced.[5]

In Shiraho and Hateruma, where the devoicing is remarkable, the 1st syllable is completely devoiced, and initial *s* is found when the following consonant is a voiced nasal which is also devoiced, so that sometimes we cannot hear the palatalization of *s* in the first syllable.

---

(4) Nakamatsu (1987), Nakamoto (1975,1976), Uemura (1992)
(5) Uemura (1993,p.98), Nakamoto (1975,p.5)

7. Interpretation of the phonological correspondence *s : k* in Yaeyama

In Yaeyama, e.g. Miyara, the initial consonant of sɪkuN is explained as follows. The phonetic shape [ksɪ] of /kɪ/ was changed to [sɪ] by devoicing the whole first syllable : [k] disappeared by devoicing and the glide [s] has replaced [k] as a new phoneme. /kɪ/ keeps its phonetical shape [ksɪ] still now in several dialects.

Miyara *sɪ(:)* (adverbial form of "*hu-N*") is considered to have developed from /*kɪ/ [ksɪ] because of devoicing and the increased prominence of its glide [s], creating the new form *sɪ(:)*. In the conjugation of *hu-N*, adverbial, prohibitive, and past forms have *sɪ* for their first syllables. They are synchronically derived from the adverbial form and their vowels are short except in the independent form. We find completely devoiced [ɪ], e.g. *sɪ tu hu* for *sɪ *du hu :*. Moreover, the adverbial form is very often followed with forms having initial voiceless consonants [s, t]. Accordingly, [s] in the adverbial form is considered as the changing of the glide to an independent phoneme just like the case of sɪku-N (to hear), that is, **kɪ → *ksɪ → sɪ*. On the other hand, *kɪsu-N* (to wear) must have had a voiced sound *r* in the next syllable. The initial *k* is kept, instead of devoicing [r] and changing it to [s]. We can find the same kind of change in other verbs of the 1-dan conjugational type.

The above facts lead us to the conclusion that *hu-* (to do) came from **ku-*.

Now, we have to examine the above-mentioned **(d)** : in Miyara, only the initial sound of the verb "*hu-*"(to do) and causative affix *hu-* correspond to *s*.

The affix which forms transitive verbs is basically the same as that of the causative except for *hu-N*, which has *sji-miru-N* as its causative form.

299

	Conclusive	Negation	Causative	Conclusive
to write	kaku-N	kaka-nu	make sb. write	kaka-hu-N
to get up	ukiru-N	uku-nu	make sb. get up	uka-hu-N

uka-hu-N is composed of [stem +*a* + *hu-N*]. It has the same composition as the 4-dan type verb *kaka-hu-N*. It is significant that the Miyara causative form is *uka-hu-N*, not **uku-hu-N* which would have the vowel pattern that would correspond to the Japanese transitive verb.[6] That causative affix has the same conjugational pattern as *hu-N*. The author posits that it must be a change from the verb *hu-N* to an affix *-hu-N*.

Thus **s→h* is denied, and both **k→h* and **k→s* are discussed. Next we have to search for the origin of Miyara *hu-N* (to do). We can think about the possibility *hu-* < **ku-*. To confirm this, we have to take the Yonaguni dialect into consideration.

8. *kiru-N* "to do" and *iru-N* "to do" in Yonaguni dialect
8.1 Preceding Research about two verbs

Miyara (1930) described *kiruN*: it means "to do", and it developed from *sjiruN* (to do). By Hirayama and Nakamoto (1964, pp. 19, 112-120), *kiru'N* and *'iru'N* are not the same word as *su'N*. Because of the change *su'N →hu'N→'N*, it became difficult to express the concept "to do" using a single phoneme *'N*, so *kiru'N* and *'iru'N* take the place of *su'N*, and he gave *iruN* and *kiruN* in his charts.

Hirayama (1967, p. 449) has only *kiruN* but not *iruN*. Hirayama (1988, p. 370) has only *kiruN*. Nakamoto (1990, p. 696) described that the verb corre-

---

(6) Examples of Iriomote-komi : *suN* "mash", *uku-huN* "to awake", *utu-huN* "to drop" The affix to make transitive verb is *-u* +*huN*. It corresponds Miyara *-a* +*huN*. The djective ending is *-haN* (*ma:haN* "delicious", *sanihaN* "happy").

sponding to CJ *suru* (to do) has disappeared in Yonaguni and has been replaced by *kirun*. In addition, Yonaguni has a synonym *irun*. Both of them have the 4-dan conjugation.

"Dialects of Ryūkyū 11" (1987, p. 162) has *iruN* as a irregular verb. "Dialects of Ryūkyū 12" (1987) does not have *iruN* but has *kiruN*.

iruN can be independently used to mean "to do so". E.g. *aŋa iruN* ("I will do it.") is offering to do something while looking at another person doing it. *kiruN* accompanied with words of actions (e.g. dance, song, smell, urinate, etc.) mean to do those actions. In other words, the former is intransitive and the latter is transitive.

The National Institute for Japanese Language "Hōgenbunpō-zenkokuchizu 2-70" has *kiruN* for the Japanese word "to do" but not *iruN*, probably because the sample sentence is "to do one's work all day long."

8.2. Conjugation of two verbs meaning "to do" in Yonaguni

Following is the conjugation of *i-ru-N* and *ki-ru-N*. It is made referring to Hirayama and Nakamoto (1964), Takahashi (1992) and "Ryūkyū no Hōgen" (1987).

	To do (intr.)	To do (tr.)	To do (farm work)[7]
Conclusive	*i-ru-N*	*ki-ru-N*	*ki-ru-N*
Negative	*i-ra-nuN*	*ki-ra-nuN*	*ki-ra-nuN*
Volitional	*i-ru:*	*ki-ru:*	*ki-ru:*
Imperative	*i-ri*	*ki-ri*	*ki-ri*
Additive	*i-ru*	*ki-ru*	*ki-ru*
Adverbial	*i-sji*	*ki*	*ki-sji*
Conjunctive	*i-sji* (*-ti*)	*ki* (*-ti*)	*ki-sji* (*-ti*)
Past	*i-ta-N*	*ki-ta-N*	*ki-sji-ta-N*
Perfect / completion	*i-sja-N*	*k-ja-N*	*ki-sja-N*

---

(7) The meaning of this form is "dig".

Following are *kag-u-* (corresponding to CJ 5-dan), *ugi-ru-* (corresponding to kami-1dan), *agi-ru-* (corresponding to shimo-1dan) and *nur-u-* (corresponding to 4-dan). We have to notice their perfect forms. There are some verbs which have two perfect forms.

	to write	to get up	to open	to ride
Conclusive	*kag-u-*	*ug-ir-u-N*	*ag-ir-u-N*	*nu-r-u-N*
Negative	*kag-a-nuN*	*ug-ir-anuN*	*ag-ir-anuN*	*nu-r-anuN*
Volitional	*kag-u*	*ug-ir-u*	*ag-ir-u*	*nu-r-u*
Imperative	*kag-i*	*ug-ir-i*	*ag-i*	*nu-r-i*
Additive	*kag-u*	*ug-ir-u*	*ag-ir-u*	*nu-r-u*
Adverbial	*ka-t-i*	*ug-i*	*ag-i*	*nu-r-i*
Conjunctive	*ka-t-i*(-*ti*)	*ug-i*(-*ti*)	*ag-i*(-*ti*)	*nu-i*(-*ti*)
Past	*ka-t-i-ta-N*	*ug-i-ta-N*	*ag-i-ta-N*	*nu-ta-N*
Perfect /Completion	*ka-t-ja-N*	*ug-u-N*	*ag-ja-N / ag-u-N*	*nwaN/nuN*

Yonaguni does not have the word meaning "to open (intr.)". People wonder why the door can <u>open by itself</u>; the door must <u>be opened</u>. Nevertheless, when the door which is difficult to open was just opened, people watching it say "*aguN!* ". Then they will tell to the others *dadu agjaN* "The door was opened.". The former shows that the speaker <u>instantaneously</u> recognized some action. Another example is *n-iru-N* "to cook". Its perfect forms are *n-ja -N /n-ju-N*. One more example is *nuru-N* (to get on) : when the speaker sees someone riding, he says : *nu-N*. When the speaker saw someone already on the deck, he will say : *nwa-N* (non-palatalized semi-vowel + *a-N*). The instantaneous intransitive verbs, such as *ug-iru-N* and *ut-iru-N*, always have -*u-N*, never -*a-N* for their perfect forms.

This -*u*-form for the perfect which is contrasted with -*j(/w)a* form is supposed to have developed from **g-j-u*, **t-j-u* etc. to *g-u*, *t-u* etc. by the phonological restriction that no sequence of palatalized consonants can be followed by back vowels. The two perfect forms of verbs ending with -*ir-u-N* (e.g. *agiru-N:ag-ja-N / ag-u-N*, *niru-N:n-ja-N / n-ju-N* "to cook") suggest that

A Study on the Formation of Luchuan (Ryukyuan) Adjective Endings

the perfect form of *i-ru-N* is supposed to have also two shapes as **ja-N* / **ju -N*.

A number of dialects have a copula whose form is *ja-*. It is supposed to be drived from a verb **i-(r-u-)* like Yonaguni. Yonaguni, however, does not have a copula, instead the verb *aru-* (to be) has that role, probably because the verb *ir-u-N* is still functioning as a verb.

The copula **ju-N* which we reconstructed just now is, in fact, found in Miyara alongside *jaru-N*. It indicates the speaker's instantaneous judgement as following. (8)

Conversation looking at a person coming toward the speaker:

(13) A: *ure: Atsuko:*. It is Atsuko. (No copula)

　B: *(ure:) Atsuko: aranu*. It is not Atsuko.

　　　B unexpectedly discovered that it is Atsuko:

　B: Atsuko *juN!*　　　It is really Atsuko.

　Later C tells to others:

　C: *(ure:) Atsuko: jaruN*. It is Atsuko.

Shuri has the copula *ja-N*, and Miyara has corresponding *jaru-N* and *ju-N*. It is considered that they have a historical relation with **i-(r-u)-*.

It is concluded that **i-a-*, a perfect form of **i-*, indicates the situation of things and another perfect form **i-u-* indicates the speaker's judgement.

Kuroshima examples of adjective endings are as follows: *jani-jaN* "bitter", *sani-jaN* "beautiful", *si:-jaN* "cold", *hau-waN* "heavy"

8.3. Parallel resemblance between affixes of perfect and adjective endings
(9)
Kuroshima verbs have affix *h-*. Verb conjugational forms are as follows:

---

(8) Izuyama(1998) See "Ryūkyū hōgen hojodōshi no kigen"
(9) The verb forms are temporaly named for 形の名は比較の為なので臨時的である。

	conclusive	completion	past	resultative	perfect	
to write	*hakuN*	*hakutaN*	*hakida*	*hakeN*	*	*hake-heN*
to get up	*hukiruN*	*hukitaN*	*hukida*	(*hukeheN*)	*huki-jaN*	*
to fall	*utiruN*	*utitaN*	*utida*	(*uteheN*)	*uti-jaN*	*
to do	*si:ruN*	*si:taN*	*si:da*	*sjeN*	*	*sje:-heN*

  The perfect form is confirmation of finishing the action, as in Miyara. At the moment of the action being completed and at once confirmed by the speaker, *hakeheN* is uttered. In the same situation, however, *hukijaN*, not *hukeheN*, is said. *hukeheN* is uttered when the speaker confirmed the result of the action a little bit later, e. g., at the moment when a baby awakes while someone is watching him, *hukijaN* is uttered. *HukeheN* is said when the baby is already awake at the moment of looking at him. *HakeN* means "being written", that is, there is something written. The usage is different from what we would suppose from the correspondence of *hake-heN* to *huki-jaN*. The intransitive verbs rarely *-heN* but often have *-jaN*.

  The Kuroshima perfect form has two kinds of endings : *-ja-N* corresponding to CJ 1dan-verb endings and *-he-N* corresponding to 5-dan verb endings. The latter has a kind of vowel harmony, that is, the vowel of *-he-N* agrees with the vowel in its stem and changes to *-ha-N*. E.g. the perfect form of *hauN* "to buy" is *hajahaN*. The ending *-ja-N*, however, is not harmonized with its stem vowel. The endings of both verb and adjective are as follows :

	verb		adjective	
to write	*hakuN*	*hake-heN*	pretty	*abare-heN*
to buy	*hauN*	*haja-haN*	high	*taka-haN*
to get up	*hukiruN*	*huki-jaN*	dirty	*jani-jaN*

  The perfect forms of verbs and the ending forms of adjectives are in parallel. We should notice the set *-h-,-h-,-j-*. The adjectives whose stems end in *-i* have the ending *-jaN* just like the verbs of 1-dan type, and stand side by side with the other adjectives which have the endings *-heN* and *-haN* (or *-hoN*), just like *-jaN* in the perfect forms of the 1-dan type stands side by side with the perfect form *-heN* and *-haN* (or *-hoN*) of the 4-dan type. Moreover, the form *-jaN* of the 1-dan type does not have vowel harmony, just as *-jaN* of adjectives does not have vowel harmony. We can not help thinking that those two parallel series have some relations.

Now we have to examine again the phonological correspondence *s* versus *h* in the adjective endings.

The adjective endings generally have the correspondence *s* : *h* between Shuri and Miyara / Kuroshima with some exceptions, e.g. *s* : *s* (Miyara), *s* : *j* (Kuroshima). The established theory could not explain cases such as Miyara *s* corresponding to Kuroshima *j*. It is difficult to conclude that Kuroshima has undergone the process of changing $*s \to *h \to *j$.

If this set (*-h-*,*-h-*,*-j-*) of adjective endings comes from $*s$ of $*sa\text{-}ari$, it must be concluded that the verb affixes *-h-*, *-h-*, *-j-* have developed from a weakening of $*s$ in the same way. We could not find any evidence for that. It seems to be impossible to reconstruct *huki-sa-N for *huki-ja-N* without any reason. Below, we will consider the $*s\text{-}$ ending in Kuroshima perfect forms.

9. Change of the verb meaning "to do" into an affix

Miyara has a special completion form with ending *-Ta*. The phonetic feature of this morpheme suggestes to us the formation of the Miyara completion form. The phonetic feature of that 1st phone [t'] (glottalized non-aspirated [t], like Japanese *sokuon*) shows that the preceding syllable is lost. Historically, the 1st syllable of *sITa* (past form of *hu-N* "to do") should be lost by devoicing. We can assume *kakiTa* <*kaki +*sIta. In a number of Yaeyama dialects, the verb meaning "to do" is functioning as an auxiliary verb. Shibata (1972, p. 47) describes that kind of auxilliary verb in Ishigaki-Kabira;

305

auxilliary *sita* in *hiki* sita means "did", and it indicates the completion of action or state. Nakamoto (1990, pp. 548, 563-564) mentions the past form of the word "to get up" in Ishigaki, Taketomi, Kabira, and Kobama as descents of *oki-sita* (to get up - did). The verb "to do" often changes to an affix in Yaeyama.

Taking those facts into consideration, it is concluded that the Kuroshima perfect endings -*he-*N ~ -*ha-*N have the same origin as Miyara *hu-*N "to do". The shapes -*he-*N ~ -*ha-*N are almost the same as Miyara resultative *he:-*N. Their grammatical meanings are almost the same and their shapes are very similar between two dialects. In Kuroshima, the verb meaning "to do" must have once been functioning as and auxilliary verb and then changed to an ending of the perfect form corresponding to Miyara he:N. The ending of the 1-dan type corresponding verbs is -ja-N. It has the same shape as was reconstructed for the Yonaguni perfect form of *iru-N: *i-(j)a-N >*ja-N. The perfect form of huk-iru-N is historically analysed as *huk-i-jaN. In the same way, the endings of emotive adjectives such as si:-jaN "sour", jani-jaN "dirty" could have developed from the perfect form of *iru-N, that is, *ja-N. Each kind of adjective ending has its own genesis. -ja-N in the emotive adjectives is *ja-N which is changed into an ending.

10. Evidentiality and personal restriction in the Yonaguni adjective

The Yonaguni adjectives are different from many other dialects. They are not divided morphologically in two groups but syntactically divided into the descriptive adjective and the emotive adjective according to the rule of evidentiality. The speaker knows his own feelings and emotions, but could not directly experience those of other people. Accordingly, looking at their appearances, he expresses their emotions by adding the verb *kiru* -N "to do" as follows.

A Study on the Formation of Luchuan (Ryukyuan) Adjective Endings

(14-1) *kanu kii ja taga-N* (15-1) *anu sjana-N*
that tree TOP high   I happy
That tree is high. (I recognize it.)   I am happy. (I feel happy.)

(15-1') *Nda sjana na?* **Nda~u ja sjana-N*.
you happy Q you~he TOP happy
You are happy? You~He is happy.

(14-2) *taga kiru-N*.   (15-2) *Atsuko ja sjana kiru-N do*
high do   Atsuko TOP happy do PRT
I insist that it is high.   Atsuko is happy, (by the look of her).

The verb phrase 'adjective stem + *kiru-N*' functions freely as a verb without any personal restriction. It also has imperative forms.

11. Yonaguni *kiru*- "to do" and Miyara *hu*- "to do"

Yonaguni *kiru-* has its perfect form *kja-*. We can however reconstruct, as stated, **k(j)u* ~ **k(I)u* ~ **k(w)u* meaning instantaneous judgement.

The formation of *kiru-* is induced as **k(u)-* + **i-ru-* > *k-iru-*. Though Yonaguni has neither /kju/ nor opposition between palatalized and non-palatalized consonants, we can assume non-palatalized **k(I)-*, which changed from **ku-* to *hu*, as a more likely development leading to the Miyara shape *hu-*"to do".

As **k(u)-* is thus reconstructed, **k(u)-a-* is expected for its perfect form. Miyara *hu-N* is supposed to mean something that comes to the attention of the speaker. In Japanese, we have the same kind of expression such as: *oto / nioi ga suru* "some sound / smell is doing" instead of hearing some sound or noticing some smell etc. Miyara *hu-* corresponds to **k(u)-* of Yonaguni as follows :

307

	nail	nouth
Yonaguni	k̠udi	k̠uci
Miyara	h̠uɴ	h̠utsɿ

All Yonaguni voiceless plosives [p, t, k, c] are unaspirated, however *kiru-ɴ* "to do" is exceptionally aspirated even in the middle of compound words. The initial consonant of *kiru-ɴ* in Yonaguni Higawa dialect is pronounced as [kh] which is very close to [χ] with strong aspiration. It shows the process of $*k > kh > \chi > h$

Even though Miyara *h* of *hu-ɴ* comes from **ku-* and *sɿ* comes from **kɿ*, we can not decide whether the consonant of *ha-, hi-, he-* of other forms were changed by the conjugational system or by a process such as *ku-a* → χ*ua* → χ*a* → *ha*. The alternation *h* and *s* of the initial sound of verb "to do" in Yaeyama indicates **k* not **s*.

12. Conclusion

The adjective in the Luchuan (Ryukyuan) dialects was historically formed by [adjective stem + ending < verb *k(ɪ)- ("to do")].

(A) The adjectives are divided morphologically or syntactically into two classes, the emotive and the descriptive.

(B) Usage of the adjectives is governed by evidentiality in almost all Yaeyama dialects.

(C) The verbs which mean "to do" participate in the syntactical usage of the adjective. Many dialects (including Miyako dialects) share this common fea-

---

(10) The initial consonant of Miyeara *ku-*"to come" keep *k*. We reconstruct **k* for the initial consonant of *hu-*"to do". In their protoforms, those two initial consonants must have had some difference of phonetic vallue, e.g. [k] or [q], consonant or vowel stem (*k-, ku-, kɿ-* etc.), the differences of following vowel or differences of accent etc.

ture.

(D) The narrow front vowel which does not palatalize preceding consonants participates in the change /kɪ/ [kɪ] to /sɪ/ [sɪ] through /kɪ/ [kˢɪ ~ ksɪ]

Luchuan (Ryukyuan) dialects are very important for the history of Japanese language and also for studies of grammar in general.

References :
Dixon, R. M. W. and Aikhenvald, Alexandra Y. (2006) Adjective classes : a cross-linguistic typology. Oxford University Press.

Izuyama Atsuko (1996) 'Ryūkyū hōgen no boin-chōwa-teki keikō [Vowel harmony in Luchuan]' *Dokkyō Daigaku Kyōyō Shogaku Kenkyū* 31-1, p. 1-13

Izuyama Atsuko (1997) 'Ryūkyū hōgen keiyōshi seiritsu no shiteki-kenkyū [A Historical Study on the Adjectives in Luchuan Dialects].' *Journal of Asian and African Studies* No. 54. Tōkyō : ILCAA

Izuyama Atsuko (1998) "Ryūkyū hōgen hojodōshi no kigen" [A Study on Copula in Luchuan Dialect]' *Dokkyō Daigaku Shogaku Kenkyū* 1-2. Dokkyō University.

Kōno Rokuro et al. (eds.) *Languages of the World*, vol. 3-2. (Sanseidō Encyclopedia of Linguistics : The Languages of the Japanese Archipelago. 1997, Sanseidō)

Kōno Rokuro et al. (eds.) *Languages of the World*, vol. 3-2. (Sanseidō Encyclopedia of Linguistics : The Languages of the Japanese Archipelago. 1997, Sanseidō)

Uemura Yukio (1992) 'Language of the Ryūkyūs (overview)' in Kamei Takeshi,

「ている」形への一考察
A Study on the Form "-te-iru" in Japanese

In Japanese, the verb has two main forms for the predicate. For instance, kak-u (I/we/you/he/she/they write (s).) and kai-te-iru (I/we/you/he/she/they am/is/are writing.) kai-ta and kai-te-ita indicate the past respectively. -te-iru forms are said to indicate the continuative or resultative aspect according to their lexical meanings.

The author proposes (1) "-te-iru" form indicates speaker's recognition or judgment. (2) Its past form indicates that the speaker recognized the action or state in the past and when he utters it the people concerned including him can not experience (see in most cases) any more that action or state. It means that the action or state might continue when the speaker mentioned it in the past form "-te-ita". Whether it indicates past or not depends on the other words included in the sentences. (3) It is important for this aspect that the action or state should have started when the speaker recognizes it. It is not necessary to recognize the moment when the action or state starts or ends. (4) In Japanese, the morpheme boundary does not necessarily coincide with the syntactic boundary.

1. 初めに

周知のとおり，金田一 (1947) の動詞分類[1]は，以下のようである。

---

(1) 金田一 (1976、pp. 7-12)

(1) 第一種　状態動詞　「ている」をつけることができない。
　　　　　　　　状態の不変化を表す。
(2) 第二種　継続動詞　「ている」をつけると動作進行中
　　　　　　　　状態の一時的変化を表す動詞
(3) 第三種　瞬間動詞　「ている」をつけると動作・作用が終わって結果が
　　　　　　　　残存している。
　　　　　　　　状態の永続的変化を表す動詞
(4) 第四種　状態を帯びることを表す動詞　いつも「ている」の形で状態
　　　　　　　　を表す。

　この分類の重要性はその後のアスペクト研究に大きな影響を与えたことで、十分理解できる。しかし、この分類は、単語ないし連語レベルのことである。その後、多くの優れた詳細且つ複雑な研究があるにも拘わらず、日本語のシンタクス的な構造を考える上では足りない点もある。[2]
　その一つは、「ている」と「ていた」の相関関係である。第二は人称によるテンス的制限である。第三は、アスペクトを論じる際に殆ど取り上げられることのない、「動作の始まり」である。「動作の始まり（出現時点）を必要としない」という特徴の重要性について触れる。第四は、以上の事実から、形態論的な境界と構文的な境界とは、別個に考察しなければならないことを示す。
　以下、例示しながら、その理由を述べ、新しい提案をする。[3]

2．普通態の「た」形と「ている」態の「た」形[4]
　先ず、金田一（1947）では、「た」が連接した場合が記されてはいるが、

（2）沖（2000, pp.62-63）の統語的アスペクトに関する指摘は、これらと関係があるかもしれない。
（3）ここでは、話ことばだけを取り上げる。書き言葉はその上にかぶさる体系であろう。
（4）「する」etc. 対「している」etcを、ここでは『普通態』対『「ている」態』と呼ぶ。

肝心の「ている」に対する「ていた」の考察が極めて不十分である。また、後続研究についても同じことが言えるのである。

普通態と「ている」態の形を、単純化して図示するなら、次のようであろう。用語は異なることがあるが、一応このように考えられている。しかしこれには問題がある。

		アスペクト	
		普通態	「ている」態
テンス	非過去	書く	書いている
	過去（／完了）	書いた	書いていた
	非過去	落ちる	落ちている
	過去（／完了）	落ちた	落ちていた

2.1 「ていた」形と「ている」形の相関関係

「する」と「している」、「した」と「していた」の対立を考察した記述は多いが、「ている」形の過去「ていた」形に対する考察は少ない。そこで、まず、この過去形「ていた」の例を検討する。

(1) マーケットで会った近所の人、
　A：貴女のうちの庭で猫が死んでいたわよ。
　　これを聞いた私は、今でも「死んでいる（死体がある）」と思って、「ああ困った。帰ってどうにかしなければ……」と家路を急ぐ。

(2) 街角で近所の人とお喋りをしているところ、家から出てきた子供が言う。
　子供：ストーブが点いていたよ。
　　　　私は「あ、大変。」今でも「点いている」と思って慌てて帰る。

（5）高橋（1985, p.33）工藤（1995, p.46）の術語は『完成相』対『継続相』

(3) 赤ちゃんの泣き声が聞こえたような気がしたので母親が見に行って来た。
　　父親：どうだった？
　　母親：寝ていた。
　　　　それを言った人も聞いた人（父親や同座の人）も、今赤ちゃんは「寝ている」と思う。

(4) 姉妹は、いつも同じ部屋にいる。姉がダイニングルームに来たので、食事の支度を済ませた母親が、妹はどうしたかと思って尋ねる。
　　母親：Aちゃん（妹の名）は？
　　姉　：作文　書いていた。
　　　　母親は今も「書いている」と思い、「じゃ、先に食べよう。」などと言う。

(5) お財布が落ちているのを見つけた子が報告する。
　　子供：あっちの道にお財布が落ちていたよ。
　　母親：あらいやね。拾って届けた方がいいかしら。（母親は今でも落ちていると思って外へ出て行く。）

　上例は、「ていた」の代わりに「ている」でも可なのであるが、自然な会話では、特に(3)の例などでは、「ていた」が好まれるであろう。その理由も後に述べる。
　重要なことは、上例の、「ている」と「ていた」は、普通態の「る」「た」と平行的ではないということである。普通態各々の対応形
　　(1)死　ぬ：死んだ　(2)点　く：点いた　(3)寝　る：寝た
　　(4)書　く：書いた　(5)落ちる：落ちた
　これらが、上述のように、同じ事実に対して相関関係をもつことはない。

　ところで、普通態が相関関係をもつのは、過去形と、非過去否定形である。参考のため次にそれを考察する。

2.2 普通態過去形と否定非過去形の相関関係

　金田一（1947, p.15）は、否定の助動詞「ない」がつく場合を挙げ、「状態動詞につくと、現在または未来の状態の否定を表す」が、「継続動詞＋『ない』は過去の事実及び未来の事実に対する否定を表す。」「『私はこの新聞を読まない』は『私はまだこの新聞をよんでいない』の意、即ち、過去の事実の否定をあらわしているか、『私は将来において読む意向がない』の意、即ち、未来の事実の否定を表しているかである。」

　しかし、『私はこの新聞を読まない』は、果たして過去の事実の否定だろうか。私（東京出身）の語感では、未来の事実の否定ならば受け入れられるが、<u>過去の事実の否定</u>としては受け入れられない[6]。しかし限られたcontextに於いてならば過去との相関関係がある。

(1) 色々な新聞が一杯散らかっている部屋にいる私を見た妹が、呆れ顔で、
　　妹：あんた、これ全部<u>読んだ</u>（の）？
　　私：えっ？　あ、スポーツ新聞は<u>読まない</u>（わよ）。あとは全部読んだ。

(2) ケタタマしく門のフォンが鳴ったと思った。慌てて出て行ったが誰もいない。そばに夫がいた。
　　私：あなたフォン<u>押した</u>？
　　夫：(怪訝な顔で) え？
　　　　<u>押さない</u>（よ）。どうして？
　　　　（私の思い違い。二階の呼び鈴の故障を息子が試していたのだった。）

(3) 塀の落書きを見て、子供に
　　私　：あんたこれ<u>書いた</u>？
　　子供：エーッ？！　<u>書かない</u>（よ）ー。やだなー。

---

(6) この考察は、東京大学角田太作教授の講義中に、大学院生の田中智子氏によって取り上げられた疑問に基づく。

(4) 3人称でも同様で、落書きを見つけ、さっきまでいたAちゃんの仕業と思い

　　私　：Aちゃん悪い子ね。こんな悪戯書き<u>して</u>！
　　息子：Aちゃんそんなこと<u>しない</u>（よ）。お母さんはすぐそういうこと言う！

　これらは、行われたという相手の<u>判断</u>を<u>訂正</u>する場合には可である。濡れ衣を着せられたときの訂正といえばいいかもしれない。つまり、過去の「事実」に対する否定ではなく、相手（話し手）の判断に対する否定ではないだろうか。これらの文の動作者を明らかにする時、「が」を入れることはできないのである。

(1)　私が<u>読まない</u>。（cf.　私　読まない）
(2)　僕が<u>押さない</u>。（cf.　僕　押さない）
(3)　僕が<u>書かない</u>。（cf.　僕　書かない）
(4)　Aちゃんが<u>しない</u>。（cf.　Aちゃん　しない）

　多くのアスペクト研究で、常にムードが問題となっている。このことは、事実の叙述と話し手の判断との区別が必要であることを示唆している。話し手の判断には、殆ど必ずムード的要素があると考えられるのである。

2.3　人称による差異

　2.1の、例(1)と(2)の動詞（死ぬ、点く）は、話し手が自分の動作に言うことはできない。そこで(3)の動作主を1人称に取り替えてみる。
(3')　私、<u>寝ていた</u>。
　　これは絶対に「寝ている」と同じだとは解釈されない。つまり、寝ている人はものを言わないからあり得ない。そこで、単語を「起きる」に取り替えてみる。

　(3)の赤ちゃんについては、「寝ていた」の場合と同様で、母親は、「起きて

いた」と答え、ミルクの準備などを始める。母親も聞いた人も、今「起きている」と解釈する。しかし

(3") 私、起きていた。

　これは、今起きていることを指しているのではなく、ある時点で起きていた（過去）を意味するのが普通ではないか。たとえ狸寝入りの場合でも、やはり、過去時点を意味していると思われる。

(4") 私、書いていた。

　これは、現在「書いている」のように理解されることは全くない。この対応例のように、ダイニングルームでこのように言ったら、それは過去の事だと理解される。

　つまり、動作者の人称によって、この同じ形式の表す事実が異なるのである。動作者が、話し手（1人称）であるか、それ以外であるかというのは、この点で実に重要なのである。
　上記のような例は特別なものではなく、継続動詞でも瞬間動詞でも同様で、例は、誰でも、いくらでも、思い浮かべることができるであろう。もう1例挙げる。

(5) 子供達が外で遊んでいる。学校から帰って来た姉娘が鞄を置き、服を着替えてから、おやつを食べにキチンに来て言う。

　姉：お母さん。Aちゃん（弟の名前）泣いていたよ。
　　　母親は今でも泣いていると思い、喧嘩でもしているのかと、外に出て行く。

(5") 私、泣いていた。

　これは、過去の事だと理解される。「泣いている」のだと理解されることは無い。
　ここで述べた諸例は、先に述べたように、動作者を、「私が」という形で出現させることはない。

　次に、動作者が話者であっても、次のように、動作が眼前に無い場合を考

えてみる。

(6”) 電話（動作が見えない）の場合[7]
 友達：あなた今何<u>している</u>の／何<u>していた</u>の？
 私　：<u>作文書いていた</u>。／<u>書いている</u>。もう少しで終わる。
 友達：じゃ、今から誘いに行くわ。40分くらいかかるからね。
　普通、対面の会話では、特別の場合を除いて、話者の動作が相手から見える。たとえ、ドアや襖で隔てられていても、気配を感じられる。質問時と同時では「ていた」で質問し、答えるということは無い。

　以上に示したように、上記のような、<u>動作者の人称</u>により、「ていた」形のテンス的な解釈が異なることを説明するのは、単語ないし連語のレベルでは、難しいのである。ここで、この問題が起こるのは１人称（即ち話し手）の動作を指し示す場合であることに注意しよう。

　無意思動詞では、当然この傾向がはっきりする。期待されるとおり、変化動詞ではその傾向が強い。
(1)　濡れて帰宅した子供に
  母親：あれ？　<u>雨降っていた</u>の？　気付かなかった。お姉ちゃんに傘持
    って行ってあげなければ。（今も降っていると思う）
(2)　水引草が好きなことを知っている友人。水引草を差し出しながら
  友人：土手で一杯<u>咲いていた</u>わ。
  私　：じゃ明日私も行ってみよう。（今も明日も<u>咲いている</u>と思う）
(3)　（電子レンジを何分かければいいか解らないで、適当にやってから）
  私　：<u>温まっていた</u>？
  子供（確かめて）：うん　<u>温まっている</u>。
　同例は多い。「乾いていた。／？」「乾いている。／？」「腐っていた。／？」「腐っている。／？」等々。

---

(7) 電話器が携帯やコードレスの場合は、手を休めず「書いている」と言うだけかもしれない。

3. 第一種動詞の「ている」形

　第一種動詞、「ている」が普通付かないといわれているものに、人称に関する差異があるかないかを検討する。
　「ある」「いる」「要る」などには「ている」の形がない。そして、これらは、単独の文では、「が」に後置されるのが普通である。「は」に後置されれば、それは対照を意味する。

　　×本が<u>あっている</u>。　　敦子が<u>いている</u>。　　お金が<u>要っている</u>。
　　本<u>が</u>ある。　　　　　敦子<u>が</u>いる。　　　　お金<u>が</u>要る。
　　本<u>は</u>ある。　　　　　敦子<u>は</u>いる。　　　　お金<u>は</u>要る。

同様に
　　×私（に）<u>は</u>～あなた（に）<u>は</u>～彼（に）<u>は</u>　<u>できている</u>。
　　　私（に）<u>は</u>～あなた（に）<u>は</u>～彼（に）<u>は</u>　できる。
　　　私<u>が</u>～あなた<u>が</u>～彼<u>が</u>　<u>できる</u>。

単独ではこのように「ている」形は不可である。そして上の3動詞と異なるのは、その動作・状態主体に「が」が後置されるのは、疑問文（誰ができる？等）への答えのような特別の場合だと考えられる。つまり上の3動詞は「が」を伴うのが普通なのだが、こちらは、「は」が普通なのである。
　これは、上の3動詞とは以下に述べるように異なる。前述した「ていた」と「ている」が交換可の場合との類似性（どういう意味で類似かは後述）があると考えられる。以下に「できる」および可能動詞を取り上げる。

(1)　漢字書き取りの練習を沢山させたら、翌日の試験は良く<u>できていた</u>。
　　母親（答案用紙を見ながら）：アラーッ。今日は、<u>できている</u>！　凄い！

(2)　発音練習授業の後
　　自信のない学生：先生これで良いですか。聞いてください。
　　先生：　　　　うん。そうそう。（ちゃんと発音）<u>できている</u>（わよ）。
　　　　　　　　　いいわ。

(3)　水泳は顔が水の中だから、初めてのときは自分がどうなっているか、よ

319

くわからない。それを見てあげながら、
　　あーっ！　今度は、うまく泳げていたわよ。ほら、もう一かきで縁に届いたのに…

(4)　ピアノのお稽古で、前回、もっと旋律を歌いなさいと注意されていた。
　　先生：練習したわね。今日は、よく歌えていました。

　これらの、動作・状態の主は、話し手以外である。このような場合が多い。しかし次のように、話し手の動作・状態についても出現するように見える。

(5)　試験を返してもらった後で、友達と
　　私　：3番の問題、難しかったよね。点数、からいし…
　　友達：そう？　私はできていた（よ）。
　客観的に見ることができる特定の物事に対してなら、このように、可なのである。

　これらは、話し手が、そういう事実を述べているのではない。これらの動作・状態主を「が」で表すことは、そぐわないのである。(1)は「試験が良くできている！」と、可のように思われるが、これは「あらーっ。(今日は)試験が良くできている。」のような発見（判断）に近い。
　このように考えると、これらは、その状態の発現を、認識・判断した時なのだと考えられる。「あっ。忘れていた！」など、「発見」や「思い出し」などと言われているが、同様に話し手の「瞬時の認識・判断」なのではないか。動作主体を「が」で出現させることは、特別な場合（疑問文の後や対比）以外できないのである。
×私が忘れていた！（cf. 私、忘れていた！）

（8）高橋（1985, p.295）非過去「ている」で言うと普通の用法で、過去は特殊な用法だとしている。

4．第四種動詞の「ている」形

次に、常に「ている」が付く第四種を検討する。これらは、動作・状態主体を示す「は」に後置され出現するが、「が」に後置される独立文は現れにくい。

(1) あら似ている！

これは、1・2・3人称と共に出現するが、もしここに「が」を付すと独立の文では、どうも座りが悪い。

  あの子（／私／あなた）は母親に似ている。
  ？あの子（／私／あなた）が母親に似ている。
    （cf.　？　私が嬉しい。）

「が」の文は、「誰が似ているの？」への返事なら可だが、独立では現れにくい。

(2) 山が聳えている。
  ？山は聳えている
  ？あの山は聳えている

もし言うことがあるなら、山を眼前にして発すると思われる（森林地帯を抜け出したら、広い谷の向こうに山があった。それを見て等）。しかし「は」の後ろや、特定の山を指して言うのは、共にどこかおかしい。強いて言えば「山は聳えている。川は流れている。鳥は鳴いている。…」のように、「この地では」と、ある地方の情景を叙して、列挙するときであろう。「山が聳えている」は、普通「(山が聳えて)(いる)」という話し手の発見に近い判断を示すと思われる。

(3) この論文は優れている。
  ？この論文が優れている。

これも、「は」で示された主体の後ろに出現する。「が」は疑問文の答えなら可であろうが単独の言い初めでは、どこかおかしい。普通は、資質とか物に関して言われることで、「あの人が優れている」は、問いへの答えならと

もかく、はじめから言うことは先ずない。「Aさんは優れている」も不自然であろう。

　優れているも話し手の判断・認識を示しているように思われる。「私の勘は優れている」。「私は勘が優れている」など。

　発見ならば、前項どうように、論文を読んで、「凄い！　例文が優れている！」のように言うこともあるだろう。(cf.「この論文は例文が優れている」)

(4)　青い顔をしている

　自分の顔は見えないから自分には言わないが、気分の悪いとき鏡を覗いて見ながらなら言える。見ての判断なのである。これも、つい先ほど会った人のことを、「伊豆山さん、青い顔をしていた」と言えば聞いている人は今なお青い顔でげんなりしているのだと思う。「は」が適切だと感じる。

　「伊豆山さんが青い顔をしている」は適切でない感じがするが、以下のように発見に似た場合なら可であろう。

(4″)　偶々廊下で、すれ違って、「あれ？！　顔色が悪い！」と思い、一緒にいた友人に、「ねー気がついた？　伊豆山さんが青い顔をしていたー。どうしたのかな。」ふり返って見た友人は言う。「ほんとだ。青い顔をしている。」

5.「ている」形と話し手

　以上のべた事実を勘案すると、「ている」は継続や動作の完了を表すのではなく、第一義的には、話し手による「動作・状態の出現の確認」ではないかと思われてくる。

　必要な特徴は出現なのである。それが継続しているか、完了しているかは、動詞の語彙的な意味によるものなのではないか。それらに関しては、金田一、工藤など、動詞分類の研究がある。

ここで言う確認は、主として「見る」ことによって行われる。だから、「ている」形は眼前での行為に用いられることが多い。「地球は自転している」のように、非日常の文語的知識は、なんらかの手段によって、それを確認していることを伝えていると考えることに支障はない。関係者の誰でもがそれを共通に確認すると言う点で、日常の「ている」と同様である。このような非日常の知識は、日常の基本の上にかぶさっていると考えられる。
　「ている」形では、必要とあれば、その発話時に、聞き手を含め誰にでもその動作・状態の出現確認ができるのである。
　例示する。
　子供が欲しいというものを以前に渡した。昨日また、欲しいと言う。母親も渡したことを忘れて、また買った。今日部屋を見たら以前渡したものがちゃんとある。一緒にいた祖母に言う。

　　母親：あらいやだ。あの子、自分でしまって、忘れている。
　　　　　私も渡しておいて、すっかり忘れていた。

　これに反し「ていた」形は、「話し手の確認が過去に行われた」ということなのである。動作の継続や完了が過去に行われたというわけではない。但し、その動作・状態は、発話時点では、話し手も含め、その発話関係者が経験・確認はできない。もし何かの科学的手段（例えばコンピューターグラフィック）で、地球が回る写真でも見たら、後で「地球が回っていたよ」と報告することができる。当然、地球は今でも回っているのである。話し手も勿論そう思っている。
　動作主が話し手と重なるとき、つまり１人称の時は、「ていた」形（「書いていた」）が「ている」形（「書いている」）と相関関係をもつことはない。これは、この形の必要な特徴の中に、「発話時に、その動作・状態が確認できない（見えない）」が含まれるからなのである。だから過去にならざるを得ない。
　つまり過去の事実なのか、今尚、そうであるかは、この形式に属する事柄ではなく、他の補助手段によって判断することなのである。

言語的手段による場合。
(1')　近所の人：あなたの家の庭で猫が死んでいた（よ）ね。
　　　私　　　：え？　何時のこと？　ああ、この前ね。
(1")　近所の人：この間、あなたの家の庭で猫が死んでいたけどどうした？
　　　　　　　（cf. あなたの家の庭で猫が死んでいたけど、どうする？）
　　　私　　　：保健所に電話した。あなたも見たの？私気がつかなかった。

　上のような言語的手段によらない場合もある。
(5)の場合、姉娘がゆっくり着替えてから来て、
(5")　姉：お母さん。Ａちゃん泣いていたよ。
　　　母：あ、どうせ玩具の取り合いでしょ。今、一度戻って、またすぐ出
　　　　　て行った。
などのように、落ち着いて答え、過去のことだと思う。
　純粋に過去を表すと言われる次例も付け加える。これも同様だと考えられる。(9)

(7)　ここに（／は）聖徳太子が住んでいた（の）。
　もし、「聖徳太子」が何者であるか全く知識を持っていなければ、「聖徳太子って誰？　私知らないよ。」「どうしてそんなこと、知ってるの？」等々の会話があるだろう。これは、知り合いについて話す次の会話と差があるとは思えない。
(7')　敦子の従姉妹どうしの会話
　「ここに（／は）敦子が住んでいた（の）。」「へー。幾つの時？」
過去を示すのは、「ていた」ではなく、「聖徳太子」なのである。

　こう考えると、先にあげた例が全部理解できる。つまり図式的に言うなら「作文を　書いている」ではなく、「作文を書いて─いる」「作文を書いて─いた」。「猫が　死んでいる」ではなく「猫が死んで─いる」「猫が死んで─

---

(9) 井上優氏のご教示による。

いた」。

　つまり、その動詞の動作主の他に、その動作への認識・判断をする主体（話し手）を想定することが必要なのである。多くの研究者がモーダルな要素を設定する必要を感じる所以である。

　このことは、工藤の（B）内的状態動詞（思考、感情、知覚、感覚）の人称制限を考える上でも都合が良い。「彼は　驚いて—いた」は、話し手の彼に対する判断なのである。「彼」は、「驚いて」の動作者であろうが、「驚いていた」の動作者ではないのである。つまり、これは、内的状態動詞という特別の場合だからなのではなく、内的状態動詞だから、はっきり本来の「話し手による認識・判断」という「ている」の機能が現れたと考える。

　このような理由で、風の強い日に、はらはら落ちる葉を見ながら「（風が強いから）木の葉が落ちている」と言うし、「あそこに、お財布が落ちている」とも言える。また同じことを「あそこに、お財布が落ちていた」とも言える。

　反復性についても同様である。木の葉がいくつ落ちていても、花が色々咲いていても、「落ちている」「咲いている」なのである。人が戦争で「大勢死んでいる」も、特に異なる特徴をもつわけではない。「落ちる」ことが起き、それを話し手が認識・判断したのである。「咲く」ことが起き、それを話し手が認識した。人が死ぬことが起き、それを話し手が認識した。日本語の動詞は、繰り返しも一体として捕らえられている。普通態（完成相）でも、「昔はよく手紙を書いた。」と言えば、繰り返されていた行為を指すのである。名詞に複数が無いのは周知の事である。

　「テレビでそう言っていた。」が「言った」よりも多く使われるように感じられるのは、同様な理由に基づく。「言うのを聞いた」という話し手の認識を示すのだと思われる。

　「ている」形は、このように、動作・状態の出現の確認・判断であると考えるが、その動作・状態の出現する瞬間（始まり）は必要な特徴ではない。つまりその出現する瞬間を見（経験す）る必要はない。話し手が見たときは

---

(10) 工藤（1995, p.45）

すでにその動作・状態は始まっている。「山が聳える」「勘が優れる」「ナイフが尖る」などの動作の始まりは不要である。既に始まっているからこそ、そう認識・判断できるのである。アスペクトを考える時、終わり方への考察は常に詳しいが、始まりの方も考察対象にしなければならない。

　「書いている」でも、妹が書き始めた時点は必要な特徴ではない。話し手の認識した時、その行為は<u>既に始まっている</u>のである。「死んでいる」でも、その死の瞬間は必要な特徴ではない。「死」は既に始まっていることが必要なのである。落ちるも同様で、「落ちる」が始まる瞬間は必要ない。結果ということが強調される所以である。しかし、「聳えている」「優れている」なども、始まりが必要ないという点では同様なのである。

　このようなことは日本語として無駄な議論のように思われるかもしれないが、琉球の方言には、その始まる瞬間がアスペクト的特徴として必要とされる形式もある。[11] タイポロジー的な観点からは重要事項であろう。

6．終わりに

　話し言葉では、無色透明の文は無い。独り言も含め、必ず誰かが誰かに話しているのである。「話し手」は常に存在する。構文における話し手は、単に1人称、2人称、3人称という同レベルにある3語彙の一つにすぎないというものではない。「ている」形の考察はそれを物語っている。

「ている」形

　動作・状態が出現しているという話し手の認識・判断を表す。その動作・状態の出現を見た（経験した）と言い換えてもいいかも知れない。但しその動作・状態は、その発話時点で、発話関係者が等しくその確認・判断に参加できる（見る／経験することができる）と理解される。しかし、その動作・状態の始まりを認識する必要はない。

---

(11) Arakaki（2002, p.26)

「ていた」形

　動作状態が出現しているという話し手の認識・判断が既に行われた（過去に認識した）ことを表す。そして発話時には、話し手を含め発話関係者が、その動作・状態を見ることができない（経験できない）。従って、話し手本人の動作・状態では、当然過去のことになる。それ以外の人／物の動作・状態なら、今もそうだ（継続／完了）と思うか思わないかは、この形式以外の要素に基づく。（例えばそう遠い過去ではなさそうだという場面状況とか、他の言語形式、「あの時、昔…」など、があるとか）。先に述べたように、一瞬前の、瞬時の判断も含むことができる。

　以上のように考えると、形態素の切れ目と構文要素の切れ目とは一致しなくなる。いくつか簡単に例示する。
(a)　犬が歩いて　いる
(b)　Ａちゃんが歩いて　いる
(b')　Ａちゃんは　歩いて　いる
(c)　鉛筆の先が尖って　いる
(c')　このナイフは　尖って　いる
(d)　山が聳えて　いる
(e)　猫が死んで　いる
(e')　この猫は　死んで　いる

　形態素の切れ目と構文的切れ目が一致しない例は他にもある。よく知られている例を挙げる。これも話し手の気持ちを表す形態素であることに注目しよう。
　　　歩きたい　　(a)　速く歩き　たい。
　　　　　　　　　(b)　とても　歩きたい。
　言語の研究には、論理もさることながら、先ず、ある実在言語に内在する論理を取り出すことが求められるのではないだろうか。そのためには、文字作品、テキストなどを研究するのは大切だが日常の話し言葉の研究がさらに重要だと思われる。

また、構文的研究には、文全体を見る必要があると思われる。日本語の場合は、特に、「は」との関連が重要である。

【参考文献】
2000年　新垣友子：Arakaki、Tomoko "The Study of Grammar in Luchuan" 消滅に瀕した方言語法の緊急調査研究（２）「環太平洋の言語」成果報告書Ａ４-012所収大阪学院大学情報学部
2000年　沖裕子：「アスペクトからみた動詞分類再考」人文科学論集34信州大学
1976年　金田一春彦：「日本語動詞のアスペクト」むぎ書房
1995年　工藤真由美：「アスペクト・テンス体系とテクスト」ひつじ書房
1985年　高橋太郎：「現代日本語動詞のアスペクトとテンス」秀英出版
1984年　寺村秀夫：「日本語のシンタクスと意味」第Ⅱ巻　くろしお出版

琉球・八重山（与那国）方言の文法基礎研究

1．与那国島の概要

　沖縄県八重山郡与那国町は、与那国島全島からなる町である。北緯24度27分東経123度00分日本最西端である。沖縄本島から南西へ509km、東京から2030kmの距離にあるが、隣接する台湾からは111kmという近さにある[1]。山があり、水が良い。海の美しさは言うまでもない島である。

　　　人口　748所帯　1,789人　　人口増加率－2.7%　　面積28.88km^2 [2]

　ここで報告するのは、行政の中心としての町役場がある祖納(そない)の方言である。他に比川(ひがわ)と港町久部良(くぶら)の2集落が各々離れて存在する。

　与那国の歴史は未詳の部分が多い。1500年頃に与那国を支配した女性、サンアイ・イソバの伝説は有名だが、史書に現れるのは鬼虎である。1522年中山王尚真時代に宮古島の仲宗根豊見親によって討伐された。その後の与那国と宮古の間の伝説哀話もいろいろある[3]。この遠い二つの島が関係をもっていたのである。

2．危機的な状況

　東洋経済新報社都市データパック2002年版によると、65歳以上の人口は21.3%だから、約383人である。久部良は港町なので、方言的にはどちらかと言えば混交的で新しい住民も多いと言われている。そのような事情を考慮

（1）位置図とも与那国町ホームページよる。与那国島地図はマピオHPによる。
（2）東洋経済新報社都市データパック2002年に基づく。Yahoo地域情報より。
（3）池間（1959）による。

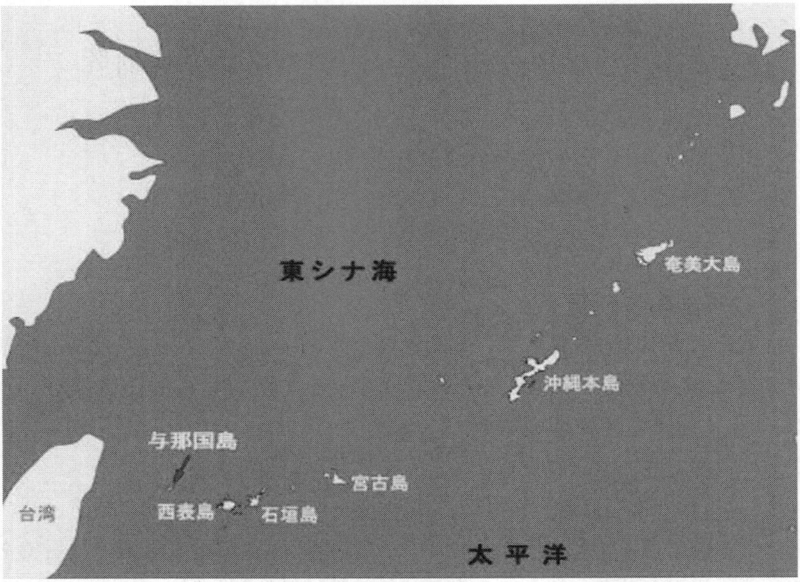
東シナ海
奄美大島
沖縄本島
与那国島
宮古島
西表島
石垣島
台湾
太平洋

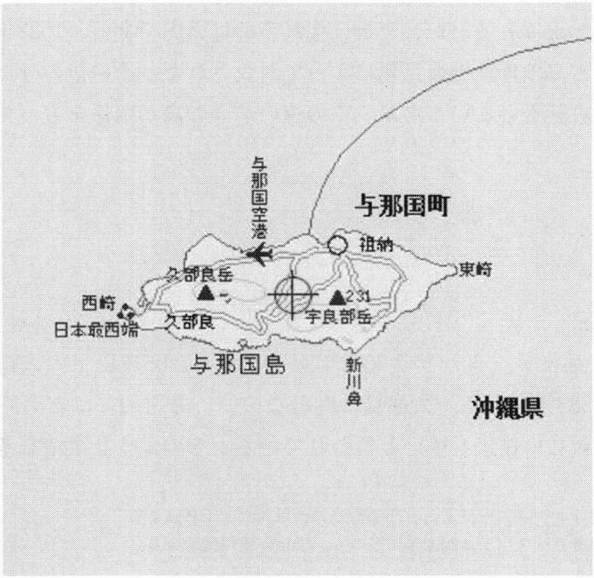
与那国空港
与那国町
祖納
東崎
久部良岳
西崎
日本最西端
久部良
231
宇良部岳
与那国島
新川鼻
沖縄県

すると、租内の方言話者数は100人前後ではないだろうか。

　人口増加率はマイナス2.7％である。25歳から64歳までの人口が略50％を占めている。15歳から24歳までは6.5％と最も少ない。これには、色々理由があろうが、一つは教育の問題がある。

　与那国では明治18年に小学校が始まった。最初の訓導は、広島県士族出身だったという。小学校は、明治17年9月設置認可を得るが、訓導の船便が遅れ、18年6月開校した。この田恕訓導は広島県士族出身で、石垣南小学校訓導を退職して来島した。18年の生徒数は、43名だったというから、教育熱が高かったと想像される。つまり、共通語教育の長い歴史があるのだと言える。(4)

　現在、与那国島には高等学校が無い。現在日本は、高校卒の資格を必要とする職が多い。15歳で中学を終えると、高等学校教育を受ける為には、高校のある石垣市か、沖縄本島に行かなければならない。この経済的負担は大きいから、一家で島を出ることに繋がるのである。

　もう一つは、医療の問題である。良い診療所があり、日常の健康管理や老人、幼児の健康管理などの施設も整っているのだが、大病の場合はヘリコプターで石垣まで行くということも起こる。高齢ともなれば、病も多くなる。どうしても大きな医療施設のあるところが好ましくなってくる。島以外で暮らす息子・娘の招きに応じて島を出ることにもなるのである。因みに、各地の郷友会（与那国出身者の会）は盛んだという。

　郷土に暮らす若年層にも、そのような事情は解っている。与那国方言は、他の八重山方言の話者達からも「解らない」と言われている。従って、子供達に、わざわざ学ばせることはないということになってしまう。与那国方言は、「石垣島を中心に行われている八重山方言とは異なる方言」だと分類する研究者もいるほどなのだから、無理からぬことである。(5)

　島の産業も変わってきた。立派な空港があり、石垣及び那覇からの直行便がある。レジャー産業としてダイビングも有名である。ということは、新し

---

(4)　以上は「与那国小学校創立百周年記念誌」による。
(5)　上村（1992, p.782）、高橋（1992, p.873）

い住民も増えることに繋がる。島が活性化すれば方言も変わらざるをえないのである。方言を話す機会も少なくなってくる。

　台湾とは距離的に本土より遥かに近い。昔から、本土から台湾へ行く大きい船が寄港していた。現在も台湾と交流が続いている。中国語の講習会もある。

　土地の方々も方言の消失には危機感があり、ありがたいことに、数年前に与那国出身で与那国在住の池間苗氏による、「与那国ことば辞典」が上梓された。氏には十余年前に初めて与那国を訪れた時からお世話になっている。

3．表記

　与那国方言は音韻的に特色がある。柴田（1959）、平山・中本（1964）などに詳しい記述がある。ここでは、簡略音声表記による。しかし、いくつか記しておかなければならないことがある。

　喉頭化・非喉頭化の対立は、語頭以外では、音韻的対立をなしていないと思われるので、語頭だけ区別して表記した。語頭で対立を持つ子音は、語中では、無気喉頭化音である。

　母音間の軟口蓋鼻音［ŋ］（［G］で転写）は、鼻音部分が長く破裂との間に音節の切れ目が無いように聞こえる。語末の成節的鼻音には2種類あるように思われる。名詞語末成節鼻音は、八重山方言の通例で口蓋垂鼻音というより軟口蓋鼻音［ŋ］に近く、jaが後接すると、渡り音［g］に近い音が聞こえることがある。ところが、動詞の語末形態素の口蓋垂鼻音［N］は、極めて緩い閉鎖で、殆ど鼻母音に近いことが多い。他の八重山方言でしっかりした［ŋ］に近い音であるのと対照的である。疑問辞のGaが後接すると、NGaだかGaだか迷うのである。現在、表記上はGにした。共通語東京方言などの「が」［ŋa］より鼻音部分が長いので、形態素の切れ目などでは特に、NGaと表すべきか、Gaと表すべきか迷うのだが、動詞ではGaに統一した。NG

――――――――――

(6) Ex. uN（扇）、muN（麦）にjaが後置した場合。

(NaNGa 波が) と Ng (Ngi 髭) と G (aGa 私が) の対立があることになる。動詞では、柴田 (1972) のテキストでも統一されず、Nŋ と ŋ が出現している。平山 (1964) は、語中では [ŋ] に統一されているようである。

　また、語末の母音は音韻論的無意味に長く且つ広くなることがある。この点もまだ諸研究者間で一致していない。例えば平山 (1964, p.35) は、「助詞／du'u／は (中略) 東京方言の [o] ほどの広さの場合もある」。池間 (1998) は [do] で短い [o] である。柴田 (1972, p.55) は／u／だけを認めている。池間氏は与那国出身なので無視できないものがある。

　この助詞に関しては、確かに広くて音声的には [o] に近い。しかも du より唇が丸められる。このような発音はもう一つ、未然形の独立した形 (志向形と呼ばれる) の語末音である。話者の内省でも、違うということもあり、似ているということもある。研究者間も一致せず高橋 (1987) は短母音の u としている。筆者は、まだ、迷っているが、僅かに異なる音であることは確かである。

　例えば「来る」の命令形が3種ある。ku:(来い) と kuba (おいで) との母音は、同じだと思われるのだが、小さい子供に優しく言う (2回繰り返されることがよくある)「おいで」は、[kɪo:] [kuo:] のようで、ku:とは違うと感じる話者も居る。筆者は、唇の丸めがあるので [kwu:] ではないかと考えている。その積りで口腔内を広くして発音すると「それでいい」と言われる。そんなわけで、／dwu／，／gwu／，／rwu／なども、考えている。この論文では、決定的ではないが、一応そういう解釈を採るが、簡略音声表記なので、音声的に [o] を用いることもあるが、音韻的解釈というわけではない。印刷の都合で以下のように書き換えた。

　ʃ→sj, tʃ→c, dʒ/ʒ→zj, Φ→hw～h, ɡ→g, ŋ→G

　成節鼻音→N, 無気喉頭化音→大文字 (語中では対立が無いので小文字)

4．人称代名詞と指示代名詞

	1人称	2人称	自己称	3人称	再帰	疑問
単数	a-nu～a-ɢa	ɴda	×	kari	sa:	ta(:)～taɢa
複数	ba:～ba-ɢa	ɴdi, ɴdiɴta	baɴta	kaɴtati	si:	taɴta:

	こ	そ	あ	疑問
単数	ku	u	kari	nu
複数	kuɴtati	uɴtati	kaɴtati	×
場所	kum-a	um-a	kam-a	mm-a
修飾	kunu	unu	kanu	×

代名詞に関する説明

(1) 1人称複数形は、<u>あなた（達）に対する私達</u>であるが、自己称は、<u>彼（等）に対する私達</u>である。⁽⁷⁾ exclusive（話し相手を含まない）、Inclusive（話し相手を含む）の対立のように言われることもあるが、そうではない。これらの代名詞と動詞形の共起関係は注意すべきである。

(2) 2人称の敬称はない。複数形の ɴdiɴta は、好ましくないコノテーションがある。

(3) 3人称代名詞がある。今見えない人を文脈指示することができる。しかし今、話し手の眼前に居る敬意持つべき人には <u>kanu tu</u>（あの人）の方が好まれる。

(4) 「どれ」「どの」のように選ぶ疑問詞はなく、<u>ta:</u>(誰)、<u>nu:</u>(何) が兼ねている。しかし多くの中から選ぶことを示す係り助詞 ba が出現することに注意すべきである。

(5) 表示しなかったが、<u>uɴni</u>（こう）<u>kuɴni</u>（そう）はあるが <u>kaɴni</u>（ああ）は無い。

(6) 指示代名詞の複数は人間に対してだけである。物に対する複数はない。

(7) ここでは「こ、そ、あ」と仮に単純に記した。琉球諸方言の常として、

---

(7) 詳しくは伊豆山（1992）参照

琉球・八重山（与那国）方言の文法基礎研究

本土共通語とは異なる。例えば手にしていながらuで指すことができる。詳細は未調査である。kaは会話者から物理的心理的に遠いものを指す。

(8)「ここ／そこ／あそこ／どこに」では、kum-a→kum-iのようにa→iと変化する。

(9) 所有を表すのには、Gaが必要なものと不必要なものがある。

(10) 人称代名詞等の語形変化形については、以下の文中に含めた。会話の流れに沿ようにしたので、区分けは大まかである。この項に関係ある語にはどの区分内でも下線を付した。

人称代名詞

(1) A： <u>ta</u>　ja:？（外で戸を叩く人へ）
　　　　誰
　　B： <u>anu:</u>.（声で知らせる）
　　　　私
　　A： <u>anu</u>　Ndi　<u>ta</u>:　kaja:.
　　　　私って　誰かね

(2) u　ja　<u>Nda</u>　iri.　kuja　<u>aGa</u>　iruN.
　　それ　は　あんた　やれ　これ　は　私が　する

(3) <u>kumi</u>　aru　munu　ja　<u>ta</u>:　munu ja:.
　　ここに　ある　物　は　誰の　物　か
　　<u>Nda</u>　munu.／<u>aGa</u>　munu.／<u>kari Ga</u>　mumu.／<u>kaNtati</u>　munu.／
　　あなたの物　　私の物　　　彼の物　／　彼等の物
　　<u>baNta</u>　　munu.
　　私達（自己称）の物
　　<u>ba</u>:　munu.／<u>ku Ga</u>⁽⁸⁾　munu.／<u>u Ga</u>　munu.／
　　私達の物　　　この（人）の物　　　あの人の物

（8）目上の人にku-は言い難い。その場にいる人ならkunu/unu/kanu Tu numunu等。KuNtati munuは殆ど使う機会が無い。

kanu ᴛu nu　munu.　／　uɴtati　munu.
　　　あの　人　の　物　　　その人達の　物
(4)　anu　aᴛa　ja　buranuɴ.　ɴda　aᴛa　ja　bu:　na？
　　　私　明日　は　居ない　　お前　明日　は　いる　か
(5)　ɴdiɴᴛa　　no ba　ki　bu　ɢa　je:.
　　　あんた達　何を　　しているの　か
　　例えば若者がたむろしているので、何か悪いことでもしているか……と言うような時目上の人が言う。見下げたような感じを伴う。
(6)　taɴta:　bu　ɢa？　誰々がいるの
　　　誰々　居るの
(7-1)　ta　ba　ɴdja　nu　　abuta　ja.
　　　　どれが　あなたんちの　お母さんか
(7-2)　ɴdja　　　nu abuta　ja　ta　ja？（上よりこの方が好ましい。)
　　　　あなたんち　のお母さん　は　どれ　か
(7-3)　子供に向かって言うなら、ɴda　　abuta　　ja　ta　ja.
　　　　　　　　　　　　　　　　あんたの　お母さん　は　どれ　か
(8)　kuja　taɢa　ka　ɢa.
　　　これは　誰が　買ったのか
　　　u　ja　aɢa　kaɴ.
　　　それは　私が　買った
(9)　taɢa　kagu　ɢa？
　　　誰が　書くか
　　　aɢa　kaguɴ.
　　　私が　書く
　　　atsuko　ɢa　kaguɴ　do.　／　atsuko　ɢa　du　kagu.
　　　敦子　が　書く　よ　　　敦子　が　書くのだ
(10)　anu　ja　numanuɴ.
　　　私　は　飲まない
(11)　anuɴ　isji　du　kiru　nai.
　　　私も　やる　ん　だよ

NdaN budi kiru na?
あんたも踊りするか
banuN iruN.
私達も する
baNtaN iru na:?
私達も やろうか

(12) kunu Nnani anu Nki turai.
この 着物 私 に 頂戴
Nda Nki ja sjiba du aru.
あんたに は 狭い

疑問代名詞・指示代名詞・人称代名詞（対格等）

(1) nu ba Nda munu ja:.
どれが あなたの 物 か

(2) ku du aGa munu
これが私の物

(3) nu Ga maci ja:. ／ nu ba maci ja:.
どれ が 良い か どれ が 良い か
（沢山の中からでも二つからでもいい）
ku du maci. ／ u du maci. ／ kari du maci.
これ が いい それ が いい あれ が いい

(4) nu: ja.
なーに？（呼ばれた時や、いきなり入ってきた人に、何の用？））

(5) nu: ba.
何だって？（聞き取れなかった時問い返して尋ねる）

(6) ta: sui hiruGa. ／ taba sui hiruGa.
誰を 連れて 行くか 誰を 連れて 行くか
Nda sui hiruN. kazu sui hiruN.
あんたを 連れて 行く 和を 連れて 行く

　　　　anu　　sui　　hiruN？
　　　　私を　連れて　行く？
　　　　u:　kuN？　それ買う？
(7)　　ta　ba　katjaGa.　（肖像画を書いている人に問う）
　　　　誰を　　書いたのか　　この場合 ta:　katjaGa はよくない。
(8)　　ta　Nki　turasjaGa.
　　　　誰に　あげたのか
(9)　　kanu　minuGa　ja　Nma　nu　Tu　ja:？　（知らない人を見かけて）
　　　　あの　女　　は　どこ　の　人　か
　　　　　　　　　　　　　　　　答えて　sakibara　Ti　nu　dumi.
　　　　　　　　　　　　　　　　　　　　崎原　（分家）の　嫁
(10)　　Nma　Nki（ba）　hiruGa？
　　　　何処　に　　　行くのか
(11)　上記は行き先を本当に尋ねているのだが、外で人に出会った時の挨拶こ
　　　とばもある。
　　　　Nda　Nma　Nki　ja:？　　　×　Nma　Nki　ba:(挨拶では無い)
　　　　あなたどちら　　へ
　　　　　　　　　　　　答えて　kama Nki:　／　uma　Nki:
　　　　　　　　　　　　　　　　あそこまで　　そこまで(近くのとき)

1 人称複数と自己称

(1)　同じ所に行くあるグループが追い越して行くので、こちらのグループの
　　一人が言う。
　　　uNtati　ja　haja　aci　sji　hiru　Ga　baNta　ja　duri:　duri　hiNdagi.
　　　彼ら　は　早足　　で　行く　が　私達　は　ゆっくり　行こう
(2)　そして追い越したグループに向かって叫ぶ。
　　　Ndi　ja　　hajagu　hiri　jo:.　banu　ja　duri　duri　hiru　juNgara:.
　　　あんた達 は 早く　行きなさい 私達　は　ゆっくり　行くんだから

338

琉球・八重山（与那国）方言の文法基礎研究

(3) しばらくしてグループの一人が思い直し、グループの皆に言う。
<u>banta</u> bagi<u>N</u> <u>uNtati</u> tu madu<u>N</u> hajagu hi<u>N</u>dagi. di:
　私達　も　　彼等と　一緒に　早く　　行こう　　さあ

(4) 待ち合わせしているのだが一人来るのが遅い。
<u>kari</u> ja madi kunu<u>N</u> gara <u>baNta</u> sati nai <u>hirwu</u>.
　彼　は　まだ　来ない　から　私達　先に　　行こう
<u>kari</u> ja madi kunu<u>N</u>gara <u>baNta</u> satinai hiru na:?
　彼　は　まだ　来ないから　私達　先に　行くか？
　そう言い出した人に
<u>Nda</u> ja satinai hiri <u>banu</u> ja mati bu<u>N</u>.
　あんたは　先に　行け　私達　は　待っている

(5) 安売りを買っているグループを見ながら
<u>uNtati</u> ja dattsaru munu kai bu <u>Ga</u> <u>baNta</u> ja <u>kuNna</u> je:
　彼等は　　安いもの　買っているけど　　私達　は　買わないよねー
Cf. <u>Nda</u> <u>kanu</u> na?　anu ja <u>kanuN</u>.　<u>Nda</u> <u>kuN</u>?
　あんた買わないの　私　は　買わない　あんた買う？
<u>Nda</u> <u>kanuN</u>?　　<u>Nda</u> <u>kuNna</u>,
　あんた買わない？　あんた買うな
<u>banu</u> ja <u>uninu</u> munu <u>kanuN</u>.　<u>hiruN</u> do:.
　私達は　　そんなもの　買わない　行くよ

(6) 隣のグループは早くから起きている（旅行中）
<u>baNta</u> <u>jauginNa</u> je:
　私達　起きないよね
　　　　　　　　　Cf. 病人を宥めて　ni<u>N</u>di buri. <u>ugiNna</u>.
　　　　　　　　　　　　　　　　　　寝ていなさい　起きるな

(7) 新しくきた嫁さんに
<u>uma</u> du <u>baNta</u> haga do:.
　ここが　私達の　墓　だ
　Cf. 家族外になら　uma ja <u>ba:</u>　haga:.（ここは私達の墓）

339

(8) 伊豆山を自宅に誘う
baja Nki kuba hai.　　　×aGa ja:,
我家に　おいでよ

Cf. 同居の孫に、「お家に帰ろう」というとき da Nki di:.　×baja(我が家)
　　　　　　　　　　　　　　　　　　　　家に　さあ

(9) 一人住いの人が自分の家を教える時
uma aGa da:.
ここ 私の 家

(10) 東京から初めて来た孫に、空港で
ita. abu da Nki. di:.
さあ ばあちゃんちに さー

そして家に着いて「ここがお家だよ」と言う。
uma du abu da do:.
ここが ばあちゃんの家だよ

(11) Ndja Nki hi:　Nsana:?
あんたの家に 行って いい

(12) 里帰りした娘に、引越し先の新築の家を指して
uma du baNta da: du.
ここが 私達の家 だ

(13) 家族（親族を含む）皆で家に帰ろうと言う時
baNta daNki di:.
自分達の 家に さあ（行こう）

その皆の中に伊豆山が混じって居れば、baNta da ではない。ただ、da Nki と言う。

再帰代名詞

　3人称に対する再帰代名詞であって、他の人称には無い。

---

(9) 建物は da:だが、家庭を指すときは baja, Ndja のように複数形の特別な形である。
(10) 単数の aGaja（我が家）はない。独身者でも用いない。
(11) baNtaja（私たちの家）とは言わない。

琉球・八重山（与那国）方言の文法基礎研究

(1) 向こうの家の人が、断りもなく、新聞を持って行った。見ていた私が言う。
　　私：　　　kari ja sjiNbuN muti hjuN do:
　　　　　　 彼は　　新聞　　持って行ったよ
　家人が答えて：
　　　　　　 kari ja sa: munu aibi du muti hjuru.
　　　　　　 あれ は 自分の もの だから 持って 行った
　そして、また、そこにあるものを指して：
　　　　　　 kuN kariGa munu. ×sa:munu（本人と照応している時だけ）
　　　　　　 これも 彼の 物

(2) kanu saNdu ja kanu da Nki hai hjuN do.（彼の家とは知らな
　　あの さんどぅ(島名)は あの 家 に 入って 行った　　　い人の言葉）
　　答えて
　　　　　　 kama ja sji: da:.
　　　　　　 あれは 自分（さんどぅ）の 家

(3) 自分の仲良しグループが出かけるのを見ながら
　　anu abiranuN ki sji bagai hiruN suja.
　　私を 呼ばないで 自分達　ばかり 行くんだな

(4) sa Ga isjiti Tsanu katarai ki:!
　　自分が やって 知らん 顔 して！（相手に言う）

(5) sji Ga isjiti Tsanu katarai ki:!
　　自分達が して 知らぬ 顔 して！（複数のあいてに言う）

(6) 母親が姉娘に、弟ができるかと心配して手伝えと言う。
　　kari Ga isjitsuru kaja:.
　　彼が　できるかね
　　姉が 答えて　sa: Tui sji iruN.
　　　　　　　　（彼は）自分一人 で する

(7) unu agamitiNta ja isjitsuru kaja:.
　　あの 子達 は できるかね（難しそうだから手伝うかなと）

341

答えて　　sji: du sji iruN.
　　　　　自分達　で　する（できる）
(8) 種を蒔かずに生えた時
　　　sa: Tui sji mui buN suja:.
　　　自分　一人　で　生えているねー　（自然に生えているねー）

5．名詞と助詞
5．1　複数形
縮小詞　-ti

agami　子供　agami-ti　小さい、可愛い子　agami-ti-Nta　小さい子供達
複数接辞　-Nta
ija-Nta:,　　　abuta-Nta:,　　asa-Nta:,　　　abu-Nta:,　　　duci Nta:
父さん達　　　母さん達　　　祖父さんたち　祖母さん達　　友人達
maju-Nta,　　inu-Nta,　　hatu-Nta
猫達　　　　　犬達　　　　鳥達　　　　　蟻など、虫には複数形は無い。

5．2　助詞
　ここでは、基礎的な文理解のための、重要なものに限って示す。その他の主な助詞については、個々の例文中にあげるように努めた。主格・対格と、あまり知られていない係り助詞相当の ba とを明示した。ba は、話し手の意図との関係で興味深い。代名詞の所有格は、人称代名詞(3)に記したので、ここでは、それ以外を簡単に記す。

所有格表示　人名及びそれに準じる呼称では無助詞。普通名詞では nu。
　　　abu munu,　　asa munu,　　ija munu,　　sjinsji: munu,
　　　祖母さんの物　祖父さんの物　父さんの物　先生の　物
　　　unu　agamiti nu munu
　　　あの子供　　の　物
主格表示　Ga 後置で、無助詞のことも多い。自動詞の時、無助詞が多いよ

うに見える。

提題の文「……は……がした。」には Ga 出現が原則のようである。

対格表示 無助詞だと考えられる。

① su:　maGu　Ga　suTaN.
　　今日　孫　　が　　来た

② u　ja　Tu　Ga　kaN　do.
　　それ　は　人　が　買った　よ

③ abu　Ga　　ara:gu　ataraki.
　　お祖母さんが　とても　大事にしてね

④ Ndi　Ga　kiditaba　agami　ugi.
　　お前達　騒いだから　子供が　起きた

⑤ Ndjanu　　agami　Ga　tinamai　ki:.
　　あんたのうちの　子　が　いたずらして

⑥ ara:gu　maisaru　ichibugu　Ga　aibi　hirarinutaN.
　　とても　大きい　大石　が　あって　行かれなかった

⑦ sjidasaru　kadi　Ga　kuN　suja:
　　涼しい　風　が　　来るね

⑧ su: ja kadi　KuN　di　do
　　今日は　風が　吹くってよ

⑨ madagaTi　ami　huruNdo.
　　やがて　雨が　降るよ

⑩ agami　maruN.
　　子供　が　産まれる

　共通語では「が」が必要そうなところに現れない場合もある。天然現象等は、特別の修飾語が無い限り、現れないようである。

　注意すべきは、主題（取り立て・対比）の助詞 ja が、主格表示の Ga と共起することである。

343

(1) anu ja numanuN.　×aGa ja　（普通に勧められた時）
　　私　は　飲まない
(2) Nda　Ga buru na ?　aGa ja buranuN.　u Ga buruN do.
　　あんた　が　折るのか　　私　は　折らない　　彼　が　折る　よ
(3) kari Ga ja buttaNtiN aGa ja buranuN.
　　彼　が　は　折っても　私　は　折らない

　もう一つ注意すべき助詞がある。質問文の中で疑問詞に後置される ba である。

(1) ici ba satja Gai.　答えて　dunaga satjaN do:
　　何時　咲いたか　　　　　　　夜中　咲いたよ
(2) ici ba hiru Ga.
　　何時　行くのか
(3) Nma Nki ba hiru Ga.　Cf. NmaN ki ja:.　×　NmaNki ba:?
　　何処　に　行くのか　　　　どちらへ　か　挨拶言葉
(4) uja Nmi ba a Ga. sakibara nu misjija ni du aru.
　　それは　何処に　あるの　崎原　の　店　に　ある
(5) ta Ga ba iru Ga.
　　誰　が　するのか
(5) nu ba iru Ga.
　　何（を）するのか
(6) nu ba NniNdi su Ga.
　　何　（を）　見に　来たか
(7) nu ba Nda munu ja:.　答えて　ku du aGa munu.
　　どれ（が）あなたの　物　か　　　これ　が　私の　物
(8) nu Ga maci ja:.　／　nu ba maci ja:.
　　どれが　良い　か　　どれ　が　良い　か　（複数の中から選ぶ）
　　ku du maci.　／　u du maci.　／　kari du maci.
　　これ　が　いい　　それ　が　いい　　あれ　が　いい

(9) ta Ga ba iTiN abjaru kaja:
　　誰　が　　一番　綺麗かね
(10) ta ba sui hirariru kaja:.
　　誰（を）　　連れて行かれるかね

今いない人を考えて誰を連れて行くかという時は ba が必要で、今居る人の中から誰かを連れて行く時は ta:でも ta ba でもいい。

これらの ba はあってもなくてもいいようだが(7)と(8)を比較すると、基本的には、対比の意味があることが知られる。(10)のように、多くの中から選ぶ意味もある。

ba に関連して、興味深い例がある。このような主格名詞と共起する ba の例は報告されていない。話し手のモーダルな面と関係する。(12)

(1) ami ba hui bi: hirarinutaN. （ba は無くてもいい）　×ami Ga ba
　　雨（が）　降ったので行かれなかった

これは、話者の意に添わない場合である。それに反し以下の場合を比較する。

(2) 大根を蒔く為には雨が欲しい。
　　話し手の意に添わない　ami ba hui bi ubuni maganinutaN.
　　　　　　　　　　　　　雨（が）　降って　大根　蒔けなかった
　　話し手の意に添う　　　ami hui bi ubuni maguN di:.
　　　　　　　　　　　　　雨（が）　降ってるので　大根　蒔く　さあ

このように意に添う時は、ba は不可である。
　　ami hui bi ubuni magariru:.　　×ba
　　雨　降って　大根　蒔ける

(3) 格助詞の代わりというわけではない。
　　uiTu (ba) nai sjikama kiraninuN.　　ba 有無は、どちらでも可
　　年寄りに　なり　仕事　　できない（望ましくないこと。）

―――――――――
(12) 伊豆山（2002, p.360-361）に、石垣宮良方言に関する同様例を報告した。

345

(4) Tsa ba paNdi buN suja:.　harai ba du naru.
　　雑草が 生えているね　取ら ねば ならない
　Cf. Tsa: Ga baburi buN suja:.　ubuni nu baipaNduN.
　　　草 が 一杯 生えてるな　大根の 芽が 出た

6．話し手の認識と優位性

　琉球諸方言では、動詞の言い切りの形（終止形を含む）は、話し手の認識に関係している。動詞・形容詞終止形の形態素Nは、話し手に属するものである。過去というのも、話し手の経験を示すものなのである。従って動作・状態の主体が話し手であるか、それ以外かで、認め方が基本的に異なる。また、話し手がその行為を直接経験している（見聞きする）か、そうでないかは、重要な示差的特徴なのである。動詞・形容詞の体系も、全てこの基本の上にある。

6.1　動詞語形と基本的用法

　動詞全体の報告は後日に譲るが、上に述べたことを理解する為に、先行研究の枠組みに従った語形変化の表をあげる。平山・中本（1964）、『琉球の方言』（1987）及び高橋（1992）に従いながら、筆者の調査で補ったり変更したりした。(13) 上記3者は各々形の名称が違う。便宜上、大体既述されている諸方言と同様な名称に従っておく。
　「する kir-・ir-」(14)、5段動詞対応の「書く kaguN」、1段動詞対応の「起きる ugiruN」

---

(13) 3者は異なる点がある。志向形を平山・中本は-u'u-と母音連続で表しているが、高橋は-uのみである。方言話者の中には、この母音とuとの違いを意識している方もおられる。音声的には、唇の丸めを伴う[u]の広め乃至[o]に聞こえる。筆者はまだ確定できないでいるが、円唇化子音の可能性を考えている。ここでは仮にその解釈を使う。
(14) kiruNは、活用型が2種ある。第2の活用型を持つものは、少数で意味が限られている。

琉球・八重山（与那国）方言の文法基礎研究

終止	否定	志向	命令	禁止	連体	連用	接続	過去	完了
kiruN	kiranuN	kirwu:	kiri	kiNna	kiru	ki	ki(ti)	kitaN	kjaN
iruN	iranuN	irwu:	iri	iNna	iru	isji	isji(ti)	itaN	isjaN
ug-iruN	-iranuN	-irwu:	-iri	-iNna	-iru	-i	-i(ti)	-itaN	-uN
ka-g-uN	-anuN	-wu:	-i	-uNna	-u	ka-t-i	-i(ti)	-itaN	-jaN

「書く ka-g-」の連用以下は、ka-t-のように語幹末音が交替する。

　先行研究の枠組みで、常に問題にしなければならないのだが、接続形（又は連用形）というのは、名前に反して独立用法がある。また、話者が単語としてあげる形は、この接続（連用）形である。その意味でもこの形は不定形的なところがある。今は、動詞体系の話には踏み込まないが、言い切りの形が解るように例示する。

　接続（連用）、過去、完了の3形には、共通語翻訳に適語が無いので特に注意を払う。例えば公民館で踊りの会がある。

① anu: su: ja budi kiruN do.
　　私　 今日は 踊り する　よ
② その夜、自宅で客に言う。
　　anu su: budi kitaN do: × kjaN do
　　私　今日 踊り　した　　よ
③ これを客が帰宅して家人に言う
　　su: ja kazu ja budi kitaN tuna:　×kitaN (do:)
　　今日 は 和 は 踊り　したってよ
④ 公民館会場で、知人との会話
　　Nda budi kja na ?　N: budi kjaN do:.
　　あんた 踊り した か　うん 踊り　したよ
⑤ 遅刻した人が、和は踊ったかと尋ねる。尋ねられた人は踊るのを見なかったが、本人も観客も踊ったと言っていたのを知っている。または、番組の順序進行も見て知っている。

347

　　　　anu ja Nnanuta Ga budi kjaN tuna:.
　　　　私　は　見なかったが　踊りしたってさ　×　kjaN
⑥　su: kazu ja ko:miNkaN ni budi kitaN do.
　　　今日　和　は　公民館　で　踊り　したよ　（見た母親の言葉）
⑦　anu su: budi kitaN do:.
　　　私　今日　踊り　した　よ　（会から帰宅した本人の言葉）
⑧　知人が遅刻した。観客席にいる母親に尋ねる
　　　kazu ja ma: budi ki: ja:?（本人は終わった後に来たようだと思っ
　　　　　　　　　　　　　　　　　　　　　　　　ている）
　　　和　は　もう　踊り　したの
⑨　踊りを見た母親が答えて、　N: ma: budi kjaN do.
　　　　　　　　　　　　　　　　うん　もう　踊り　した　よ
⑩　息せき切って来た人が母親に尋ねる
　　　kazu budi ki:?　答え kjaN do:. ／ nai kjaN.　×ki:
　　　和　踊りしたか　　　　 した　よ　／　今　した
⑪　nai kjaN. といわれたのに対して、もう一度 budi ki:. と独り言する。
⑫　番組の順を知らず、見に来た人が客席に居る本人に尋ねる
　　　NdaN budi ki:?
　　　あんた踊り　したの（踊ることは知っていたが、済んだかどうかの確認
　　　の質問）
⑬　上に答えて　naigara du kiru.
　　　　　　　　　今から　する
⑭　久しぶりで来島した知人が、何も知らずに見に来て、丁度踊り終わって
　　　衣装を脱いだり化粧落しをしている和さんを見て、独り言を言う。
　　　Kazu ja budi kjaN suja:.
　　　和　は　踊り　した　んだな
⑮　NdaN budi kiru na ?　　　答えて　kiranuN.
　　　あんたも　踊り　するか　　　　　　　しない
⑯　幼児がおしっこをし終わった所で尋ねる

348

　　　　Nda　Nbai　ki:？　　　　　　　答えて　Nbai　kjaN.　　×ki:.
　　　　あんた　おしっこ　した　　　　　　　　おしっこ　した
⑰　幼児がおしっこ終わって、母親に
　　　Nbai　kjaN　do.
　　　おしっこしたよ
　　　　　　　　　　　それを聞いた母親が　Nbai　ki:？
　　　　　　　　　　　　　　　　　　　　おしっこした（えらいねー）
⑱　　Ndja　　nu　　agami　Ga　tinamai　ki:.
　　あんたのうちの　子　が　いたずらして　（抗議に行った時）
⑲　　abu　Ga　ara:gu　aTaraki　（ju:）.
　　　お祖母さんが　とても　大事にしてね
⑳　　Ndi　　Ga　kiditaba　　　agami　ugi.
　　　お前達　が　騒いだから　子供が　起きた

　以上のように、接続（連用）形というのは、独立して、行為の出現だけを指し示している。質問・問い返し、現状言及などである。その意味で不定形的であり、方言話者が、単語として辞書形にあげるのも理解できるのである。
　『与那国ことば辞典』は、そのような方言話者の気持ちが表れている。辞書形の例。
　　ティ　吹く、ティ　聞く、フイ　降る（雨が）、クルビ　転ぶ、カイ　買う
　これらは、『琉球の方言11，12』によれば、その見出し語は、各々次のようである。
　　k'uN　　　k'uN　　　huruN　　　　kurubuN　　kuN
　前者の動詞見出し語には、終止形もあるが、このように接続（連用）形と呼ばれている形も見られる。
　もう一つ接続（連用）形について述べておかなければならないことがある。琉球諸方言で有名だが、この形が、行為の出現を指し示す例であり、後の形容詞の文法に必要なのである。

	ある	書く	起きる
① 肯定	a-N	kag-u-N	ug-ir-u-N
② 否定	a-ra-N	kag-a-nuN	ug-ir-a-nuN
③ 無い	mi-nu-N	kat-i minu-N	ug-i minu-N

　この③の形は、事態が、話し手の期待に反して起こったのを意味することができる。

例文　書き物を頼んだ人に会って

(a)　Nda katja na？　答えて　madi kati-minuN.／madi kaga-nuN.
　　　あんた　書いたか　　　　　未だ書いてない　／　まだ書かない

(b)　孫の落書きを見て、da: nu kubi N kati minuN suja:.
　　　　　　　　　　　家　の　壁　に　書いちゃった　なー

(c)　natta Ga du kadi Tibi buru uti minuN.
　　　実ったけど　風　吹き　皆　落ちちゃった（せっかく楽しみにしてたのに……）

　通常の否定では、まだ動作は起こらない。③は起こった行為に関する話し手の期待はずれの気持ちが表れている。

6.2　動作の認識と行為結果

動作の認識

　話し手が直接その動作を経験（見聞）しかかどうかということは、先ず基本である。前節6.1の③、⑤はそのことを示している。もう一つ例を加える

　孫が生まれたので酒を飲まないが、お祝いなので酒を飲んだ話。（以前の事でもいい）

①　kanu abu　　ja maGu Ga maritaba　　sagi numi ju:.
　　あの　お祖母さんは　孫　が　生まれたので　酒　飲んだ　よ

①'　kanu abu　　ja maGu Ga maritaba sagi numitaN do:
　　　あの　お祖母さんは　孫　が　生まれたので　酒　飲んだ　よ

---

(15) 同じ状況で、自分の事は numitaN do: は言い難い。その動作見聞が話題だからであろう。

② 自分のことを語る　maGu Ga maritaba　　sagi numi ju:.
　　　　　　　　　　　孫　が　うまれたので　酒　飲んだ　よ
③ その情景を、宴席では見られなかったが、そう聞いたので、帰宅してから話す。
　　kanu abu 　ja sagi numitaN di:.　×　numi ju:
　　あの　お祖母さんは 酒　飲んだ　って
④ gisama 　　 ja sagi numanuN do:
　　ぎさま（人名）は　酒　飲まないよ　（話し手が経験上知っている）
⑤ 奥さんから飲まないと聞いていれば
　　gisama ja sagi numanuN tuna:
　　ぎさま　は　酒　飲まない　とさ
⑥ kama Nki bagiN naN Ga sutaN tuna.
　　あそこに まで 波 が 来た とさ　（昔の津波の話）
　その動作が起こったのが遥か昔であろうが、つい先ほどであろうが、動詞テンスに関わりなく、話し手の<u>直接経験</u>（見聞）という、モダリティー的要素が、動詞形態に含まれていると考えられる。直接経験でないときは、tuna, di:などが必要になる。

動作の認識と結果の関係

　次に、完了形と呼ばれる形を検討する。[16]
(1)　人の行為、他動詞の場合、例　kag-～kat-（書く）
① tarumja:ru munu katjaN ?
　　頼んだ　　物　書いた　　　答えて
② katjaN.
　　書いてある
　このkatjaNという形は、結果相断定[17]、完了形[18]、融合形[19]などの名前で呼ば

---
(16) 平山（1964, p.144）高橋（1987, p.194）（1992, p.418）は等しく「書き（連用形＋あり）としている。その通時的解釈は受け入れ難いし、翻訳も誤解をまねくものである。
(17) 高橋（1992, p.879）
(18) 高橋（1987, p.546）
(19) 平山（1964, pp.144-146）

れている。しかしこれらの書で言われているような「書いてある」とは、かなり異なっている。他動詞の場合は、結果だけではなく、動作の認知が必要なのである。

　上のようにkatjaNと答えることができるのは、書いた本人か、書くのを見ていた家族なのである。留守番のものなら、そうはいかない。

　もし留守番が、それらしい書類の置いてあるのを見て知っていても、katjaN.（書いてある）と言うわけにはいかない。書くところは見ていなかったのだから、そのような場合は、次のように言う。

③　kati　　aN.
　　書いて　ある

例えば、娘が留守番している。母親の書いているところは見ていないが、書いたものがあることは知っている。そのような時は、取りに来た人と顔見知りの娘との間に次のような会話があるだろう。

④　atsuko　　　　ja　tigami　katjaN[20]?
　　敦子（母親の名）は　手紙　書いた

⑤　katjaru　munu　Nnita　Ga　turi　ku:　na:.
　　書いた　もの　見たが　取って　来るか

⑤'　katjaru　munu　aru　juNgara　turi　ku:　je.
　　書いた　もの　ある　から　取って来るね

　⑤⑤'のように答えてkatjaNとは言わないのである。

　また、母親の書いているところを見てしかも詳しい事情（何の書類で何時誰が取りに来る等々）も知っていたとするなら、katjaNもまあ可だが、それにしても

⑥　Nnu:　kati　butaru　juNgara　　aN　do:.
　　昨日　書いて　いた（のを見た）から　あるよ

このように言うのが好まれる。つまり、客観的事実を述べるだけに止め、katjaNではないのである。

　その動作は今見えないが、その動作から結果に至るまでの一連の行為が起

----

(20) 娘が事情を知らないと思った場合は katja na？「書いたか」

こったことが明瞭に解っている、確かである、そういう場合にのみ、この-N形が用いられる。従って話し手本人（か常に共に居る家族）の行為に対して多用されるのである。

　動作は見ていないが、その行為の起こったことが明瞭で、一般的に（話し手以外にも）解る場合は-ru形なのである。この点も他の八重山方言と共通である。

⑦　taGa　katja　Ga ?
　　誰が　書いたか　（書を前にしながら尋ねる）
⑧　aGa　du　katjaru.
　　私が　書いた

(2) 人の行為ではない自動詞の場合。

　話し手の行為ではないから、その行為に関して、話し手もそれ以外の人も差異はない。しかし、経験が違う。

　島以外から来て見たら、島は台風の後らしく木が倒れていたりして荒れている。

⑨　ja:　ubu　kadi　TjaN　suja:.
　　あれ　大風　吹いた　ん　だね

と独り言を言い、島のことを何も知らないで一緒にきた友人に次のように教える。（彼は台風の痕がどうなるかを知らないのである）

⑩　ubu　kadi　du　Tjaru　do:.
　　大風　が　吹いたんだよ（吹いた様子だよ）

その友達が答えて

⑪　je:　ubu　kadi　Ti:[21]　ja: ?
　　え　大風　吹いたの

そこへ島の人が迎えに来て言う。

⑫　buduti　ubu　kadi（du）Ti:　ju:.
　　一昨日　大風　　が　　吹いてねー

または

---

(21) この形は従来「連用形」と呼ばれ、このような独立用法に関する報告は無い。池間（1998）はこの形が辞書形である。

⑬　buduti　ubukadi　du　ataru　do:.
　　一昨日　大風　で　あった　んだよ

　大風が吹くところは見なかったが、その痕跡がある。そこで「吹き」からその痕跡までの一連の行為を認め「吹いたんだな」と、動作（吹き）が出現したと判断をする。そして⑩のように吹いたと認められると言う。実際にその行為を経験した人は、Ti:(ju:)と言い、それが出現したことを告げる[22]。

⑭　朝、戸を開けたら外が濡れている。
　　dubi　ami　du　hwaN　suja:(⑨と同じ型)
　　昨夜　雨　降ったんだね

それを聞いて、夜中まで起きていた人は、雨だったことを知っているので
　　ami　hutaN　do:.
と教えてくれ、更に前出と同じパタンで

⑫'　dubi　ubu　ami　hui　ju:.　／　⑬'dubi　ubu　ami　du　ataru　do:.
　　昨夜　大　雨　降ってね　　　　昨夜　大　雨　だったよ

事実を知っている人は、hwaNとはいわない。

⑮　既述した例をもう一度ここであげる。

　久しぶりで来島した知人が、何も知らずに踊りの会を見に来た。丁度、踊り終わって衣裳脱いだり化粧落しをしている和さんを見て、独り言を言う。
　　kazu　ja　budi　kjaN　suja:.
　　和　は　踊り　した　んだな　（踊るところは見ていない）

⑮　綺麗に掃除してある所に訪れて
　　sudi　kjaN　suja:.　答えて　N:　kjaN　do.　kazu　Ga　du　sudi　ki:　ju:.
　　掃除　したんだ　な　　　　うん　した　よ　和　が　掃除　した　よ

　以上、完了という名称も相応しいとは言えないことが解るであろう。「書いてある」も「吹いてある」も誤解を招く。共通語の「書いてある」に対応するのは、kati aNの方なのである。

　これらの事実は、本島から先島までの琉球諸方言に広く認められる。それ

---

(22) TitaN do:も可だが意味異なる。これはそういうことが起こったという報告である。こちらは、ubu kadi の方が言いたいのである。「大風さん」のなら TjaN do:. かもしれない。

琉球・八重山（与那国）方言の文法基礎研究

それの方言語形が違うので、一層歴史的に受け継がれた形だと考えられる。形の類似からだけで、直ちに歴史的解釈をするのは慎まなければならない良い例である。

6.3 補助動詞（コプラ）

　琉球諸方言には、補助動詞（コプラ）（「だ、である」に相当）があるが、与那国にはこれに対応する形はない。「だ、である」に相当する語は、aNで、これは動詞「ある」と同じ形で、同じ語形変化を示す。この否定「ではない」に当たる語は、他の諸方言同様、「ある」の否定形で、aranuNである。この「である」相当の語は、duの結びでなければ、出現しないのが普通である。以下に例示する。

① u　ja　sagi.
　　それ　は　酒

② u　ja　sa:　aranuN.　sagi　du　aru.
　　それ　は　茶では　ない　酒　で　ある

他方言のコプラに、用法的に対応するのは、以下である。

③ uja　sata　aNdagi:.
　　これは　サタ　アンダギー（砂糖揚げ菓子）　（だ）

④ u　bagiN　sata　aNdagi:　na?
　　これ　も　サタアンダギー　か

⑤ aranuN.　sata　aNdagi:　aranuN.
　　違う　サタアンダギー　じゃない。

⑥ u　ja　nu　ja:.
　　これは　何か　（何が入っているか分からない小包を前にして）

⑦ sa:　hadi　(do).
　　お茶（の）　筈　（だ）

⑧ sa:　du　aru　hadi.
　　お茶　で　ある　筈

⑨ sa:　aranu　kaja:.
　　お茶　じゃない　かな

355

⑩　sa:　du　aN　sai.
　　お茶　で　ある　さ
⑪　nu:　arubaN　minuna.
　　何　であっても　無いか（何か無いか）

　上記のように、本土方言の「…だ」相当の場合は普通出現しないが、du の結びなどに「ある aN」の活用形が現れる。そこで「ある aN」の活用と一般的用法を参考に記す。活用形の名は伝統的なものを用いた。高橋（1992）によって表示する。

否定	志向(23)	連用	終止	禁止	連体	命令	条件	過去	結果
(aranuN)	aru	ai	aN	×	aru	x	arja	ataN	×

Ａ：sata aNdagi:　haibusa Ga　Ndjani a na ?
　　サタアンダギー　食べたいけど　お前の家に　あるか
Ｂ：umi aN do.
　　ここに　あるよ
Ｃ：baja　ni　arja　Ndasji　ku:　je:.
　　我が家　に　あるから　出して　来ようね

また次のような会話もあり得る。

Ａ：sata aNdagi: minu na ?
　　サタアンダギー　無いか
Ｂ：aN.
　　ある
Ａ：Ndani irara a(:)na ?
　　お宅に　鎌　あるか
Ｂ：minuN.
　　ない

それから探したら見つかった

―――――――――
(23) 志向形の用法は不明

356

umi　ataN.
ここにあった

aranu(-N)に関して注意することがある。その意味上の肯定形が、次の形を持つことである。

isji　kaja　aranu　kaja:.
そうかな　そうじゃないかな

　このisjiは、動詞iruN（する）の活用形の一つである。つまり、「そうじゃないか」の肯定の対語は「そうして（いる）かな」なのである。与那国では、「ある」が他方言のコプラの代わりを勤めていること、他方言にないir-という動詞があることは、コプラの起源を考える上で参考になる。[24]

7．形容詞

　形容詞は、2種類に大別される。1類を描写形容詞と呼び、2類を気分形容詞と呼ぶ。気分形容詞では、その性質・状態の主体は1人称だけである。
　従来形容詞の終止形とされている形は、この点で再考されなければならない。他の八重山方言同様、形態素Nが話し手の認識判断を表していると考えられるからである。

7．1　語形と問題点
7．1．1　語形
　与那国方言の形容詞語形を伝統的枠組みであげれば以下のようで、その2大類別が反映されているのがわかる。

---

(24) 伊豆山（1998）参照

	語幹	否定	連用	終止	連体	已然(25)	命令
1類	taga-	taga-minuN	tagagu	taga-N	taga-ru	taga-rja	?
2類	sjana-	sjana-minuN	1＊	sjana-N	sjana-ru	2＊	3＊

過去の形　語幹＋taN　taga-taN, sjanataN　否定　taga-minu-taN, sjana-minu-taN

　1・2類共に揃っている否定・連用には、動詞の項で述べた話し手の優位性が直接関係してくる。
＊標の項は後述する。
　このように整理すると、全ての項に問題があるが、簡単な事項を下記する。
(1) 語幹の用法2類では不可

　　taga-ki　　　　　　　　　×sjana-agami
　　高　木　　　　　　　　　嬉しい子供
(2) 連体形
　　1類　(a)　tagaru ki:　　　×sjanaru　agami
　　　　　　　高い　木　　　　嬉しい　子供
　　　　　　　tagaru ki: Nki nui buN suja. （高い木に登っているね）
　　　　(b)　tagaru hadi.　　○sjanaru　hadi.
　　　　　　　高い　筈　　　嬉しい　筈
　　　　　　　kari N sjanaru hadi do:
　　　　　　　彼　も　嬉しい　筈　だよ
　　　　(c)　kanu ki Ga du tagaru.　×kari Ga du sjanaru.
　　　　　　　あの　木　が　高い　　彼　が　嬉しいのだ

7.1.2　言い切りの形

　1類、描写形容詞と2類、気分形容詞とでは、語形変化が並行的でないのを見て来たが、気分形容詞では、その主体が話し手かそれ以外かで、先ず、

---

(25) 高橋（1992）は条件形の一つとしている。平山（1964）には無い。

言い切りの形が異なる。自分以外の人の内的状態は直接経験することはできない。様子から判断する他は無い。形容詞語幹に動詞 k-ir-（する）を後接した派生語でしか表現し得ない。ところが、この形は1人称とも共起する。つまり制約が少ない。動詞的機能のある形容詞的表現なのである。逆に描写形容詞にはこのような事は無い。つまり、taga-ki は無い。

　過去といわれている形は、話し手の経験した時間的過去のこともあるが、もっと一般的に言うなら、話し手がその状態を確認したという報告なのである。今尚その状態は続いている可能性もある（続いていない可能性もある）。

描写形容詞

① kanu ki: ja tagaN （suja:）.
　　あの 木 は 高い　　　　独り言には suja:が現れる。
　　kama ja tagaN suja:.
　　あそこ は 高い なー
② tagagu cimi.
　　高く 積め （石垣などを作る時）
　　unu agamiti ja tagagu budui tsuNNsuNN ja:.
　　その子 は 高く 踊りあがれる ね
③ tagaru ki: Nki nui buN suja.
　　高い 木 に 登っているね
　　kanu ki: ja tagaru ki: du aN suja:.
　　あの木 は 高い 木 であるなー
④ kari tu ku tu nuGa ba tagaru kaja:.
　　あれ と これ と どれが 高い かねー
　　ku Ga du tagaru. u ja tagaminuN.
　　これ が 高い それは高くない
⑤ 已然形 kuma tagarja nuigurisa:.
　　　　　ここは高いから 登り難い
⑥ 原因 tagabi kanuN. ／ kanutaN. ×tagaki は無い
　　　　高いので 買わない 買わなかった

⑦ 仮定　dattsaruba　ku:munu　tagabi　kanuN.
　　　　安ければ　買うのに　高いので買わない
　　　　mabitati　hudu　Ga　tagaruba　NsarumunU.
　　　　もう少し体　が　　高ければ　いいのに
　　　　mabitati　hudu　Ga　　tagataruba　NsarumunU.
　　　　もう少し　体（背）が　高かったら　いいのに
⑧ 条件　dattsataja　ku　Ga　　tagataja　kanuN.
　　　　安かったら　買うが　高かったら　買わない

気分形容詞
主体による制限がある。
　1人称とは共起する。2人称とは質問文でのみ共起する。
① Nda　sjana　na？　② anu　sjanaN　do.　③ anu　ja　sjanaminuN.
　　あんた　嬉しい　　　私　嬉しいよ　　　　　私　は　嬉しくない
④ banuN　sjanaN　do.
　　私達　嬉しいよ
⑤ kantati　ja　sjana　kibu　Ga　baNta　bagiN　sjanaN　sa:.
　　彼等　　は　嬉しくしてるけど　私達　も　嬉しいんだ
　3人称主体の場合は大きく異なる。先ず、「敦子は嬉しい atsuko sjanaN」は不可である。自分以外の人に対しては、以下に例示するように、客観的な表現を用いる。また、動詞同様、直接経験でなく、そのように「聞いている／言われている」という表現を用いる。
⑥ 否定の形。③で anu　ja　sjanaminuN.（私は嬉しくない）と言った敦子の話を人にする。
　　atsuko　ja　sjanaminuN　tuna.　　×atsuko　ja　sjaminuN.
　　敦子　　は　嬉しくない　ってよ
⑦ その人が、家に帰ってから、家人に今日のできごとを話して、
　　su:　ja　buru　ja　sjana　ki　butaGa　atuko　ja　sjanaminutaN　tuna.
　　今日　は　皆　は　嬉しくして　いたけど　敦子　は　嬉しくなかったってよ

⑦' buru ja sjana ki butaGa atsuko ja sjana ki buranutaN.
　　皆　は　嬉しく　して　いたが　敦子　は　嬉しく　して　いなかった

7.1.3　語幹＋動詞「する kir-」と主体制限の緩和（附過去の意味）

　自分以外の人の気持ちは解らないから、形容詞は出現できない。kir-を伴って、「その気持ちになっている」、「その気持ちがこみ上げている」のような意味を添えて、この動詞連語が現れる。

① 今、嬉しい様子をしている人を見て
　　atsuko ja sjiana ki buN suja:.　×sjanaN
　　敦子　は　嬉しく　している　な（喜んでいるな）
② 客から子供にと菓子を貰った。それを子供に上げてから、
　　kazu ja kaci turataba　sjana ki ju:.
　　和　は　菓子　あげたから　嬉しくしてる
②' kazu ja kaci turataba sjana ki butaN.
　　和　は　菓子　あげたので　嬉しく　して　いた　（喜んでいた）
③ 珍しいものなど頂いて
　　anu ara:gu sjanaki ju:.
　　私　とても　嬉しくしている　（頂いた物を見ながら）
④ 頂いた時、見て直ぐ言う。
　　anu ar:gu sjanataN.
　　私　とても　嬉しいかった　（嬉しいと認識した。嬉しく思った）
⑤ 頂いた時、直ぐ始めから sjanaN は言い難い。尋ねられた時なら可。
　　Nda sjana na?　答えて　ara:gu sjanaN.
　　あんた嬉しいの　　　　とても　嬉しい
⑤' Nda sjana na?　答えて　hugarasa: ara:gu sjanataN.
　　あんた嬉しい？　　　　ありがとう　とても　嬉しかった

　この②'④⑤'は過去と言われる形だが、その本人は今尚嬉しい状態なのである。この -taN の形は、その時点での、話し手の確認を表していると考えられる。その時点で「その状態を経験し（見）た」のである。

7.1.4 語幹＋動詞「する kir-」の動詞としての機能

先に例示した「踊りをする」と同じ動詞の、接辞化だと考えられる。動詞として機能する。命令形もある。以下の例にそれらを示す。

① anuN sjana ki du buru.
   私も 嬉しくして いる（喜んでいる）（他人に告げる時、人の慶事を聞いて等）

② kari Ga du da:sa ki: buru.
   彼 が ひもじくとしている（お腹へったと言っている）

③ baNtaN sjana kirwu:.
   私達も 嬉しくしよう（喜ぼう）（彼等が喜んでいるのを知って）

④ NdaN sjana kiri.
   あんたも 嬉しくしなさい（喜びなさい）

⑤ anuN sjana ki NdaN sjana ki turai.
   私も 嬉しくしてて あんたも 嬉しくしてください
   （私も嬉しいから あんたも 喜んで 頂戴）

⑥ 頼んだ事をしてくれている。それを誉めて、人に言う
   kazu ja sjana ki isji buN sai.
   和 は 嬉しく（喜んで）やっている

⑦ ata ja budi kiri Ndi sutaGa Nda sjana kirja:.
   明日 踊り して と 来たけど あんた 嬉しいンでしょ

⑧ anu sjanabi budi ki buN. ×sjana ki
   私 嬉しいので 踊り している

⑨ kazu ja sjana ki   budi ki buN sai. ×sjanabi
   和 は 嬉しく（し）て 踊り しているね

⑩ anu ja ar:agu sjanabi budi kitaru. ×sjana ki
   私は とても嬉しいので踊り した （自分が踊り終わってから言う）
   Cf. kazu ja ara:gu sjana ki budi kitaN sai. ×sjana bi
       和 は とても 嬉しく（し）て 踊り したのだ （和が踊り終わってから）

⑪　条件　Nda　sjanataja　bud　kiri.
　　　　あんた　嬉しいなら　踊り　しろ
　　　　kazu　ja　sjanataja　budi　kiruN　sa:.
　　　　和　は　嬉しかったら　踊り　するよー
⑫　おいしいお菓子がある。
　　食べた人が言う　　　u:　ma:bi　hataN.
　　　　　　　　　　　　これ　美味しいので　食べた
　　まだ食べていない人　mataja　hu　kaja:.
　　　　　　　　　　　　美味しいのなら食べようかね
　　　　　　　　　　　　maru　juNgara　hai.
　　　　　　　　　　　　美味しいから食べろ
　　　　　　　　　　　　u:　ma　ki　hai　butaN
　　　　　　　　　　　　それ美味しく（て）食べていた

　sjanagu という形が無い理由が解るであろう。この sjana ki という動詞の連用（接続）形といわれている形が、言わば連用修飾的な機能を果たしているのである。また、主体が１人称の時は、原因を表す -bi が共起するが、3人称の時は共起しない。

7.1.5　kir-による語幹選択の自由度と生産性
　本土共通語の「……がる」と似ているところがあるが、そればかりではない。「そのように常々言っている」という場合にも可なので、共通語「……がる」より自由度が高い。例えば「綺麗がる」のような形もある。
①　敦子が自分の家の花のことを話す
　　baja　nu　hana　satiti　ara:gu　abjaN　do.
　　我が家の　花　咲いて　とても　綺麗よ
　それを聞いた人が、他の人に言う
　　atsuko　ja　sija　nu　hana　ara:gu　abja　ki　buN.
　　敦子　は　自分の家の　花を　とても　綺麗としている（思って／言っている）

② 敦子に食事を出したら　ku ja maN suja. と言って食べた
　　　　　　　　　　　　　これは美味しい
あとでその人が他の人に言う
　　atsuko ja ma: ki hataN do:
　　敦子　は　美味しく　食べたよ　（美味しいと言って食べた）
③ su:　ja kama Nki hita Ga diNkuru Kati ina munu.
　　今日　は　あそこに　行ったが　財布　落として　残念だ
　　atsuko ja diNkuru Kati Ndi inamunu ki: buN sai.
　　敦子　は　財布　落としたとて　残念がっているよ

7．2　連体修飾と中間的な形容詞

　気分形容詞の説明が終わったところで、連体修飾について触れておくことがある。先に次のような関係を述べた。tagaru ki:　　× sjanaru agami
　　　　　　　　　　　　　　　　　　　　高い　木　　　嬉しい　子供
　　　　　　　　　　　　　　　　　　　　tagaru hadi.　○ sjanaru hadi.
　　　　　　　　　　　　　　　　　　　　高い　筈　　　嬉しい　筈
形容詞の2大別が理解されれば形容詞とその被修飾名詞との意味関係が理解されるだろう。

　　　　× sjanaru Tu　　○ niguraru Tu
　　　　　嬉しい　人　　　　恐い　人
① niguraN do:.　（逃げた牛が疾走している時など道端の子供に言う）
　　恐いよ
② 大きな包丁を持って歩いている男を見たら呟く　niguranu.
　　　　　　　　　　　　　　　　　　　　　　　　恐い
③ 怪談などを聞いたあと、暗い夜道を一人で歩いて帰るとき
　　da Nki hiru basu niguragu nai:.
　　家　に　行く　時　恐く　なってね
④ ……を振り回している男がいる。
　　niguraru Tu do:.
　　恐い　人　だよ（私が恐いと感じる対象の人。恐がっている人ではない。）

364

琉球・八重山（与那国）方言の文法基礎研究

sjanaN も niguraN も、共に話し手の気持ちを表しているが、niguraN は、対象に対して話し手が持つ気持ちなのである。従ってその対象に対しては、連体修飾が可能になる。また、niguragunai に対して sjanagunai（嬉しくなって）は無い。嬉しい気持ちは瞬間的に生じるからではないだろうか。この niguraN のように、中間的な形容詞もある。

7.3　描写形容詞の言い切りの形 -nu

① ara:gu taganu.　kanuN.　×sjana-nu
　　とても　高い。　　買わない

② u ja taganu.　u ja dattsaN suja:.（店などで安い品をあさりながら）
　　これ は 高い　これは 安い　な

気分形容詞を用いるなら、次のようである。

③ kazu ja sjananu Ndi budi ki butaN
　　和 は 嬉しい とて 踊り した

これらの例から見ると、話し手の判断に関わる形なのであろう。話し手が主体の場合

　　anu　sjananu　あまり言わないと。
　　anu　sjananu　Ndi　話者の感じでは、ありそうな言葉だが使う場合が見つからない。
　　anu　sjanabi　（嬉しいので）　これが普通。

話し手主体の時はこの他 du aru と連語をなす。

④ ara:gu sjana du aibi Nda Nki TamiruN.
　　とても　嬉しい（状態な）ので　あんた　に　知らせる

⑤ 大きな包丁を持って歩いている男を見たら呟く　niguranu.
　　　　　　　　　　　　　　　　　　　　　　　　恐い

⑥ anu da:sanu.
　　私　ひもじい（お腹へった）　　（子供が何か食べたい時）

気分形容詞の中にも下位分類がある。この項目と連体修飾の項を調べる

と、更に詳しく形容詞の性格が解る。

	嬉しい	高い	恐い
動詞化	○sjana kir-	×taga kir-	○nigura kir-
状態	○sjana du aru	×taga du aru	?（未調査多分可）
判断	×sjananu	○taganu	○niguranu
語幹修飾	×sjana agami	○taga ki	×niguraTu
已然形	×sjanarja	○tagarja	?（未調査）
連用修飾	×sjanagu	○tagagu	○miguragu

気分形容詞にも、「da:sa-（ひもじい）」のように、意味によって、判断形が現れ得る。

　kir-（する）という動詞は、知られている方言の中では、与那国にだけある。この動詞による形容詞の動詞化は、注目に値する。これによって、1人称以外の主体の状態を、表すことが可能になるのである。宮古（平良）や、上代日本語の形容詞を思い出さずにはいられない。

　確定的ではないが、仮に、今まで検討した言い切りの形を整理して表示する。

	話し手認識	話し手判断	否定	一般確認
taga-	tagaN	taganu	tagaminuN	tagaru
sjana-	sjanaN	sjana ki	sjanaminuN	sjana ki buru

7.4　特殊な形の形容詞

　平山（1964, p.148-149）に別の要素が接して用いられる終止形が載っている。これらは文例がないのだが、そのminuNによる否定形は誤りである。動詞のところでも述べたが、minuNは、「話し手の期待に反して……なってしまった」を意味することができる。

(1) **tai** 変化して……となっている　　例 agaNtai buN　赤くなっている
　　　　aga Nnani 赤-着物　　×agaNtai Nnani
　① 夕日が沈むのを見ながら
　　　iri tidaN agaNtai buN su ja:.
　　　夕日　赤く　なっているね
　② Nda cira agaNtai buN su ja:.
　　　あんた　顔　赤くなっているね（酒、日焼け、擦れなどで）
　③ agaNtai minuN.　　赤くなってしまった、赤すぎてしまった。
　　　おこわ作る時や、かまぼこを作るとき食紅を入れる。
　　　a： agaNtai minuN！
　　　あ　赤く　なっちゃった
　　　kamabugu agaNtai minuN.
　　　蒲鉾　赤すぎてしまった
　④ agaNtai na?
　　　赤がすぎたかな　（染めつけ終わって、出来栄えを尋ねる）
　⑤ agaNtai ja？
　　　赤すぎたか（問い返す）
　⑥ agaNtai ti ja naranuN
　　　赤くしては　　　ならない
　⑦ 否定は agaNtai minuN ではない。色をもっと着けたい時は動詞を用いる。
　　　agami buranuN／agaminuN
　　　赤くなってない　赤らまない
(2) **cici**（agacici（赤）という言葉はない。）
　① hurucici buN,　hurucici du buru
　　　（汚れ等で）　　　黒くなった
　　　hurumi du buru　（黒くなっている）に似ている
　② hurucici minuN　（染色の時よく言う）
　　　黒く　なっちゃった　黒すぎてしまった

③ huruCiCi buranuN　（黒く染まっていない）これが否定を意味する。
　　黒く　なってない

(3) tati

① hiCitati buN.
　　薄くして　いる

② hiCitati nu Nnani
　　薄い　　　着物　夏物の薄物

③ Nda Nnani hiCitati buN suja:.
　　あんたの着物　薄いね

④ hiCitati Tsji:.
　　薄く　切れ（蒲鉾の切り方を言う。逆は atsagu Tsji 厚く切れ）

⑤ ma:biN hiCitati naruN.
　　もう少し　薄く　なる　（急に客が増えたので１本の蒲鉾を人数分に切る時）

⑥ hiCitati minuN.　（否定形ではない）
　　薄くなっちゃた　／　薄すぎちゃった

(4) その他

① tsudari nu munu　cf. u ja tsu:munu
　　白い　　もの　　　これは　白い（初めからもともと白い）

② unu kabi tsudari buN suja:.
　　この　紙　白い　な

③ arataba tsudari buN.
　　洗って　白く　なっている

④ umuKiCi arataja tsudari naruN.
　　思い切り洗ったら　白く　なる

⑤ tsudari minuN.
　　白く　なっちゃった　（色物が洗ったら色落ちした時）

⑥ tsudari buranuN.
　　白くなってない

⑦　蕾では白かと思っていたのに、花には色がついていたとき
　　unu　hana　ja　tsudari　buranuN　suja:.　　agami　buNsuja:.
　　この　花　は　白く　していないな　　　　赤くなっている
⑧　喪の時など、色をつけないで寒天を作るとき
　　tsudari　na？
　　白か（色つけないのか）

　以上の特殊な形の形容詞は、動詞の継続形と呼ばれる形を持っていると思われる。意味の上からも、動詞からの派生だと考えられる。このような特殊な形のものだけではなく、一般的に形容詞は動詞との類似点がある。

【付記】

　この文法の研究・発表に関しては、宮岡伯人大阪学院大学教授と真田信治大阪大学教授に深く感謝する。国立国語研究所主任研究員大西拓一郎氏及びそのグループの方々との学問的交流は支えとなり、いつも感謝している。与那国町役場の新城好美氏には、その出会いから現在まで、長年にわたりお世話いただいて本当に有難い。続けられたのも氏に負うところが多い。そして面倒な質問を受けて考えてくださる話者の方々のお名前を記して深い感謝を表したい。

【方言話者のお名前と生年】（敬称略、順不同）

　池間　苗　大正8年　　喜久山ミヨ　大正15年　　崎原トシ　大正13年
　宮良保全　大正7年　　宮良節（故人）

【参照文献】

池間栄三（1959）『与那国の歴史』私家版
池間苗（1998）『与那国ことば辞典』私家版
伊豆山敦子（1992）「琉球方言の1人称代名詞」『国語学』171
伊豆山敦子（1997）「琉球方言形容詞成立の史的研究」『アジア・アフリカ言語文化研
　　究54』東京外語大AA研

伊豆山敦子（1998）「琉球方言補助動詞（コプラ）の起源」『独協大学諸学研究』1－2
伊豆山敦子（2001）「琉球・八重山（石垣宮良）方言条件表現のアスペクト・モダリティー的側面」『マテシス・ウニウェルサリス』2－2 獨協大学外国語学部言語文化学科
伊豆山敦子（2002）「琉球・八重山（石垣宮良）方言の文法」文部省科学研究費補助金「特定領域研究（A）『環太平洋の「消滅に瀕した言語」にかんする緊急調査研究』成果報告書 A4-004
柴田武（1959）「琉球・与那国方言の音韻」『ことばの研究』国立国語研究所
柴田武監修（1962）『全国方言資料』第11巻琉球編Ⅱ日本放送協会
髙橋俊三（1992）「与那国方言」『言語学大辞典』4巻　p.873－882 三省堂
髙橋俊三（1986－7）「八重山・与那国島」『琉球の方言』11,12 法政大学沖縄文化研究所
平山輝男・中本正智（1964）『琉球与那国方言の研究』東京堂
与那国小学校百周年記念誌編集委員会（1985）『与那国小学校創立百周年記念誌』与那国小学校百周年事業協讃会

琉球方言の母音調和的傾向
A Kind of Vowel Harmony in
Luchuan Dialects

1．初めに
　琉球方言では、語幹の母音にの出現、ある種の制限があるようにみえる方言がある。沖縄本島北部方言・辺土名などがそういう傾向をもつ。[1]

　八重山方言では、接尾形式（助詞・助動詞など）の母音が語幹末音に呼応して交替する現象がある。これは、琉球方言の史的研究にとって重要であり、上代の関連語に対する参考資料ともなる。

　この論文は、八重山方言の上記のような現象を、母音調和的傾向として、八重山黒島・石垣宮良方言を中心に報告する。

2．八重山方言の地域
　日本の最西南に位置するのが八重山諸島である。これらの島々で話されている方言が琉球方言の一派で、八重山方言と呼ばれている。（次頁地図参照）

3．助詞の母音交替　（本土方言の「へ」「に」及び「から」に相当する語）
3.1　黒島方言
　黒島は、面積9.83平方キロ、海岸線延長12.62km の珊瑚礁に囲まれた美しい島で、平成2年の人口は約200人、所帯数約100である。西表島から水道

（1）伊豆山（1996）p. 9

琉球列島位置図

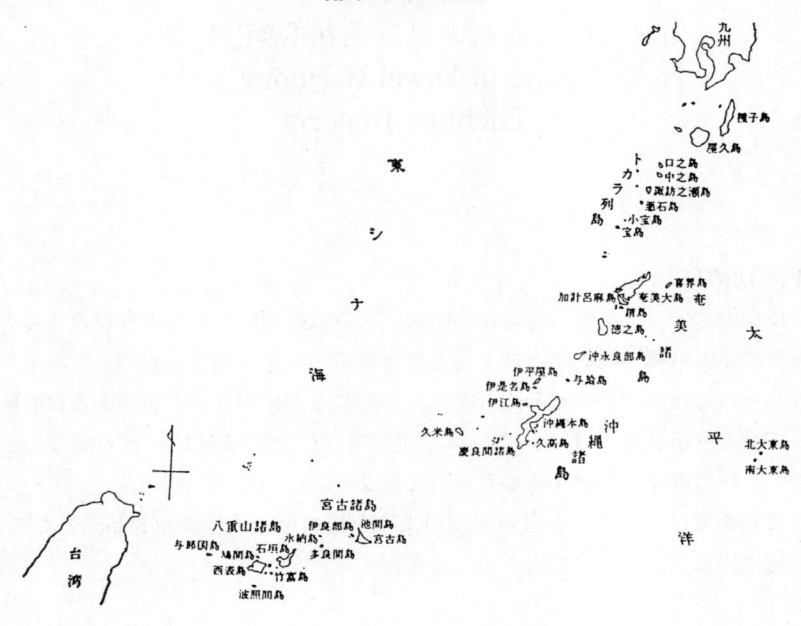

八重山諸島

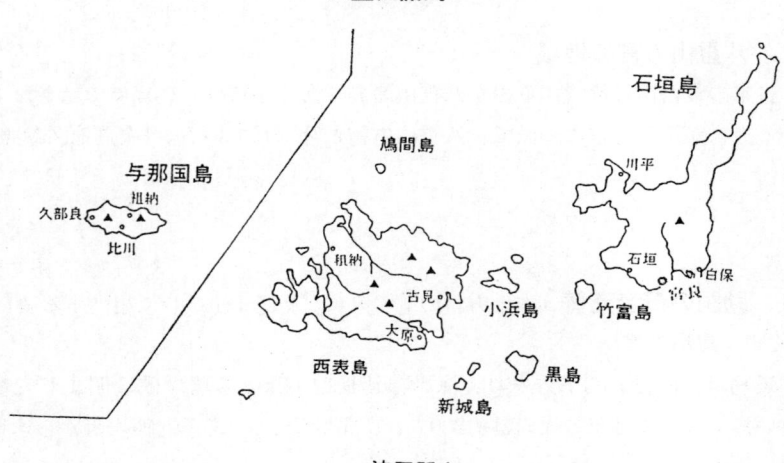

琉球方言の母音調和的傾向

を引いた現在は、畜産を営み、人口より牛の方が10倍程多い。

近来まで5つの集落があったが、宮里に住人がいなくなり、現在は4つの集落があって、少しづつ方言差がある。この論文では東筋（a:suN）を主とし仲本（nahaNtu）を参照する。

黒島（東筋）方言は、首里方言などと異なり、短母音/o//e/をもつ。〔I〕は音声的には認められることもあるが、音韻的には、/rI/だけであろう。[2]

行為の方向・目的等を表す助詞（「へ」「に」に相当する）に3つの形 ha～he～ho がある。また「から」に対応する助詞にも3つの形 hara～hera～hora がある。

これら3形の母音は、その接する語の末音に呼応している。末音が i か e なら he、u か o なら ho、それ以外なら ha である。hara etc もこれに準じる。そして、これらが接尾するとき、その接する語の末母音が狭母音なら、i→e、u→o のように広くなる。但し1音節語は、e:の場合だけ he で、他は全て ha が接尾する。

以下に例を示す．共通語の訳は、主として形による。

（簡略音声表記による。記号書き換え：

　ʃ→sj、β→v、Φ→hw、tʃ→c、tʔ→、kʔ→、→TK、ｷ→I、音節末 n、m、ŋ→N）

　pataki→patake he paruN.　　pataki→hatake hera du ke:.
　　畑　　畑　　へ　行く　　　　畑　　　から　　来た
　maci→mace he paruN.　　usji→usi he isjiba jaretta:.
　　町　　町　　へ　　行く　　牛　　牛　へ　石を　投げた
　garas(j)i→garas(j)e he、me: he→me: he　he、
　　鳥　　　鳥　　　へ　　墓　　　墓　　へ
　gakko(:)→gakko ho、iso→iso ho、jamatu→jamato ho、
　　学校　　学校　へ　磯　磯　へ　大和　　大和　へ

（2）東筋の/rI/に、仲本では/N/が対応する。尚〔I〕は中舌ではなく前舌母音であるが、ここでは習慣に従っておく。

373

izu→izo ho
魚　魚　へ

hama→hama　ha、　tumarı→tumarı　ha、　Kumurı→kumurı　ha、
あっち　あっち　へ　海　　　海　へ　（海の)溜り　　溜り　へ

kaNgarı→kaNgarı ha、　tiN→ tiN　ha、iN→iN　ha
　鏡　　　鏡　へ　　天　天 へ　犬 犬 へ

miN→miN　ha、pe: →pe:　he、
耳　　耳　へ　織器具　織器具　へ

pi:→ pi: ha、 to:→to: ha、 tu:→tu: ha、 ha:→ ha: ha
リーフ リーフ へ 唐 唐 へ 渡 渡 へ 井戸 井戸 へ

また、本土方言の「に」に相当する例

banı he tabo:ri.　banta ha tabo:ri.
私　　に　下さい。　私達　に　下さい。

名詞以外にも接尾する。動詞に接する例をあげる。

hauN hajahara　　　hwukiruN hwukihera
買う　買ってから　　　起きる　起きてから

　この母音の交替は、「学校」のような新しい語彙の場合にも見られるので、productive であろうが、更に化石化していると思われる例もある。

	明日	明後日	明明後日（4日)	5日目
黒島	atsaha	asjitoho	jo:ho	isıka
宮良	atsa	asutu	ju:ga	itsıka

黒島にも stsa、asjitu という語もある。
これらは、未来方向には -ha etc を伴うが、過去方向には伴わない。

	昨日	一昨日	去年	一昨年	来年	再来年
黒島	kino	busjitui	kuzu	mi:ti	jeNha	mi:tehe
宮良	kInu	bududui	kuzu	mi:dinadi	eN	mi:di

jeNha 以下は常に -ha etc. を伴う。明々後日以降は、4日、5日等の -ka

374

に対応すると思われる。

このような傾向からすると、黒島方言一人称代名詞のいわゆる inclusive の bija-ha の -ha の起源は、これと同じではないかと思われる。

bijaha の -ha は、複数語尾ではなく、bija（bë）ja:（我が家）のように-ha なしで用いられることがある。いわゆる inclusive 代名詞は、「彼ら」（uttsa）に対する「我ら」なのであるからおそらく、「あちら側」に対する「こちら側」を意味した ha が bija に接尾したものだと考えられる。[3]

3.2 その他の八重山方言と従来の研究

琉球方言の、「へ」に相当する助詞の形は、以下に記すように様々である。まず次の章で取り上げる宮良方言は、ge(:)で母音は交替しない。

また黒島と似た形 he(:)をもつ川平では、母音を変えることはないが、野原（1975 p.96）によれば語幹末の短母音 -u が -o:に変わるようである。そうなら、黒島との接点もあることになる。

例　uma: he: あそこへ、me:ko: he　宮古へ（me:ku 宮古）

3.2.1　黒島方言に関する先行研究の記述

黒島方言に関する記述はいくつかあるが、上述したような母音の交替に触れたものは皆無である。

その事実に気がつかなかったものか、理由を示さずに、ただ1形だけをあげている。以下にそれらを記す。

平山・中本（1964　p.158）は次のように多くの方言を記している。（下線筆者）

　　　'NKi（与那国）　　Qti, ti（船浮）　　ci、ga（波照間）
　　　ka'a（新城）　　　'Nge'e（小浜）　　'i（竹富）
　　　ha（黒島・真栄里）　he'e（川平）　　ka'i（石垣・大浜）
　　　ge'e（平得・宮良）　go'o（白保）

そして「カイ系統とカチ系統があり、これらはカイ系統に相当する形が、

（3）伊豆山（1992）p.2

いろいろな音韻変化をたどったものだが、波照間はカチ系統か。」と述べている。黒島については ha だけをあげ、異なる母音の形の記述は何もない。

野原（1986　p.10～12）は、場所・目標などを表すカイ系、カチ系などを記し、黒島については ha だけをあげている。なお同頁の宮良 ga: は ge: の誤りである。小浜に ge: を記しているところからみると、場所を示す Nga と間違ったものであろう。

中松（1987　p.215）は「ヘ」の項に ho だけをあげている。しかし kumaha:(こちらへ)、hamaha:(あちらへ) を記している。

また中松（1976　p.120）は（ヘ）格の助詞として NgeR だけあげている。これは黒島のどの方言かわからない。

以上に見られるように、琉球方言は、助詞に関してさえまだ研究が十分でないのに、大きく変貌しつつある。残念ながら、研究はむずかしくなるばかりである。

3.2.2　波照間方言と白保方言

波照間は日本有人島では最南端の島で、面積12.46平方キロ、平成2年現在の人口687である。

白保は、波照間からの移住の村である。明和の大津波（1771年）で壊滅的な被害を被った白保は、波照間から強制移住した人々により復興した。生存者28人のところに415人移住したといわれる。(4) 従って基本的に両者は同じ方言に属すと言える。

この200年間で、この2方言がどのような変化をしたか、壮大な実験場のようなものなので、比較研究できれば多くの学問的収穫があると思われる。白保の方言も、消失寸前なので、調査研究は急がなければならない。(5) 人口約1600と多いが、本来の方言話者は少なくなってくる一方である。

波照間方言については、以下に記すように、研究書により記述が異なって

---

(4) 八重山歴史 p.269
(5) 白保と宮良は、歴史的に異なる方言に属していて、長く互いに特殊性を保っていた。しかし近来、中学校がこの2村に対し1校配置されたこと、高校は石垣の八重山高校1校であることなども影響し、本来の方言の研究は高齢者によるしかない状態である。

いる。
   平山・中本（1964）　　　ci、ga
   中松（1987 p.214-215）　～ci（へ、に）
                       mo:ga（こちらへ）、haga（あちらへ）
   野原（1986 p.11）　　ga
   野原同書同ページは、波照間にgaだけをあげているが、p.413以下の波照間方言の文例には、ciが4例ある。それは以下の通りである。
çigaci（家へ）、　ʔusina:ci（沖縄へ）、ʔisasjimaci（石垣島へ）、nahaci（那覇へ）
   平山（1988 p.771-773）は波照間方言の格助詞の項があり、全く同じ文例「沖縄に行く」に対して、区別を明記することなく、3つの助詞を次のように記している。
動作・作用の帰着するところ　ウシゥナガ　ングン。ウシゥナナガ　ングン。
動作・作用の向けられる方向・目標または帰着するところウシゥナチ　ングン。
   波照間と同系統の白保については、平山・中本（1964）ではgo'oだけをあげている。
   野原（1986）は白保に触れていない。
   白保は筆者の調査によると次のように2形ある。

go-　kuma　go　ku:jo:.　pi: go NguN.　phama go NguN.
　　　ここ　へ　来い　　リーフ　へ　行く　浜　へ　行く
　　　mo:　go　ku:jo.
　　　こっち　へ　来い
　　　inu（犬）、maja（猫）、usji（牛）go
(ko) -　nisji ko（du）NguN.（-sji 無声化）
　　　北（西）へ行く

gaci-　bahi　gaci　ku:jo:.
　　　私の家　に　来い　(hi: 家)

　　　　　ON　　　gaci　NguN.
　　　　　お願いに　　行く　（ON 御嶽）
（Kaci)-　isasI　Kaci　Ngara.
　　　　　石垣　に　　行こう　（isasI 石垣　-sasI　無声化）
　　　cf. me:ra（宮良）go Ngara、sIsabu（白保）go、junoN（与郷国）go

　g～Ko の方が g～Kaci より遙かに多く用いられる。後者は、場所方向を示す時、場所以上の抽象的な意味があると用いられるように見受けられる。
　家に行くのは、話したり遊んだりする意味あいがある。御嶽も拝んだり祭りのために行く。石垣も賑やかな町として他の集落にはない特殊性がある。
　この点では、波照間でも何らかの違いがあったのではないかと思われる用例が、柴田（1972）に載っている。
　　　　　'isasIkaci（石垣へ）：　'isasImaci（石垣島へ）
　波照間の用例を見ると、場所の方向を示すときは ci で、行為の目的を示すときは ga が多いようにみえる。分化しているのかもしれない。
　白保の gaci は、化石化しつつあるのかもしれない。白保では go が圧倒的に有力だが、波照間に比べると次のような興味深い事実が分かる。
　柴田（1972　p.320）には moaga（そのへんに）がある。これは白保の mo:go（こちら）に対応すると思われる。波照間では -ga の前で -a が挿入されたか -o- の音価が変わったのではないだろうか。同書では、場所の方向を表すには ci が多く、ga は moaga 以外では zagaru（どこへ）1例あるだけである。
　mo:go（こちらへ）の形を持つ白保で -go が優勢であり、mo:ga の方を持つ波照間では、場所に関して -ci が -ga より優勢と見えるのは偶然であろうか。嘗て go が語幹末音と呼応したことがあって ga と交替したのではないかと疑われる。なお調査を要する。

3.2.3　鳩間方言

　鳩間は面積1.01平方キロ、平成2年現在の人口54という可愛い島である。嘗て、黒島から移住が行われたことがある。
　加治工（1983　p.125-126）によれば、方向格の助詞は上接語の末尾音の

種類によって次のように変化する。また、-ra（空間的時間的起点、手段「から」に対応する）も同様である。
（イ）-i＋へ→Ce:(C＝子音)　　（ロ）-a＋へ→Ca:(C＝子音)
（ハ）-u＋へ→Co:(C＝子音)

　何故「＋へ」なのか、例がないので解らないが、恐らく1音節語の場合には出現するのであろう。
　同書の例を見ると、黒島のように母音調和的であった3つの交替形の、語頭子音 h- が母音間で失われ融合した形である。
　野原（1986　p.11）は、鳩間を黒島とは全く違う系統（A-4　と A-1）として分類しているが、誤りであろう。通時的には、黒島同様、語幹末音に呼応していた助詞の *h- が消失した形である。

　以上みた語幹末音と呼応する接尾形式は、h で始まるという共通点がある。そしてそれは、*k- に由来すると考えられる。

4. 石垣宮良方言の形容詞語尾

　石垣市宮良は、人口1294、石垣市から7キロほど離れた、農業を主としている海沿いの集落で、1771年の津波の後、小浜島からの移住者を迎えた。生存者171のところへ小浜から320人移住したといわれる[6]。従って宮良方言は、基本的には小浜島と同系である。
　既述のように宮良の ge:(へ) の母音は交替しないが、形容詞語尾は語幹末音と呼応している。
　語幹末母音が a であるか、u 又は o であるか、i 又は e であるかに応じて、haN～hoN～heN のように母音が交替し、語幹末母音が -ɨ なら -saN、また1音節の -i なら -sjaN である。これにはまず例外がない[7]。

---

(6) 注(4)と同じ。
(7) 宮良の/I/の母音の音価は中舌とは言いがたい前舌なのだが、今は慣習に従っておく。上村（1993）も、石垣、波照間、白保等に中舌的音色の舌先的母音を認めている (p.97-98)。

形容詞の終止形として -N の形をあげることには、躊躇いを感じるが、習慣に従っておく。

同じような傾向を示す黒島では、更に異なる語尾を持っている。以下に表示する。

意　味	宮　良	黒　島
赤い	akahaN	akahaN
悪い	janahaN	janahaN
うまい	NmahaN	ma:haN
黒い	hwhwohoN	vo:hoN
広い	pɪsohoN	pisohoN
弱い	jo:hoN	jo:hoN
固い	ko:hoN	ko:hoN
強い	co:hoN	su:waN
痒い	bjo:hoN	bju:waN
遠い	to:hoN	tu:waN
青い	auhoN	auhaN
大きい	maiheN	ubohoN
可愛い	apareheN	abareheN
涼しい	pirɪgeheN	pi:rakeheN
苦い	NgahaN	NgeheN
汚い	janeheN	janijaN
うれしい	saneheN	sanijaN
美しい	kaiheN	haijaN
寒い	pi:sjaN	pi:jaN
酸っぱい	sɪ:saN	sji:jaN
薄い	pɪsaN	pisjaN
薄くなった	pɪsa:pɪsa（h）i [8]	pisjiheN

宮良の -o: に対応する黒島 -u: 語幹へ接尾するのは、-ho ではなく -wa である。これらは、偶々1音節語幹だから助詞の場合と同様だとみなすことができる。

すなわち、通時的には、助詞の場合と同様、e: 以外の1音節語幹では *-haN

---

(8) 盛山マントさんによると -hi である。この事実は、通時的に形容詞語尾を考える際に重要である。

380

が接尾したのだが、uの後ろで*hが消失し-wとなったと考えることができる。

　黒島で-heが接尾するのは-e語幹であり、-iで終わる2音節語幹および長母音の-iで終わる1音節語幹には-jaが現れる。

　-saは宮良以上に出現し、とどちらでも良いという場合が、特に1音節語幹に見られる。

　例　su:saN、jo:saN、p(I)saNの他ja:saN（ひもじい）など

　また、熟語的や派生語幹的と見られるものには-saが思われる。その例をあげる。habasaN香しい、atarasaN可愛い、hamarasaN悲しい、pirumasaN不思議な、hasamasaNうるさい、hama: rasaN悲しい、kucisaN苦しい

　互いに母音調和的傾向を持つこの2方言の形容詞語尾を比較すると、これらが通説のように「さ＋あり」に由来するとは考えにくい。

　特に、宮良のe-heNに対する黒島のi-jaNを通説で説明することは困難である。

　更に言えば、宮良でも黒島でも、他方言のsにhが対応する例は見いだせない。形容詞語尾の起源は、他に求められるであろう。[9]

5．その他の母音調和的現象

5.1
黒島方言の完了を表す動詞語尾は、形容詞語尾と極似している。4段動詞対応の動詞語尾は、次のように語幹の母音に呼応する。

　　書く　hakuN hake-heN　買う　hauN haja-haN

参考に2段動詞対応の動詞語尾を記すと次のようである。

　　起きる　hwukiruN hwuki-jaN

　ここでは、この動詞語尾と既述した形容詞語尾の、形の類似性に注意を喚起するにとどめておく。

（9）伊豆山（1996b）p.113以下参照

5.2 鳩間方言の形容詞語尾は、黒島と類似している。加冶工（1984 p 330）で示せば次の通りである。

　　　語幹の末尾が cvcv 構造の時　　-a＋aN→-a: N、-i＋aN→e: N、
　　　　　　　　　　　　　　　　　　-u＋aN→-o: N、
　　　語幹の末尾が cvv 構造の時　　 -i＋aN→ijaN、-u＋aN→uwaN

これは -ijaN を除けば、前述した「ヘ」相当の助詞の場合とほぼ平行している。通時的には、黒島のような -h- が消失したものであろう。

同上書は、形容詞語尾を「語幹＋さ＋あり」という構成だとする通説に対して、「鳩間方言の形容詞は語構成上、語幹に直接「アリ」が下接したものとみなければ説明がむつかしい。」と正当な疑問を呈している。

5.3 次に、与那国祖内方言の「ので」を意味する動詞接辞があげられる。
これは -bi と -ba の2形がある。-i（非過去、いわゆる連用形）に接する時と、-a（過去）に接する時とで、母音が交替している。

　　　bui-bi　　いるので　　　buTa-ba　　いたので、
　　　kaTi-bi　 書くので　　　kaTiTa-ba　書いたので

5.4 宮良の複合語にも類似例がある。
　　　ki: 木　 kuru-kI　黒木　 so-gI ki: 白木（木）

「黒」「白」に対応する方言語彙は、形容詞の -a 語尾と共存するのを嫌い、母音調和的に語尾の母音を変えるということがない方言では、動詞形をとる傾向がある。「白い」で例示する。

　　黒島　dzo: hoN、宮良　sIsohoN、辺土名　sju: ro: N、与那国　tsuda: ri

余談にわたるが、宮良の90余りの高齢者の一人が、自分が年をとって役にたたなくなったのを嘆いて（実際は丈夫で農業に従事しているのだが）、次のように言った。

　　　「mu:ru　sukurupu　nati」
　　　　全く　　　？　　　なって

老人の悪口をいう珍しい単語があると思って、2・3回繰り返してもらったら、実は「スクラップ」であった。その時はがっかりしたが、すぐ思い直

琉球方言の母音調和的傾向

した。
　宮良には /su/ も /ku/ も /ra/ も /pu/ もある。しかし cucacu のような語幹は少ないのである。多分ないのかもしれない。
　このようなことも、70代の方々の言葉では観察することはできない。共通語がすっかり浸透しているからである。

6．終わりに
　八重山方言に広くみられる母音調和的傾向を報告した。このような現象は琉球方言のみならず、一般言語学的に、日本語全体の研究の参考資料となるものである。
　また琉球方言の歴史的研究において、考慮すべき現象である。
　琉球方言は劇的な変化を経験しつつある。それは、勿論、新しい方言が生まれる興味ある現象を提供するものではあるけれども、多様で比較研究の絶好の場がまだ残っている今、文化財とも言うべき高齢者の体系を捉えておかなければ、後生に悔いを残すことは間違いない。
　日本語の歴史研究にとって、琉球方言の全体的且つ詳細な研究の緊急性・重要性を大きく訴えたい。

【付記】　この論文は平成8年国語学会春季大会（於東京、青山学院）で、「琉球方言の母音調和的傾向―八重山黒島方言と石垣宮良方言―」という題で、口頭発表したものの一部を基に、書き変えたものである。他の部分に関しては、改めて発表するつもりである。

【方言話者の御氏名および生年（敬称略）】

宮良　　　田盛宇津良　明治44年　同　ハル　大正3年　東成底光秀　大正2年
盛山　信八　昭和3年　同　シズ　昭和5年　盛山マント　明治38年
嵩原　チヨ　大正6年

白保	宮良　マツ　明治38年		
黒島東筋	神山　仲蔵　大正5年　同　トミ　大正8年　比屋定小町　大正5年		
黒島仲本	宮喜　清　昭和3年　小浜伸光　大正11年　同　トヨ　大正10年		
小浜　キク	大正15年		
与那国祖内	池間　苗　大正8年　新城好美　昭和20年		
与那国比川	前粟蔵ヲナリ　明治39年		

【参考文献】

伊豆山敦子（1992）「琉球方言の1人称代名詞」『国語学』171

伊豆山敦子（1966a）「辺土名方言が示す琉球方言研究の問題点」獨協大学教養諸学研究30巻2号

伊豆山敦子（1966b）「琉球方言の母音調和的傾向」国語学会平成8年度春季大会要旨集

上村幸雄（1993）「音声の現状　琉球列島」『国際化する日本語』第7回「大学と科学」公開シンポジウム組織委員会

加冶工真市（1983）「八重山鳩間方言の助詞」『琉球の方言8』法大沖文研

加冶工真市（1984）「八重山方言概説」『講座方言学10—沖縄・奄美地方の方言』国書刊行会

柴田　武（1972）『全国方言資料』第11巻　琉球編Ⅱ

中松竹雄（1976）『南島方言の記述的研究』根元書房

中松竹雄（1987）『琉球方言辞典』那覇出版社

野原三義（1986）『琉球方言助詞の研究』蔵野書院

野原三義（1975）「八重山石垣島川平方言（助詞の部）」「琉球の方言」法大沖文研

平山輝男・中本正智（1964）『琉球与那国方言の研究』東京堂

平山輝男　et al（1988）『南琉球の方言基礎語彙』桜楓社

八重山歴史編集委員会（1953）『八重山歴史』八重山歴史編集委員会

Evidentiality
―琉球語の場合―

要旨

琉球諸方言では、Evidentiality（証拠様態）が、文法範疇として存在する。石垣宮良と宮古平良では、語の形態は全く異なるが、陳述ごとに情報源が特定される。1．直接、2．推論、3．伝聞の三項対立である。

1．Evidentiality（証拠様態）(1)について

Alexandra Y. Aikhenvald（2003）を引用する。In a number of languages, the nature of the evidence on which a statement is based must be specified for every statement-whether the speaker saw it, or heard it, or inferred it from indirect evidence, or learnt it from someone else. This grammatical category, referring to an information source, is called 'evidentiality' (p. 1). そして、(p. 4)には、VISUAL(or DIRECT), INFERS, REPORTED の三項対立を挙げている。これは、琉球諸方言にとって有効で、先島諸方言では、以下のように陳述ごとに、証拠のあり方（Evidentiality 証拠様態）を特定する。固有の文字が無い言語であることを特に記しておく。

（1）工藤真由美（2004）に、証拠性（evidentiality）がある。本稿では、陳述毎に特定される証拠のあり方という文法システム範疇の evidentiality（証拠様態）である。

2．宮良方言（動詞語形変化表。伝統的な表と方言体系による表とを続けてあげる。）

Ⅰ型	未然	連用	終止	連体	已然	命令	接続
書く	kak-a	kak-ɪ	kak-u-N	kak-u	kak-ja	kak-i	kak-i
起きる	uk-u	uk-i	uk-ir-u-N	uk-ir-u	uk-ir-ja	uk-ir-i	uk-i
Ⅱ型	未然	連用	終止	連体	已然	命令	接続
（書いてる）	kak-ira	kak-i	kak-iN	kak-ir-u	kak-ir-ja	kak-ir-i	kak-ir-i /kak-ir-ir-i
（起きてる）	uk-ira	uk-i	uk-iN	uk-ir-u	uk-ir-ja	uk-ir-i	uk-ir-i
Ⅲ型	未然	連用	終止	連体	已然	接続	
（書いた）	kak-e:r-a-	kak-e:-	kak-e:-N	kak-e:r-u	kak-e:r-ja	kak-e:r-i	
（落ちた）	ut-e:r-a-	ut-e:-	ut-e:-N	ut-e:r-u	ut-e:r-ja	ut-e:r-i	

		不定（連用）	確認（連体）[2]	已然	未然
Ⅰ群	認識型	kak-ɪ	kak-u	×	kak-a
	生起型	kak-i	×	kak-ja	×
	生起認識型	kak-ir-i /kak-ir-ir-i	kak-ir-u	kak-ir-ja	kak-ir-a
Ⅱ群	生起型	uk-i	×	×	uk-u (uka-)
	生起認識型	uk-ir-i	uk-ir-u	uk-ir-ja	uk-ir-a
Ⅲ群	生起型	kak-e:-	×	×	×
	生起認識型	kak-e:-ri-	kak-e:r-u	kak-e:r-ja	kak-e:r-a-

　伝統的文法枠組みによる活用表では、-N はⅡ・Ⅲ型連用、Ⅱ型連体と全已然形に後接する。方言体系に基づく語形変化（活用）表では、-N は全生起型不定形、全已然形、Ⅰ・Ⅱ群の確認（連体）形に後接。-da は、認識型不定形、全生起型不定形に後接。Ⅲ群の不定（連用）形は独立せず -N／-da／-so: が後接し、-N は -so:／-da と共起しないが、-so: は-da にも後接する。

2.1　終止形と宮良方言の言い切り形

　-N 形は、話し手の認識・判断が伴う。2 人称動作主体の質問は可だが陳述・断定は不可。

（2）連体形という用語は、琉球語には相応しくないが、日本語との関係上用いた。

Evidentiality —琉球語の場合—

① ba: kakuN.　　wa: kakuN?
　　私　書く　　あんた　書く？（質問辞は無い。イントネーションで表す）
② wa:　kaki.　可　×　wa:　kakuN.　不可
　　お前　　書け　　　　お前（は）書く
　　相手（wa:）のことは、相手本人が一番よく解る。話し手が、相手本人以上に解る筈はない。
③ ta: du kaku?　ba: du kaku./(Atusko Ndu kaku.)　×wa: du kaku.
　　誰　が　書く？　私　が　書く／（敦子　が　書く。そう決まっている時）
④ no: du kaku?　　kunu zI: du kaku.
　　何　を　書く　　この　字　を　書く
　　「書く」行為が行われることは、見て（筆を持って紙を広げている）、あるいは確実な根拠により（ポスターを作る集会だ等）当事者全員（話し手、聞き手）が認めている。問題は、焦点の「書き手」或いは「書く対象」である。係り結びというのは単なる規則ではないのだ。
⑤ ami hwo:N.　　⑤'　×　ami hwo:N?
　　雨　降る　　　　　　雨　降る？（人間には答えられない質問。）[3]
⑥ ami hwo: N kaja:.　疑問の語を用いて問うべきである。
　　雨　降る　かねー
⑥' 例えば木を見ながら　kunu ki: ja hana sakuN?　この木は花咲く？
　　花木のことをよく知っている人は答える。　sakuN.　咲く

-N 後接の、文を終止すると言われる形式は、発話者（話し手）の判断・認知を表しているのであり、質問は、相手がその形で答えられるか、相手の判断を問うているのである。[4]話し手は、自分の行動なら確実に解っている。他人の行動でも確実な事実に基づく推論なら可能だ。しかし聞き手のことは、聞き手以上に確実な陳述をすることはできない。

　3人称が動作主体の場合は、「そうである」と確実に判断される状況証拠があるなら「Atuko: kakuN.（敦子書く）」も可だが、そうでなければ、hazI

（3）黒い雲が湧いて来るのを見ながら jagati ami hwo:N?（やがて雨降る？）なら可。構文的な切れ目が単語の切れ目と一定しない例になるかもしれない。
（4）Ⅰ・Ⅱ群生起型不定形に後接する -N については伊豆山（2005）参照

を加えるのが普通である。
⑦　ure:　kaku hazɪ.
　　彼は　書く　だろう。　これは、日本語の「筈」とは異なり、状況による推測である。

2.2　宮良方言の過去

　Aikehenvald（p. 4）に、VISUAL（or DIRECT），INFERS，REPORTED の三項対立がある。

　琉球の「過去（-da~ta）」というのは、無限の過去ではない。<u>自分の経験範囲</u>での過去である。その行為が実現したことを、<u>話し手の体験（見聞）により確認した状態</u>にある。数回にわたる行為も、丸ごと一体として捉えられる。以下、過去（接辞-da）の例。

(1)　**Visual（Direct）見聞（直接経験）**
①　ba: kɪnu　tigami　<u>kakɪ-da</u>.
　　私　昨日　手紙　書いた
②　もし自分が必要な手紙を書いたかどうか忘れたなら、
　　ba: tigami　<u>kakɪ-da</u>　kaja:.　必ず答えられると限らないから、kaja: が必要。
　　私　手紙　書いた　かねー　　　答えは<u>二通り</u>ある。
③　wa: tigami　<u>kakɪ-da</u>　(-so:).
　　あんた手紙　書いた（さ）（<u>手紙を書くのを見た。</u>）
②'　taniɴgasa: nu tigami　kaki-da-soɴga ta: du　<u>kaki-da</u>　kaja:.
　　誰か　　が　手紙　書いていたけど　誰が　書いていたのかなー
　　（人が書いているのは見たけれど、名前が分からなかったか忘れた時）

(2)　**Infers 推論**
④　書く<u>動作は見ていなかった</u>が、書いた<u>手紙を見た</u>時。
　　wa:　tigami　kake:　-so:.
　　あんた　手紙　書き終わった（状態だ）
「動作」は見なかったが、書く行為の付随事象として手紙があるのだから、「書く行為（動作及びその付随事象）」は起こり、終わったと推論できる。

388

Evidentiality ―琉球語の場合―

参考に、事体・状態を述べ、-N と対立する -so が、他の語幹に出現する例を挙げる。

(1) 皆が、早い者勝ちで何か書く場合 （彼が書きそうなのを見ながら）
　　uri nu kakɪ-so:.　　　wanuN higu kakja:.
　　彼が　書くよ　　　お前も　早く　書け

(2) ure:　kaki-da-so:
　　彼は　書いていた　よ　（書いているのを見た）

(3) **Reported** 伝聞

経験外の事柄を述べる。生まれた日の出来事は、見聞（経験）してはいない（生まれたばかりで解らない）。誰かに告げられ（reported） 知ったことである。

⑤　ba: maridakeN ja kazji Ndu huki-da　co:.
　　私の　生まれた時　は　大風　が　吹いていたって

このように、co: (とさ) という語を付け加えなければならない。huki-da と言った人は、暴風だったのを経験している。この co: は、次例のような伝聞の語と同じである。

⑥　ami nu　huiri-ki　mukaina:　ku-N co:.
　　雨　が　降っているから　迎えに　来るって

経験（主に visual evidence）の有無で、同じ事実に、異なる表現をとらなければならない。

例えば方言話者から昔の苦労話を聞いたとする。実際経験した話者は言う。

⑦　mukasa:　jamaNgarasɪ sa: ri tamunu putso: -da.
　　昔は　　山刀　　で　薪　取った（拾った）

この話を筆者が「宮良地方の昔の生活」として報告するなら、

⑦'　mukasa:　jamaNgarasɪ sa: ri tamunu putso: -da co:.
　　昔は　　山刀　　で　薪　拾った　そうだ

歴史的なできごと、明和の大津波（1771）事件についても次のようでなければならない。

⑧ mukasɪ takarabe: kɪɴ di aɴzu pɪtu nu ta: ɴga sjigutu hi:
　　昔　　タカラベークィンと　いう　　人　　が　田　で　仕事　して
　　o: ruɴkeɴ du naɴ nu kɪtara: du takaharu kata ge: nuburuɴ di:
　　いられたら　　津波　が　来たから　高い　　方　　へ　登ろう　と
　　o: ruɴkeɴ du haɴ ba a: rai unu naɴ ja haq-ta co:.
　　していられると　足　を　洗い　その　津波　は　去った　とさ。

2.3　動作目撃の有無

　動作を見なかった場合は少し複雑な事情がある。言い切りの時、三つの形態素（-so:, -da, -ɴ）が後接する語幹 kake: - は、同じ形態素が後接する他の語幹とは異なり、独立しない。
(1) -so: が後接する場合。その動作は見ていないが、今は見えない、終わった行為を、現在見ている状態だけから推論して述べることができる。既述例に、いくつか追加する。
　① 朝、戸を開けたら、今、陽は射しているが、水たまりがあり、木々も濡れている。
　　　ami　（nu）　hui-e: -so:.
　　　雨　（が）降ったんだ。（雨が降り終わった状態だ）
　② 今日は静かな天気なので、畑に行ったら植えた韮が倒れている。
　　　kazji ɴdu　huk-e:-so:.
　　　風　　が　　吹いたんだ
　③ 枯れ木かと思っていた木の下に、花びらが散っている所に行き合わせた。
　　　hana　（nu）　sak-e:-so:.
　　　花　（が）　咲いたんだ
(2) -ru が後接する場合。発話者が、既に終わった動作を、原則、見ている。推論で、略確実だが、見ていない時は、na: を付すのが好ましい。
　④ 名前書き忘れの書類を見せながら尋ねる
　　　kure: ta: du kake: -ru?
　　　これは　誰が　書いたの？

Evidentiality —琉球語の場合—

⑤　ba: du　kake: -ru.（書いた本人が名乗り出る）
　　私　が　　書いたのだ（書類を見て、自分が書いたのだと解った）
⑤'　atsuko Ndu　kake: -ru.（敦子が書いたところを見ていた）
　　敦子　が　　書いたのだ
⑤"　展覧会などでよく見たら名前が書いてある場合。
　　A：ta: du　kaki-kaja:.
　　　　誰　が　書いたのかねー
　　B：na: nu　ariki　atsuko Ndu　kake: -ru　na:.
　　　　名　あるから　敦子　が　書いたんだ　ね
書くところは見ていなかった。名前が敦子だから、そうと決まっているが、見たわけではないから断定的でなく、na:をつける。

⑥　uQtaNga　cibisjike: nu　putsari-so:. hwa: Ndu　mare: -ru　na:.
　　彼等のうちに　おしめ　が　干されている。子供　が　生まれたんだな
　　（おしめが見えるし、若夫婦がいて、妊娠していたことも知っている等々）
(3) -Nが後接する場合。発話者が、既に終わった動作を、原則見ている。発見の時など推論で、そうと認識することも可だが、見ていない時は、na:を付す方が好ましい。

⑦　ami　hwuie: -N　na.
　　雨　降ったんだ　な（朝窓を開けたら、夜中に雨が降ったらしいと解って）

⑧　敦子が来るとか来ないとか言っていた。なかなか来ないので、ちょっと外出し、帰宅したら、敦子からの届け物が置いてあるのを発見して、
　　ku: nu di antasoNga　ke: -N！
　　来ないと　言ったけど　来たんだ。

書き物を頼んでおいた相手本人に道で出会った時や、取りに行った時の入り口で、

⑨　ba: taraNdaru muno:　kake: -N？
　　私の　頼んだ　ものは　書いた（てある）？　　　答えて
⑩　kake: -N.　　　⑩' me: da kaka-nu.　⑩" nama du　kaki-ru.
　　書いた（書き終えてある）　まだ　書か（いて）ない　今　書いている

391

その頼んだ本人が留守で、顔見知りの親類の者が留守番していたとする。
⑪　ba:　taraNdaru muno:　atsuko:　kake:-N　kaja:.
　　　私の　頼んだ　ものは　　敦子　　　書いた　かね

頼んだ相手ではないので、kake:-N？と言えず、疑問辞 kaja:が必要である。留守番は、「机の上にあったのがそれか」と思い見ると、やはりそれである。しかし、kake:-N. は不可。書くのを見ていたわけではないので、kake:-N とは言えない。

　　　kamaNga　urita:na:　nu munu nu assonga　ba:　ja bagaranu.
　　　あそこに　それらしい　もの　が　　あるけど　私　　は　分からない

と言って断る。「頼まれたわけではないから、もう一度、居る時に来てください」となる。

しかしこの留守番が、頼まれた敦子の子供か夫で、書くのを確実に見て、事情を知っていたならば kake:-N（書いてある）も可である。

類例をあげる。特別良いほうれん草の種類を庭に植えている家がある。その評判を聞きつけて、見知らぬ人がその種でも分けて貰おうかと訪ねて来る。

⑫　wacca Nga　ho:reNso:　ibe:-N？　　⑬　ibe:-N.
　　　あんたんち　ほうれん草　　植えてある？　　植えてある

植えた本人か、自分では手を下さなくても植えるのを見ていた妻が上のように答える。筆者が昨日から泊って、留守番をしている。昨日来たので、その、自慢のほうれん草畑を既に見て知っている。訪問者は、留守番とは知らず ibe:-N？と尋ねるが、答えて ibe:-N. は不可である。aruN.（ある）と答え、また来てくださいのように言う。「植えてある」ことは知っていても、「植える」動作は見ていないからである。

⑭　夜中に、敦子の車が音を立てて入って来た。家人が音で目が覚める。
　　　ba: kuruma nu utu ba sjiki du　uke:-ru na:.
　　　私の　車　の　音　を　聞き　起きたんだね（目覚まさせてごめんね）
⑭'　ba: kuruma nu utu ba sjiki du　uke:-ru？
　　　私の　車　の　音　を　聞き　起きてしまったの
　　×　ba: kuruma nu utu ba sjiki uke:-N？

Evidentiality ―琉球語の場合―

⑮　食事準備ができたと妹が姉を呼びに行くが、戻って来て母親に言う。
　　　jo: ko:　nongasa: ba　kaki　uruN.
　　　洋子は　　何か　　　を　書いて　いる（のを確認している）
⑯　再び見に行ったら、丁度鉛筆を置き片付けていた。立ち上がったのを見て、
　　　jo: ko　kake: -N.　（独り言、または、一緒に見に来た弟に言う）
　　　洋子　書き終わったんだ　　　　　　それから洋子に尋ねる
⑰　jo: ko:, wa:kake: -N ?　　答えて　　kake: -N.
　　洋子　あんた　書き終わった？　　　書き終わった
⑱　戻って、母に　jo: ko　kake: -N.　（そこで母はご飯を温めなおす）
⑲　書く動作は見なかった弟が、洋子の書いた書を持ってきて、母に渡して言う。
　　　jo: ko:　　kake: -so:　　　mi: mori.
　　　洋子　書いたんだ　　　見て御覧なさい

この -e: -N 形は、話し手自身の行為であれば、常に問題なく出現できる。自分の行為は経験（見聞）認知しているものなのだから。

(4) 仮定　（動作を見ることない、動作終了の仮定）
　①　kake: -ru　pIto:　ja:　ge:　kair-i　mishaN.
　　　書き終わった　人は　家　に　帰って　いい
　②　年寄りを騙して署名させる悪徳業者が来た時に、注意されたので署名しなかった。
　　　atsuko nu　anzanare: ru-ka:　ba:　jagati　kake: -N .
　　　敦子　が　言わなかったら　私は　もう少しで　書いた。（書かないですんだ）

393

3．宮古平良方言

宮古平良方言も evidentiality（証拠様態）の文法範疇を持っている。動詞変化形を示す

意味	語幹	（終止形） 不定(非過去)	（継続形） 出現(未完了)	（志向形） 未然(未来性)	(—)[5] 已然	（命令） 命令
書く	kak-	kak-I	kak-i	kak-a	kak-ja	kak-i
起きる	uk-	uk-i- (Z)	uk-i	uk-i	uk-ir-ja	uk-ir-u

1段対応動詞過去形形成と連体修飾形形成の相違に注目必要。–Z が話し手の認識を示す。

過去形　　不定形＋ta-z　　kak-I-ta-z,　　uk-i-ta-z　（書いた、起きた）
連体修飾　不定形＋名詞　　kak-I pazI,　　ukiz pazI　（書く筈、起きる筈）
否定形　　未然形＋N　　　kakaN,　　　　ukiN　　　（書かない，起きない）

3．1　非過去（複雑なので、特徴的な概略だけ記す）[6]

① ba:ja kakadja:N.
　　私　は　書かない（書く積りはない）　×　atsuko: kakadja: N.

話し手の意図に関わるから2・3人称主体では不可である。自分以外の人の気持ちは、判定できないのだ。その場合は次のようである。

② atsuko: kakadja: N　ti du uz.
　　敦子は　書かない　とて　いる　（書かないと言っているのを見て知っている）

②' atsuko: kakadja: N tsa.
　　敦子は　書かない　ってさ

3．2　過去

平良方言でも、「過去」というのは、話し手の直接経験（話し手の見聞）

（5）平山（1967）と狩俣（1992, p. 858）には無い。
（6）伊豆山（2002c）（pp. 53–69）参照

である。話し手以外が動作主体である時は、話し手がそれを直接経験（見聞）している。

(1) **Direct** 直接経験

① ta: ga kakɪtarja.
誰　が　書いたか

② atsuko ga du kakɪtaz.（書く動作を見た。）
敦子　が　書いた

②' ba: ja kakattaN（〜m）.⁽⁷⁾
私　は　書かなかった

②" atsuko: kakattaN（〜m）.
敦子　は　書かなかった．（敦子が書かなかったことを見て知っている）

(2) **Reported** 伝聞

① atsuko: kakattaN（〜m）tsa.
敦子は　書かなかった　って　（書かないのを見て知ったのではない）

② 歴史的事実（明和津波1771）は、経験していないから、「過去」では語れない。

meiwa nu tukjanna husaciNmi gami su: nu du agaztaz tsa:.（必ずtsaが必要）
明和　の　時には　ふさちん　まで　潮　が　あがった　とさ

③ 自分の経験と、他人の経験

jarabi pada: agata nu uriga: Nkai tago: katami mizɪ hum ga kaju: taz.
子供　頃は　向こうの　降り井戸に　桶　担いで　水　汲み　に　通った

この話者夫人が、何度も話を聞き、当時の状況も良く知り、このuriga: も見て知っていても、karja:（彼は）を付け、この通りに言うことはできない。tsaを付すことが必要である。

（7）1人称動作主体kakadja:N（書かない）の過去は無い。否定過去形末尾音は古い世代では[m]。

④ 自分で実際経験しもしないのに知った振りしてあれこれ言う人に
　　vva　mi: nu　sɪtarja？
　　あんた　見　た　のか
返すことばもないので、仕方ないから次のように言う。　　　　tsa.
　　　　　　　　　　　　　　　　　　　　　　　　　　（そう）だってさ
⑤　A：kɪno takanohana　makidu　sɪtaz.
　　　　昨日　貴乃花　　　負けた　んだよ　実際に（テレビを含む）見
た の意味。
昨日その時間には他のところで仕事をしていた筈なのにと思い、
　　B：vva　ma: nti　mi:　nu　sɪtarja？
　　　　あんた　本当に　見　　たのか
　　A：tsa:. ／anci: tsa　（実は聞いたか、読んだか、しただけだった）
　　　　だとさ。　そうだってさ

3.3　行為終了（動作終了後、その動作に伴った現象から、行為終了を推論する）

(1)　直接経験
　書いた書類を見せながら（書類完成は書く行為が終わった事を示す）
　　①　ta: ga kaki ukɪ（〜ukja）？　　答えて　baga du kaki ukɪ.
　　　　誰が　書いたの　か　　　　　　　　　　私が　　書いたのだ
　　②　atsuko ga　du　kaki ukɪ.　　　　　（敦子が書く動作を、見た）。
　　　　敦子が　　　書いたのだ
(2)　伝聞　前項質問に対し、動作を見なかったが、見た他人から聞いて知っていた時
　　②'atsuko ga du　kaki ukɪ tsa:.　　　敦子が書いたそうだ。
(3)　推論　動作は見ていないが、字でそれと分かるか、よく見たら名前がある場合
　　②"atsuko ga du　kaki ukɪ　pazɪ.
　　　　敦子　が　書いた　のだろう
(A)　動作目撃の有無　（動詞が focus）

Evidentiality —琉球語の場合—

① 自分が、書いたかどうか、よく覚えていないとき
　　ba: tigami　kakɪ du sɪtaz　　be: ja.
　　私　　手紙　　（ちゃんと）書いた　　かなー
奥さんが答えて　　　　vva　kaki　utaz.
　　　　　　　　　　あんた　書いて　いた（書いているのを見た）
①' 書くところは見ていないが、書いた手紙は見た時
　　vva　kaki du　ukɪtaz.　　　　×vva tigami kakɪtaz.
　　あんた　書いてしまったのだ（書いたもの＝手紙を、見た）続けて以下
　　handai nu wa:buɴ du ari utaz.　～　　ari uz.
　　飯台　の　上　に　あった（あるのを見た）～　ある（今でもあるのが見える）utaz なら手紙を出し終わったか、今もまだあるかは解らない。兎に角見た。
② 苦瓜　作りの上手な家に、苗を貰いに訪ねてきた人が言う。
　A：　go:ra ibi nu ukɪ？
　　　苦瓜　　植えて　　ある？
　B：　ibi du ukɪ.　　　　（植えた本人か見ていた家族の答え）
　　　植えて　ある
其の日に留守番で居た人は、その苦瓜畑を見ていても、同様に答えられない。
植えるのを見ていないから、次のように答える。
③ ba: ja uma nu ja:　nu pɪtu aranniba　sɪsain.
　　私　は　ここ　の　家　の　人　でないから　知らない
④ 頼んだ書類を取りに来た人が言う。
　baga tanumtaz muno: kaki nu ukɪ？
　　私が　頼んだ　もの　書いてある？
⑤ kaki du ukɪ.　　　　（頼まれた本人の答え）
　　書いて　ある
⑥ 本人が留守で里帰りした娘が留守番でいた。彼女は⑤で答えられない。尋ね方も違う。
　atsuko ja baga tanumutaz muno:　kaki du ukɪ be: ja.

397

敦子　は　私が　頼んだ　もの　は　書いておいたかね
⑦　<u>kaki ukɪ garamai sɪsaɪN</u>.　　　× <u>kaki du ukɪ</u>.
　　書いてある　　かも　しれない
　　tsukue nu wa: buN du no: gara nu ari uiba kai be: ja.
　　机　の　上　に　何か　が　あるけど　あれかね
それが「書いてある」事は解っていても、<u>kaki du ukɪ</u>. とは言えない。

(B)　動作目撃の有無　（動詞が focus ではない）
①　近所で泥棒の噂がある。家に足跡があり、家が荒らされているのを見て
　　nusutu nudu <u>pazji ukɪ</u>.
　　泥棒　　が　　入ったのだ
②　家では降っていなかったが、畑は湿っていた。雨が降ったと分かる。
　　ami nu du <u>huri ukɪ</u>.
　　雨　が　降ったのだ
　　(cf. 他所から来た人　ame:huri nu ukɪ?　当地の人　huri du ukɪ.)
　　(　　　　　　　　　雨は降ったの？　　　　　　　降った　)
③　韮をとりに行ったら、みな倒れているのを見て、
　　kazji nu du　<u>huki ukɪ</u>.
　　風　　が　吹いたのだ
④　大工の造作が悪くてちょっとの地震で天井が落ちた
　　tinzjo: nudu <u>uti ukɪ</u>. ／ uz.
　　　天井　が　落ち　ている　（落ちたままになっているのを見ている）
　　　落ちる瞬間は見ていない　　　　cf. 見ていれば　<u>utitaz</u>
⑤　動作を見ることない行為の終了
　　<u>kaki ukɪ</u>　pɪto: pirjamai zjo: buN.
　　書き終わった　人　は　帰っても　いい

4．終わりに

　文法範疇としての証拠様態に関する報告は、琉球諸方言に関しても、殆ど無い。今後の調査研究が望まれる。日本語の歴史的研究、及び類型論的研究に貢献するに違いない。

【参考文献】

伊豆山敦子（2002a）「琉球・八重山（石垣宮良）方言の文法」ELPR A4-004　科研費特定領域研究報告書

伊豆山敦子（2002b）「琉球・八重山方言における「行為の認知」と「行為の結果」『マテシス・ウニウェルサリス』　第4巻　第1号　獨協大学外国語学部言語文化学科

伊豆山敦子（(2002c)「琉球・宮古（平良）方言の文法基礎研究」ELPR A4-012　科研費特定領域研究報告書

伊豆山敦子（2005）「琉球語 i-＊　の文法化」『日本語の研究』（武蔵野書院）

狩俣繁久（1992）「宮古方言」『言語学大辞典』4巻　pp.848-863　（三省堂）

工藤真由美（2004）『日本語のアスペクト・テンス・ムード体系』（ひつじ書房）

平山輝男（1967）『琉球先島方言の総合的研究』（明治書院）

Alexandra Y. Aikhenvald (2003) 'Evidentiality in typological perspective' "Studies in Evidentiality" Edited by A. Y. Aikhenvald. & R.M.W. Dixon. "Typological Studies in Language 54" John Benjamins publishing Co.

著者略歴

伊豆山敦子（いずやまあつこ）

東京に生まれる。
1955年東京大学文学部フランス文学科卒業。同大学大学院言語学専攻修士課程終了。
ハーヴァード大学大学院言語学科留学。
1966年3月東京大学大学院人文科学研究科言語学専門課程 博士課程単位取得満期退学。
東京女子大学・独協大学・文教大学等で教鞭をとる。

琉球のことばと人―エヴィデンシャリティーへの道―

平成23年6月30日　初版発行　　　　　Printed in Japan

著　者	伊豆山敦子
発行者	株式会社真珠書院 代表者　三樹　敏
印刷者	藤原印刷株式会社 代表者　藤原愛子
製本者	藤原印刷株式会社 代表者　藤原愛子
発行所	株式会社真珠書院 東京都新宿区大久保1-1-7　郵便番号169-0072 電話　03-5292-6521 振替　00180-4-93208

ⒸAtsuko Izuyama 2011
ISBN 978-4-88009-506-6